This is Tsutsui. This is volume 17.

This volume marks one possible ending to our story.

Thanks to all of your support for more than three years now, I have succeeded in drawing ___ story thus far! My heart is bursting with ___ I LOVE YOU!

___ e thrilled if you'd ___ to the exam-stressed, ___ slightly strange ___ the very last page!

• Taishi Tsutsui •

We Never **Learn**

We Never Learn

Volume 17 • SHONEN JUMP Manga Edition

STORY AND ART **Taishi Tsutsui**

TRANSLATION Camellia Nieh
SHONEN JUMP SERIES LETTERING Snir Aharon
GRAPHIC NOVEL TOUCH-UP ART & LETTERING Erika Terriquez
DESIGN Shawn Carrico
EDITOR John Bae

BOKUTACHI WA BENKYOU GA DEKINAI © 2017 by Taishi Tsutsui
All rights reserved.
First published in Japan in 2017 by SHUEISHA Inc., Tokyo.
English translation rights arranged by SHUEISHA Inc.

Printed in the U.S.A.

Published by VIZ Media, LLC
P.O. Box 77010
San Francisco, CA 94107

10 9 8 7 6 5 4 3 2 1
First printing, August 2021

viz.com

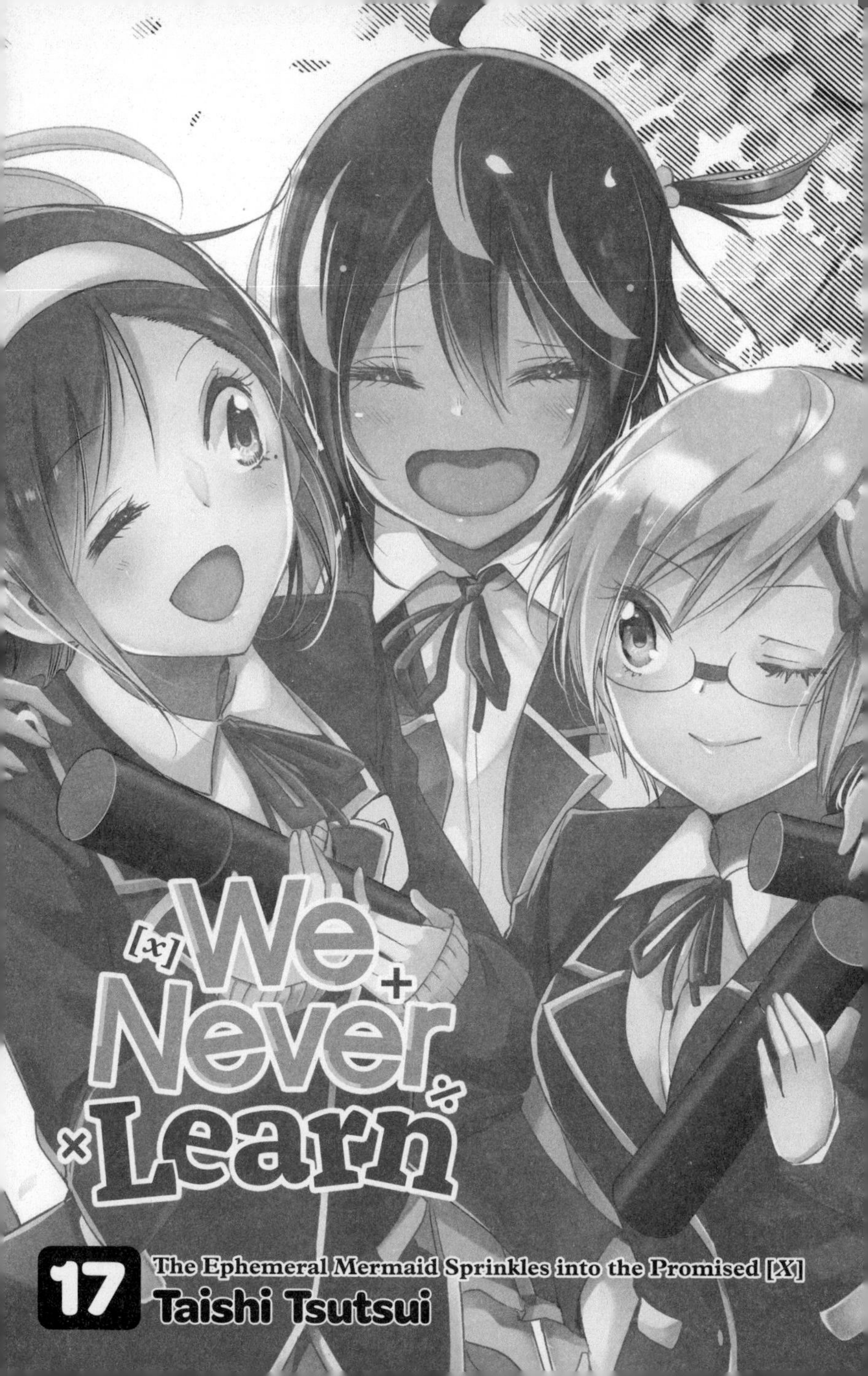
[x] We + Never ÷ × Learn
17
The Ephemeral Mermaid Sprinkles into the Promised [X]
Taishi Tsutsui

We Never Learn

Nariyuki Yuiga and his family have led a humble life since his father passed away, with Yuiga doing everything he can to support his siblings. So when the principal of his school agrees to grant Nariyuki the school's special VIP recommendation for a full scholarship to college, he leaps at the opportunity. However, the principal's offer comes with one condition: Yuiga must serve as the tutor of Rizu Ogata, Fumino Furuhashi and Uruka Takemoto, the three girl geniuses who are the pride of Ichinose Academy! Unfortunately, the girls, while extremely talented in certain ways, all have subjects where their grades are absolutely rock-bottom. How will these three struggling students ever manage to pass their college entrance exams?!

Uruka finally musters the courage to give Nariyuki his Valentine's Day chocolate—something she's struggled with for years! Before their exams, Nariyuki gives each girl a final study notebook and all of them manage to successfully pass their tests! With their exams behind them, Uruka finally manages to confess her feelings to Nariyuki!

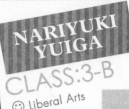

NARIYUKI YUIGA

CLASS:3-B

☺ Liberal Arts
☺ STEM
☹ Athletics

A bright student from an ordinary family. Nariyuki lacks genius in any one subject but manages to maintain stellar grades through hard work. Agrees to take on the role of tutor in return for the school's special VIP recommendation.

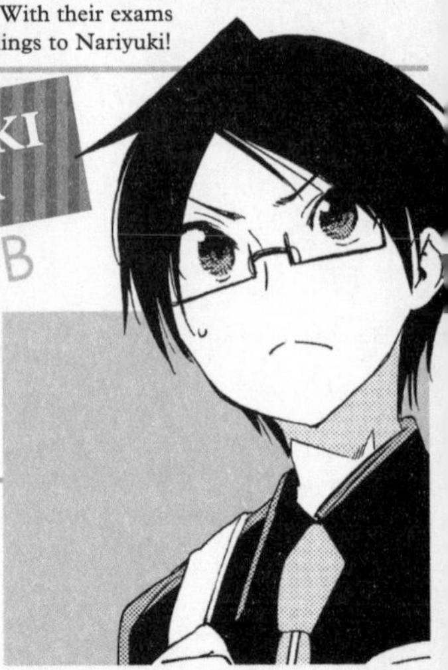

The Yuiga Family

A family of five, consisting of Nariyuki, his mother and his siblings, Mizuki, Hazuki and Kazuki.

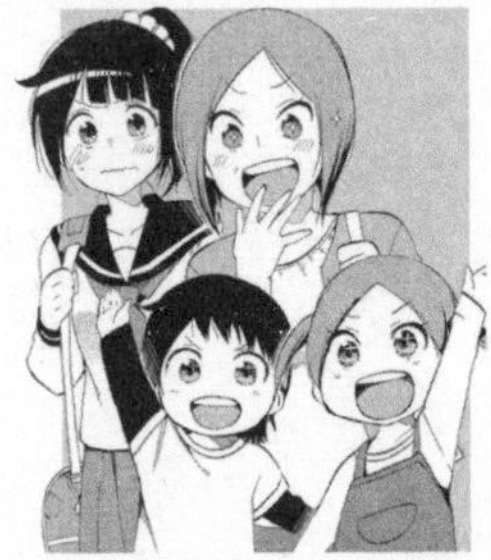

Kobayashi and Omori

Nariyuki's friends.

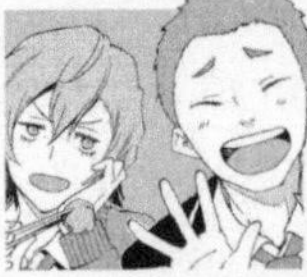

Miharu Kirisu

The head of the science club and a rival of Rizu's, who in fact adores Rizu.

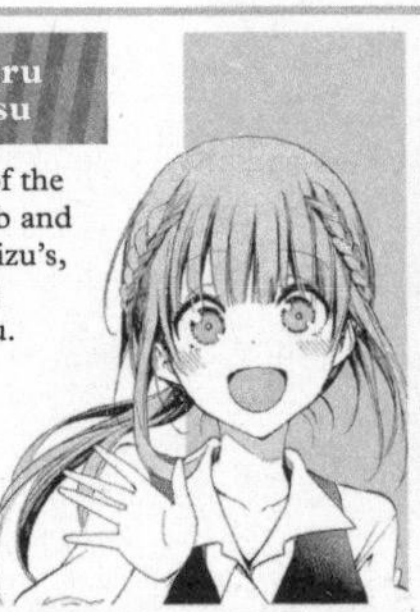

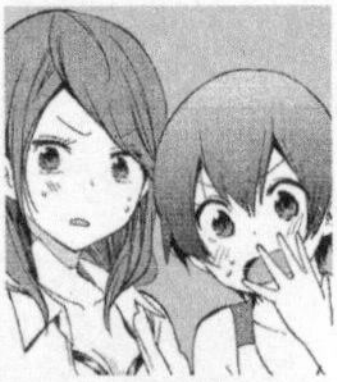

Kawase and Umihara

Uruka's friends.

Sawako Sekijo

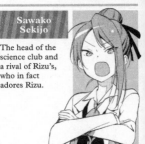

The head of the science club and a rival of Rizu's, who in fact adores Rizu.

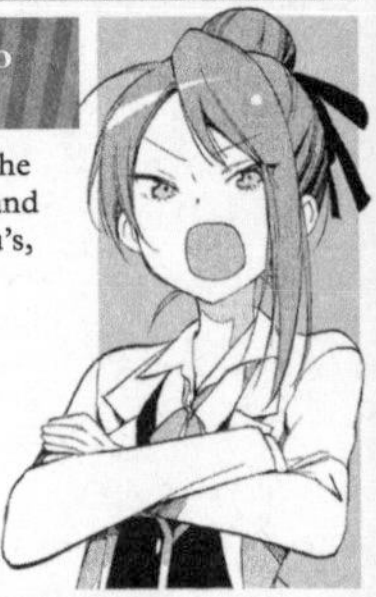

RIZU OGATA

CLASS:3-F

☹ Liberal Arts 😀 STEM ☹ Athletics

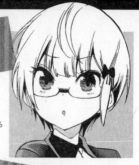

Known as the Thumbelina Supercomputer, Rizu is a math and science genius, but she's a dunce at literature, especially when human emotions come into play. She chooses a literary path to learn about human psychology—partially because she wants to become better at board games.

FUMINO FURUHASHI

CLASS:3-A

😀 Liberal Arts ☹ STEM ☺ Athletics

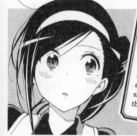

Known as the Sleeping Beauty of the Literary Forest, Fumino is a literary wiz whose mind goes completely blank when she sees numbers. She chooses a STEM path because she wants to study the stars.

URUKA TAKEMOTO

CLASS:3-D

☹ Liberal Arts ☹ STEM 😀 Athletics

Known as the Shimmering Ebony Mermaid Princess, Uruka is a swimming prodigy but is terrible at academics. In order to get an athletic scholarship, she needs to meet certain academic standards. She's had a crush on Nariyuki since junior high.

MAFUYU KIRISU

TEACHER

😀 Pedagogy ☹ Home Economics

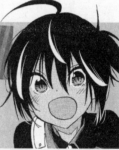

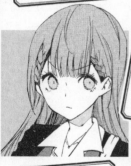

A teacher at Ichinose Academy, and Rizu and Fumino's previous tutor. She believes people should choose their path according to their talents.

ASUMI KOMINAMI

OG

☹ Science ☺ Service

A graduate of Ichinose Academy. Works at a maid cafe and attends cram school in order to get into medical school and take over her father's clinic one day.

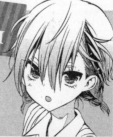

TITLE

We Never Learn

CONTENTS

VOLUME **17** The Ephemeral Mermaid Sprinkles into the Promised [X]

NAME **Taishi Tsutsui**

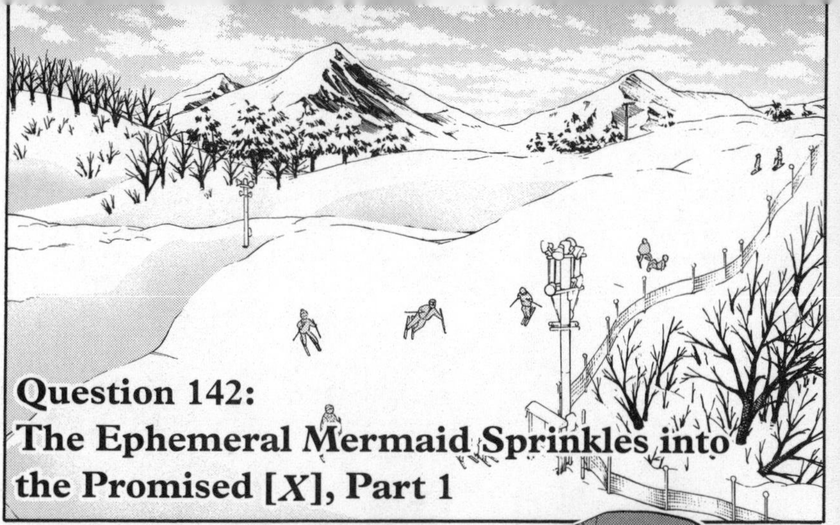
Question 142:
The Ephemeral Mermaid Sprinkles into the Promised [X], Part 1

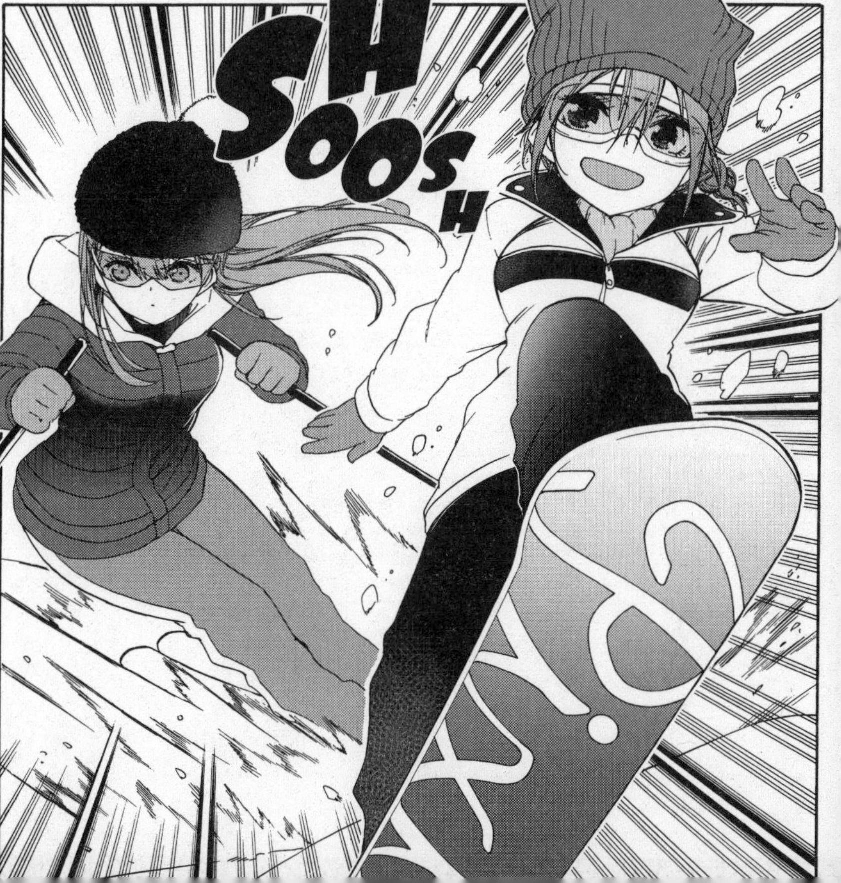
SH SOOSH

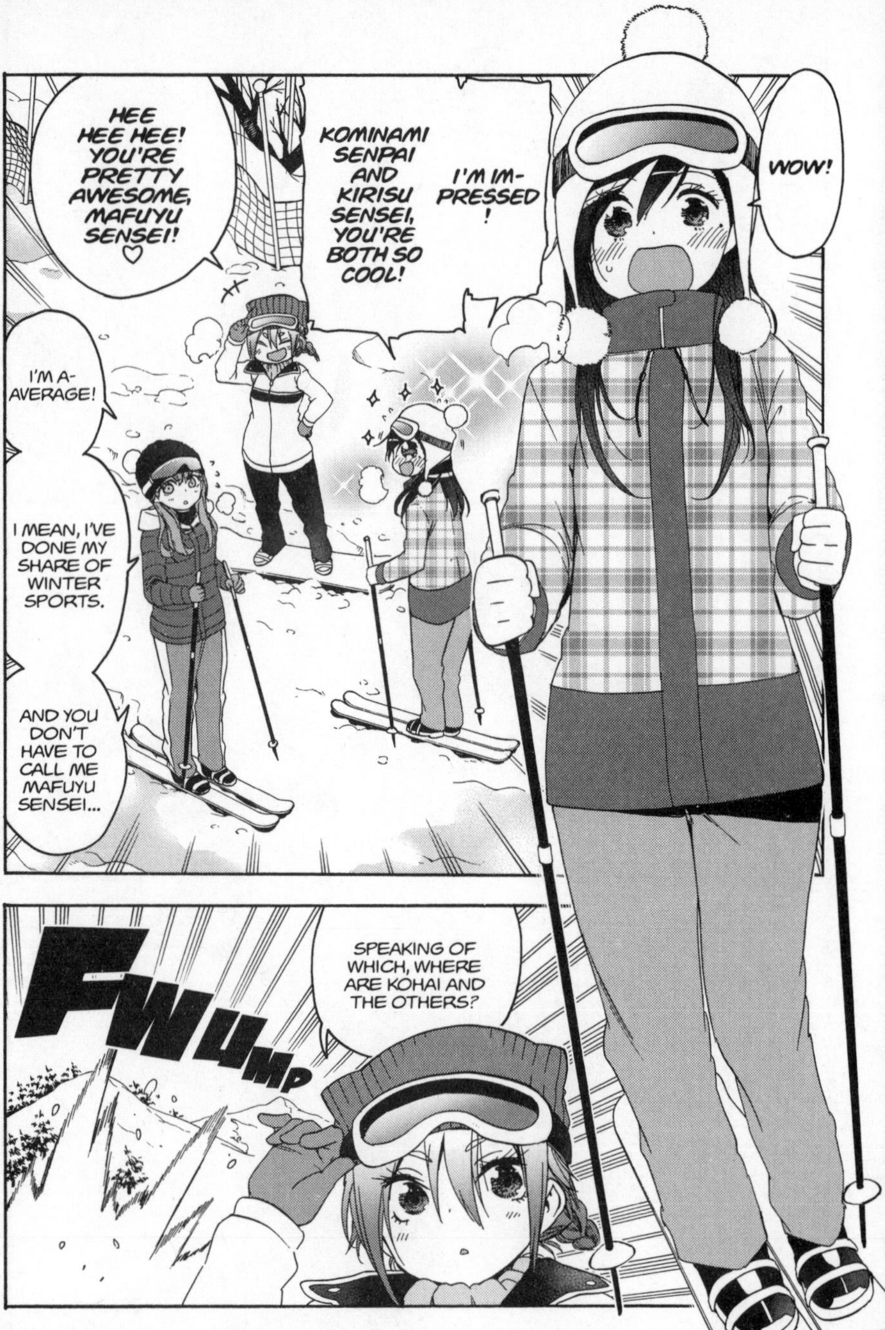
WOW!
I'M IM-PRESSED!
KOMINAMI SENPAI AND KIRISU SENSEI, YOU'RE BOTH SO COOL!
HEE HEE HEE! YOU'RE PRETTY AWESOME, MAFUYU SENSEI! ♡
I'M A-AVERAGE!
I MEAN, I'VE DONE MY SHARE OF WINTER SPORTS.
AND YOU DON'T HAVE TO CALL ME MAFUYU SENSEI...
SPEAKING OF WHICH, WHERE ARE KOHAI AND THE OTHERS?
FWUMP

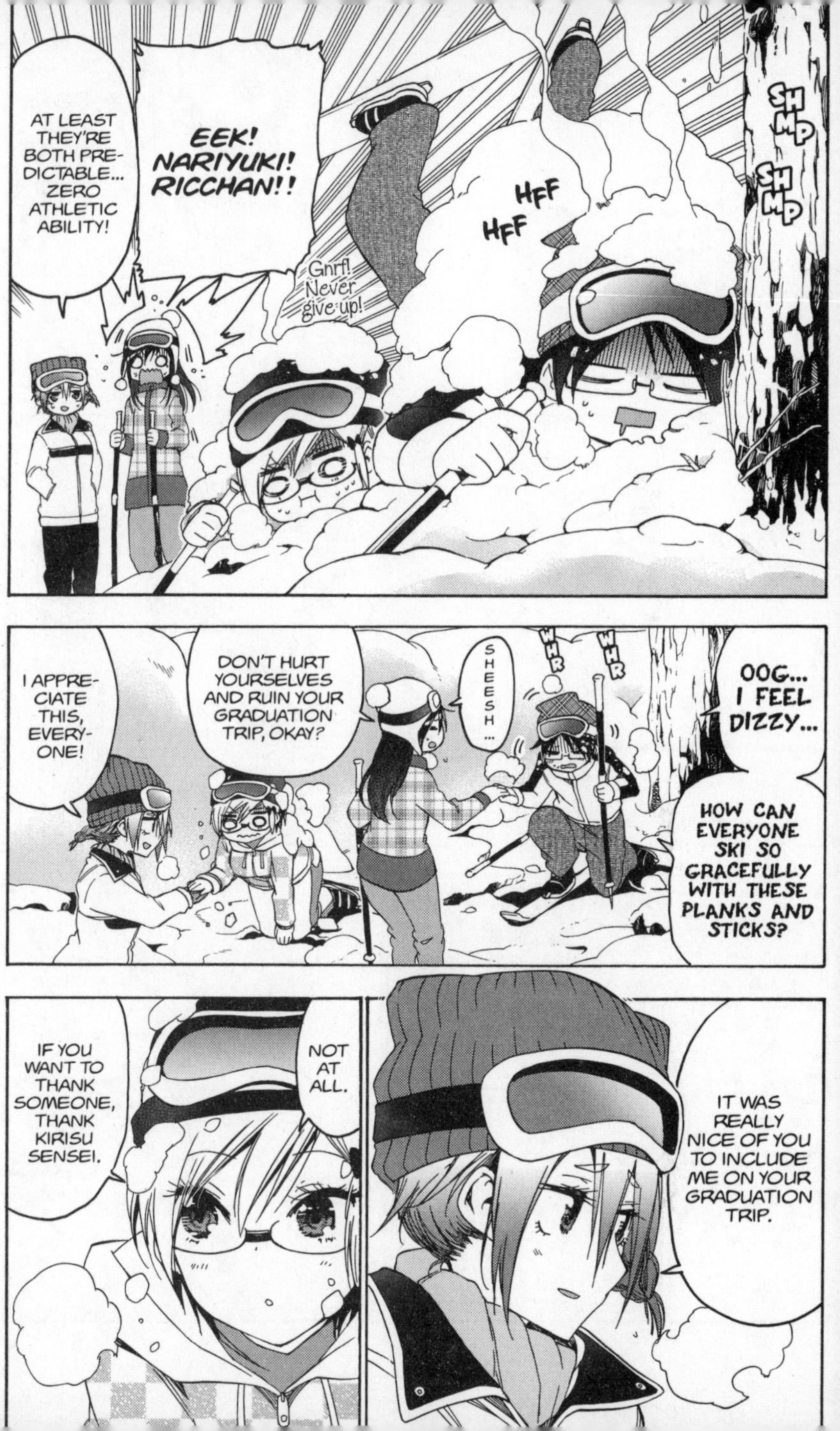
SHMP
SHMP
HFF HFF
Gnrf! Never give up!
EEK! NARIYUKI! RICCHAN!!
AT LEAST THEY'RE BOTH PREDICTABLE... ZERO ATHLETIC ABILITY!
OOG... I FEEL DIZZY...
HOW CAN EVERYONE SKI SO GRACEFULLY WITH THESE PLANKS AND STICKS?
WHR
WHR
SHEESH...
DON'T HURT YOURSELVES AND RUIN YOUR GRADUATION TRIP, OKAY?
I APPRECIATE THIS, EVERYONE!
IT WAS REALLY NICE OF YOU TO INCLUDE ME ON YOUR GRADUATION TRIP.
NOT AT ALL.
IF YOU WANT TO THANK SOMEONE, THANK KIRISU SENSEI.

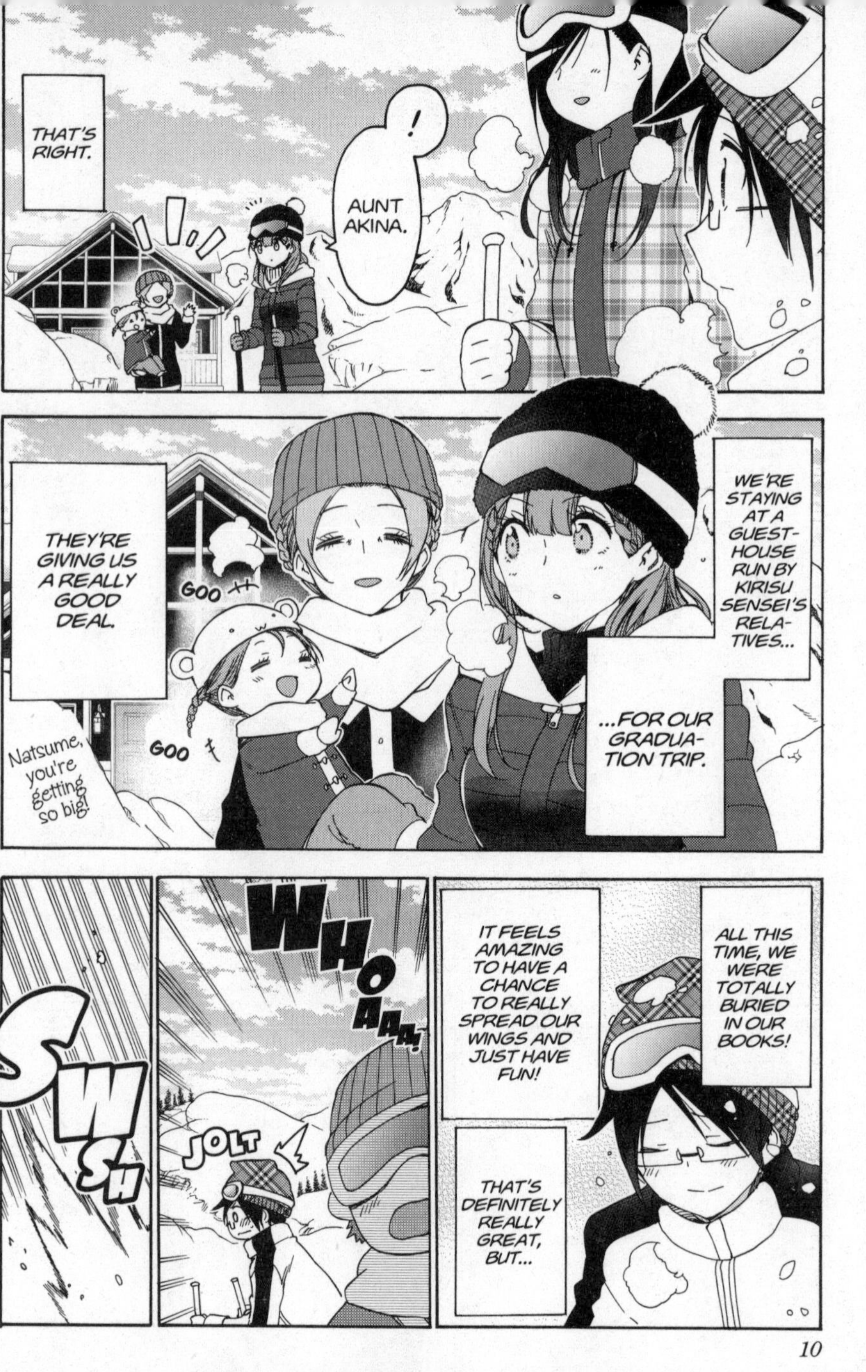
!
AUNT AKINA.
THAT'S RIGHT.
WE'RE STAYING AT A GUEST-HOUSE RUN BY KIRISU SENSEI'S RELATIVES...
...FOR OUR GRADUATION TRIP.
THEY'RE GIVING US A REALLY GOOD DEAL.
GOO
GOO
Natsume, you're getting so big!
ALL THIS TIME, WE WERE TOTALLY BURIED IN OUR BOOKS!
IT FEELS AMAZING TO HAVE A CHANCE TO REALLY SPREAD OUR WINGS AND JUST HAVE FUN!
THAT'S DEFINITELY REALLY GREAT, BUT...
WHOAAA!
JOLT
SWISH

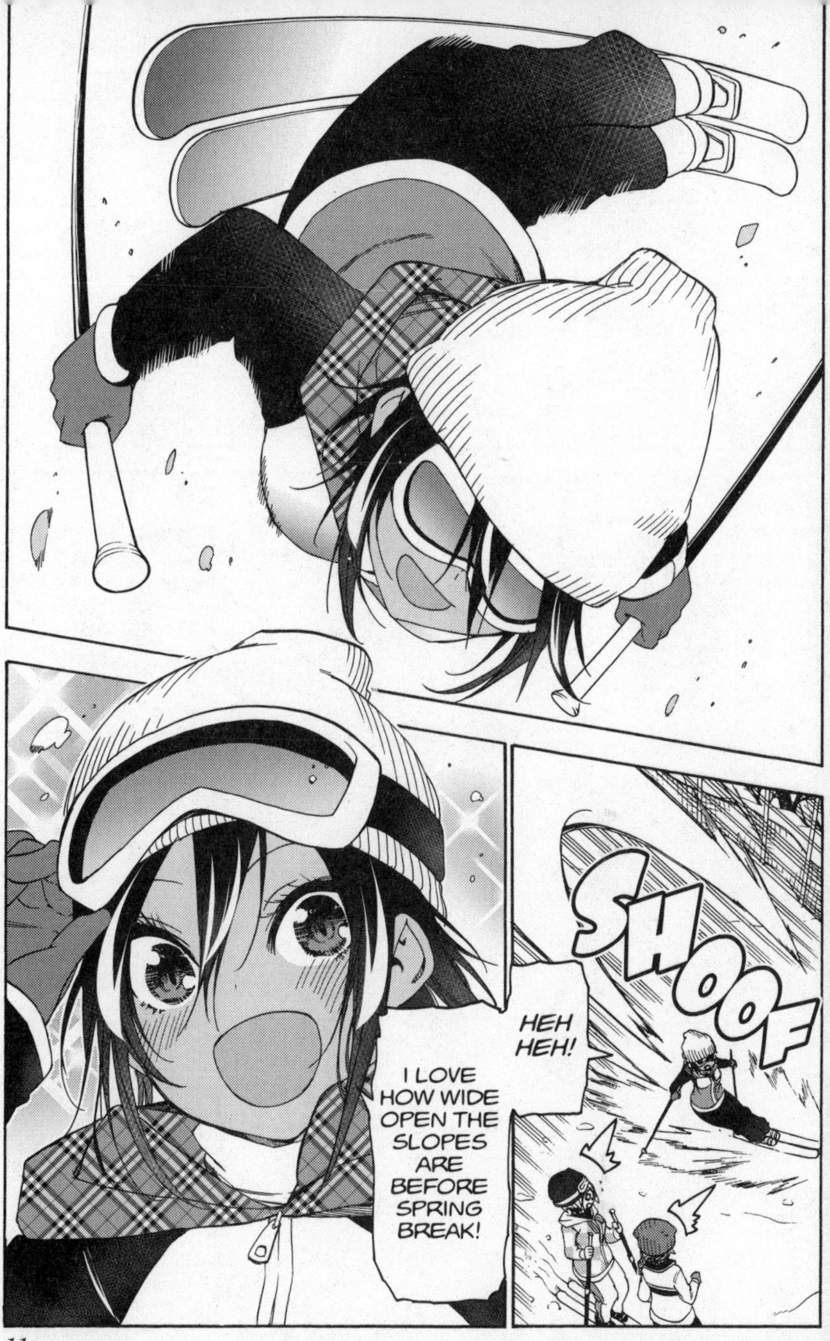
SHOOF
HEH HEH!
I LOVE HOW WIDE OPEN THE SLOPES ARE BEFORE SPRING BREAK!

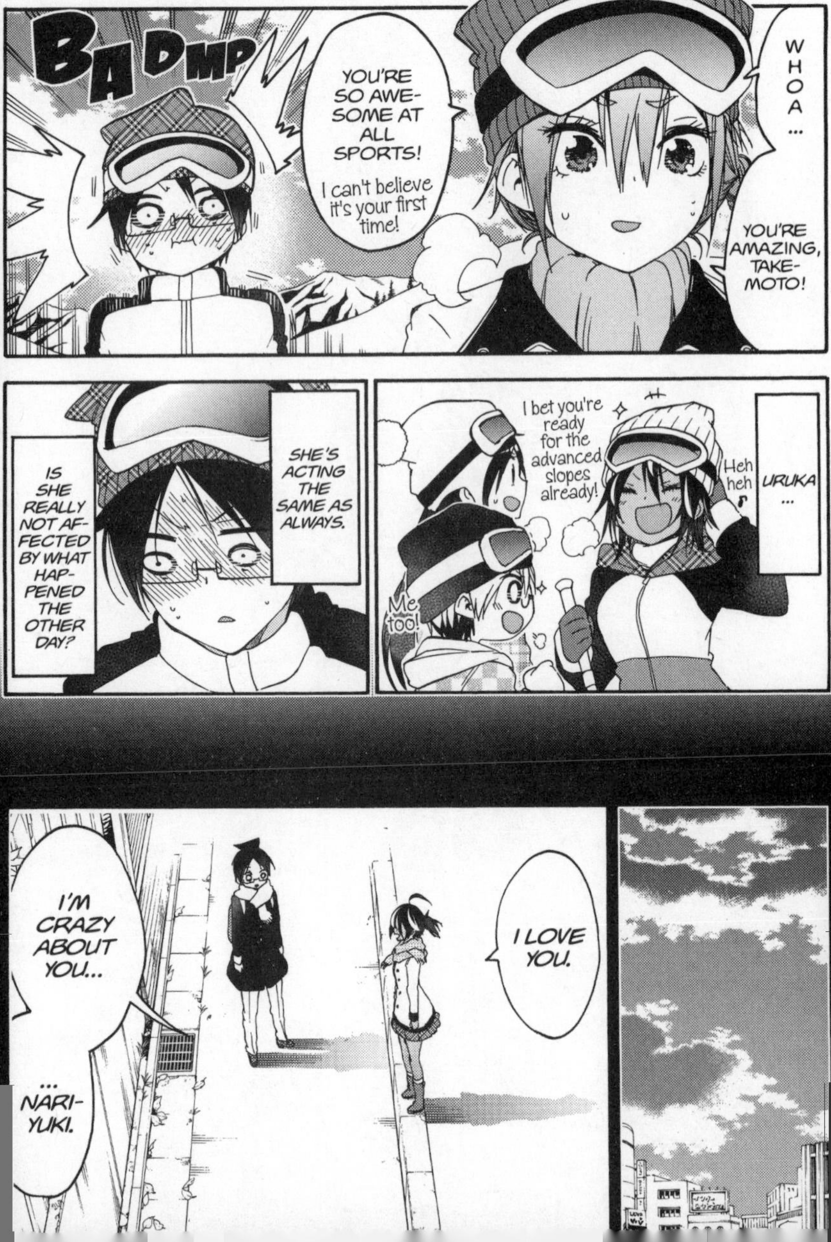
WHOA...
YOU'RE AMAZING, TAKE-MOTO!
YOU'RE SO AWE-SOME AT ALL SPORTS!
I can't believe it's your first time!
BADMP
URUKA...
Heh heh
I bet you're ready for the advanced slopes already!
Me too!
SHE'S ACTING THE SAME AS ALWAYS.
IS SHE REALLY NOT AF-FECTED BY WHAT HAP-PENED THE OTHER DAY?
I LOVE YOU.
I'M CRAZY ABOUT YOU...
...NARI-YUKI.

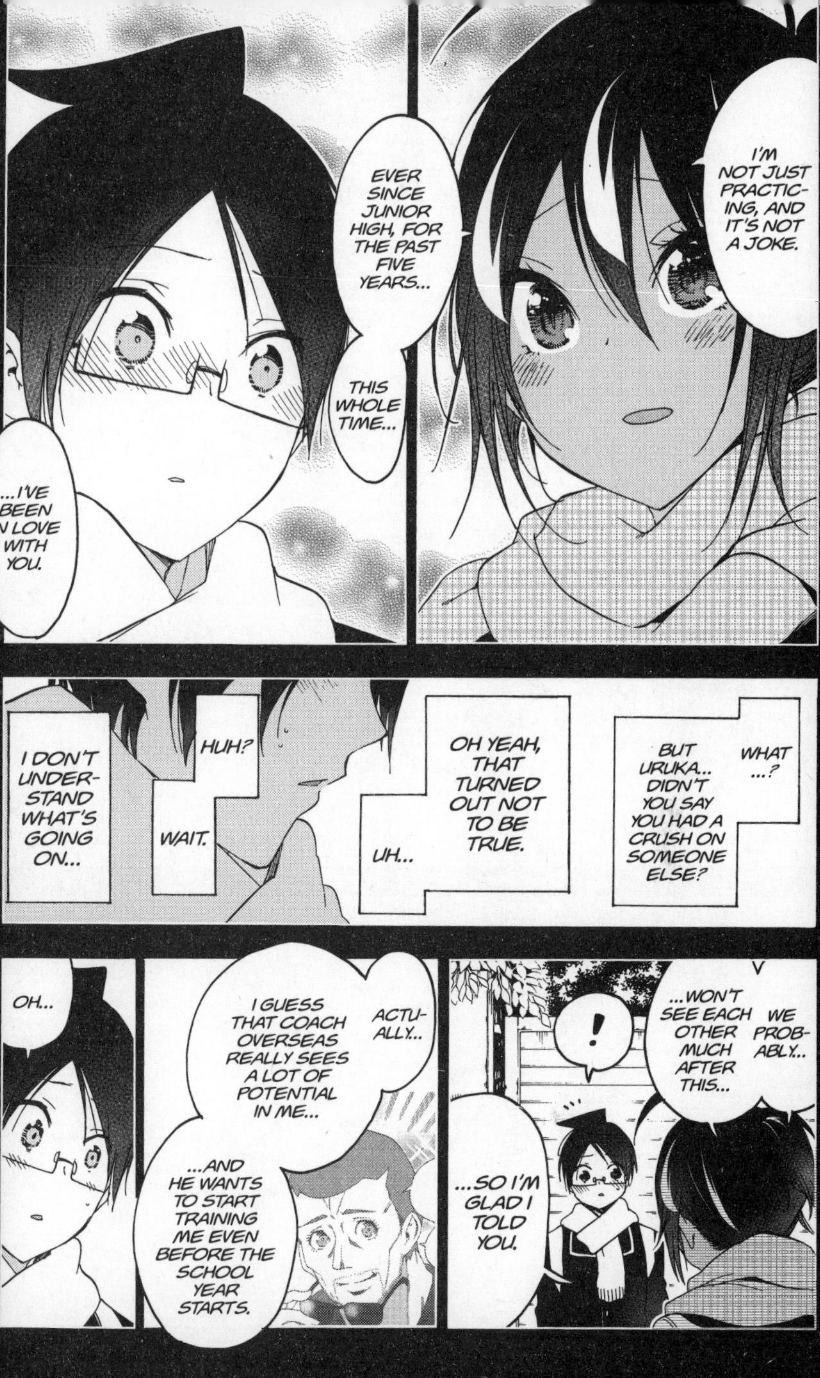
I'M NOT JUST PRACTIC-ING, AND IT'S NOT A JOKE.
EVER SINCE JUNIOR HIGH, FOR THE PAST FIVE YEARS...
THIS WHOLE TIME...
...I'VE BEEN IN LOVE WITH YOU.
WHAT ...?
BUT URUKA... DIDN'T YOU SAY YOU HAD A CRUSH ON SOMEONE ELSE?
OH YEAH, THAT TURNED OUT NOT TO BE TRUE.
UH...
HUH?
WAIT.
I DON'T UNDER-STAND WHAT'S GOING ON...
WE PROB-ABLY...
...WON'T SEE EACH OTHER MUCH AFTER THIS...
!
...SO I'M GLAD I TOLD YOU.
ACTU-ALLY...
I GUESS THAT COACH OVERSEAS REALLY SEES A LOT OF POTENTIAL IN ME...
...AND HE WANTS TO START TRAINING ME EVEN BEFORE THE SCHOOL YEAR STARTS.
OH...

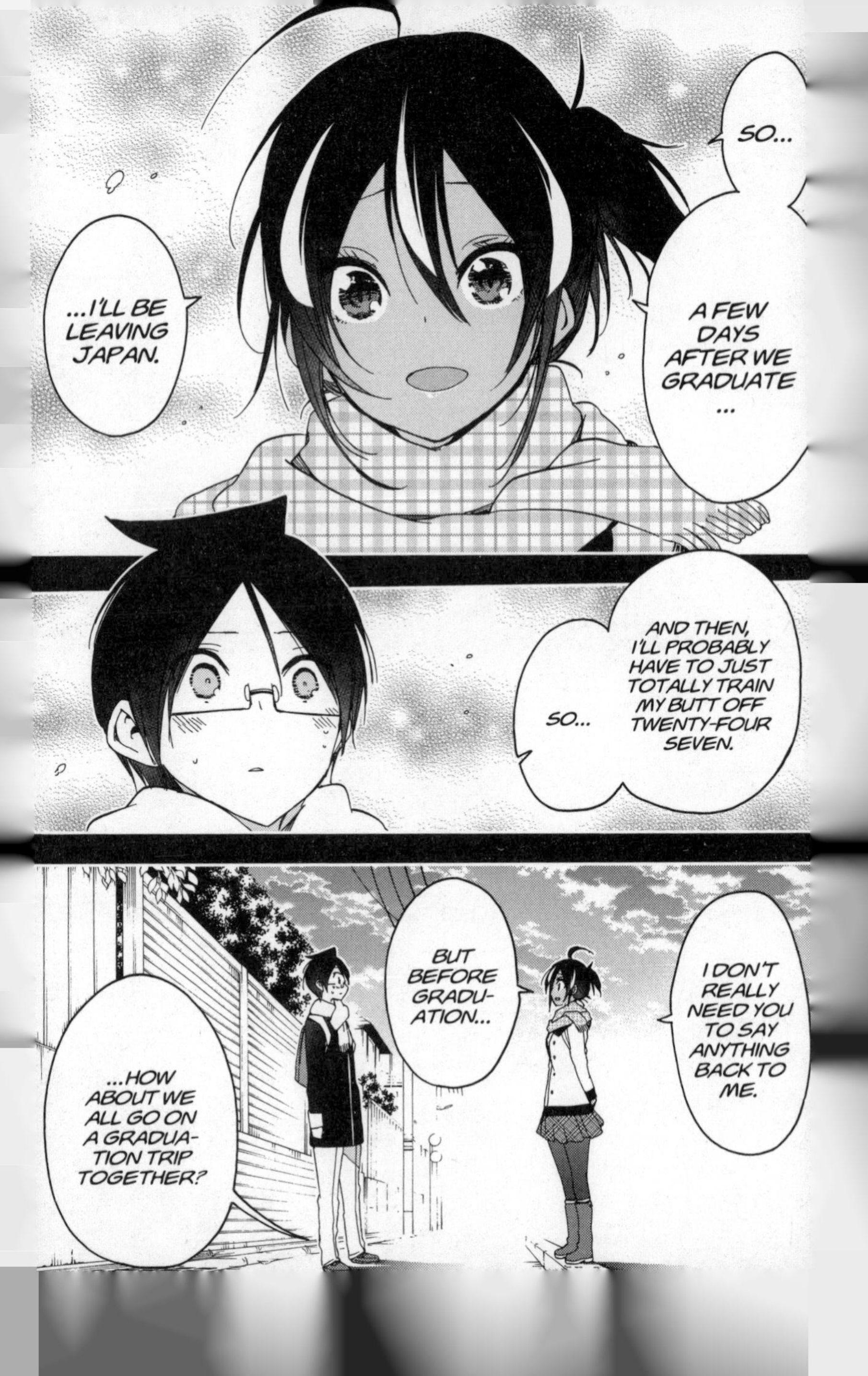
SO...
A FEW DAYS AFTER WE GRADUATE ...
...I'LL BE LEAVING JAPAN.
AND THEN, I'LL PROBABLY HAVE TO JUST TOTALLY TRAIN MY BUTT OFF TWENTY-FOUR SEVEN.
SO...
I DON'T REALLY NEED YOU TO SAY ANYTHING BACK TO ME.
BUT BEFORE GRADU-ATION...
...HOW ABOUT WE ALL GO ON A GRADUA-TION TRIP TOGETHER?

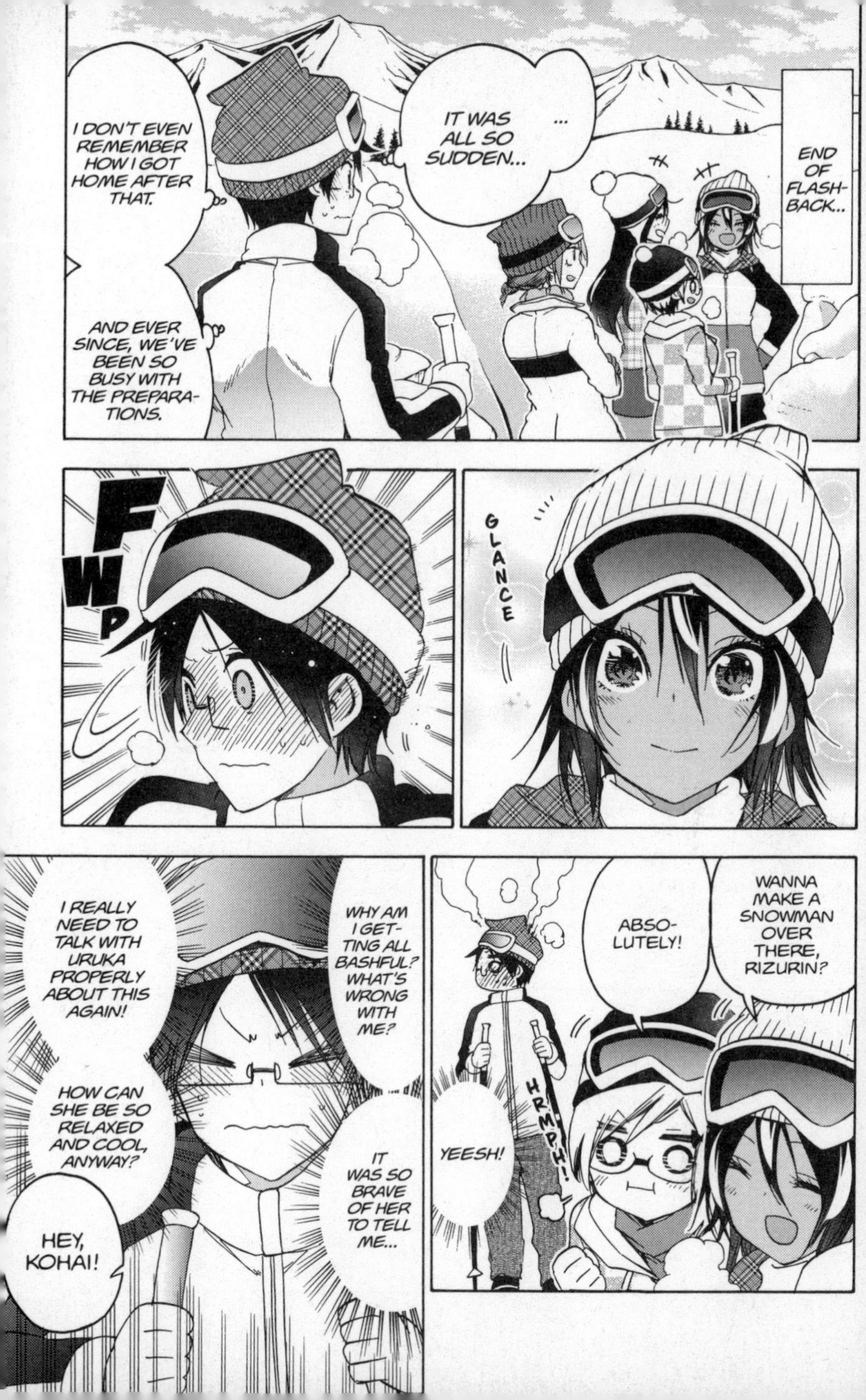
END OF FLASH-BACK...
...
IT WAS ALL SO SUDDEN...
I DON'T EVEN REMEMBER HOW I GOT HOME AFTER THAT.
AND EVER SINCE, WE'VE BEEN SO BUSY WITH THE PREPARA-TIONS.
GLANCE
FWP
WANNA MAKE A SNOWMAN OVER THERE, RIZURIN?
ABSO-LUTELY!
HRMPH!
YEESH!
WHY AM I GET-TING ALL BASHFUL? WHAT'S WRONG WITH ME?
I REALLY NEED TO TALK WITH URUKA PROPERLY ABOUT THIS AGAIN!
IT WAS SO BRAVE OF HER TO TELL ME...
HOW CAN SHE BE SO RELAXED AND COOL, ANYWAY?
HEY, KOHAI!

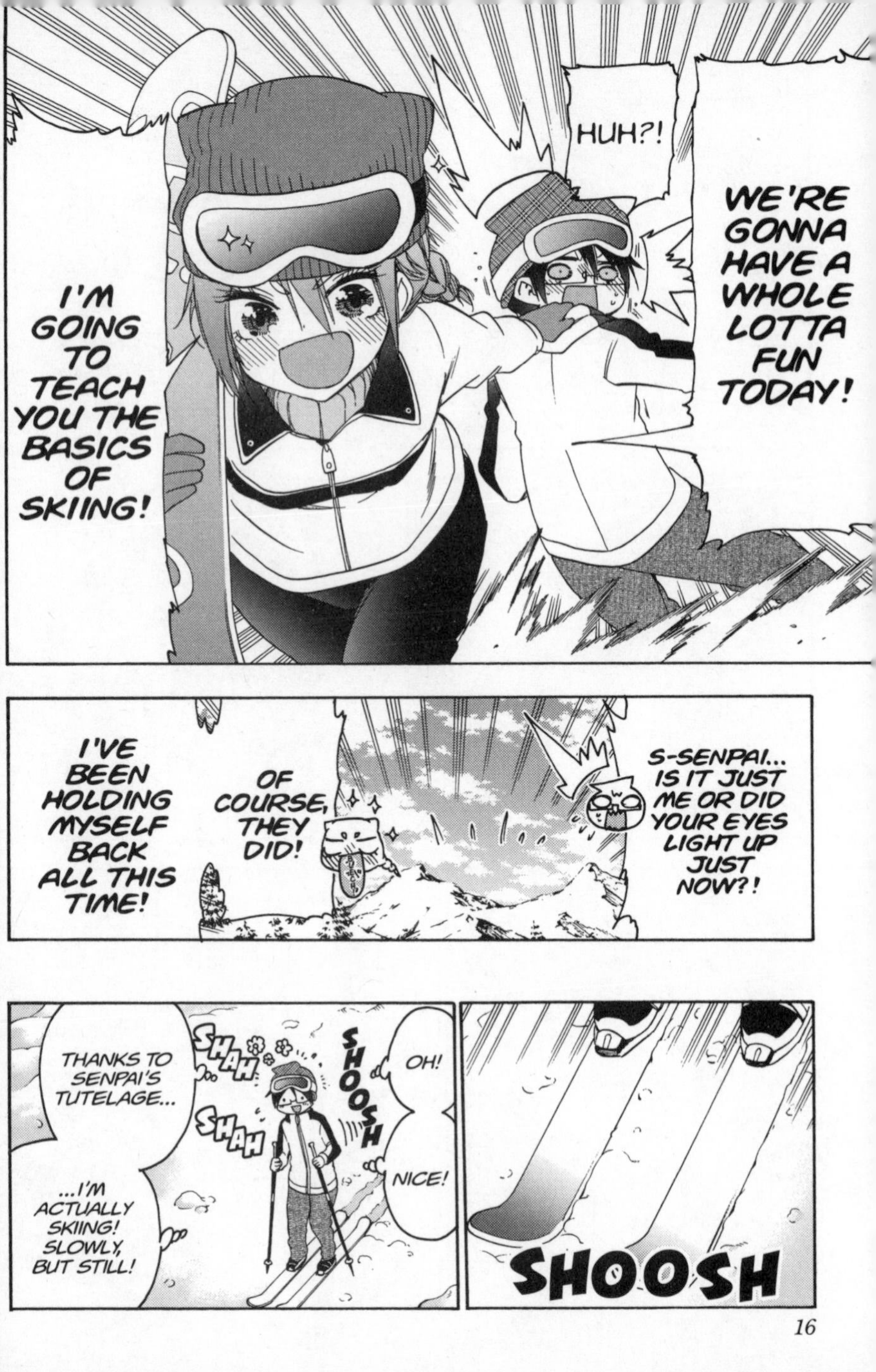
HUH?!
WE'RE GONNA HAVE A WHOLE LOTTA FUN TODAY!
I'M GOING TO TEACH YOU THE BASICS OF SKIING!
S-SENPAI... IS IT JUST ME OR DID YOUR EYES LIGHT UP JUST NOW?!
OF COURSE, THEY DID!
I'VE BEEN HOLDING MYSELF BACK ALL THIS TIME!
SHOOSH
SHOOSH
OH!
NICE!
SHAH
SHAH
THANKS TO SENPAI'S TUTELAGE...
...I'M ACTUALLY SKIING! SLOWLY, BUT STILL!

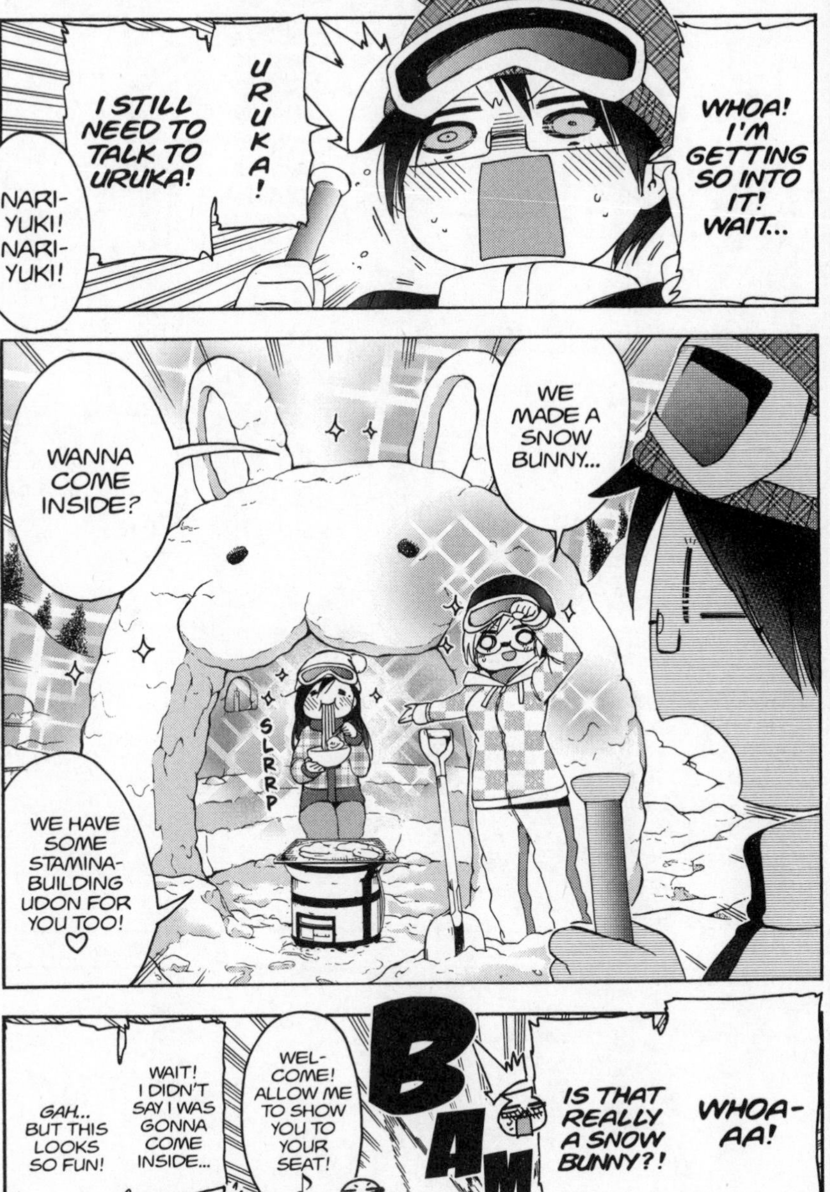
WHOA! I'M GETTING SO INTO IT! WAIT...
URUKA!
I STILL NEED TO TALK TO URUKA!
NARI-YUKI! NARI-YUKI!
WE MADE A SNOW BUNNY...
WANNA COME INSIDE?
SLRRP
WE HAVE SOME STAMINA-BUILDING UDON FOR YOU TOO! ♡
WHOA-AA!
IS THAT REALLY A SNOW BUNNY?!
BAM
WEL-COME! ALLOW ME TO SHOW YOU TO YOUR SEAT! ♪
WAIT! I DIDN'T SAY I WAS GONNA COME INSIDE...
GAH... BUT THIS LOOKS SO FUN!
WHRR

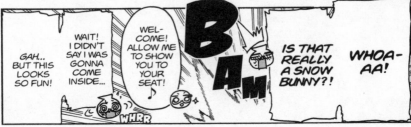

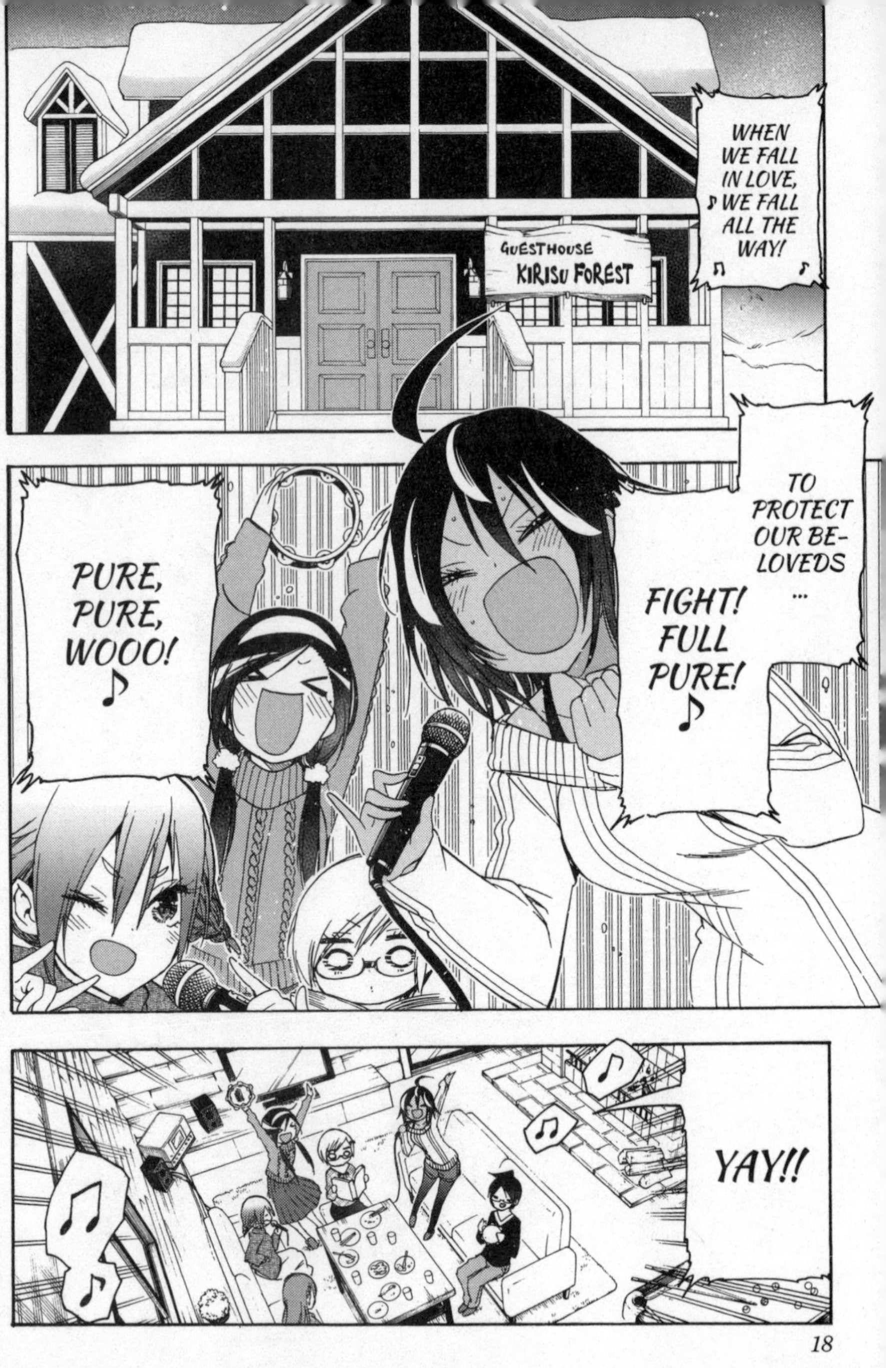
GUESTHOUSE KIRISU FOREST
WHEN WE FALL IN LOVE, ♪ WE FALL ALL THE WAY! ♫ ♪
TO PROTECT OUR BE-LOVEDS ...
FIGHT! FULL PURE! ♪
PURE, PURE, WOOO! ♪
YAY!!

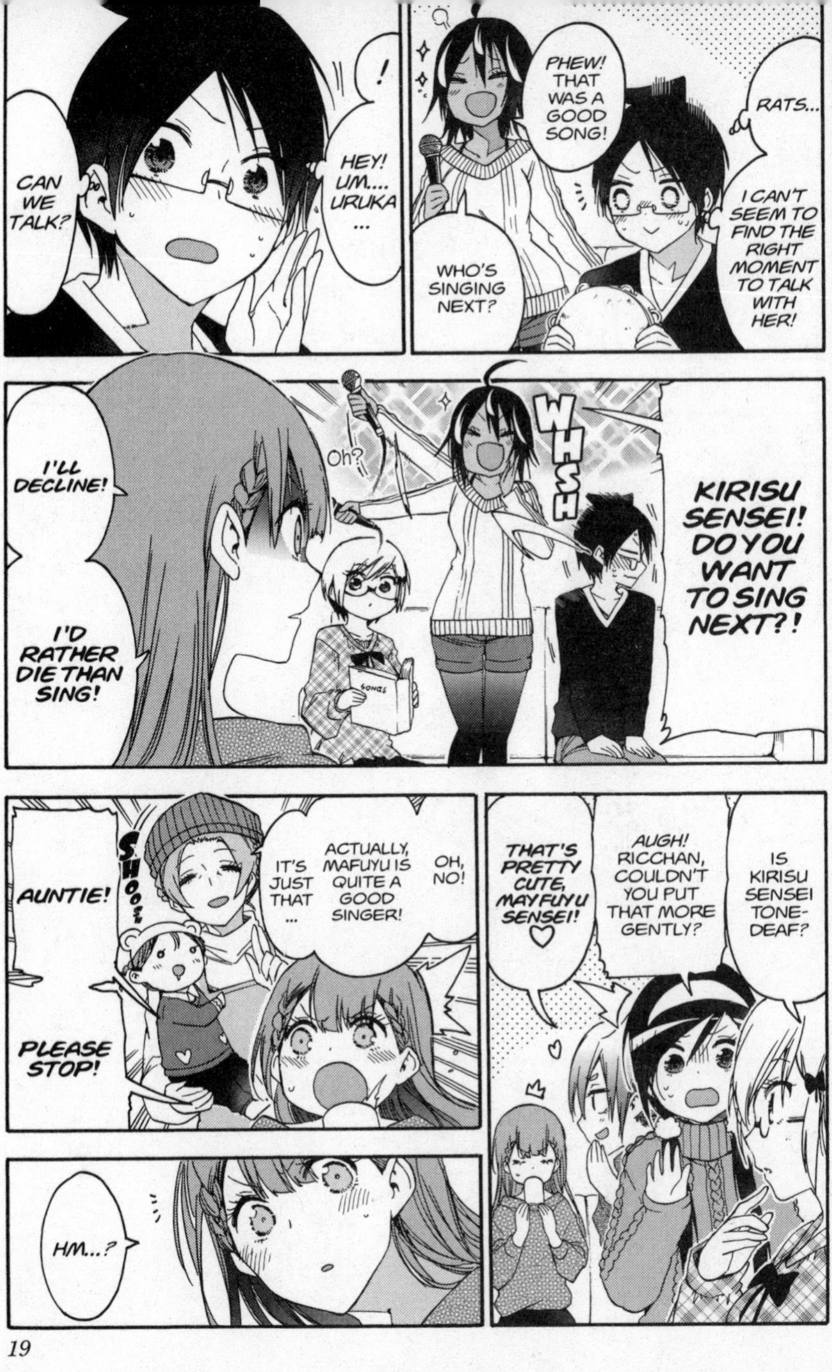
RATS...
PHEW! THAT WAS A GOOD SONG!
I CAN'T SEEM TO FIND THE RIGHT MOMENT TO TALK WITH HER!
WHO'S SINGING NEXT?
!
HEY! UM.... URUKA ...
CAN WE TALK?
KIRISU SENSEI! DO YOU WANT TO SING NEXT?!
WHSH
Oh?
I'LL DECLINE!
I'D RATHER DIE THAN SING!
SONGS
IS KIRISU SENSEI TONE-DEAF?
AUGH! RICCHAN, COULDN'T YOU PUT THAT MORE GENTLY?
THAT'S PRETTY CUTE, MAYFUYU SENSEI! ♡
OH, NO!
ACTUALLY, MAFUYU IS QUITE A GOOD SINGER!
IT'S JUST THAT ...
SHOO
AUNTIE!
PLEASE STOP!
HM...?

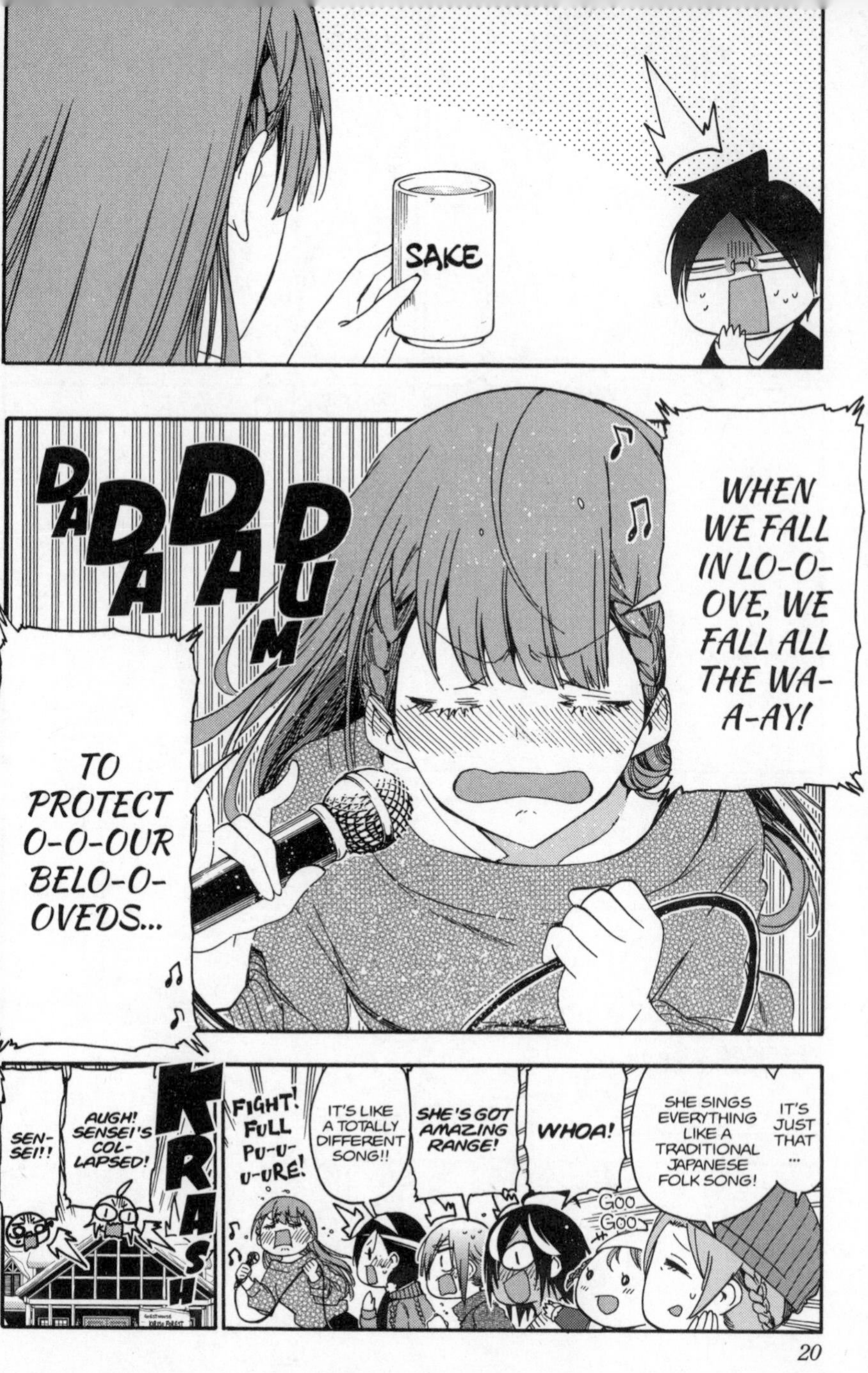
SAKE
WHEN WE FALL IN LO-O-OVE, WE FALL ALL THE WA-A-AY!
DADADADUM
TO PROTECT O-O-OUR BELO-O-OVEDS...
IT'S JUST THAT ...
SHE SINGS EVERYTHING LIKE A TRADITIONAL JAPANESE FOLK SONG!
GOO GOO
WHOA!
SHE'S GOT AMAZING RANGE!
IT'S LIKE A TOTALLY DIFFERENT SONG!!
FIGHT! FULL PU-U-U-URE!
KRASH
AUGH! SENSEI'S COL-LAPSED!
SEN-SEI!!

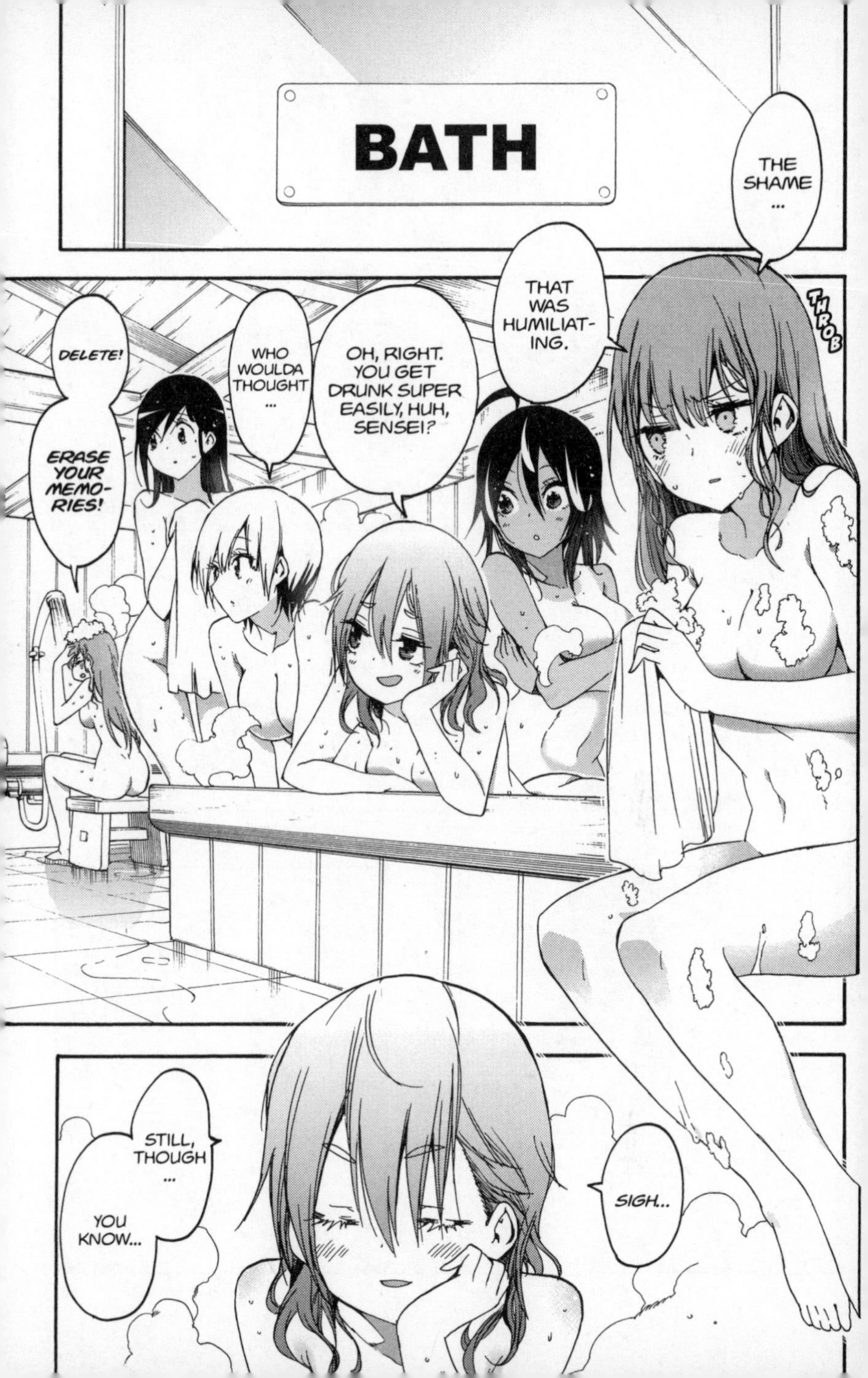
BATH
THE SHAME ...
THROB
THAT WAS HUMILIAT-ING.
OH, RIGHT. YOU GET DRUNK SUPER EASILY, HUH, SENSEI?
WHO WOULDA THOUGHT ...
DELETE!
ERASE YOUR MEMO-RIES!
SIGH...
STILL, THOUGH ...
YOU KNOW...

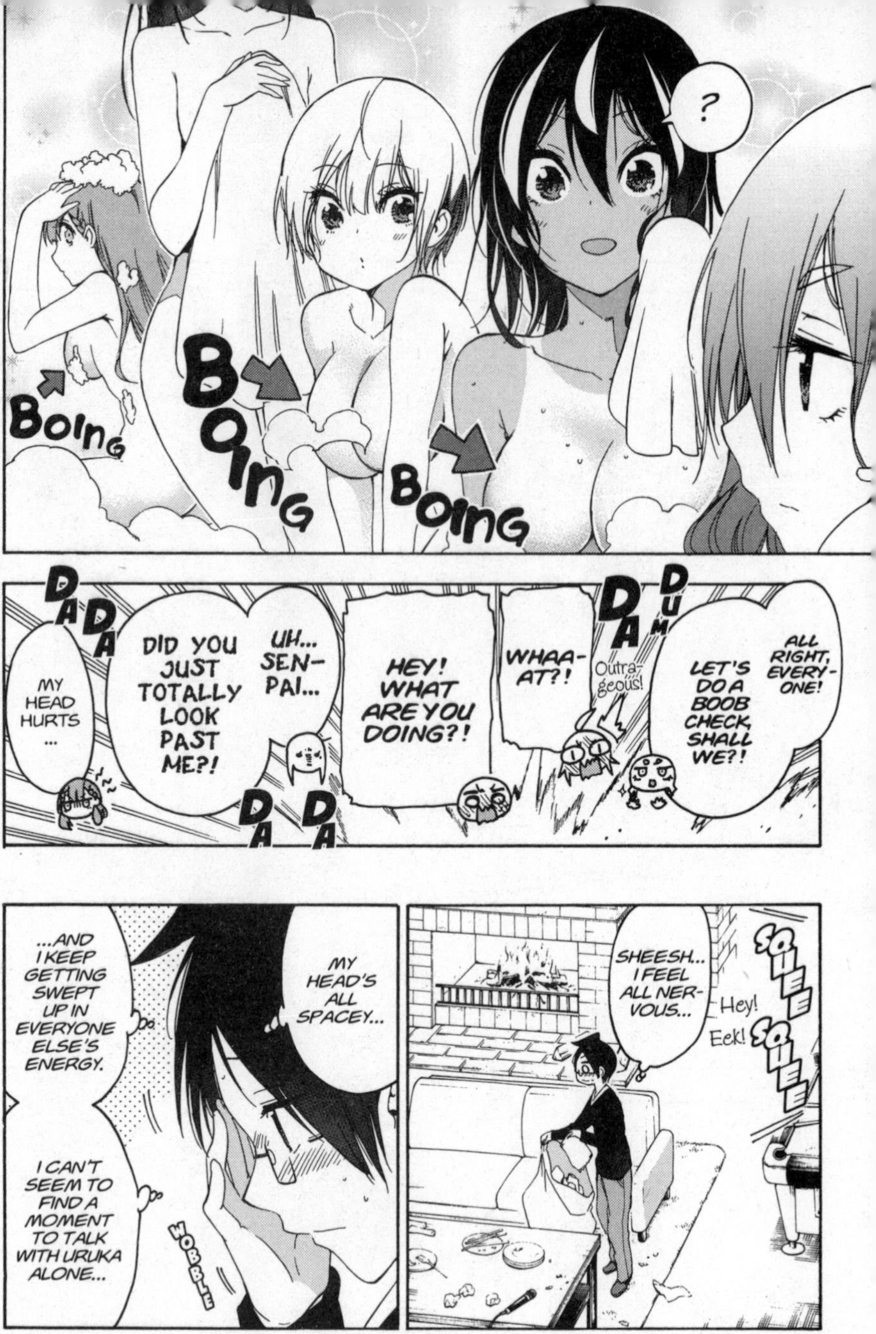
?
BOING
BOING
Boing
DUM
DA
ALL RIGHT, EVERYONE!
LET'S DO A BOOB CHECK, SHALL WE?!
Outrageous!
WHAAAT?!
HEY! WHAT ARE YOU DOING?!
UH... SENPAI...
DID YOU JUST TOTALLY LOOK PAST ME?!
DA
DA
DADA
MY HEAD HURTS...
SQUEE SQUEE
Hey!
Eek!
SHEESH... I FEEL ALL NERVOUS...
MY HEAD'S ALL SPACEY...
...AND I KEEP GETTING SWEPT UP IN EVERYONE ELSE'S ENERGY.
I CAN'T SEEM TO FIND A MOMENT TO TALK WITH URUKA ALONE...
WOBBLE

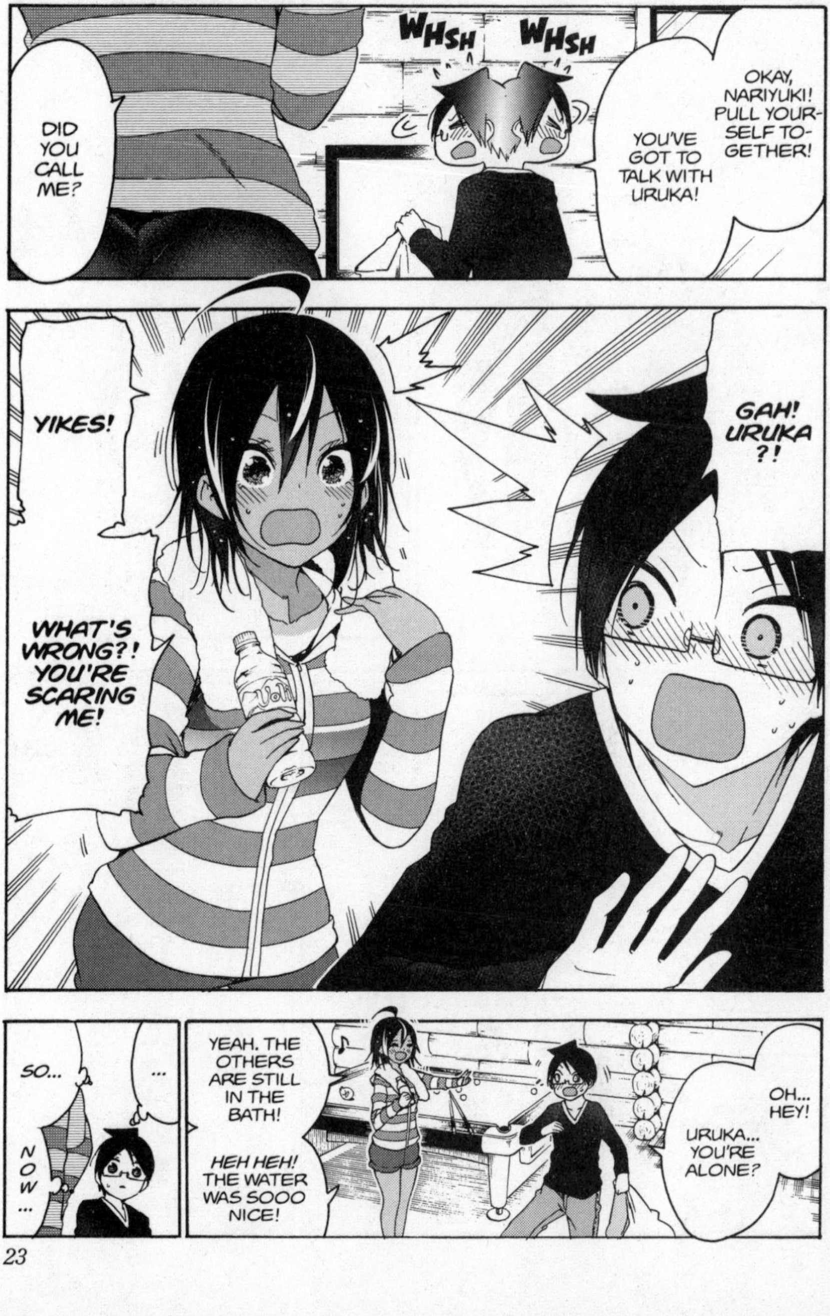
OKAY, NARIYUKI! PULL YOURSELF TOGETHER!
YOU'VE GOT TO TALK WITH URUKA!
WHSH WHSH
DID YOU CALL ME?
GAH! URUKA?!
YIKES!
WHAT'S WRONG?! YOU'RE SCARING ME!
OH... HEY!
URUKA... YOU'RE ALONE?
YEAH. THE OTHERS ARE STILL IN THE BATH!
HEH HEH! THE WATER WAS SOOO NICE!
...
SO...
NOW...

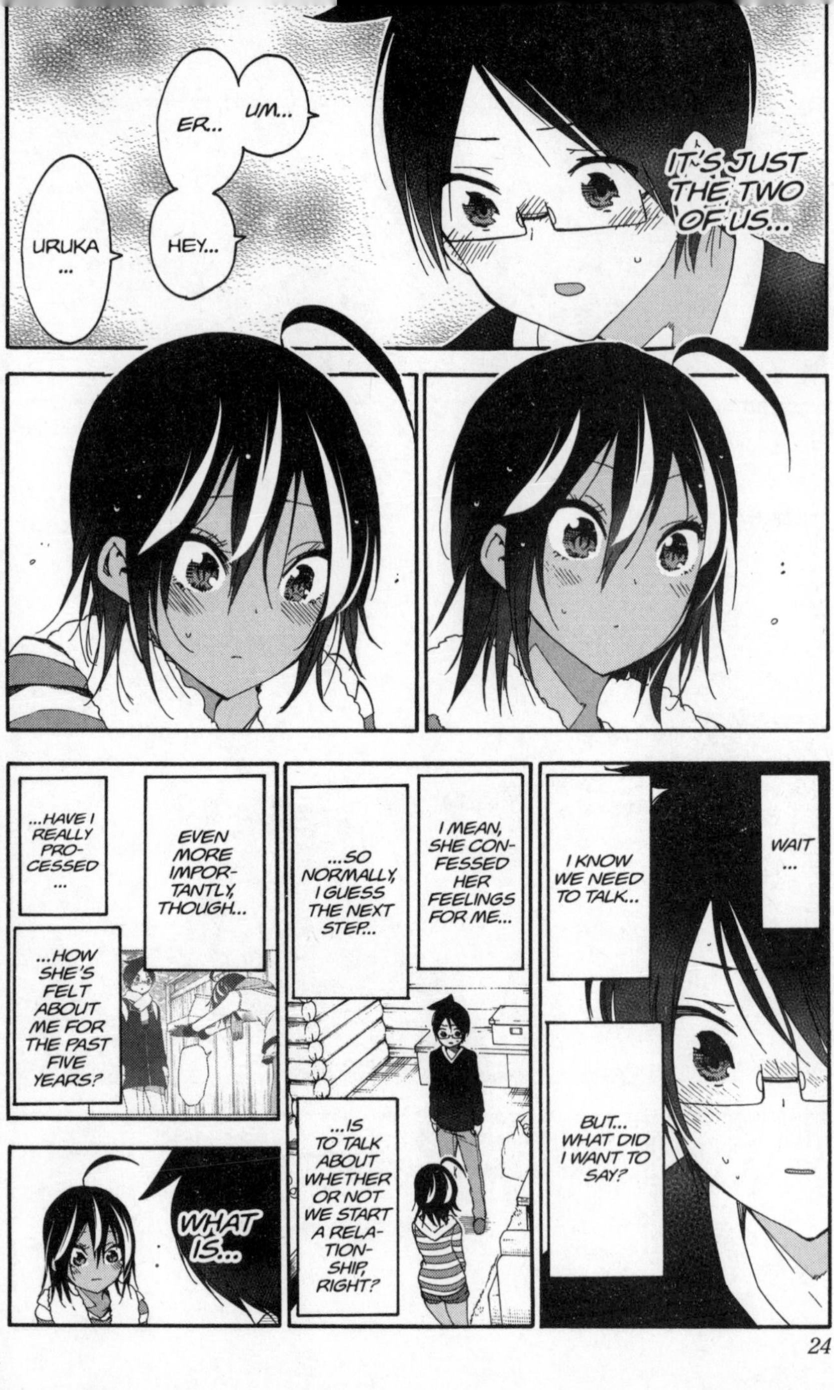
IT'S JUST THE TWO OF US...
UM...
ER...
HEY...
URUKA...
WAIT...
I KNOW WE NEED TO TALK...
BUT... WHAT DID I WANT TO SAY?
I MEAN, SHE CONFESSED HER FEELINGS FOR ME...
...SO NORMALLY, I GUESS THE NEXT STEP...
...IS TO TALK ABOUT WHETHER OR NOT WE START A RELATIONSHIP, RIGHT?
EVEN MORE IMPORTANTLY, THOUGH...
...HAVE I REALLY PROCESSED...
...HOW SHE'S FELT ABOUT ME FOR THE PAST FIVE YEARS?
WHAT IS...

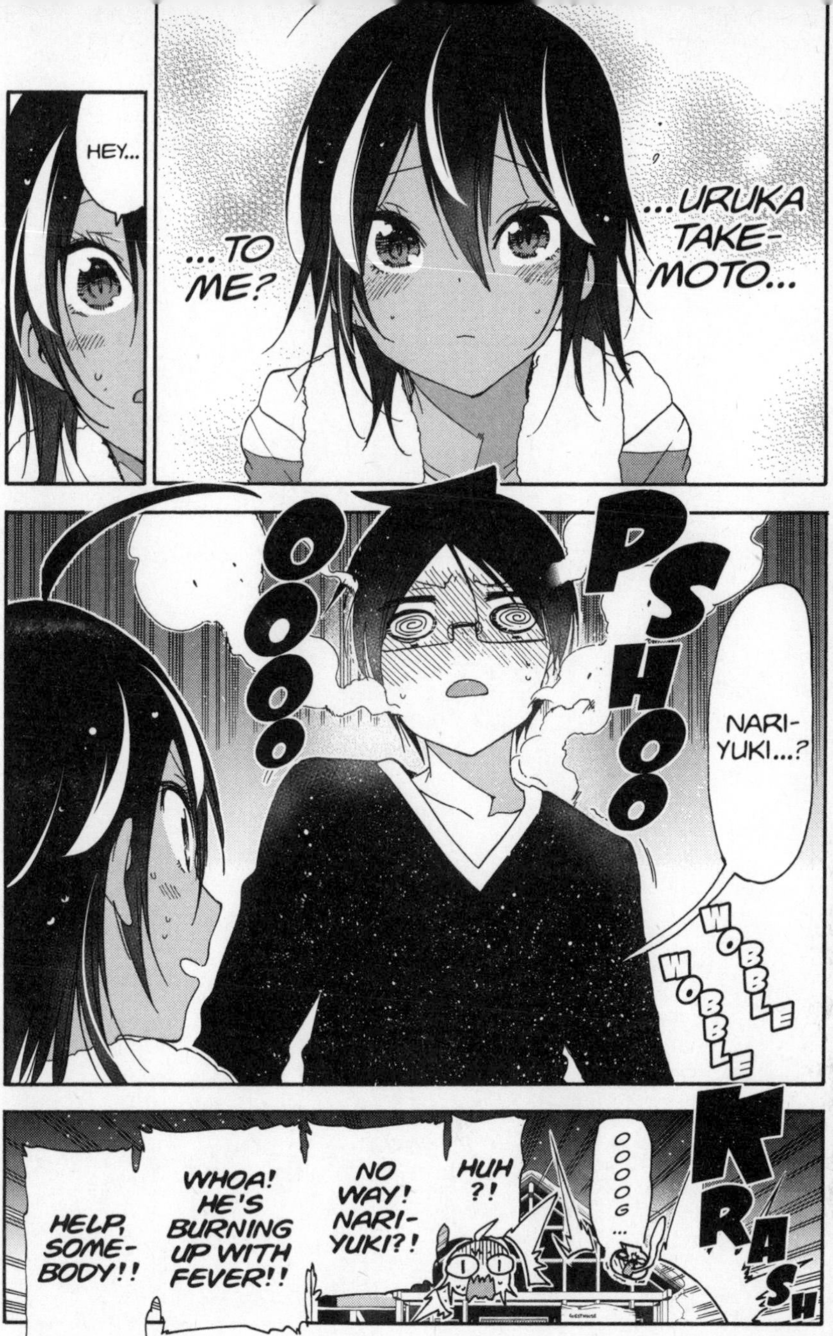
...URUKA TAKE-MOTO...
...TO ME?
HEY...
PSHOO
OOOOO
NARI-YUKI...?
WOBBLE
WOBBLE
KRASH
OOOOG...
HUH?!
NO WAY! NARI-YUKI?!
WHOA! HE'S BURNING UP WITH FEVER!!
HELP, SOME-BODY!!

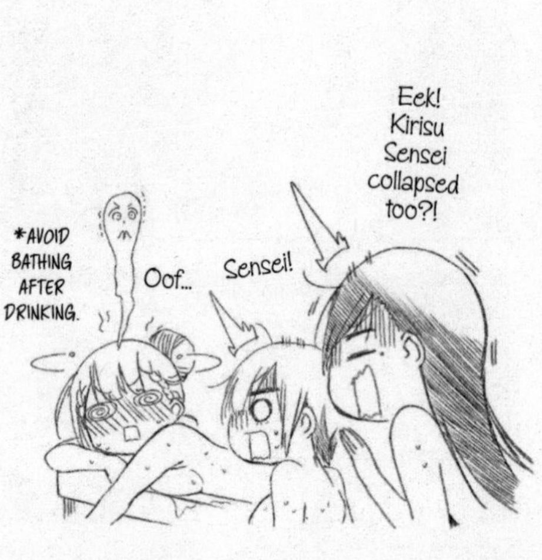
Eek! Kirisu Sensei collapsed too?!
Sensei!
Oof...
*AVOID BATHING AFTER DRINKING.

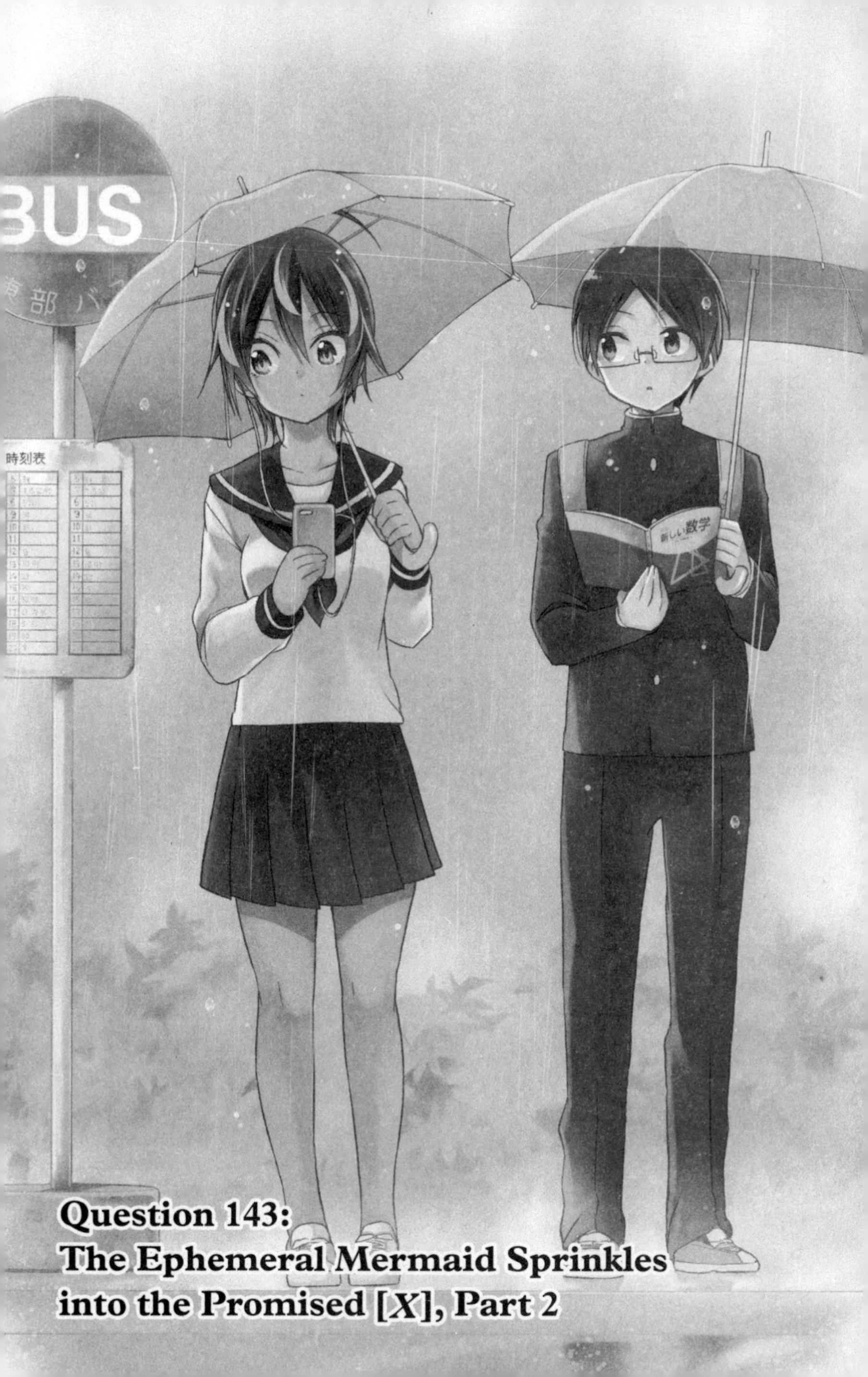
BUS
時刻表
新しい数学

Question 143:
The Ephemeral Mermaid Sprinkles into the Promised [*X*], Part 2

[x] We
Never
Learn

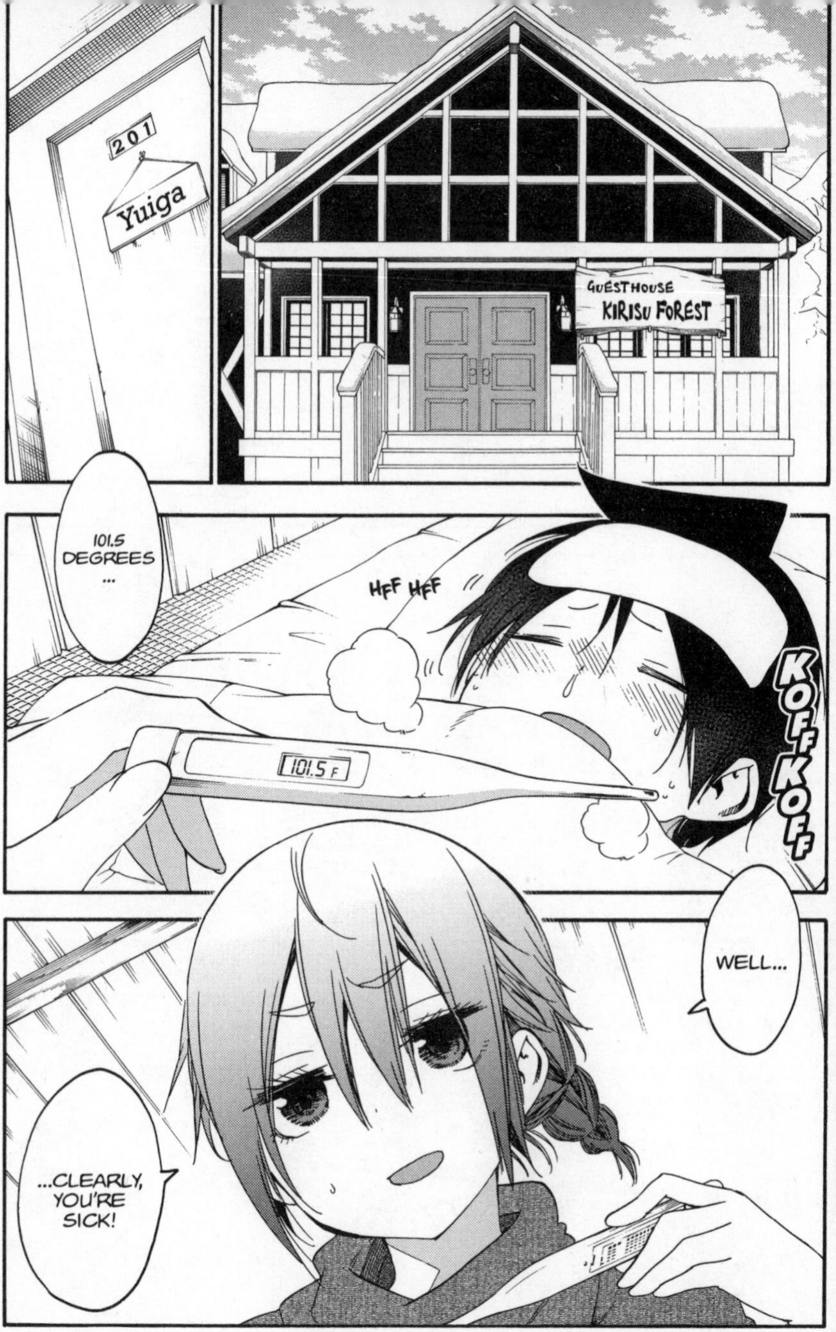
GUESTHOUSE
KIRISU FOREST
201
Yuiga
KOFF KOFF
HFF HFF
101.5 DEGREES ...
101.5 F
WELL...
...CLEARLY, YOU'RE SICK!

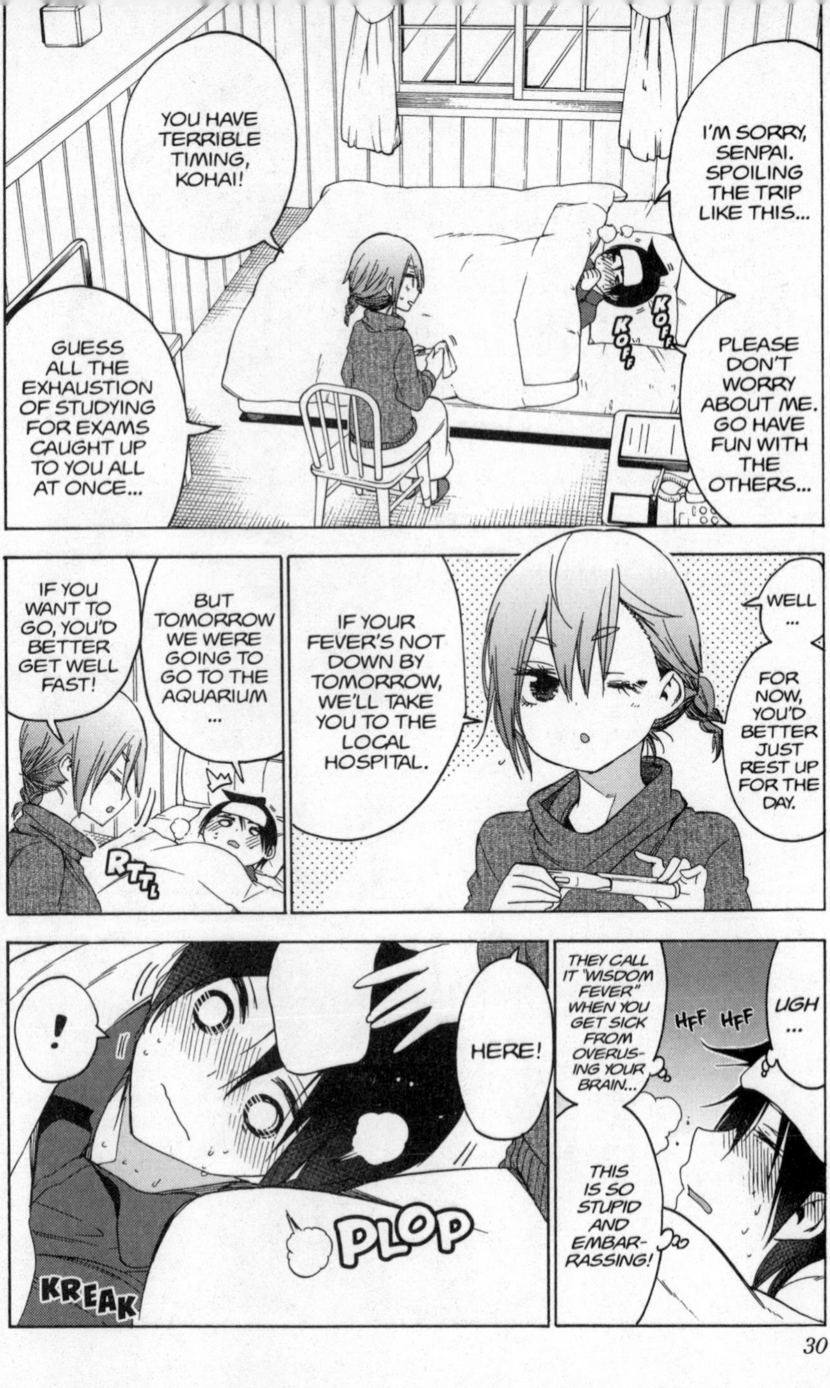
I'M SORRY, SENPAI. SPOILING THE TRIP LIKE THIS...
YOU HAVE TERRIBLE TIMING, KOHAI!
KOFF KOFF
PLEASE DON'T WORRY ABOUT ME. GO HAVE FUN WITH THE OTHERS...
GUESS ALL THE EXHAUSTION OF STUDYING FOR EXAMS CAUGHT UP TO YOU ALL AT ONCE...
WELL ...
FOR NOW, YOU'D BETTER JUST REST UP FOR THE DAY.
IF YOUR FEVER'S NOT DOWN BY TOMORROW, WE'LL TAKE YOU TO THE LOCAL HOSPITAL.
BUT TOMORROW WE WERE GOING TO GO TO THE AQUARIUM ...
IF YOU WANT TO GO, YOU'D BETTER GET WELL FAST!
RTTL
UGH ...
HFF HFF
THEY CALL IT "WISDOM FEVER" WHEN YOU GET SICK FROM OVERUS-ING YOUR BRAIN...
THIS IS SO STUPID AND EMBAR-RASSING!
HERE!
!
PLOP
KREAK

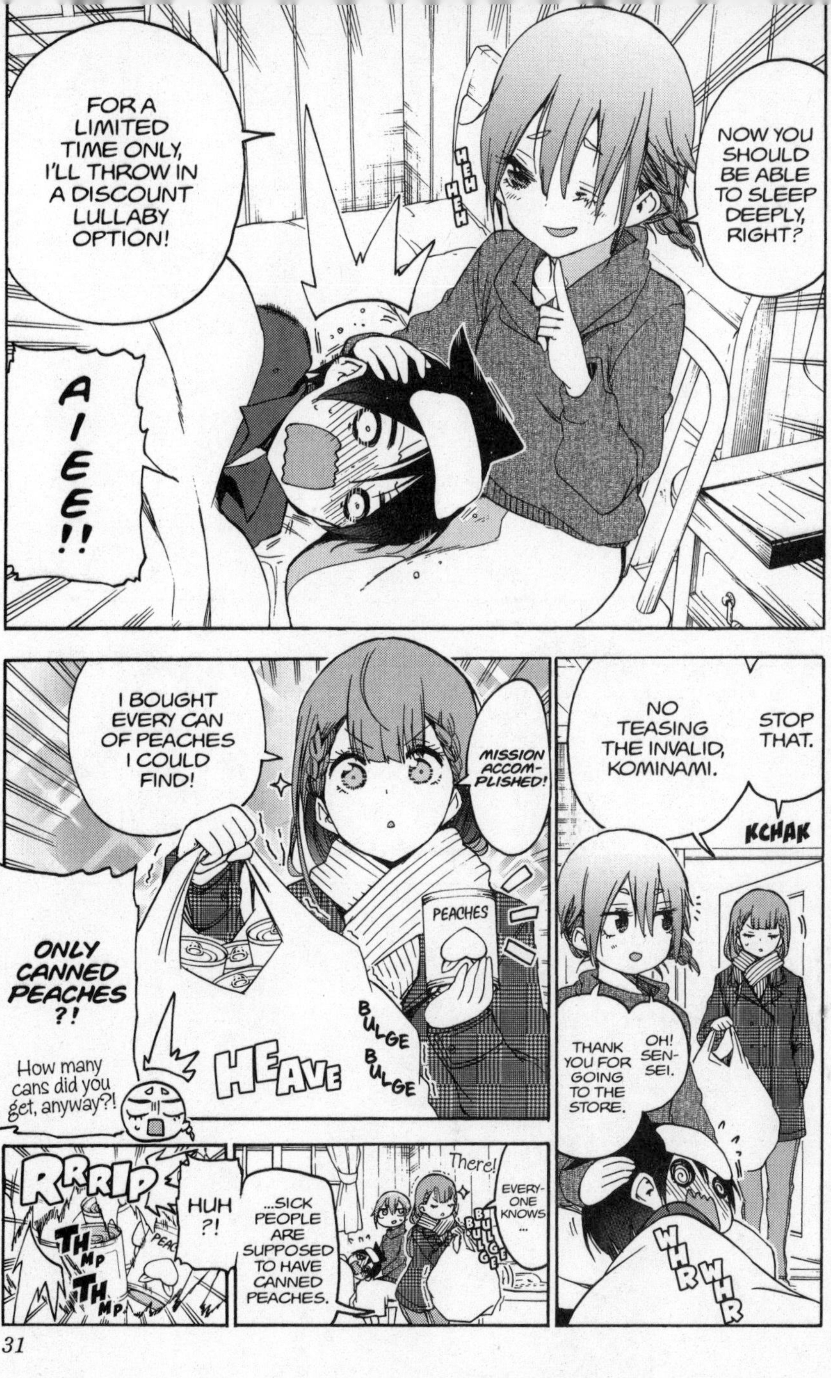
NOW YOU SHOULD BE ABLE TO SLEEP DEEPLY, RIGHT?
HEH HEH
FOR A LIMITED TIME ONLY, I'LL THROW IN A DISCOUNT LULLABY OPTION!
AIEEE!!
STOP THAT.
NO TEASING THE INVALID, KOMINAMI.
KCHAK
OH! SEN-SEI.
THANK YOU FOR GOING TO THE STORE.
WHR WHR
MISSION ACCOMPLISHED!
I BOUGHT EVERY CAN OF PEACHES I COULD FIND!
PEACHES
BULGE BULGE
HEAVE
ONLY CANNED PEACHES?!
How many cans did you get, anyway?!
There!
EVERY-ONE KNOWS ...
BULGE BULGE
...SICK PEOPLE ARE SUPPOSED TO HAVE CANNED PEACHES.
HUH ?!
RRRIP
THMP THMP

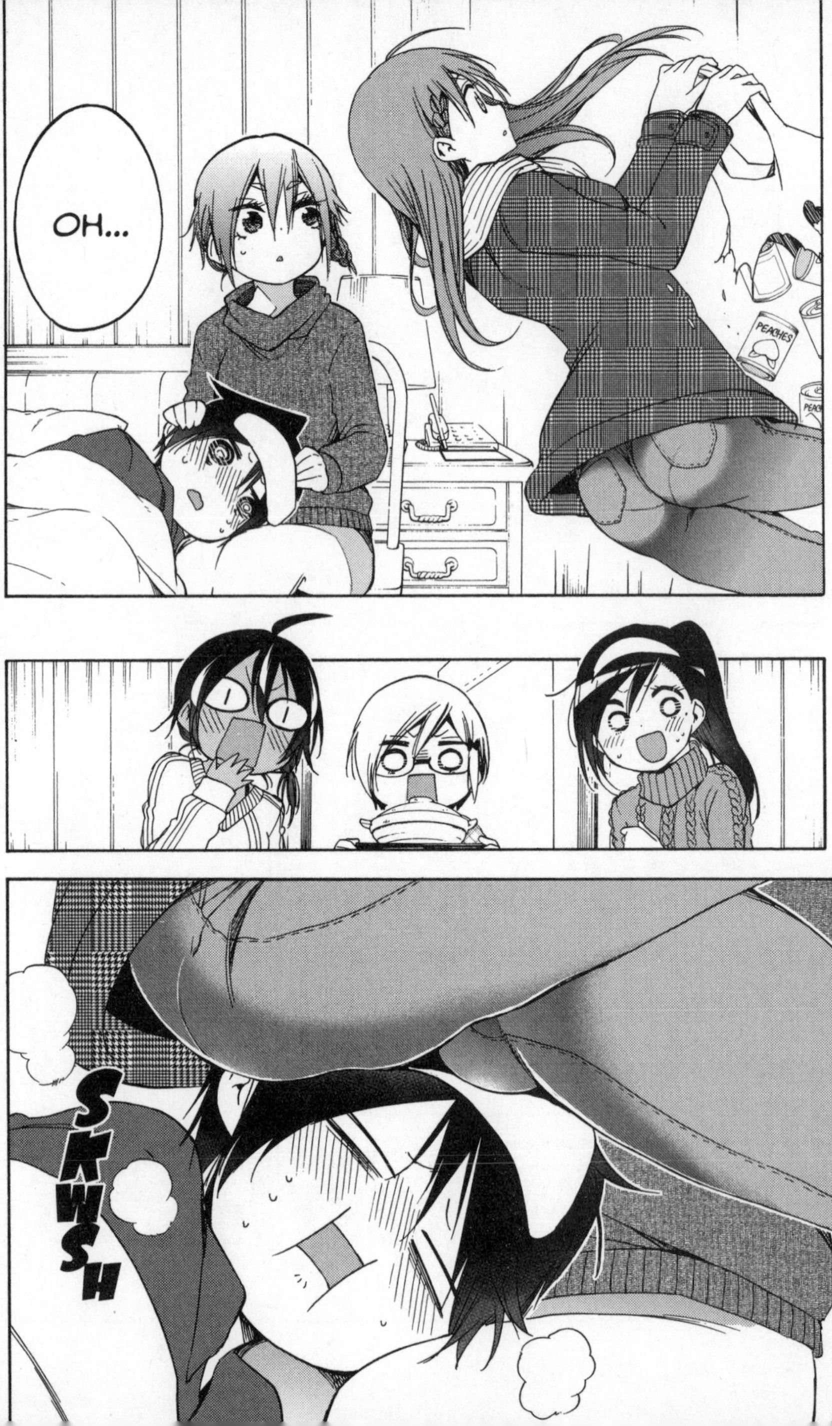
OH...
PEACHES
SKWSH

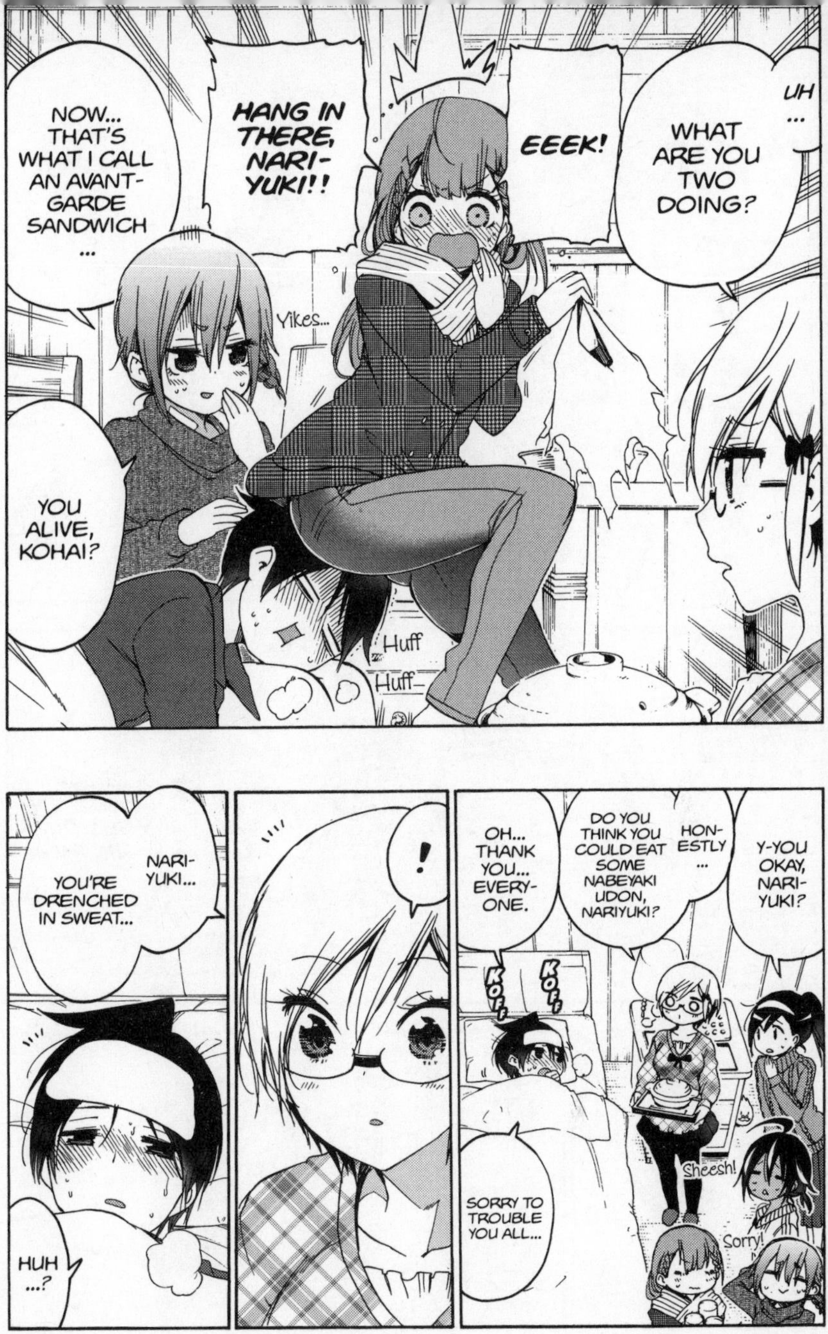
UH ...
WHAT ARE YOU TWO DOING?
EEEK!
HANG IN THERE, NARIYUKI!!
NOW... THAT'S WHAT I CALL AN AVANT-GARDE SANDWICH ...
Yikes...
YOU ALIVE, KOHAI?
Huff
Huff
Y-YOU OKAY, NARIYUKI?
HONESTLY ...
DO YOU THINK YOU COULD EAT SOME NABEYAKI UDON, NARIYUKI?
OH... THANK YOU... EVERYONE.
KOFF
KOFF
Sheesh!
SORRY TO TROUBLE YOU ALL...
Sorry!
!
NARIYUKI...
YOU'RE DRENCHED IN SWEAT...
HUH ...?

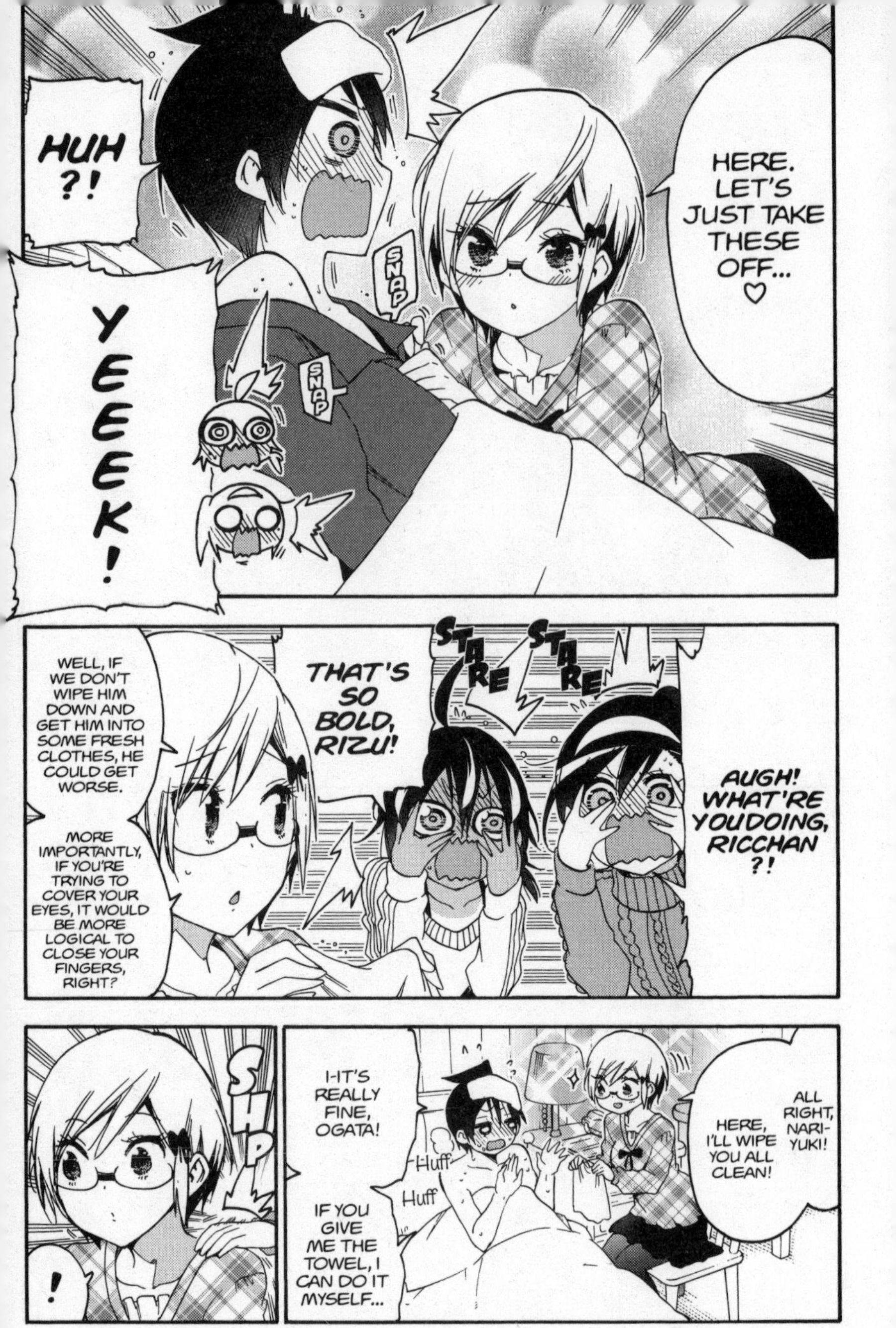
HERE. LET'S JUST TAKE THESE OFF... ♡
SNAP
SNAP
HUH ?!
YEEEEK!
AUGH! WHAT'RE YOUDOING, RICCHAN ?!
STARE
STARE
THAT'S SO BOLD, RIZU!
WELL, IF WE DON'T WIPE HIM DOWN AND GET HIM INTO SOME FRESH CLOTHES, HE COULD GET WORSE.
MORE IMPORTANTLY, IF YOU'RE TRYING TO COVER YOUR EYES, IT WOULD BE MORE LOGICAL TO CLOSE YOUR FINGERS, RIGHT?
ALL RIGHT, NARI-YUKI!
HERE, I'LL WIPE YOU ALL CLEAN!
I-IT'S REALLY FINE, OGATA!
Huff
Huff
IF YOU GIVE ME THE TOWEL, I CAN DO IT MYSELF...
SHP
!

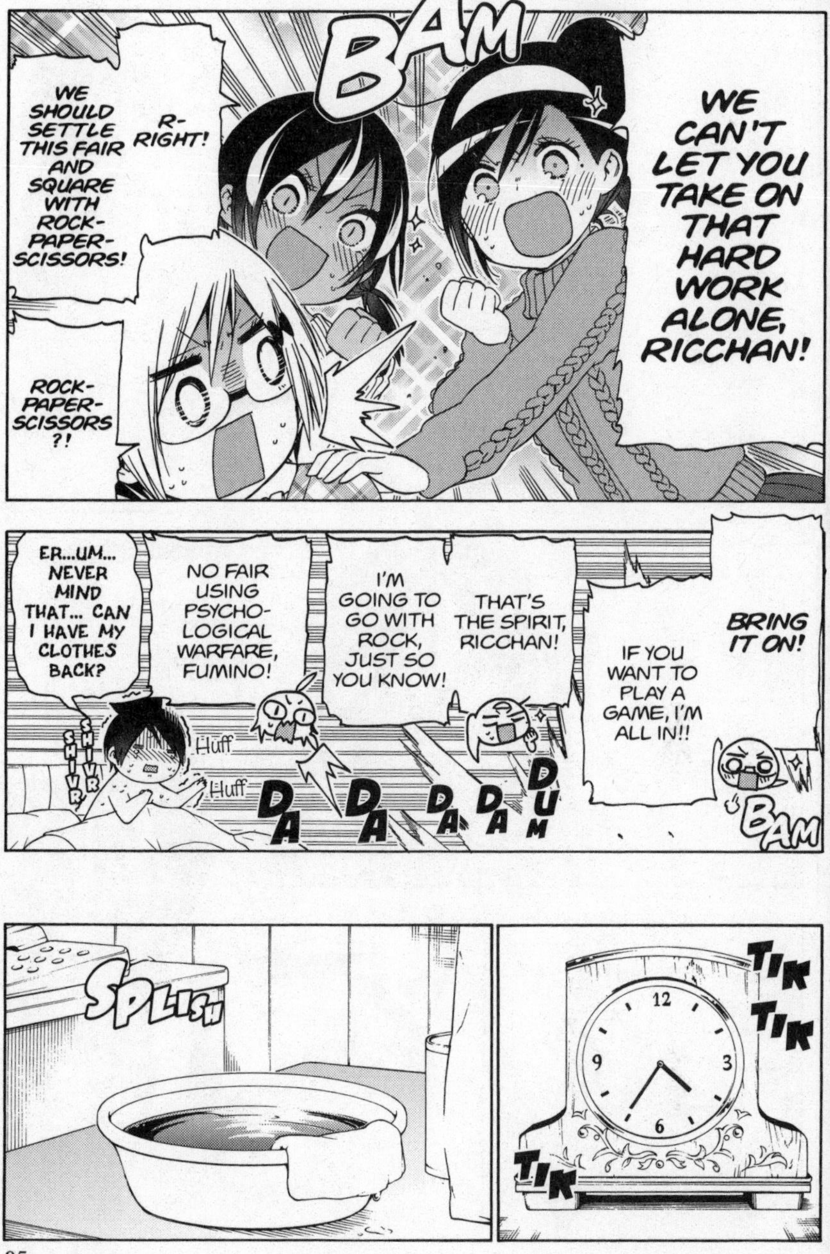
BAM
WE CAN'T LET YOU TAKE ON THAT HARD WORK ALONE, RICCHAN!
R-RIGHT!
WE SHOULD SETTLE THIS FAIR AND SQUARE WITH ROCK-PAPER-SCISSORS!
ROCK-PAPER-SCISSORS?!
BRING IT ON!
IF YOU WANT TO PLAY A GAME, I'M ALL IN!!
BAM
THAT'S THE SPIRIT, RICCHAN!
I'M GOING TO GO WITH ROCK, JUST SO YOU KNOW!
NO FAIR USING PSYCHOLOGICAL WARFARE, FUMINO!
DA DA DA DA DUM
ER...UM... NEVER MIND THAT... CAN I HAVE MY CLOTHES BACK?
Huff
Huff
SHIVR SHIVR
TIK TIK
TIK
SPLISH

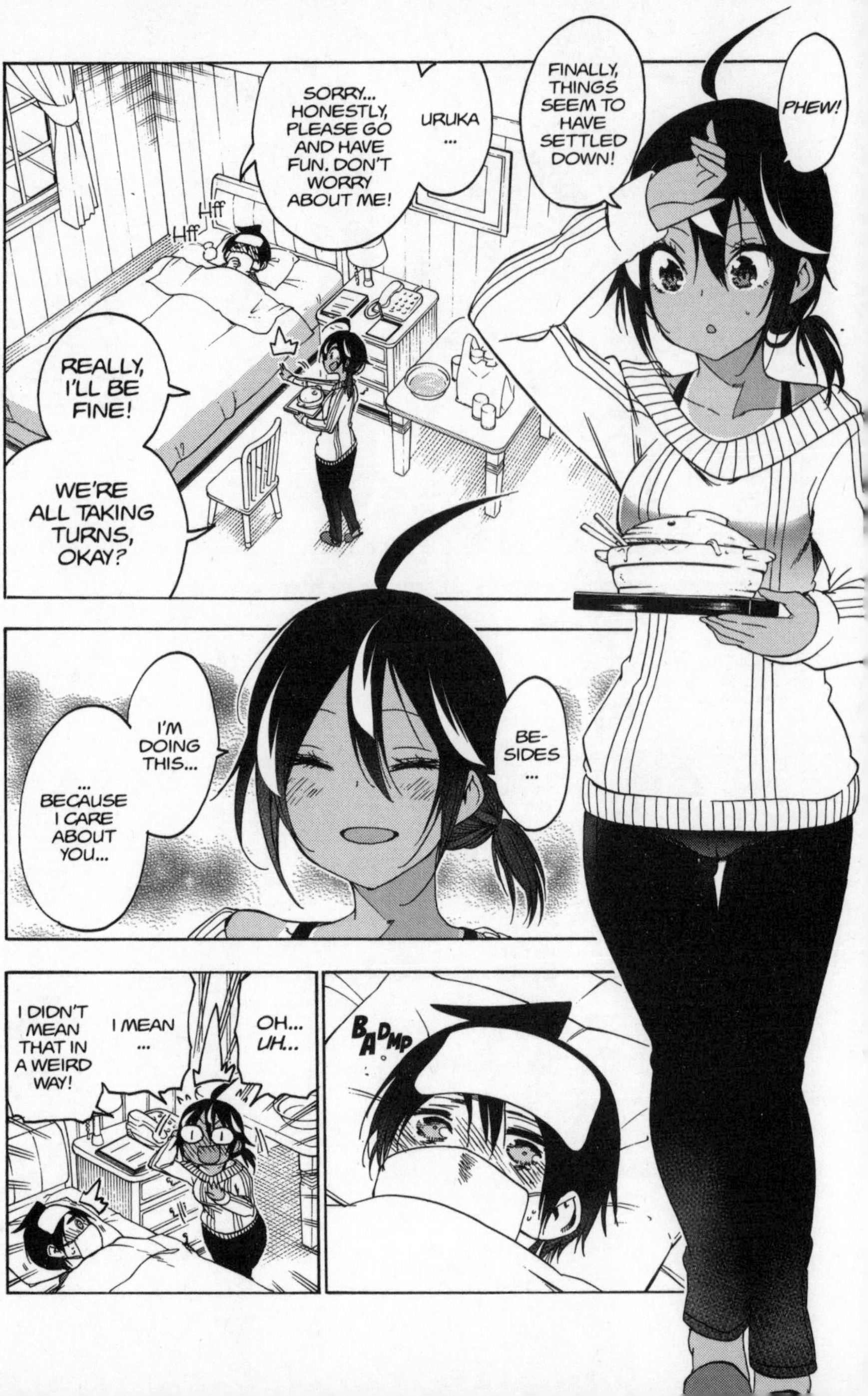
PHEW!
FINALLY, THINGS SEEM TO HAVE SETTLED DOWN!
URUKA ...
SORRY... HONESTLY, PLEASE GO AND HAVE FUN. DON'T WORRY ABOUT ME!
Hff Hff
REALLY, I'LL BE FINE!
WE'RE ALL TAKING TURNS, OKAY?
BE-SIDES ...
I'M DOING THIS...
... BECAUSE I CARE ABOUT YOU...
BADMP
OH... UH...
I MEAN ...
I DIDN'T MEAN THAT IN A WEIRD WAY!

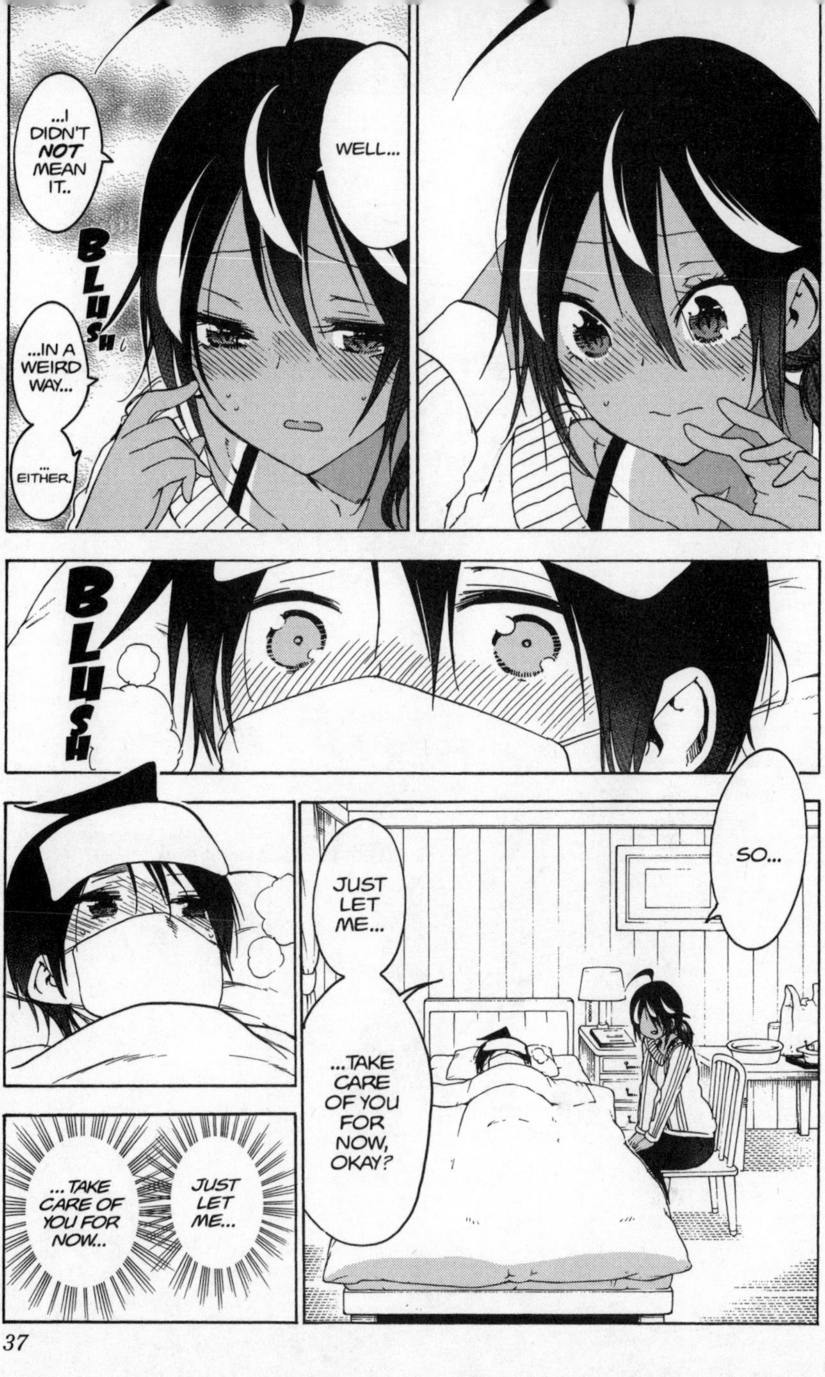
WELL...
...I DIDN'T NOT MEAN IT..
BLUSH
...IN A WEIRD WAY...
... EITHER.
BLUSH
SO...
JUST LET ME...
...TAKE CARE OF YOU FOR NOW, OKAY?
JUST LET ME...
...TAKE CARE OF YOU FOR NOW...

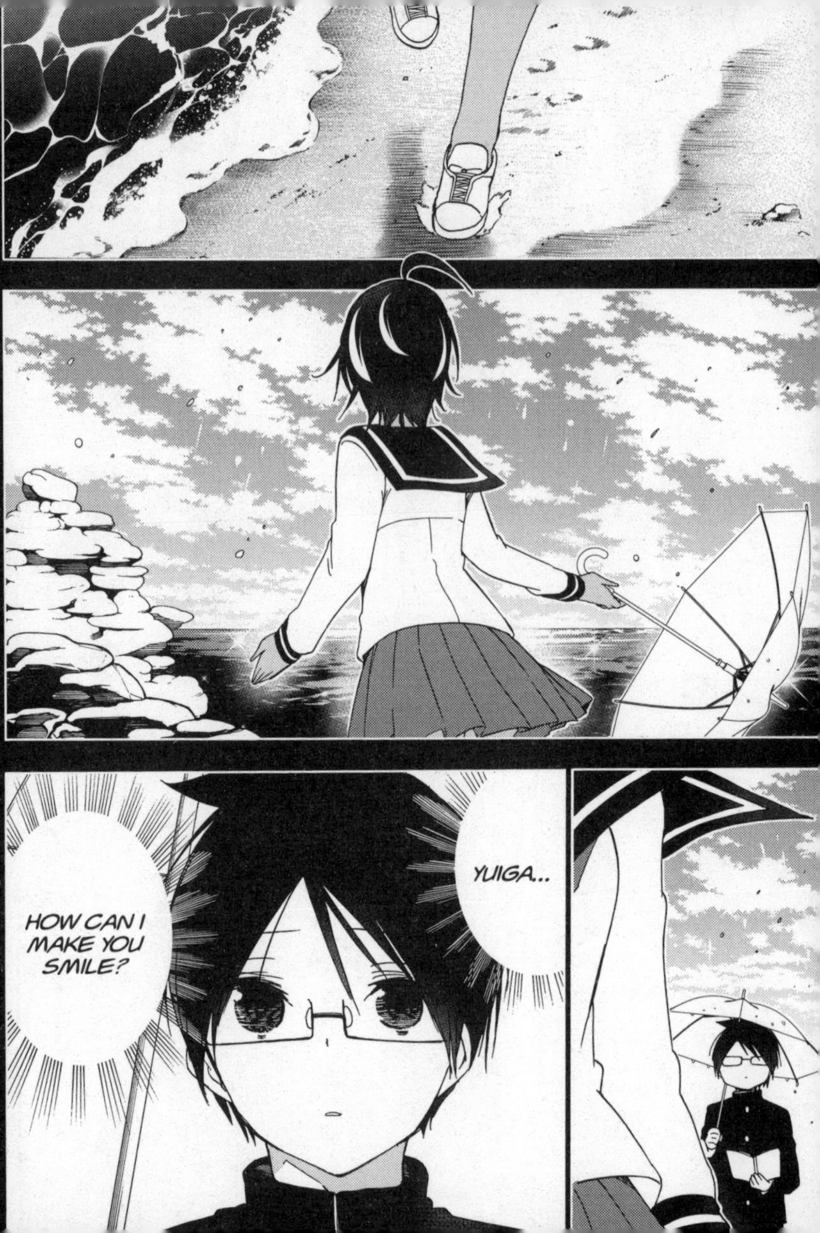
YUIGA...
HOW CAN I MAKE YOU SMILE?

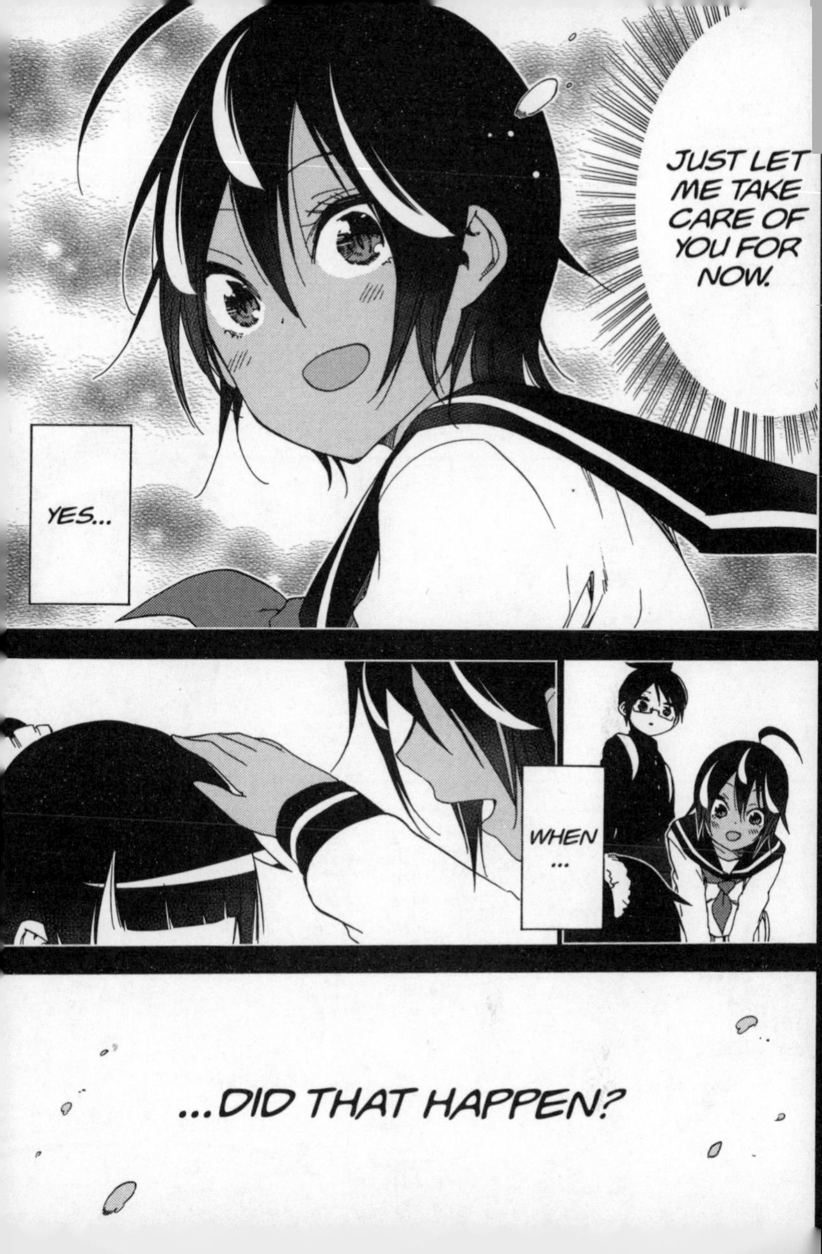
JUST LET ME TAKE CARE OF YOU FOR NOW.
YES...
WHEN ...
...DID THAT HAPPEN?

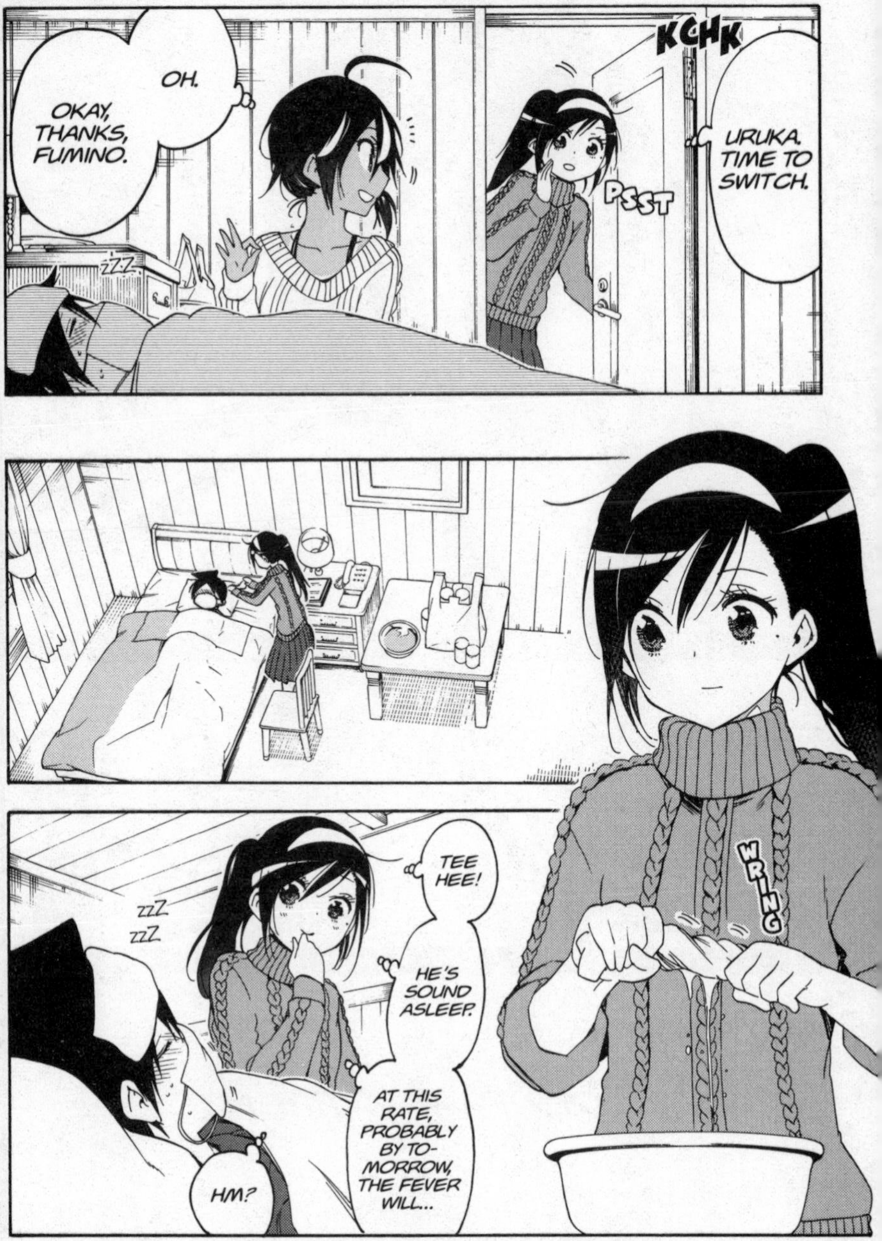
KCHK
URUKA. TIME TO SWITCH.
PSST
OH.
OKAY, THANKS, FUMINO.
ZZZ
WRING
TEE HEE!
HE'S SOUND ASLEEP.
zzZ
zzZ
AT THIS RATE, PROBABLY BY TO-MORROW, THE FEVER WILL...
HM?

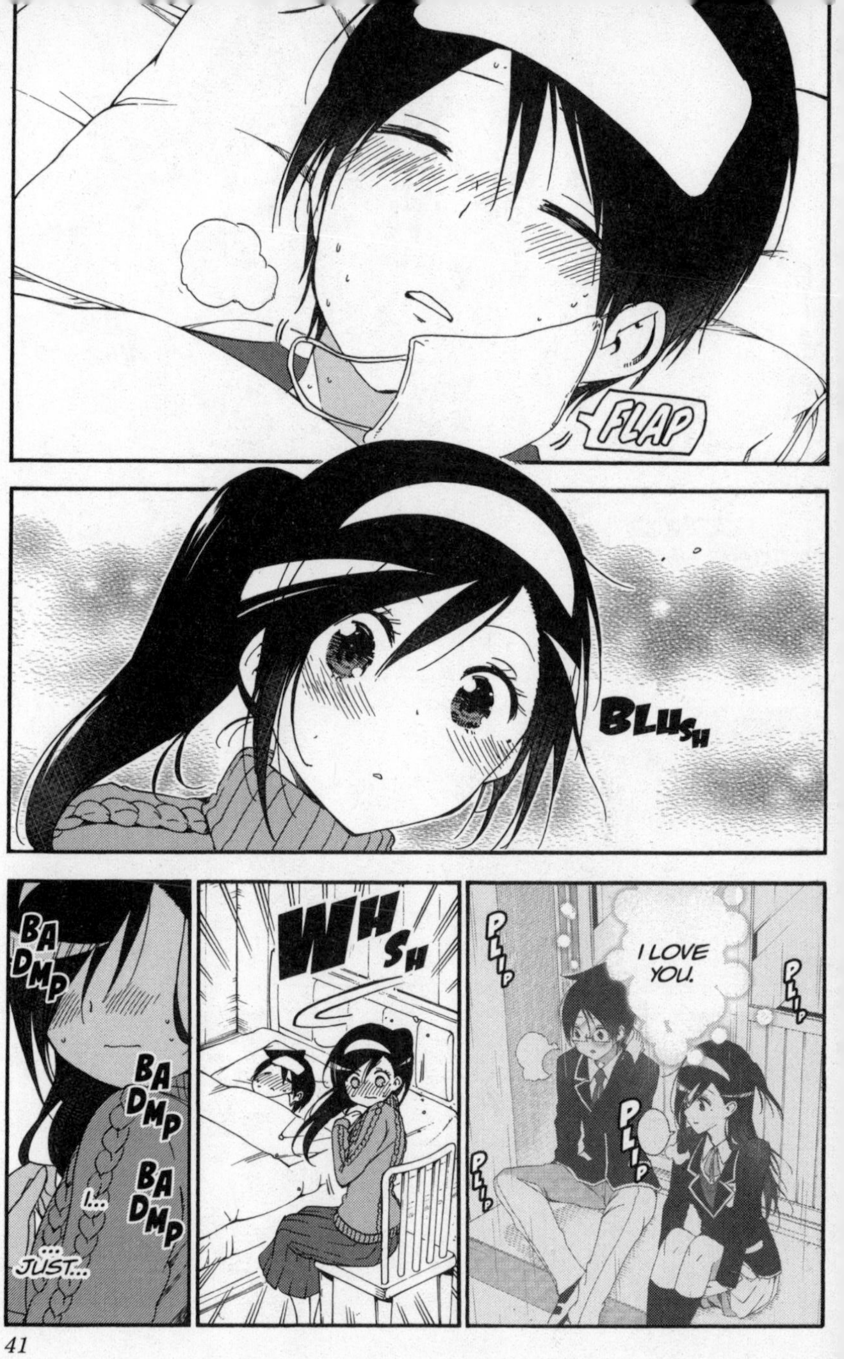
FLAP
BLUSH
I LOVE YOU.
PLIP
PLIP
PLIP
PLIP
WHSH
BA DMP
BA DMP
BA DMP
I...
...JUST...

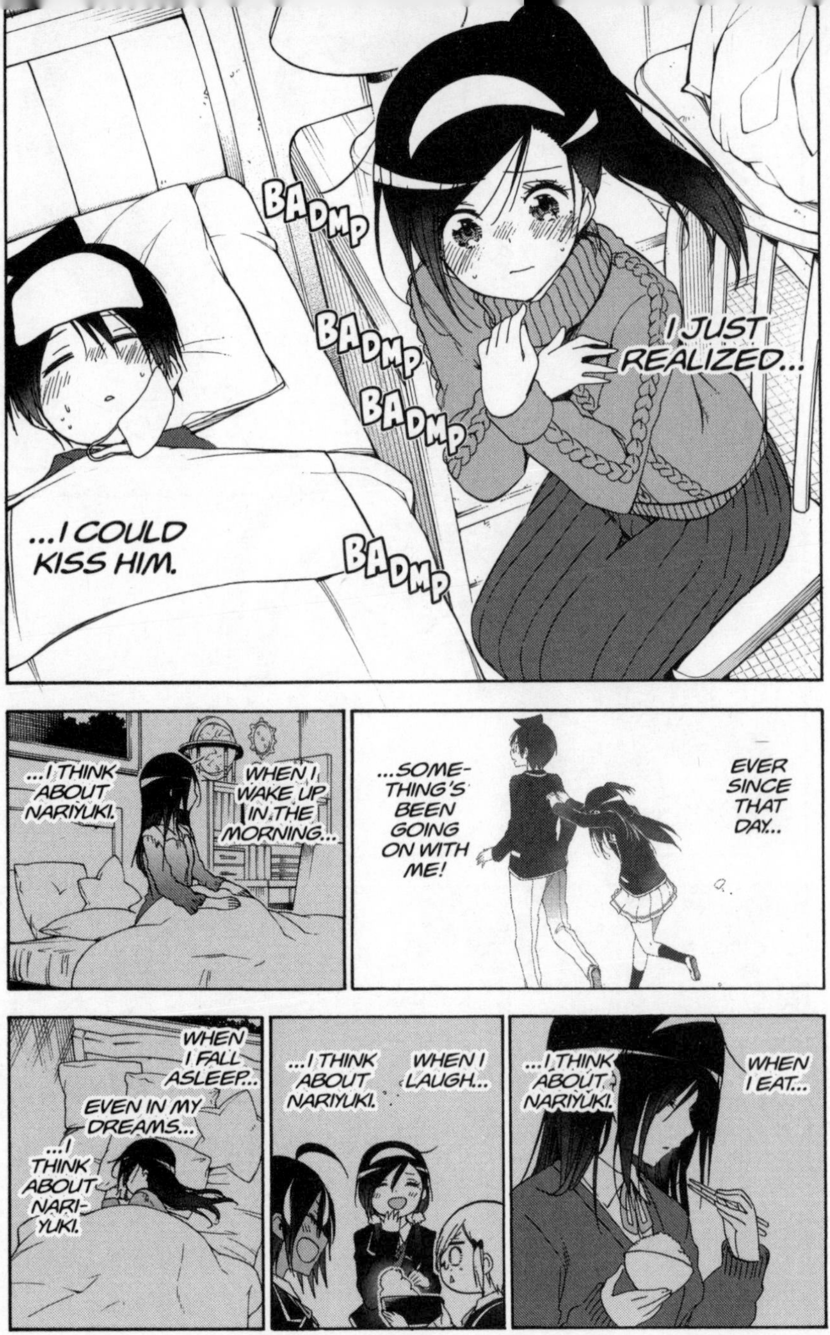
I JUST REALIZED...
BADMP
BADMP
BADMP
BADMP
...I COULD KISS HIM.
EVER SINCE THAT DAY...
...SOME-THING'S BEEN GOING ON WITH ME!
WHEN I WAKE UP IN THE MORNING...
...I THINK ABOUT NARIYUKI.
WHEN I EAT...
...I THINK ABOUT NARIYUKI.
WHEN I LAUGH...
...I THINK ABOUT NARIYUKI.
WHEN I FALL ASLEEP...
EVEN IN MY DREAMS...
...I THINK ABOUT NARI-YUKI.

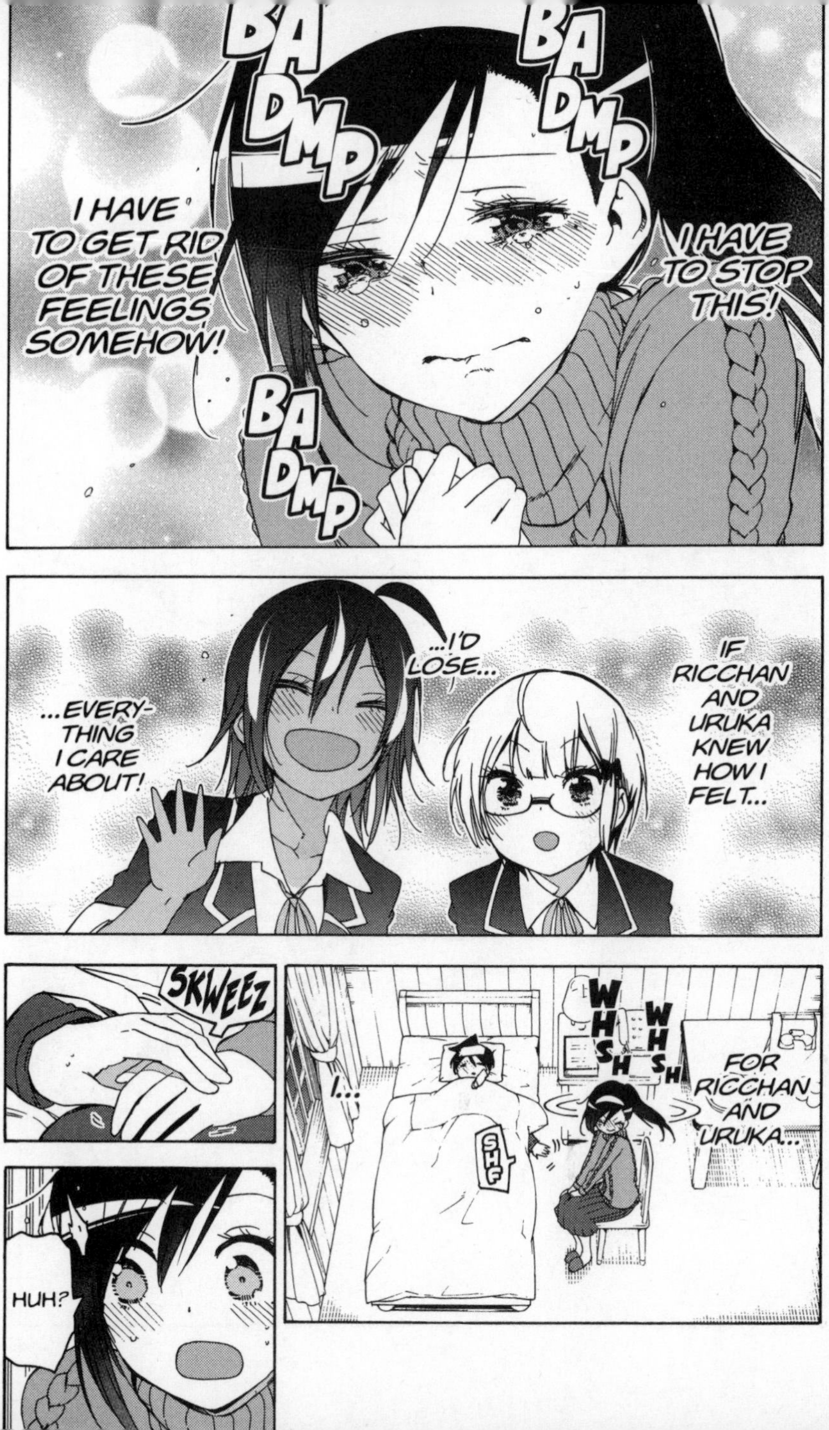
BA DMP
BA DMP
I HAVE TO STOP THIS!
I HAVE TO GET RID OF THESE FEELINGS SOMEHOW!
BA DMP
IF RICCHAN AND URUKA KNEW HOW I FELT...
...I'D LOSE...
...EVERY-THING I CARE ABOUT!
WHSH
WHSH
FOR RICCHAN AND URUKA...
I...
SHF
SKWEEZ
HUH?

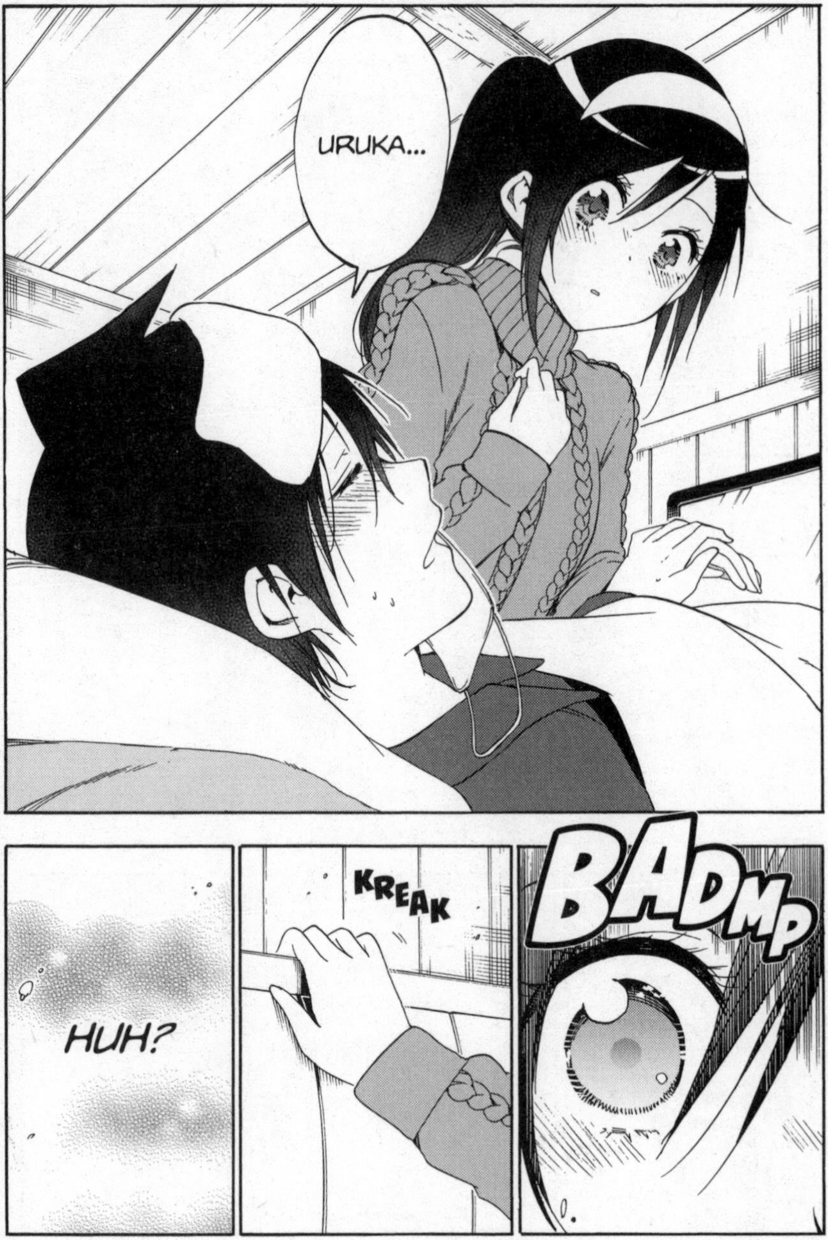
URUKA...
BADMP
KREAK
HUH?

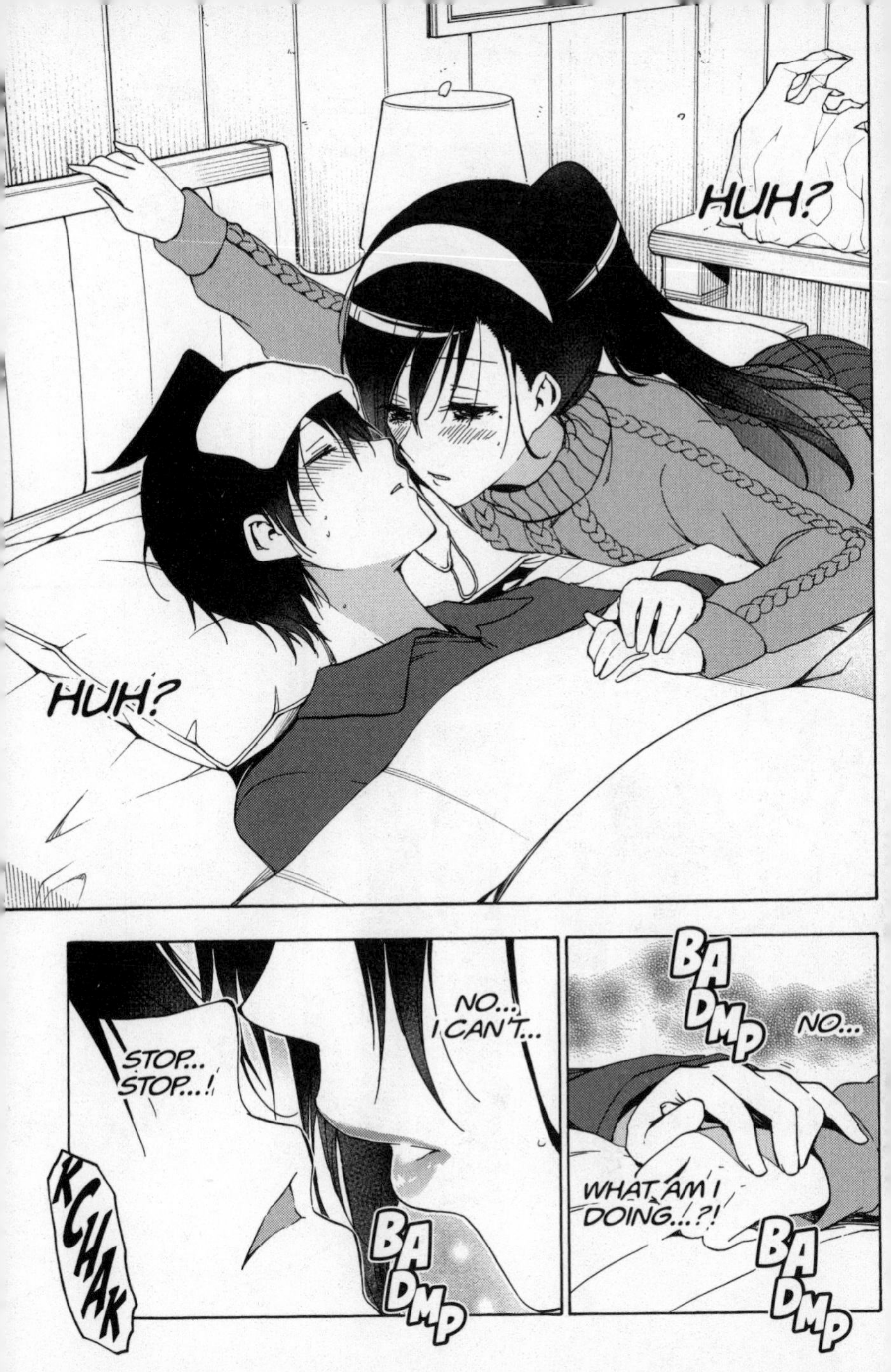
HUH?
HUH?
BA DMP
NO...
WHAT AM I DOING...?!
BA DMP
NO... I CAN'T...
STOP... STOP...!
BA DMP
KCHAK

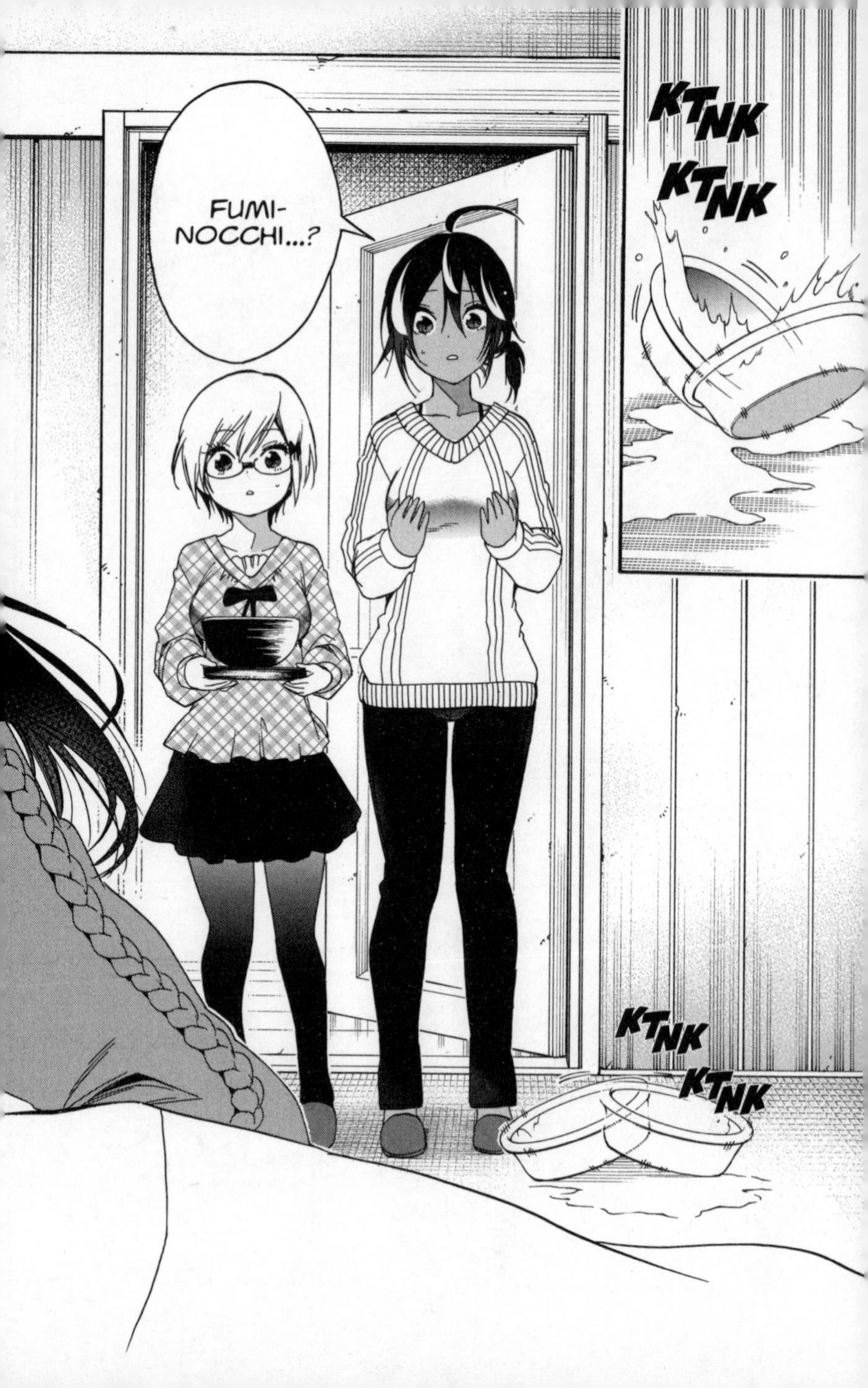
KTNK
KTNK
FUMI-NOCCHI...?
KTNK
KTNK

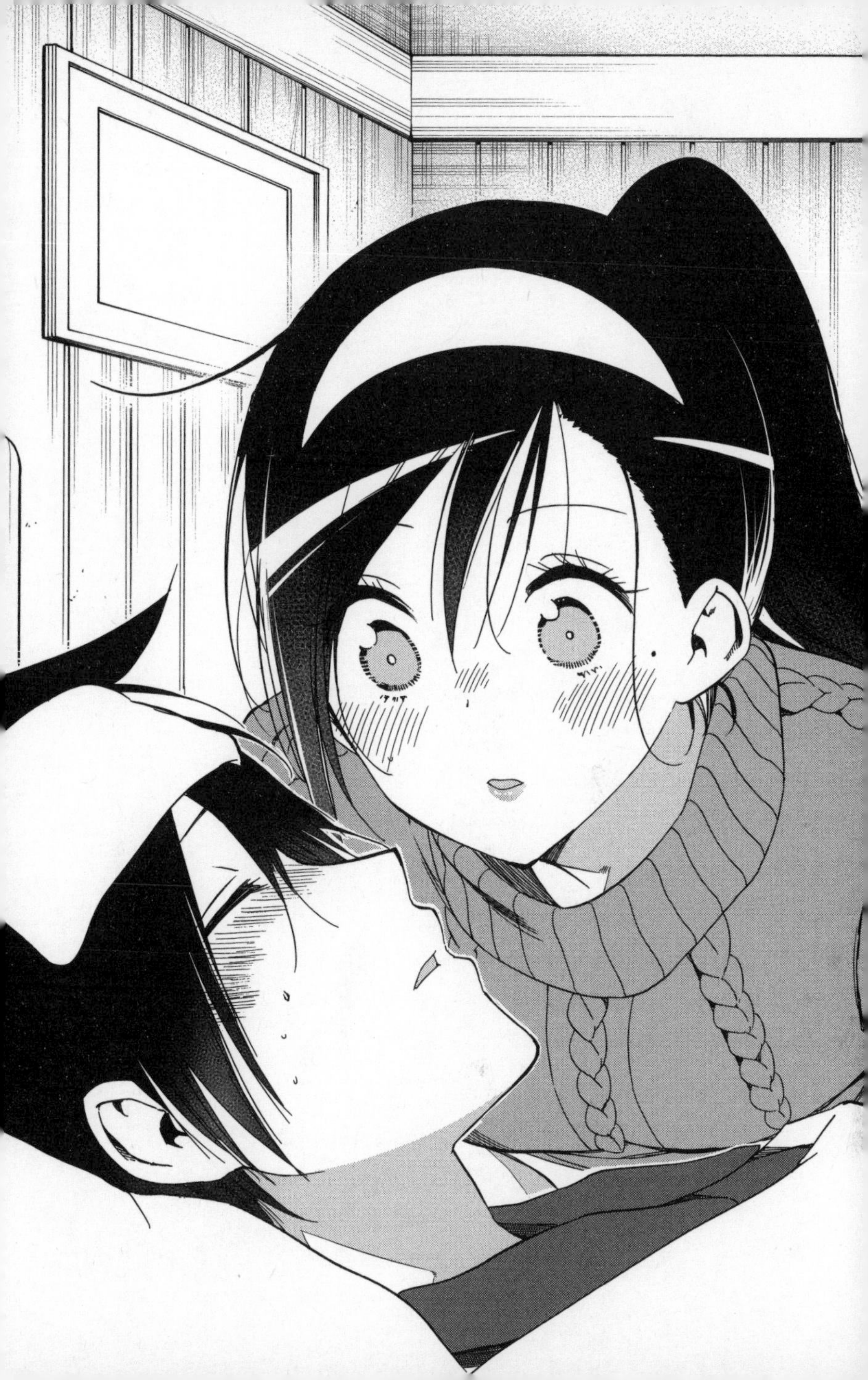

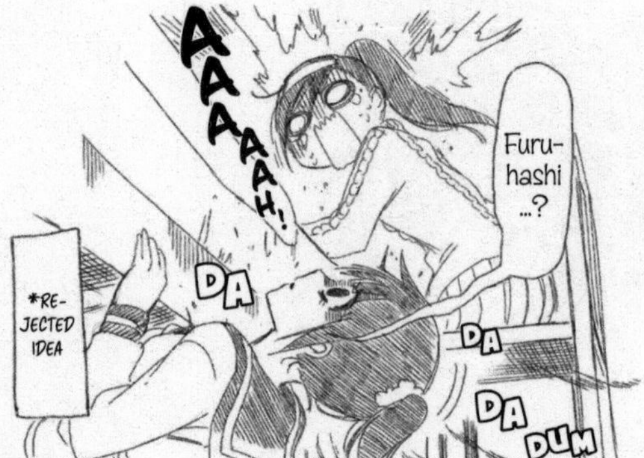
Furu-
hashi
...?
AAAAAH!
DA
DA
DA
DUM
*REJECTED IDEA

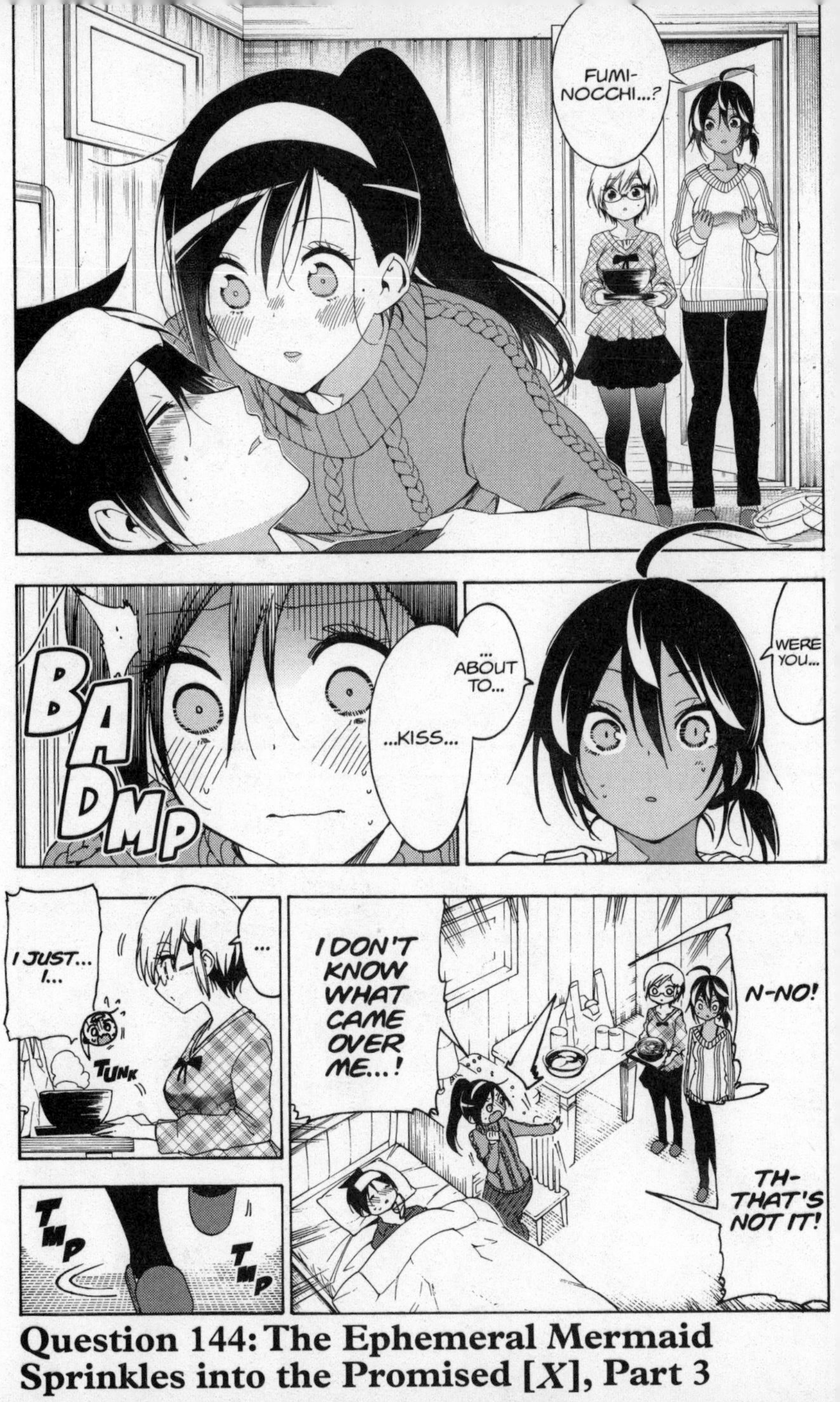
FUMI-NOCCHI...?
WERE YOU...
...ABOUT TO...
...KISS...
BADMP
N-NO!
I DON'T KNOW WHAT CAME OVER ME...!
TH-THAT'S NOT IT!
...
I JUST... I...
TUNK
TMP
TMP

Question 144: The Ephemeral Mermaid Sprinkles into the Promised [X], Part 3

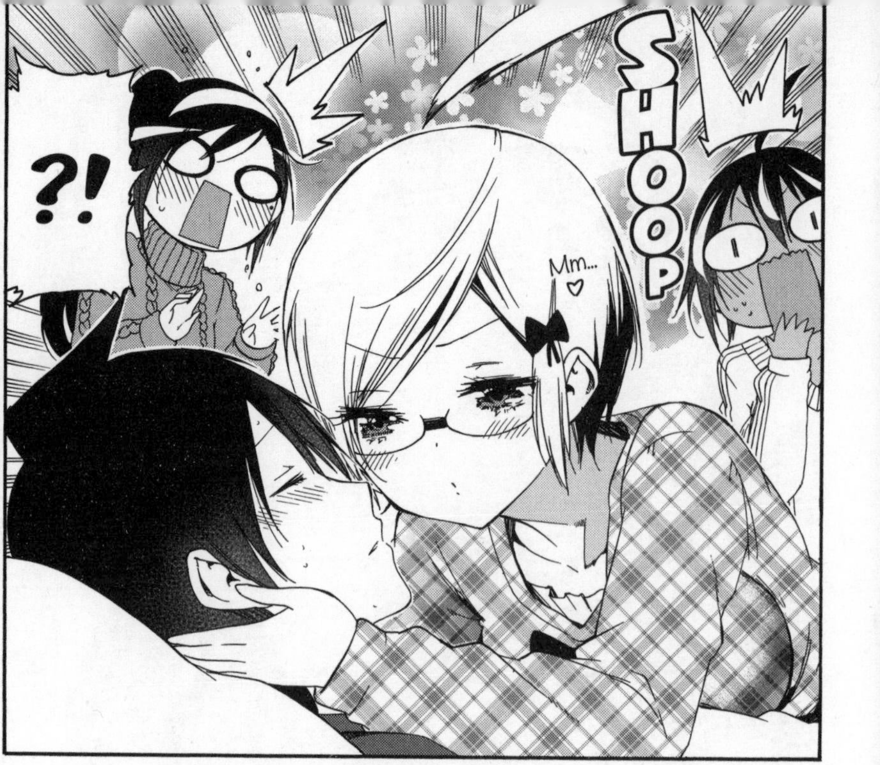
SHOOP
Mm... ♡
?!

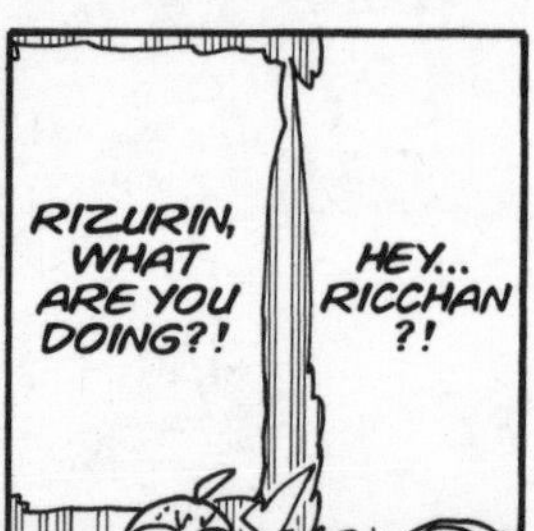
HEY... RICCHAN?!
RIZURIN, WHAT ARE YOU DOING?!
Stop! Stop!
BUT IT'S NOT FAIR!

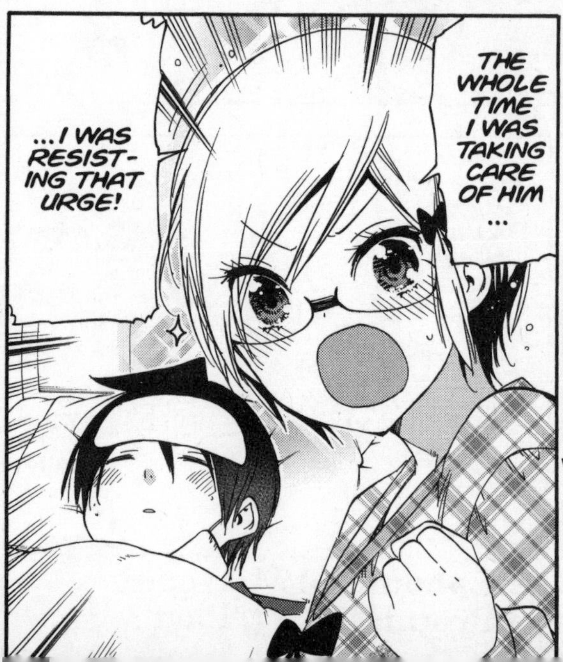
THE WHOLE TIME I WAS TAKING CARE OF HIM...
...I WAS RESISTING THAT URGE!

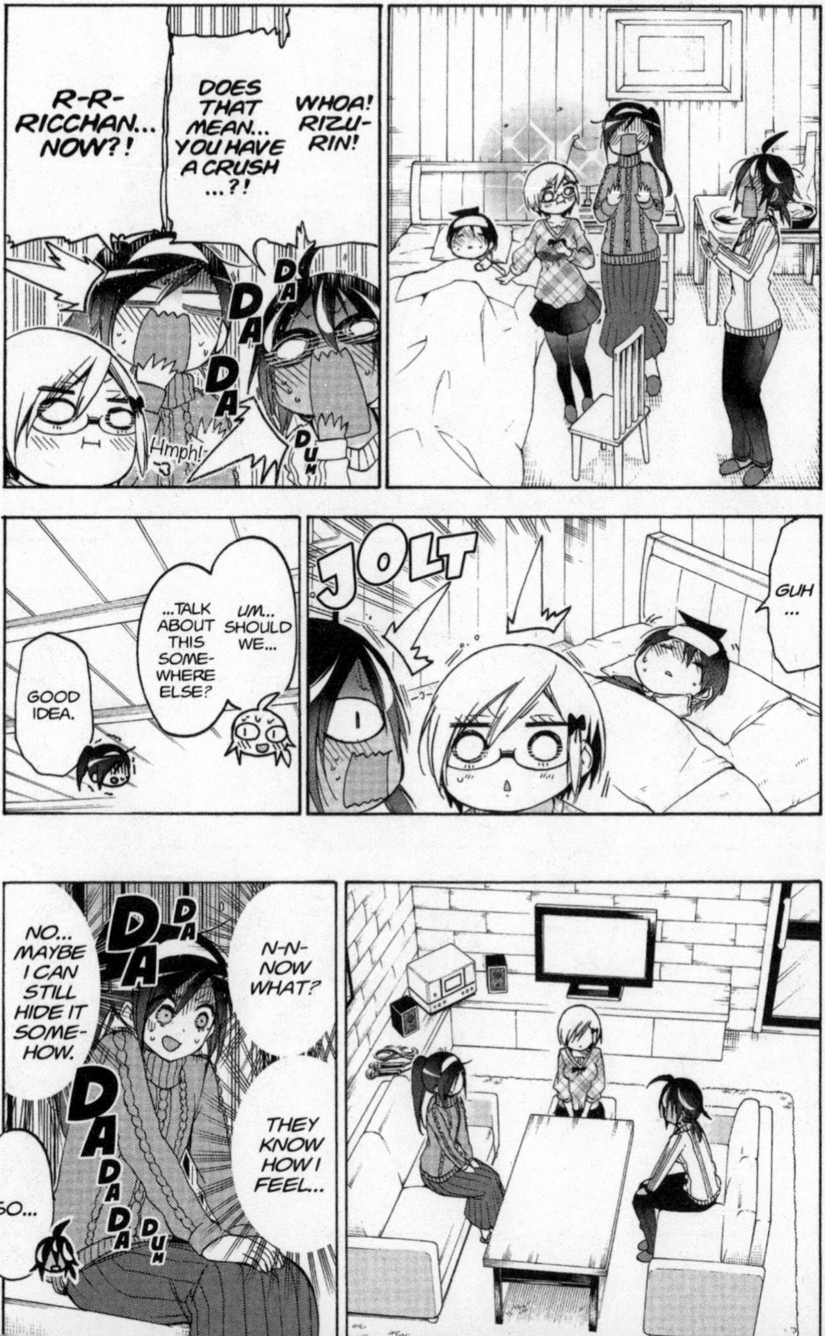
WHOA! RIZU-RIN!
DOES THAT MEAN... YOU HAVE A CRUSH ...?!
R-R-RICCHAN... NOW?!
DA DA DA DA
Hmph!
DUM
GUH ...
JOLT
UM... SHOULD WE...
...TALK ABOUT THIS SOME-WHERE ELSE?
GOOD IDEA.
N-N-NOW WHAT?
DA DA
NO... MAYBE I CAN STILL HIDE IT SOME-HOW.
THEY KNOW HOW I FEEL...
SO...
DA DA DA DA DUM

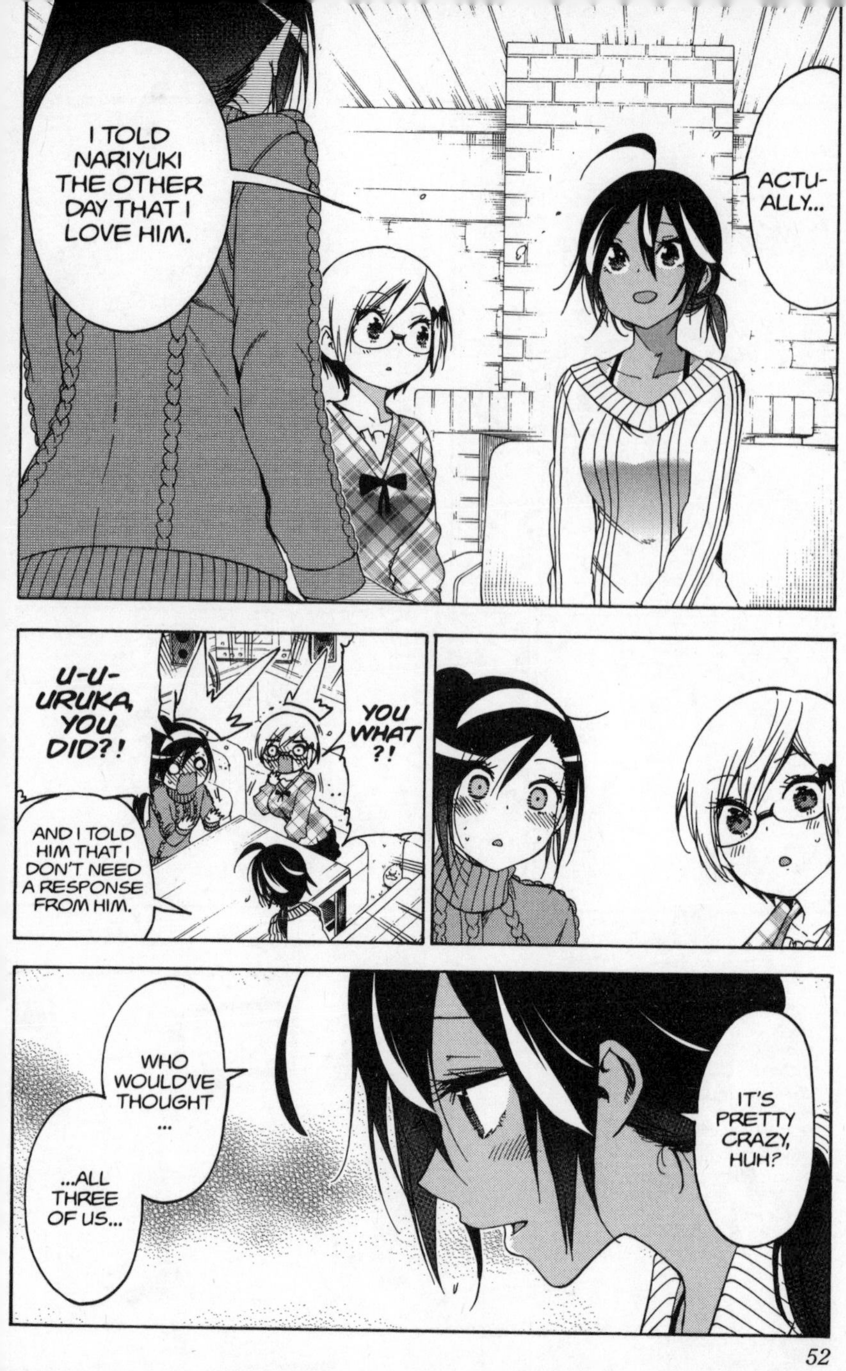
ACTU-ALLY...
I TOLD NARIYUKI THE OTHER DAY THAT I LOVE HIM.
YOU WHAT?!
U-U-URUKA, YOU DID?!
AND I TOLD HIM THAT I DON'T NEED A RESPONSE FROM HIM.
IT'S PRETTY CRAZY, HUH?
WHO WOULD'VE THOUGHT ...
...ALL THREE OF US...

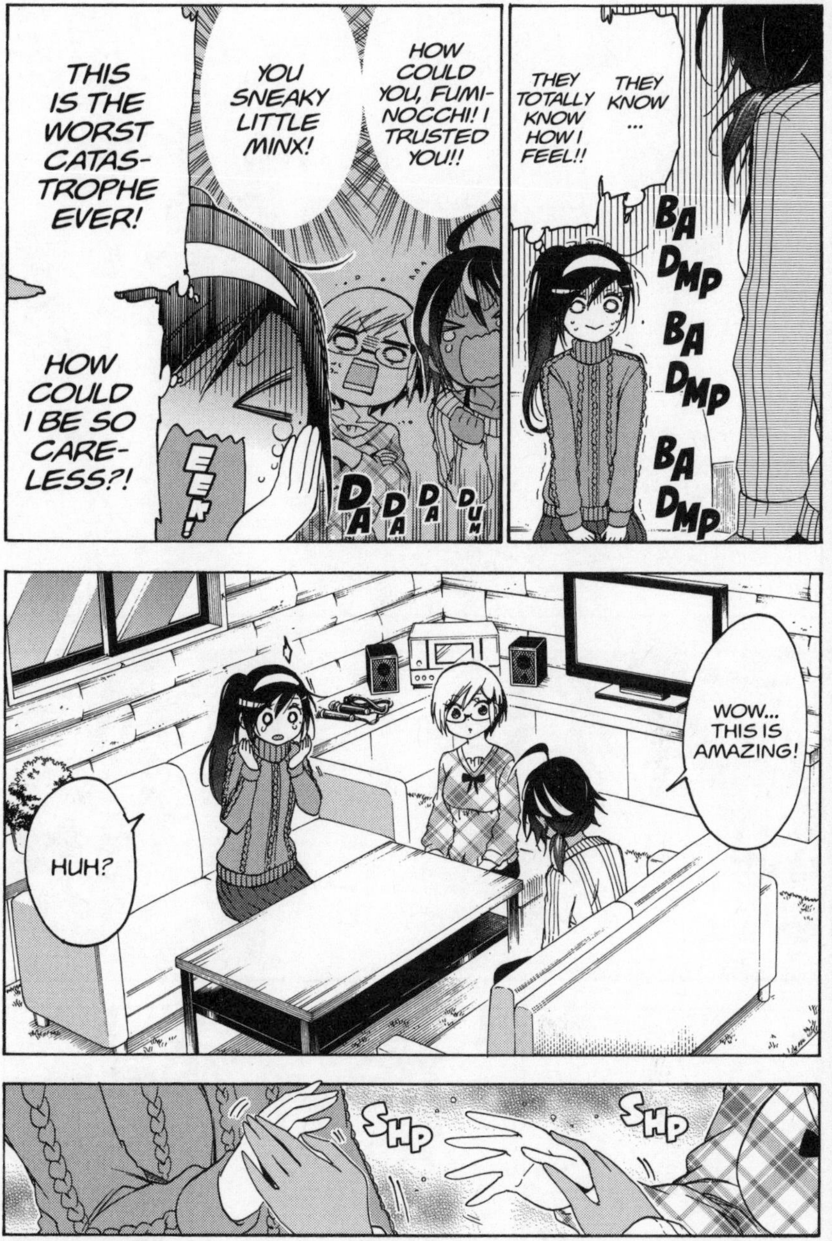
THEY KNOW ...
THEY TOTALLY KNOW HOW I FEEL!!
BA DMP
BA DMP
BA DMP
HOW COULD YOU, FUMI-NOCCHI! I TRUSTED YOU!!
YOU SNEAKY LITTLE MINX!
THIS IS THE WORST CATAS-TROPHE EVER!
HOW COULD I BE SO CARE-LESS?!
EEK!
DA DA DA DUM
WOW... THIS IS AMAZING!
HUH?
SHP
SHP

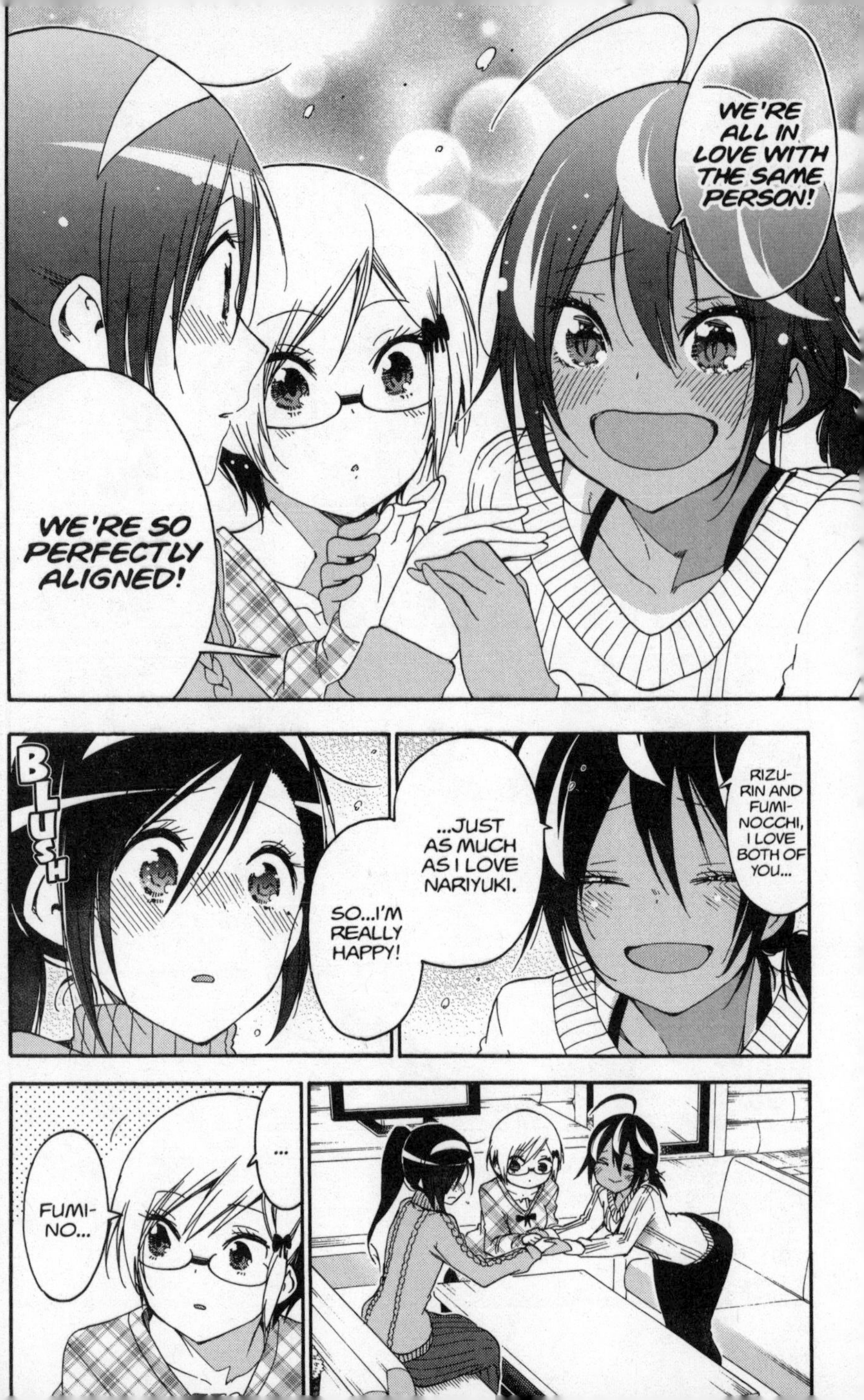
WE'RE ALL IN LOVE WITH THE SAME PERSON!
WE'RE SO PERFECTLY ALIGNED!
RIZU-RIN AND FUMI-NOCCHI, I LOVE BOTH OF YOU...
...JUST AS MUCH AS I LOVE NARIYUKI.
SO...I'M REALLY HAPPY!
BLUSH
...
FUMI-NO...

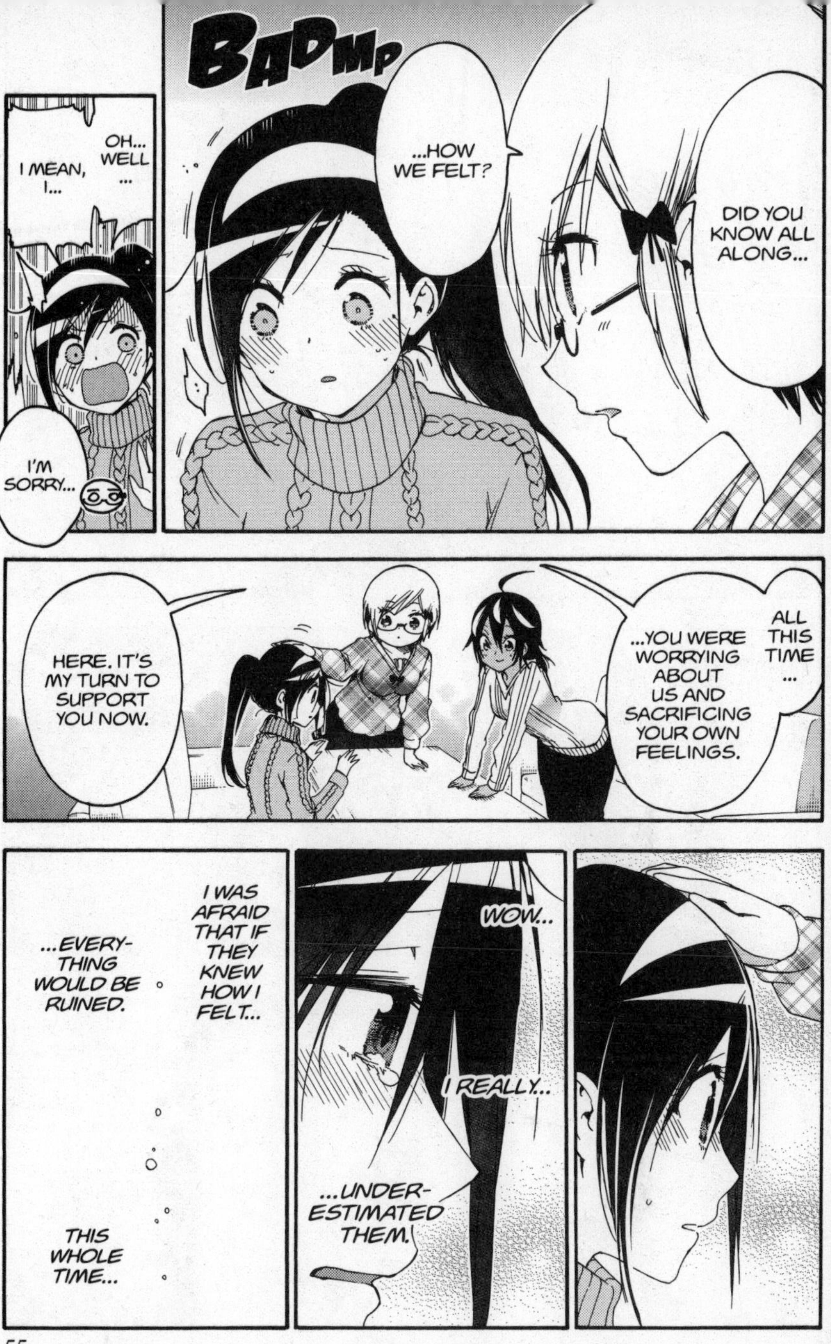
DID YOU KNOW ALL ALONG...
BADMP
...HOW WE FELT?
OH... WELL ...
I MEAN, I...
I'M SORRY...
ALL THIS TIME ...
...YOU WERE WORRYING ABOUT US AND SACRIFICING YOUR OWN FEELINGS.
HERE. IT'S MY TURN TO SUPPORT YOU NOW.
WOW...
I REALLY...
...UNDER-ESTIMATED THEM.
I WAS AFRAID THAT IF THEY KNEW HOW I FELT...
...EVERY-THING WOULD BE RUINED.
THIS WHOLE TIME...

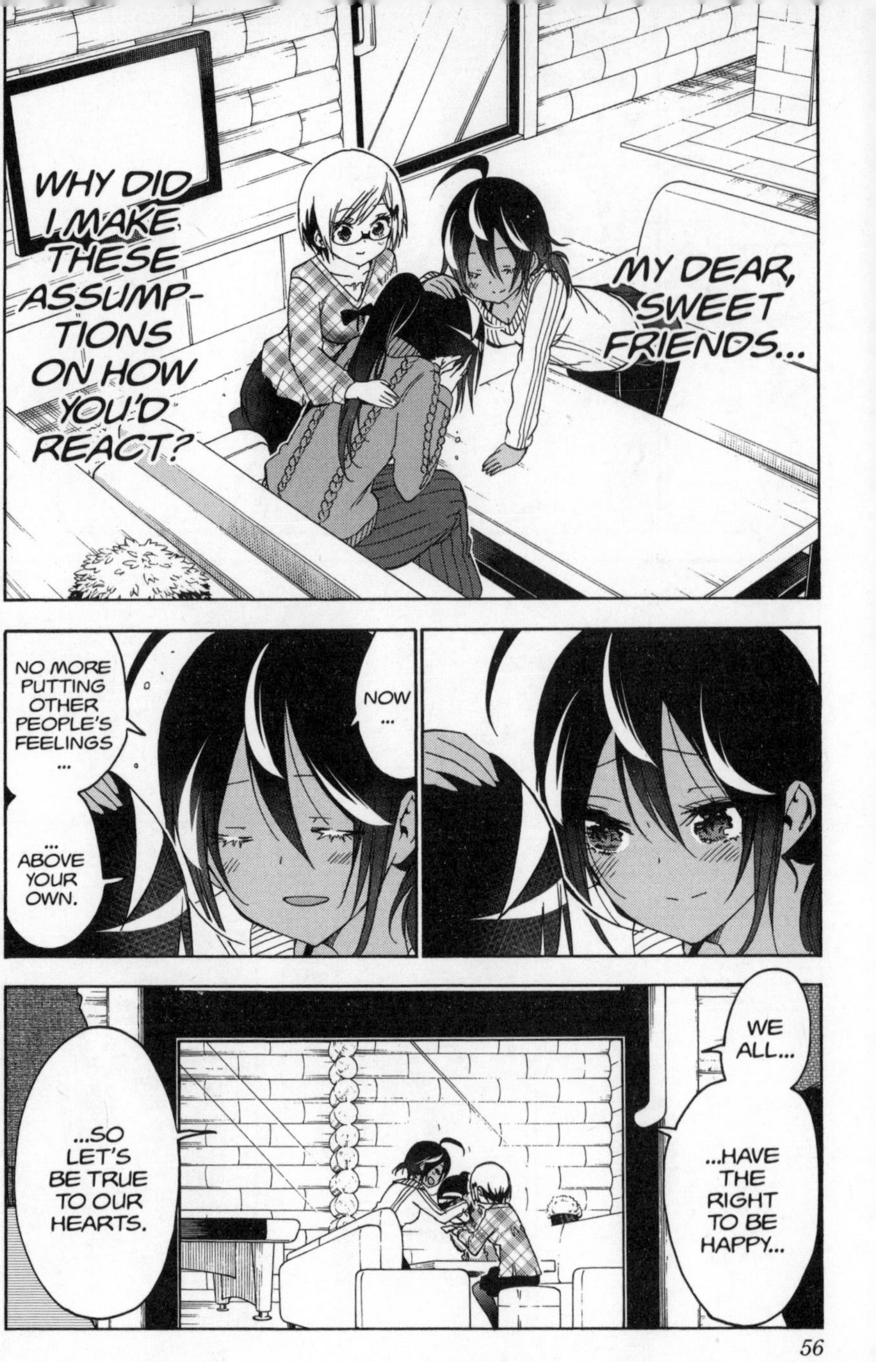
MY DEAR, SWEET FRIENDS...
WHY DID I MAKE THESE ASSUMP- TIONS ON HOW YOU'D REACT?
NOW ...
NO MORE PUTTING OTHER PEOPLE'S FEELINGS ...
... ABOVE YOUR OWN.
WE ALL...
...HAVE THE RIGHT TO BE HAPPY...
...SO LET'S BE TRUE TO OUR HEARTS.

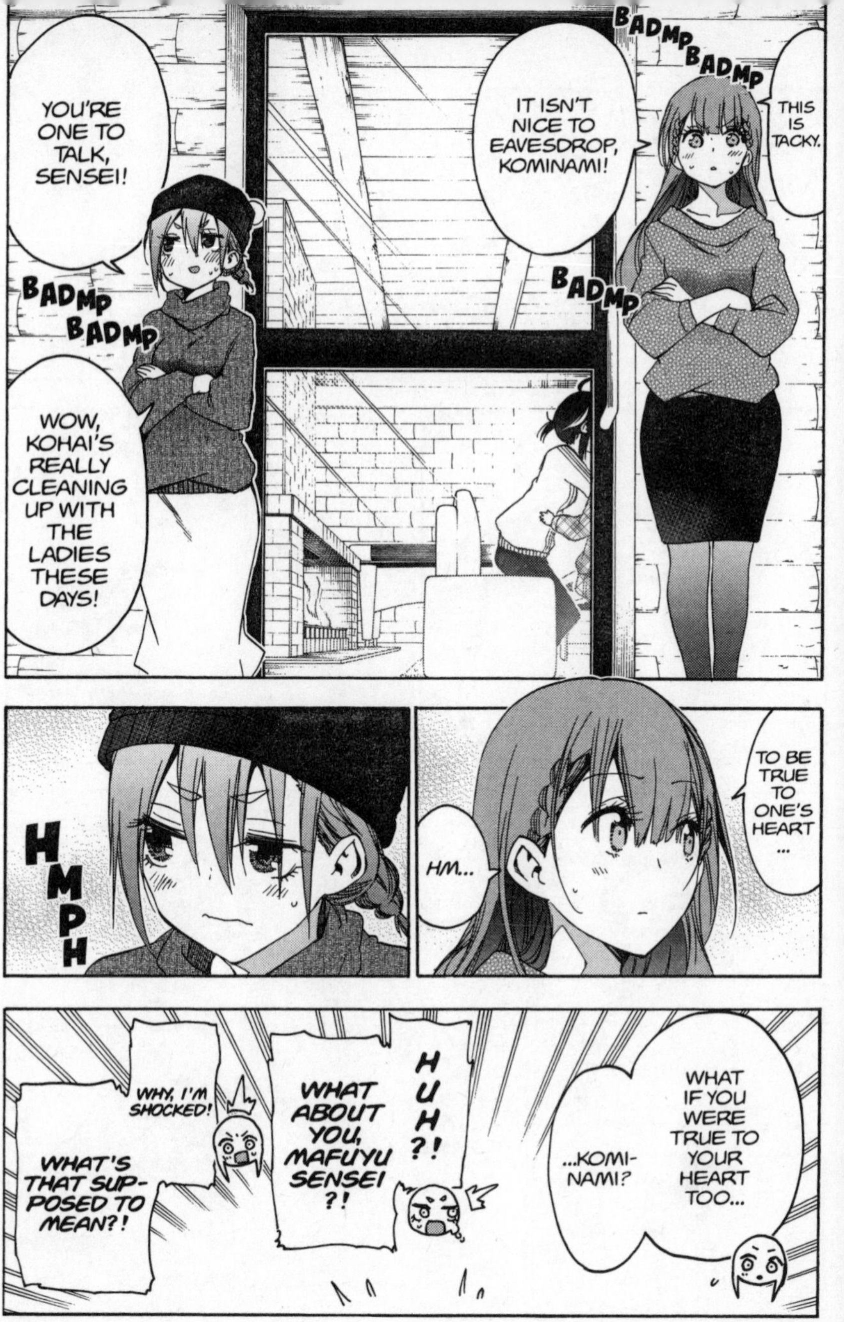
BADMP BADMP
THIS IS TACKY.
IT ISN'T NICE TO EAVESDROP, KOMINAMI!
BADMP
YOU'RE ONE TO TALK, SENSEI!
BADMP BADMP
WOW, KOHAI'S REALLY CLEANING UP WITH THE LADIES THESE DAYS!
TO BE TRUE TO ONE'S HEART ...
HM...
HMPH
WHAT IF YOU WERE TRUE TO YOUR HEART TOO...
...KOMI-NAMI?
HUH?!
WHAT ABOUT YOU, MAFUYU SENSEI?!
WHY, I'M SHOCKED!
WHAT'S THAT SUP-POSED TO MEAN?!

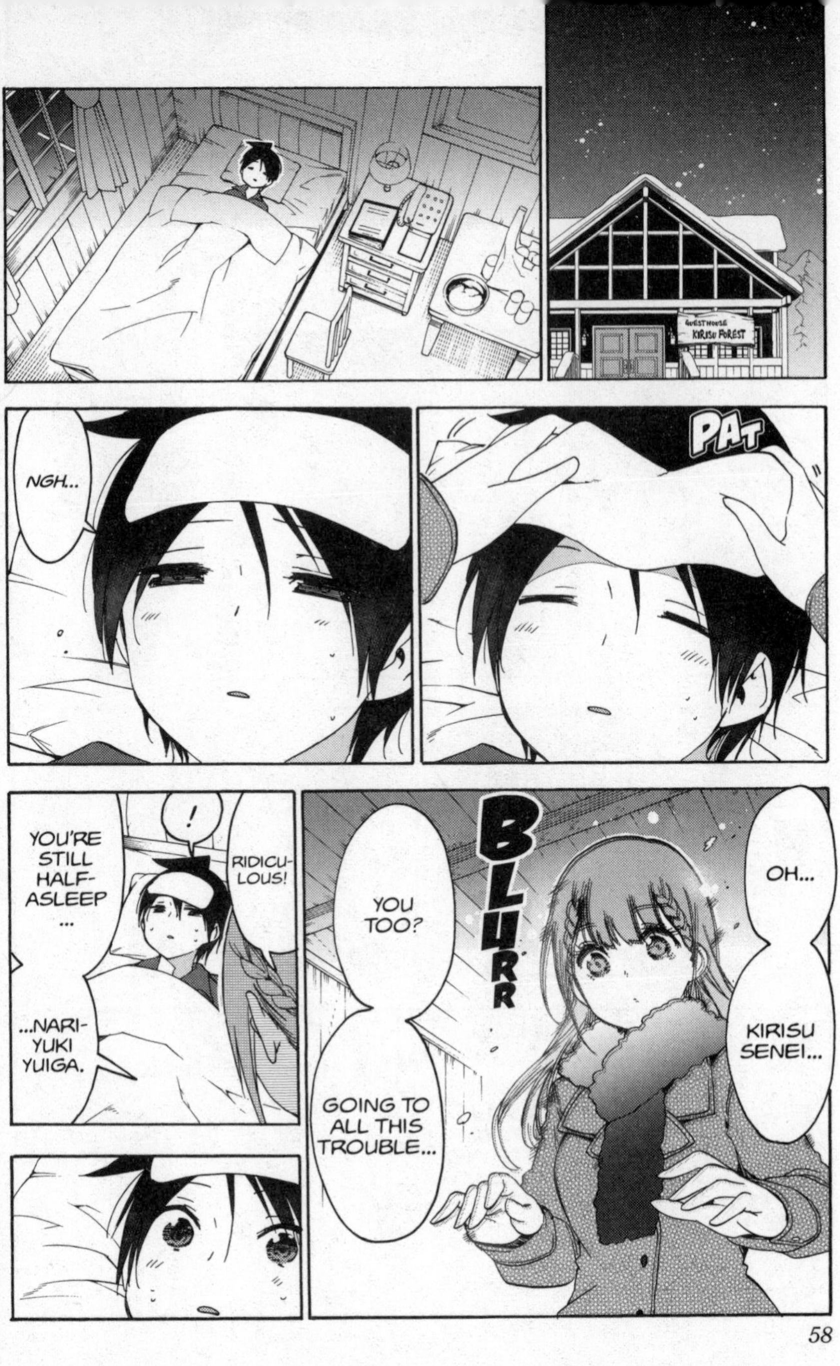
GUESTHOUSE
KIRISU FOREST
PAT
NGH...
OH...
KIRISU SENEI...
BLURR
YOU TOO?
GOING TO ALL THIS TROUBLE...
!
RIDICULOUS!
YOU'RE STILL HALF-ASLEEP ...
...NARIYUKI YUIGA.

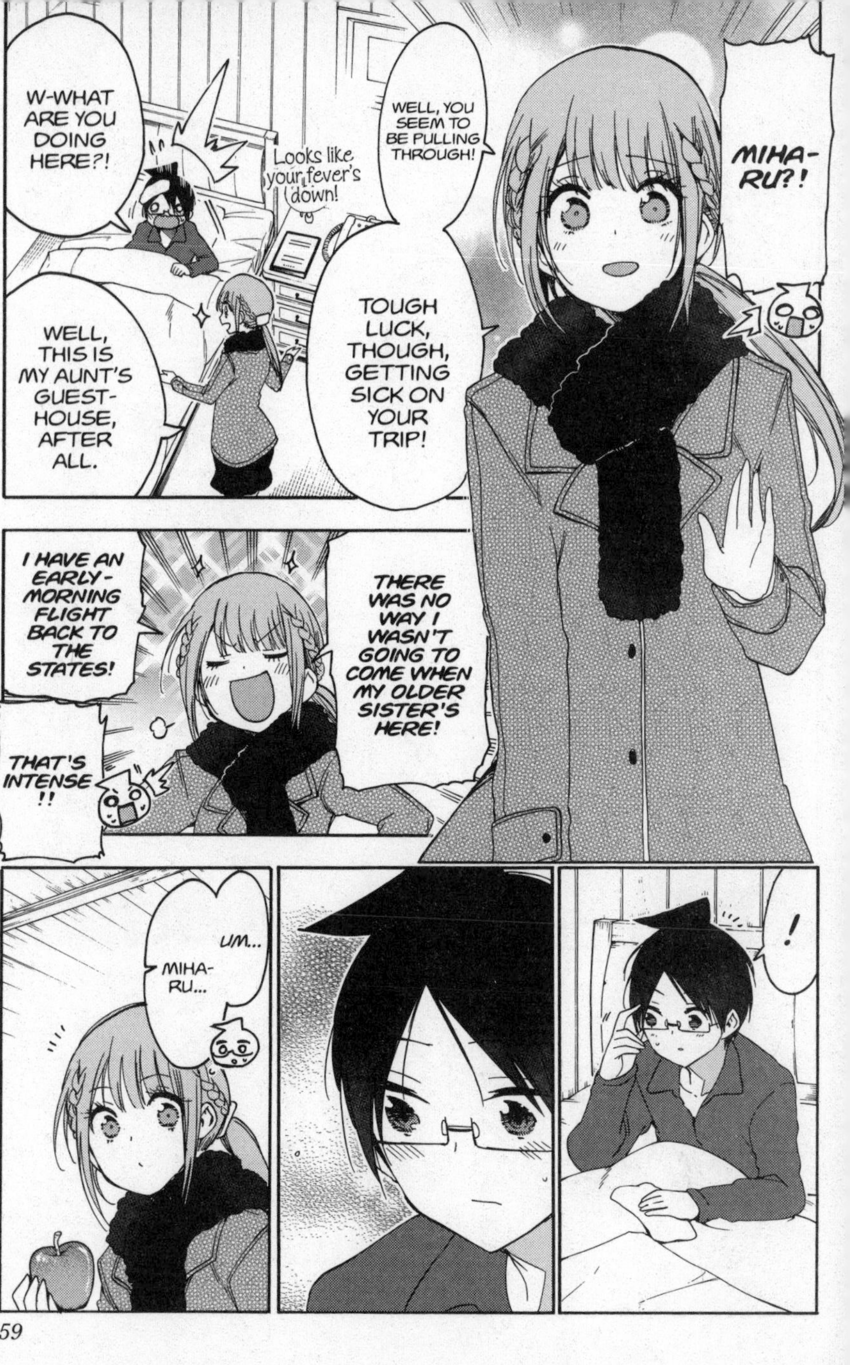
MIHA-RU?!
WELL, YOU SEEM TO BE PULLING THROUGH!
Looks like your fever's down!
TOUGH LUCK, THOUGH, GETTING SICK ON YOUR TRIP!
W-WHAT ARE YOU DOING HERE?!
WELL, THIS IS MY AUNT'S GUEST-HOUSE, AFTER ALL.
THERE WAS NO WAY I WASN'T GOING TO COME WHEN MY OLDER SISTER'S HERE!
I HAVE AN EARLY-MORNING FLIGHT BACK TO THE STATES!
THAT'S INTENSE!!
!
UM...
MIHA-RU...

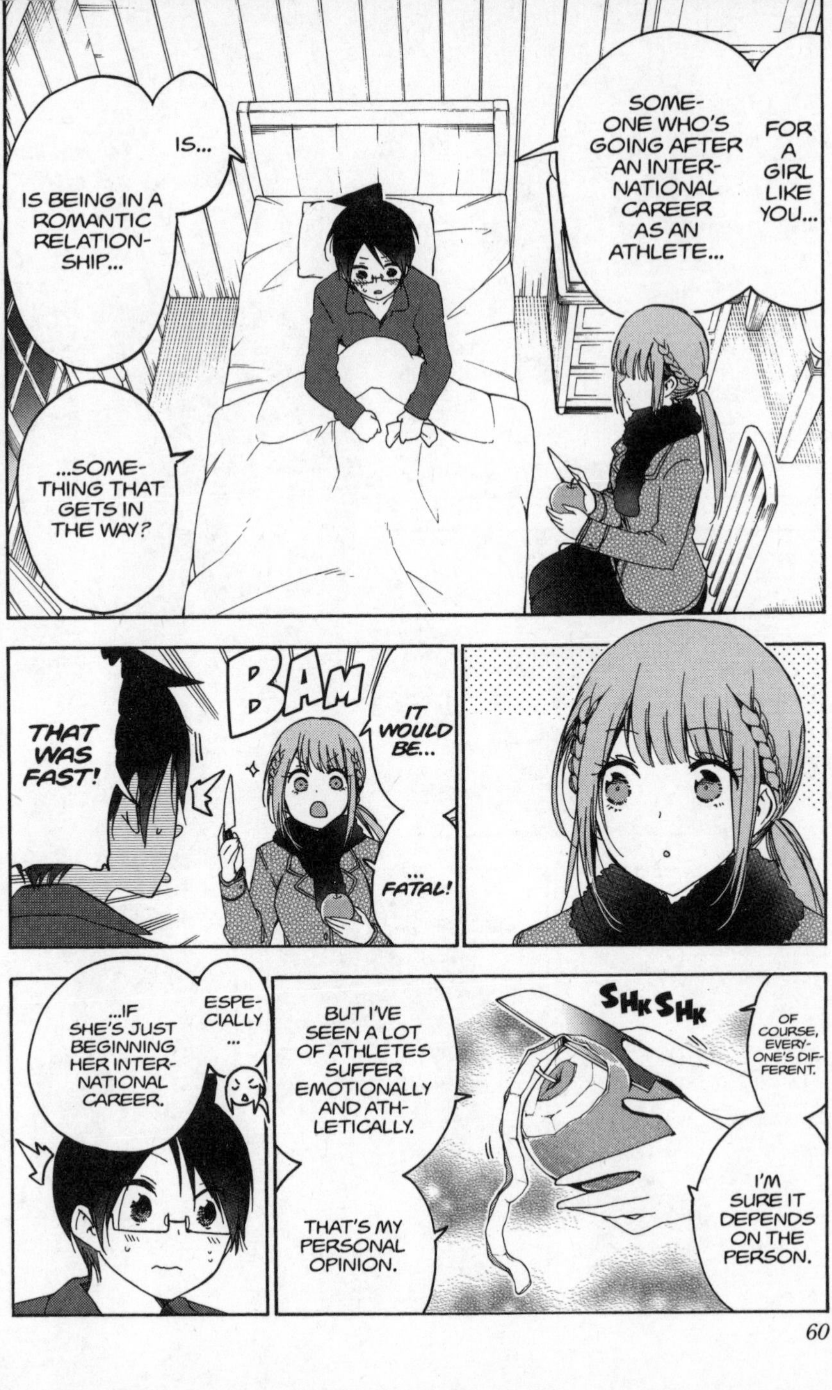
FOR A GIRL LIKE YOU...
SOMEONE WHO'S GOING AFTER AN INTERNATIONAL CAREER AS AN ATHLETE...
IS...
IS BEING IN A ROMANTIC RELATIONSHIP...
...SOMETHING THAT GETS IN THE WAY?
BAM
IT WOULD BE...
...FATAL!
THAT WAS FAST!
SHK SHK
OF COURSE, EVERYONE'S DIFFERENT.
I'M SURE IT DEPENDS ON THE PERSON.
BUT I'VE SEEN A LOT OF ATHLETES SUFFER EMOTIONALLY AND ATHLETICALLY.
THAT'S MY PERSONAL OPINION.
ESPECIALLY...
...IF SHE'S JUST BEGINNING HER INTERNATIONAL CAREER.

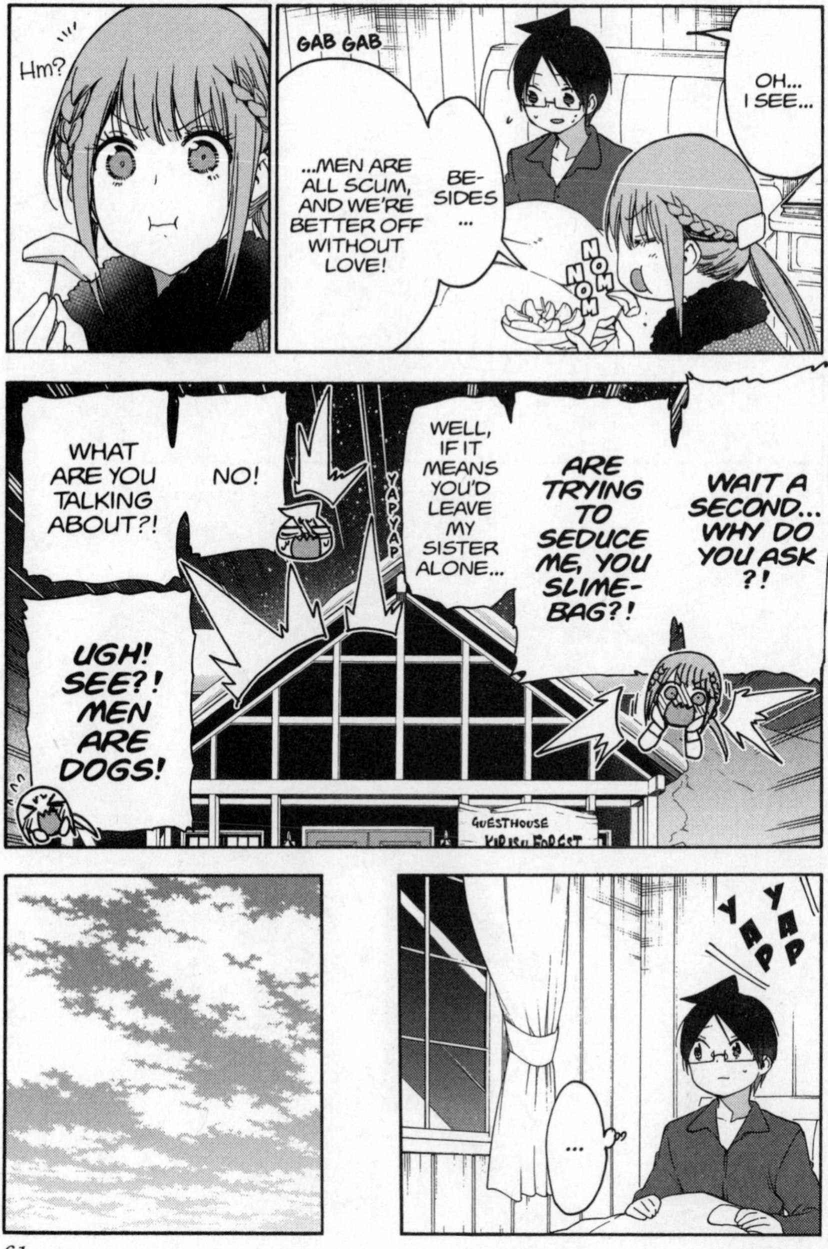
OH... I SEE...
GAB GAB
BE-SIDES...
...MEN ARE ALL SCUM, AND WE'RE BETTER OFF WITHOUT LOVE!
NOM NOM
Hm?
WAIT A SECOND... WHY DO YOU ASK?!
ARE TRYING TO SEDUCE ME, YOU SLIME-BAG?!
WELL, IF IT MEANS YOU'D LEAVE MY SISTER ALONE...
YAP YAP
NO!
WHAT ARE YOU TALKING ABOUT?!
UGH! SEE?! MEN ARE DOGS!
GUESTHOUSE
YAP YAP
...

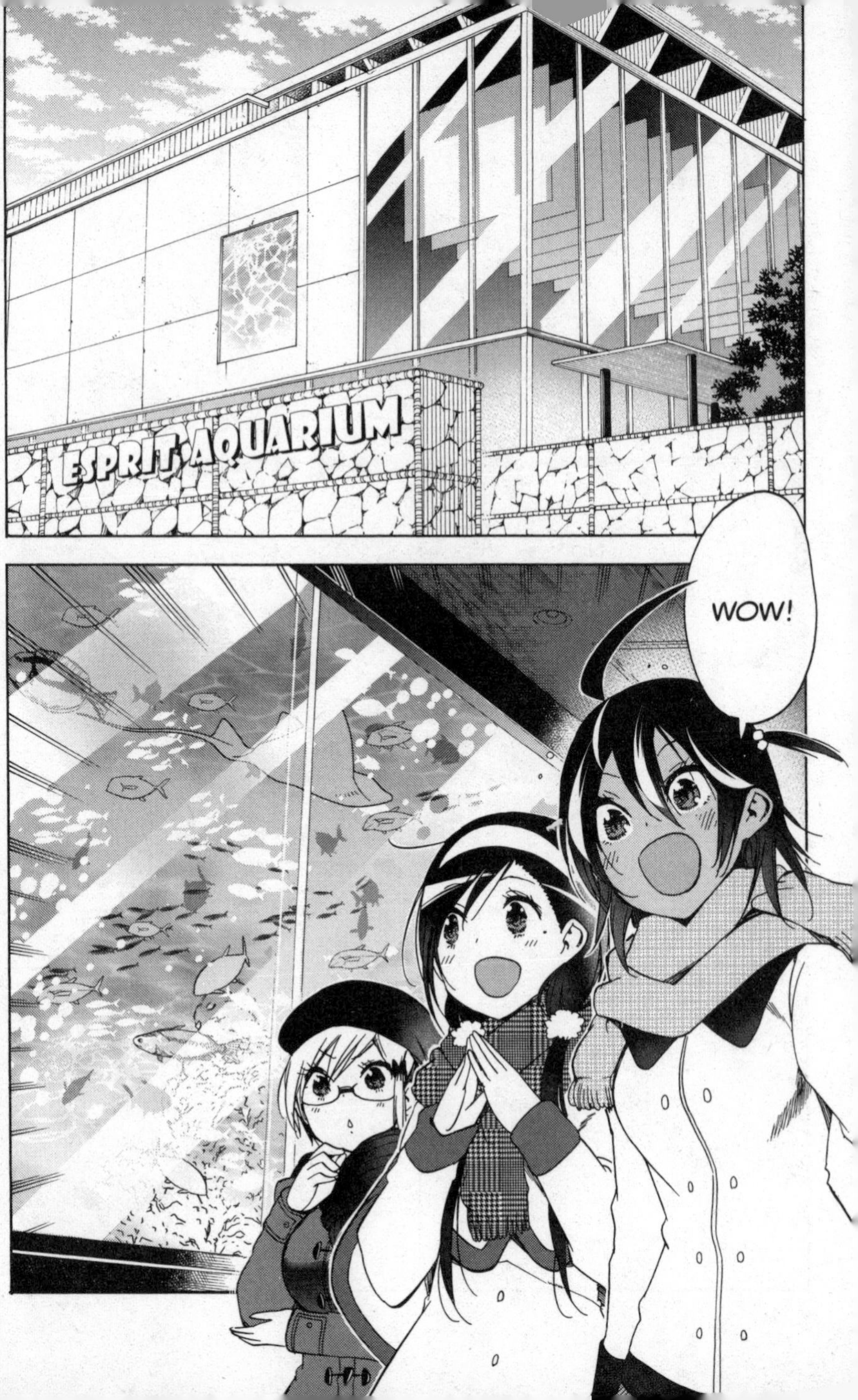
ESPRIT AQUARIUM
WOW!

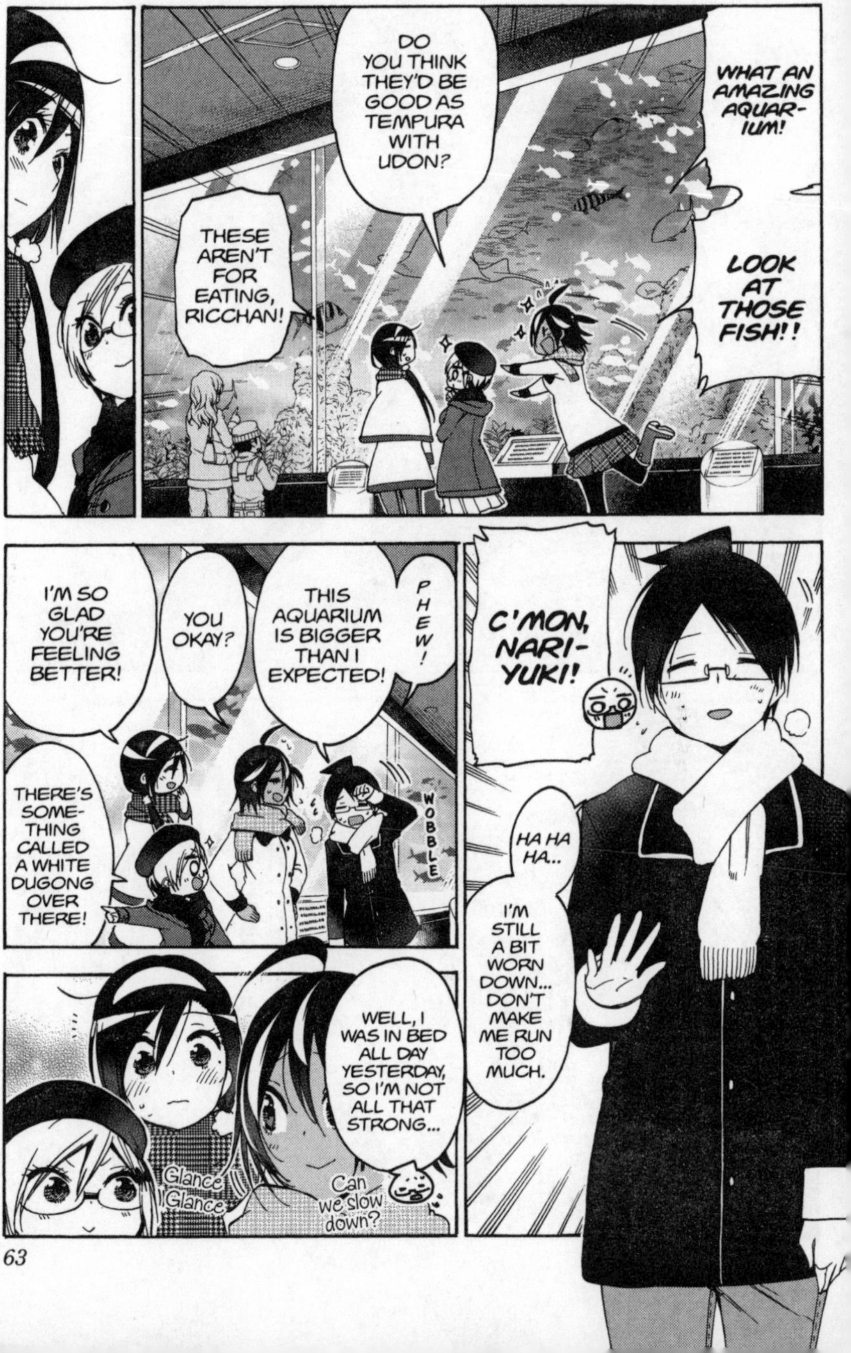
WHAT AN AMAZING AQUARIUM!
LOOK AT THOSE FISH!!
DO YOU THINK THEY'D BE GOOD AS TEMPURA WITH UDON?
THESE AREN'T FOR EATING, RICCHAN!
C'MON, NARIYUKI!
HA HA HA...
I'M STILL A BIT WORN DOWN... DON'T MAKE ME RUN TOO MUCH.
PHEW!
WOBBLE
THIS AQUARIUM IS BIGGER THAN I EXPECTED!
YOU OKAY?
I'M SO GLAD YOU'RE FEELING BETTER!
THERE'S SOMETHING CALLED A WHITE DUGONG OVER THERE!
WELL, I WAS IN BED ALL DAY YESTERDAY, SO I'M NOT ALL THAT STRONG...
Can we slow down?
Glance Glance

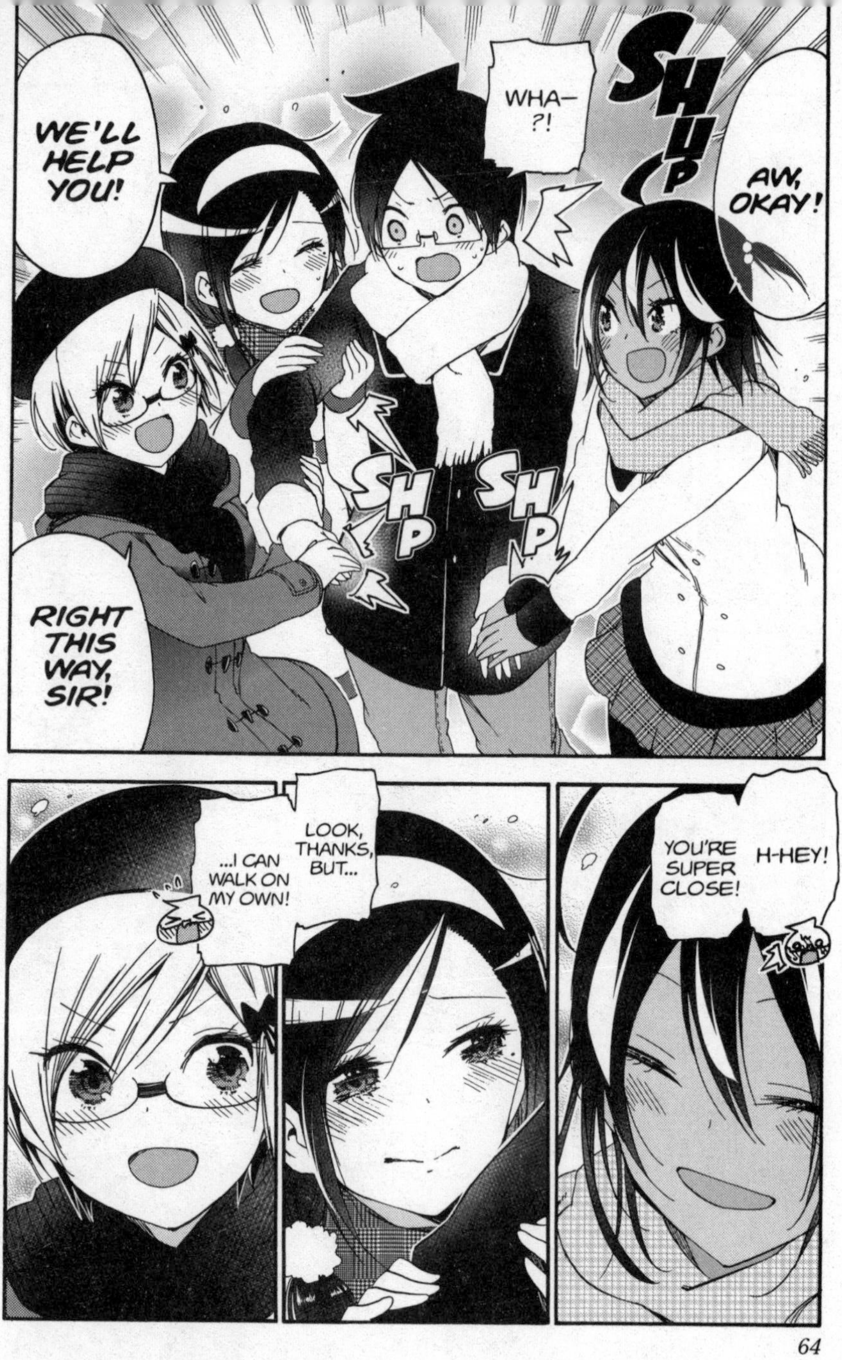
SHUP
AW, OKAY!
WHA—?!
WE'LL HELP YOU!
SHP
SHP
RIGHT THIS WAY, SIR!
H-HEY!
YOU'RE SUPER CLOSE!
LOOK, THANKS, BUT...
...I CAN WALK ON MY OWN!

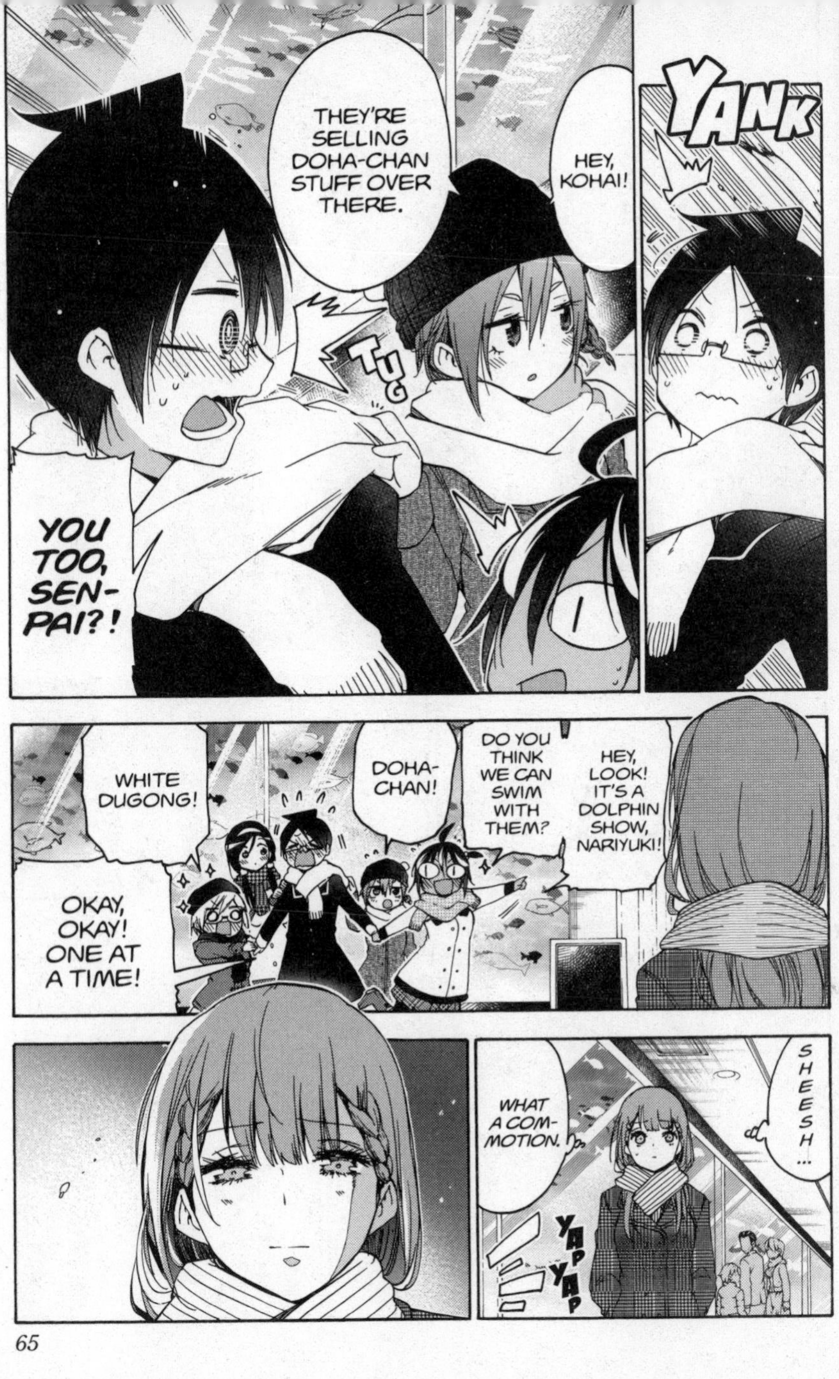
YANK
HEY, KOHAI!
THEY'RE SELLING DOHA-CHAN STUFF OVER THERE.
TUG
YOU TOO, SEN-PAI?!
HEY, LOOK! IT'S A DOLPHIN SHOW, NARIYUKI!
DO YOU THINK WE CAN SWIM WITH THEM?
DOHA-CHAN!
WHITE DUGONG!
OKAY, OKAY! ONE AT A TIME!
SHEESH...
WHAT A COM-MOTION.
YAP YAP
YAP YAP

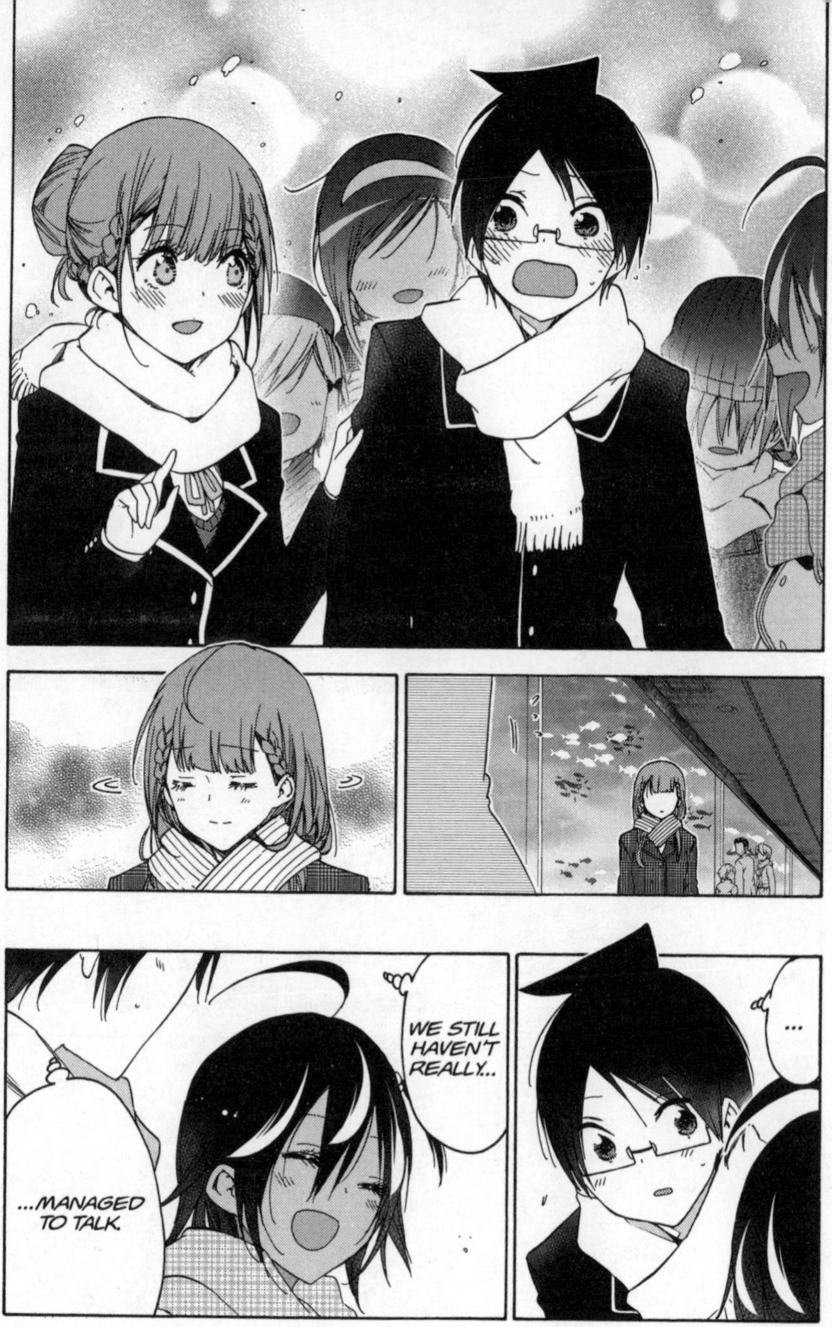
...
WE STILL HAVEN'T REALLY...
...MANAGED TO TALK.

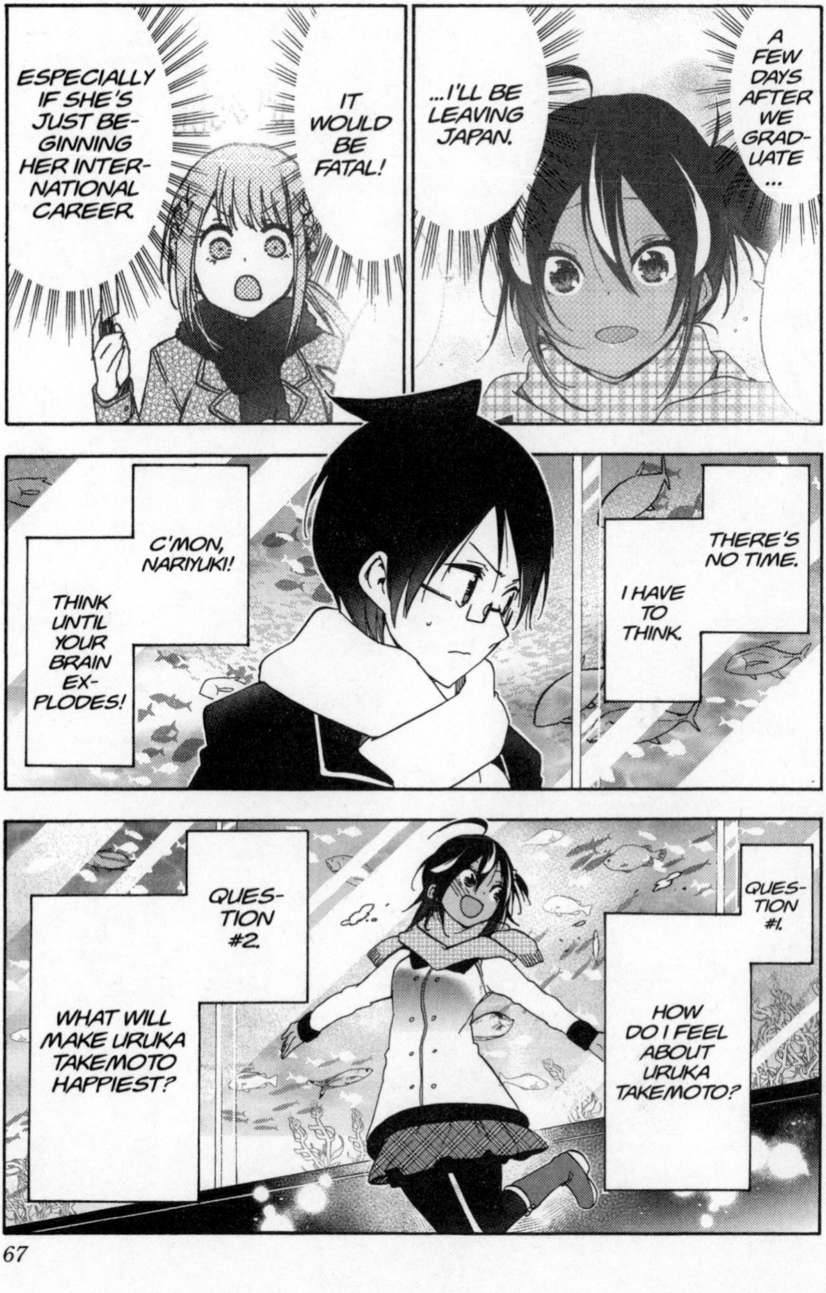
A FEW DAYS AFTER WE GRADUATE...
...I'LL BE LEAVING JAPAN.
IT WOULD BE FATAL!
ESPECIALLY IF SHE'S JUST BEGINNING HER INTERNATIONAL CAREER.
THERE'S NO TIME.
I HAVE TO THINK.
C'MON, NARIYUKI!
THINK UNTIL YOUR BRAIN EXPLODES!
QUESTION #1.
HOW DO I FEEL ABOUT URUKA TAKEMOTO?
QUESTION #2.
WHAT WILL MAKE URUKA TAKEMOTO HAPPIEST?

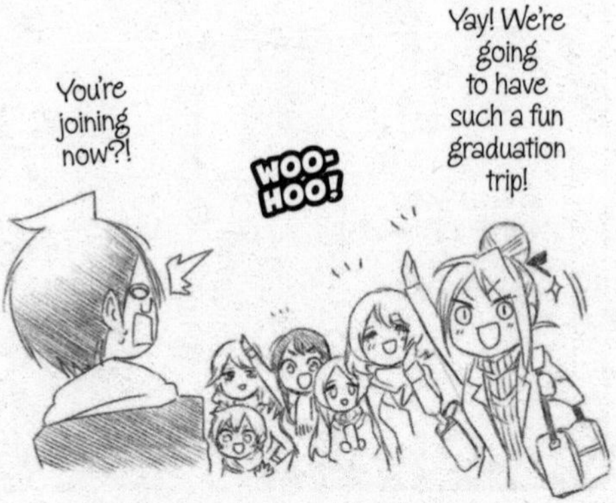
Yay! We're going to have such a fun graduation trip!
WOO-HOO!
You're joining now?!

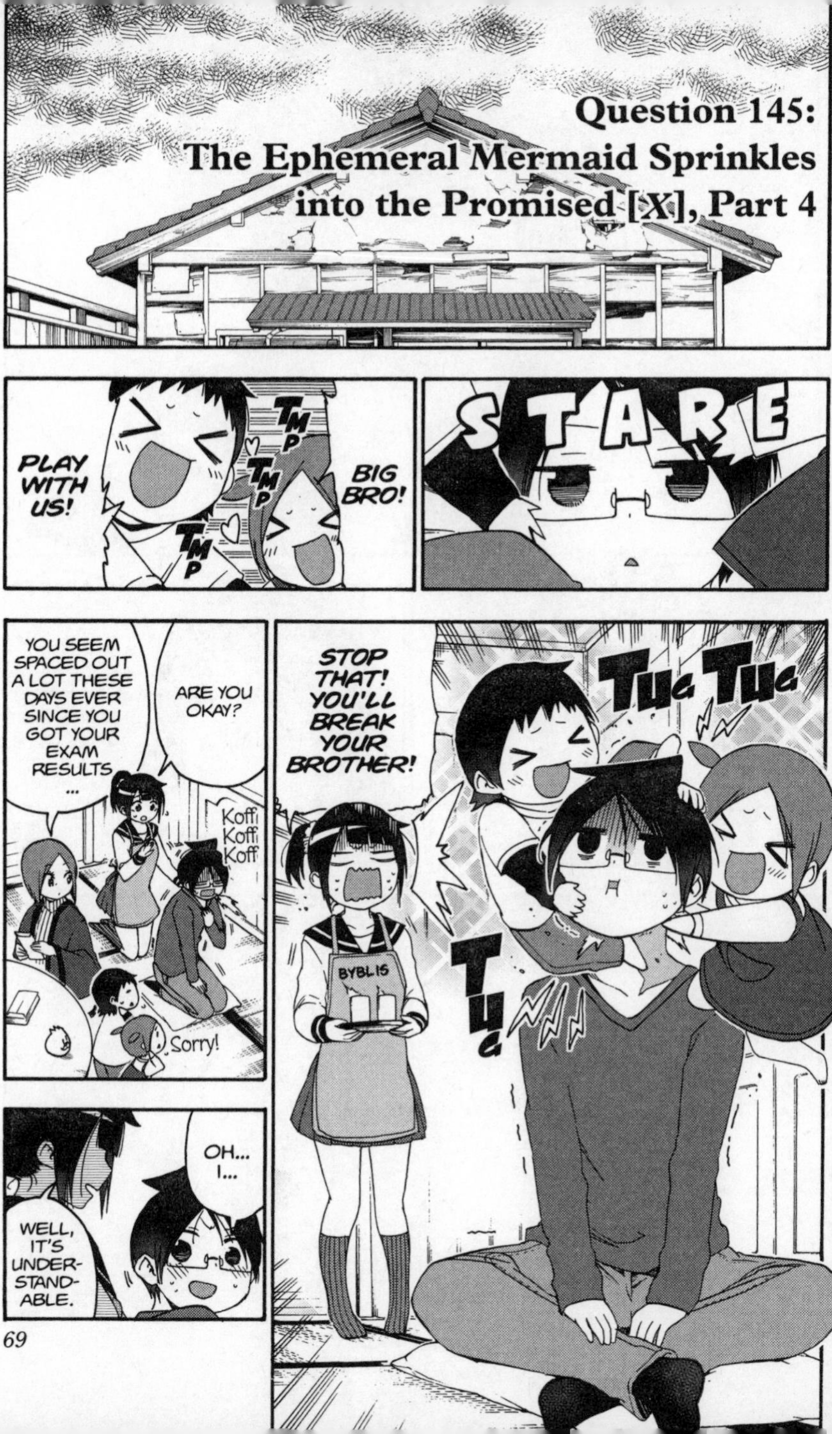
Question 145:
The Ephemeral Mermaid Sprinkles into the Promised [X], Part 4
STARE
BIG BRO!
TMP TMP TMP
PLAY WITH US!
STOP THAT! YOU'LL BREAK YOUR BROTHER!
TUG TUG
TUG
ARE YOU OKAY?
YOU SEEM SPACED OUT A LOT THESE DAYS EVER SINCE YOU GOT YOUR EXAM RESULTS ...
Koff Koff Koff
BYBLIS
Sorry!
OH... I...
WELL, IT'S UNDERSTANDABLE.

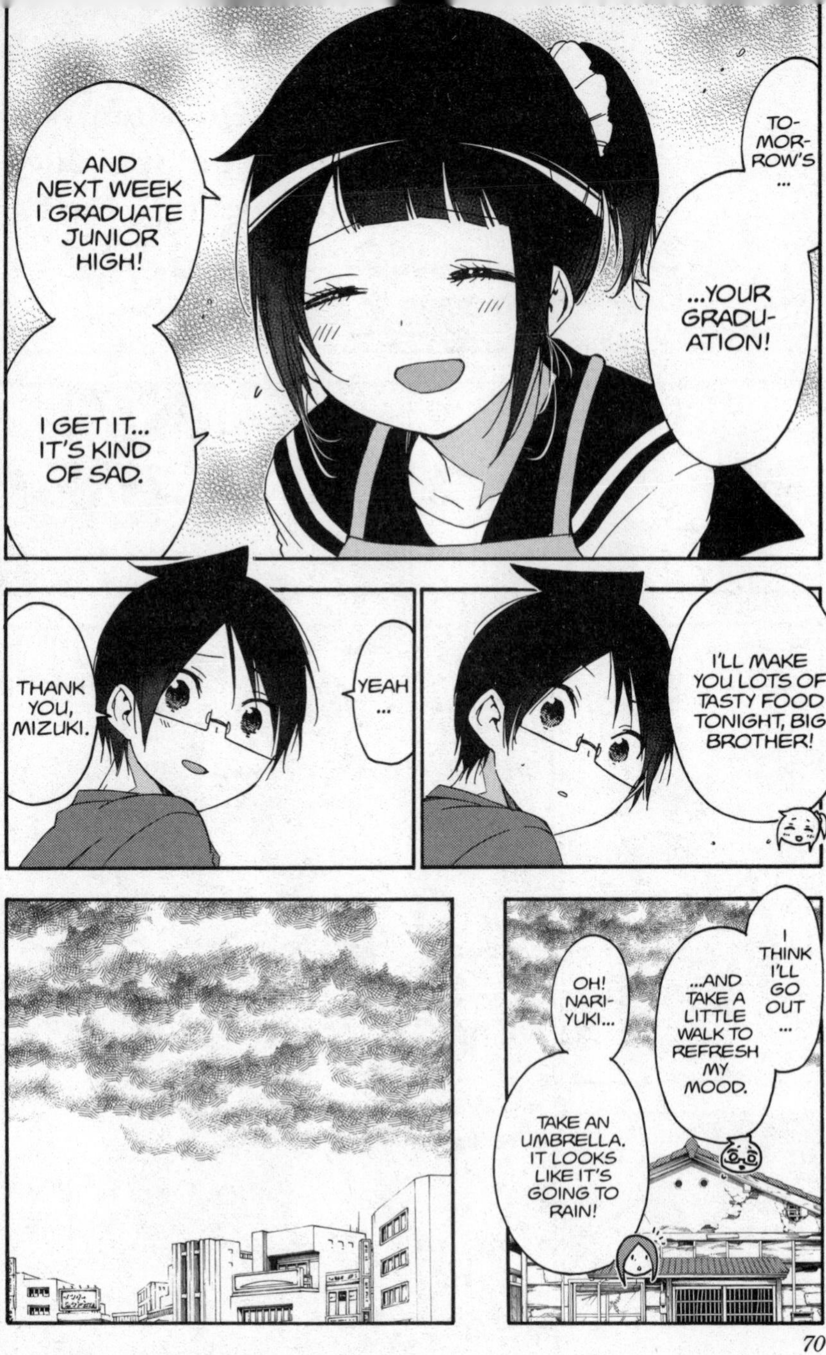
TO-MORROW'S...
...YOUR GRADUATION!
AND NEXT WEEK I GRADUATE JUNIOR HIGH!
I GET IT... IT'S KIND OF SAD.
I'LL MAKE YOU LOTS OF TASTY FOOD TONIGHT, BIG BROTHER!
YEAH...
THANK YOU, MIZUKI.
I THINK I'LL GO OUT...
...AND TAKE A LITTLE WALK TO REFRESH MY MOOD.
OH! NARI-YUKI...
TAKE AN UMBRELLA. IT LOOKS LIKE IT'S GOING TO RAIN!

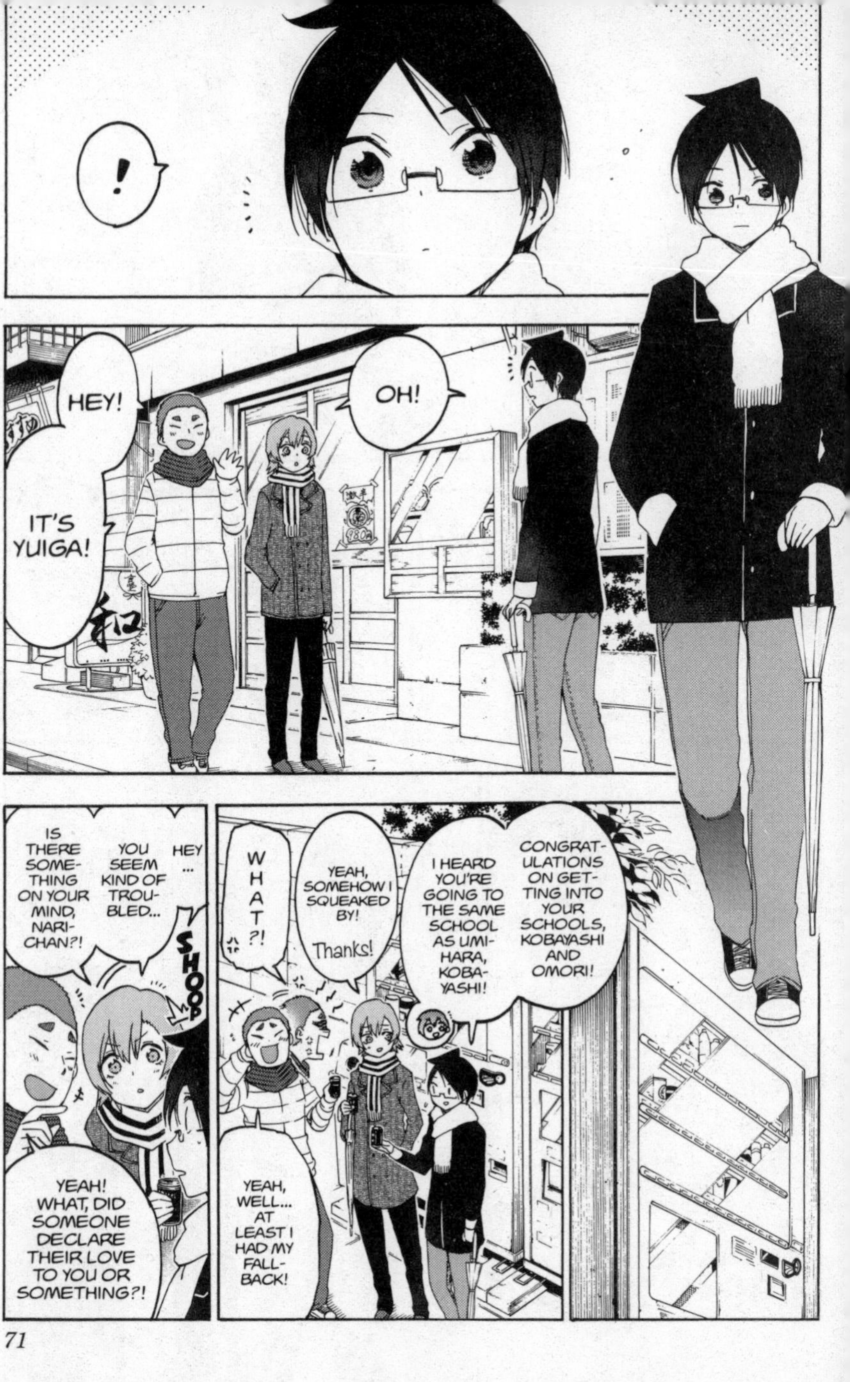
!
OH!
HEY!
IT'S YUIGA!
CONGRATULATIONS ON GETTING INTO YOUR SCHOOLS, KOBAYASHI AND OMORI!
I HEARD YOU'RE GOING TO THE SAME SCHOOL AS UMIHARA, KOBAYASHI!
YEAH, SOMEHOW I SQUEAKED BY!
Thanks!
WHAT?!
YEAH, WELL... AT LEAST I HAD MY FALLBACK!
HEY...
YOU SEEM KIND OF TROUBLED...
IS THERE SOMETHING ON YOUR MIND, NARI-CHAN?!
SHOOP
YEAH! WHAT, DID SOMEONE DECLARE THEIR LOVE TO YOU OR SOMETHING?!

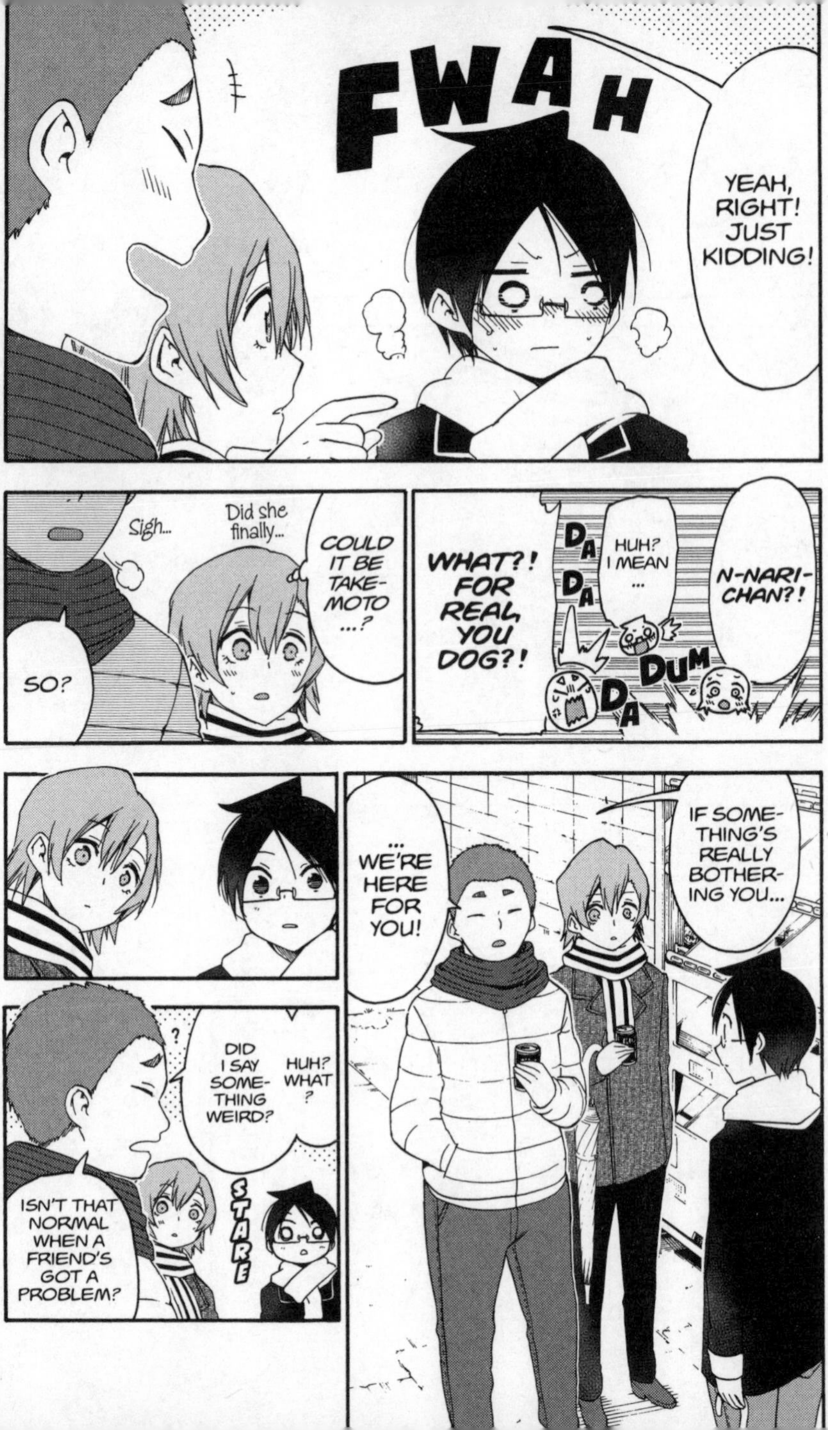
FWAH
YEAH, RIGHT! JUST KIDDING!
N-NARI-CHAN?!
HUH? I MEAN ...
DA DA DUM DA
WHAT?! FOR REAL, YOU DOG?!
COULD IT BE TAKE-MOTO ...?
Did she finally...
Sigh...
SO?
IF SOME-THING'S REALLY BOTHER-ING YOU...
... WE'RE HERE FOR YOU!
HUH? WHAT?
DID I SAY SOME-THING WEIRD?
?
STARE
ISN'T THAT NORMAL WHEN A FRIEND'S GOT A PROBLEM?

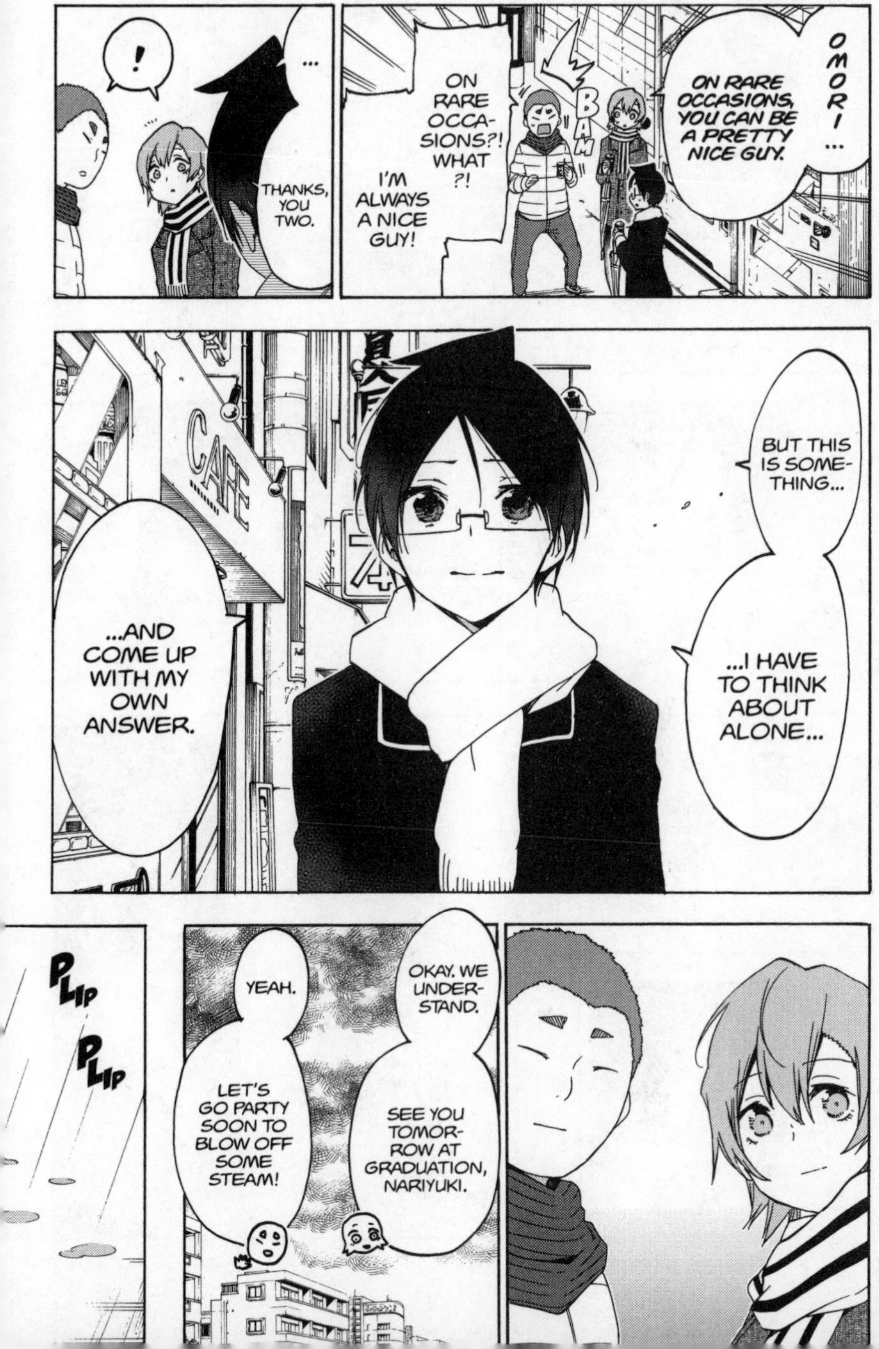
OMORI...
ON RARE OCCASIONS, YOU CAN BE A PRETTY NICE GUY.
BAM
ON RARE OCCA-SIONS?! WHAT?!
I'M ALWAYS A NICE GUY!
...
!
THANKS, YOU TWO.
BUT THIS IS SOME-THING...
...I HAVE TO THINK ABOUT ALONE...
CAFE
...AND COME UP WITH MY OWN ANSWER.
OKAY. WE UNDER-STAND.
SEE YOU TOMOR-ROW AT GRADUATION, NARIYUKI.
YEAH.
LET'S GO PARTY SOON TO BLOW OFF SOME STEAM!
PLIP
PLIP

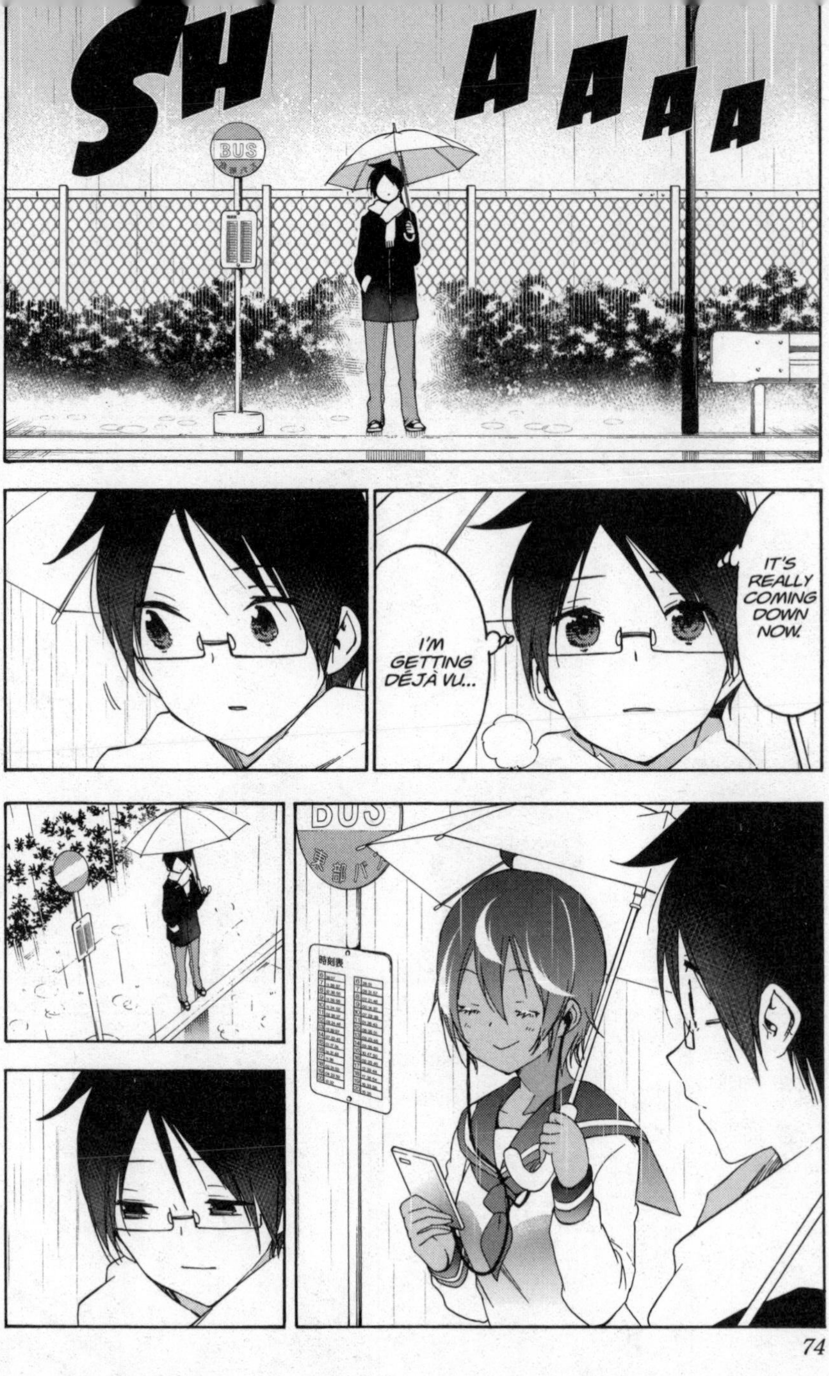
SHAAAAA
BUS
IT'S REALLY COMING DOWN NOW.
I'M GETTING DÉJÀ VU...
BUS

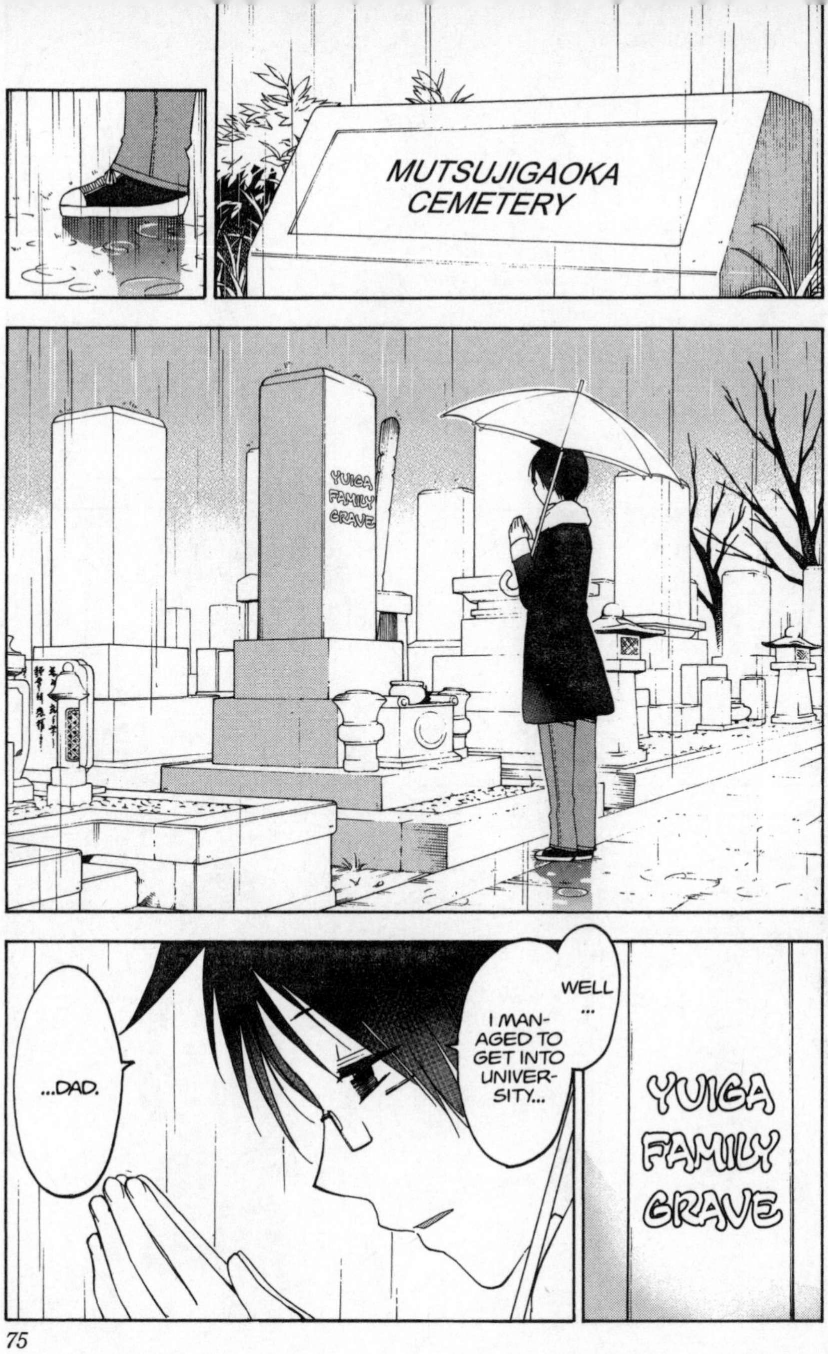
MUTSUJIGAOKA CEMETERY
YUIGA FAMILY GRAVE
YUIGA FAMILY GRAVE
WELL...
I MANAGED TO GET INTO UNIVERSITY...
...DAD.

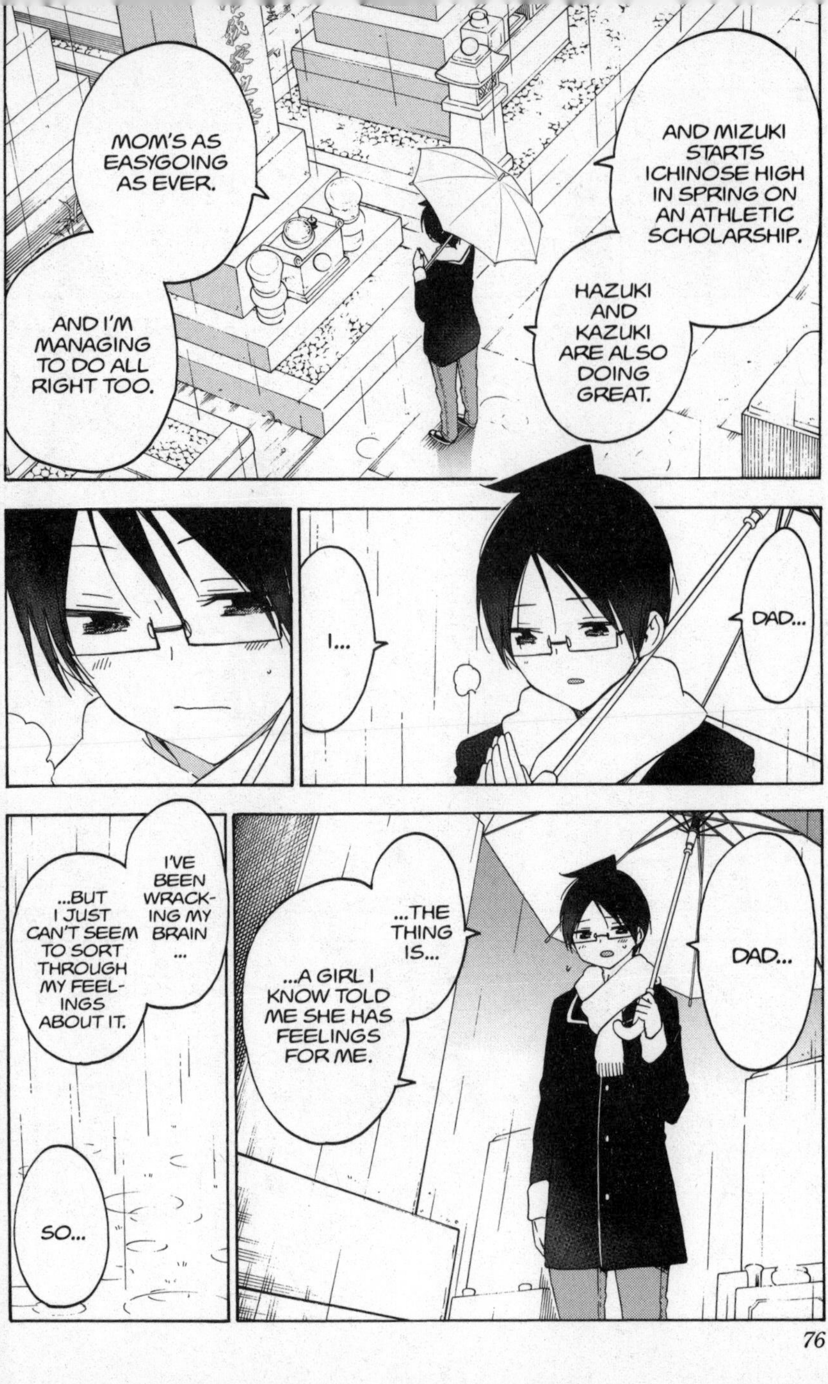
AND MIZUKI STARTS ICHINOSE HIGH IN SPRING ON AN ATHLETIC SCHOLARSHIP.
HAZUKI AND KAZUKI ARE ALSO DOING GREAT.
MOM'S AS EASYGOING AS EVER.
AND I'M MANAGING TO DO ALL RIGHT TOO.
DAD...
I...
DAD...
...THE THING IS...
...A GIRL I KNOW TOLD ME SHE HAS FEELINGS FOR ME.
I'VE BEEN WRACKING MY BRAIN...
...BUT I JUST CAN'T SEEM TO SORT THROUGH MY FEELINGS ABOUT IT.
SO...

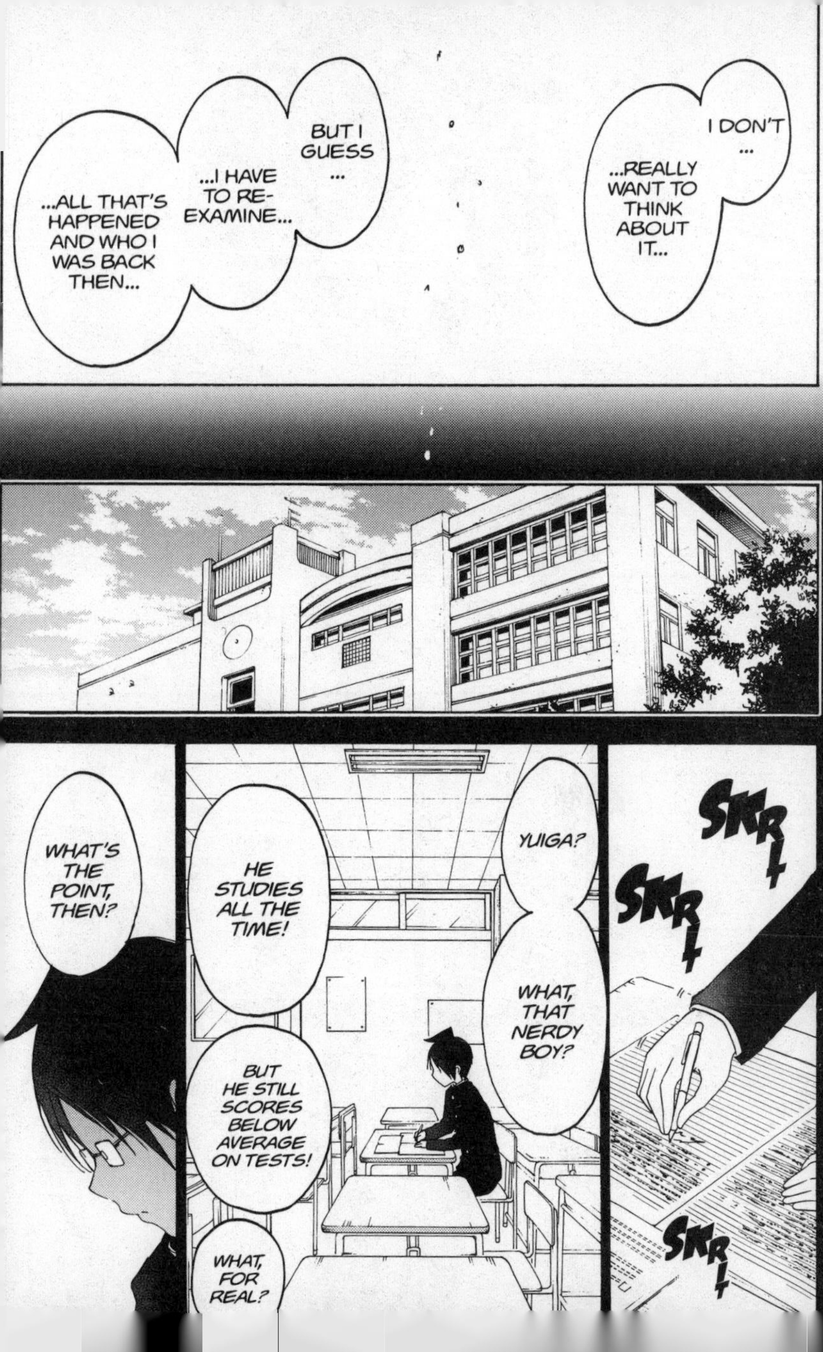
I DON'T ...
...REALLY WANT TO THINK ABOUT IT...
BUT I GUESS ...
...I HAVE TO RE-EXAMINE...
...ALL THAT'S HAPPENED AND WHO I WAS BACK THEN...
SKRIT
SKRIT
SKRIT
YUIGA?
WHAT, THAT NERDY BOY?
HE STUDIES ALL THE TIME!
BUT HE STILL SCORES BELOW AVERAGE ON TESTS!
WHAT, FOR REAL?
WHAT'S THE POINT, THEN?

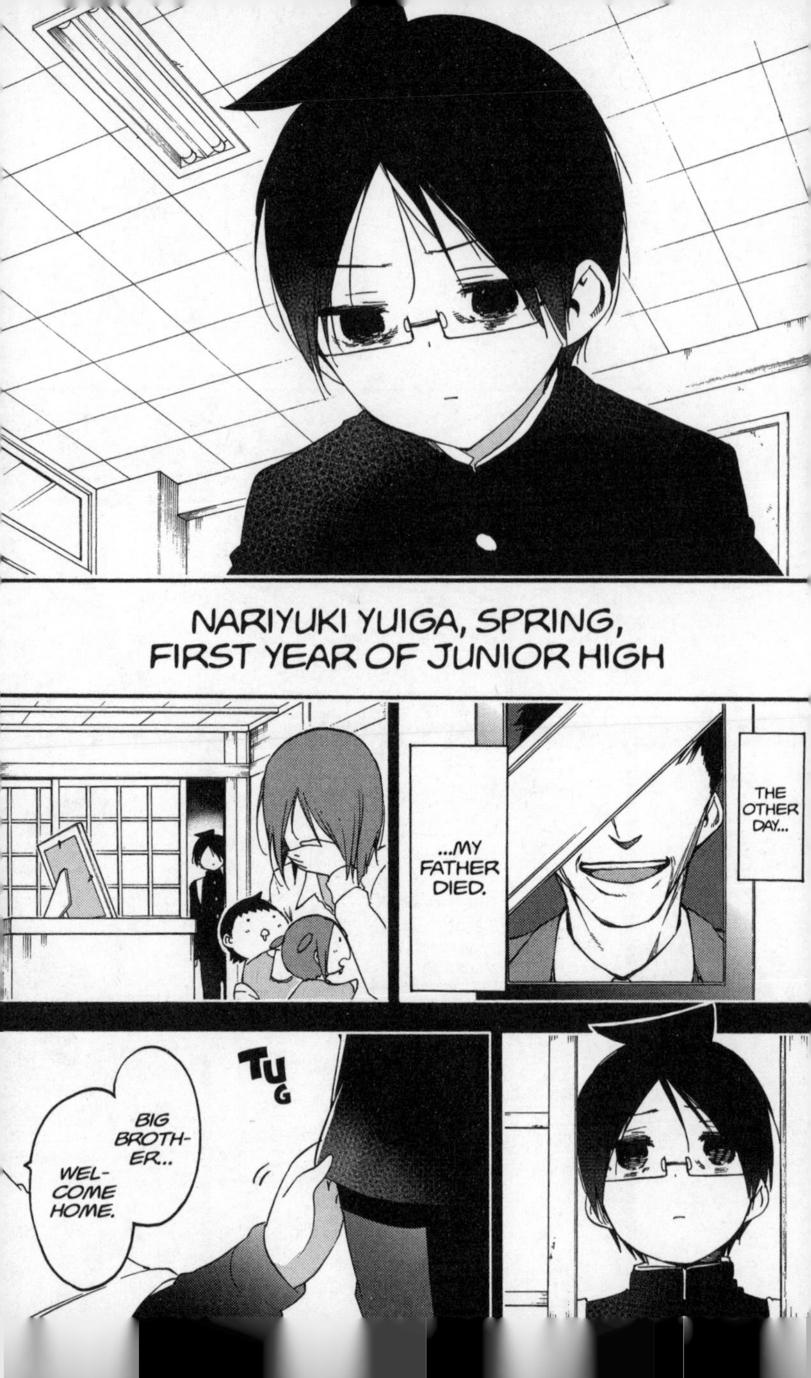
NARIYUKI YUIGA, SPRING, FIRST YEAR OF JUNIOR HIGH
THE OTHER DAY...
...MY FATHER DIED.
TUG
BIG BROTH-ER... WEL-COME HOME.

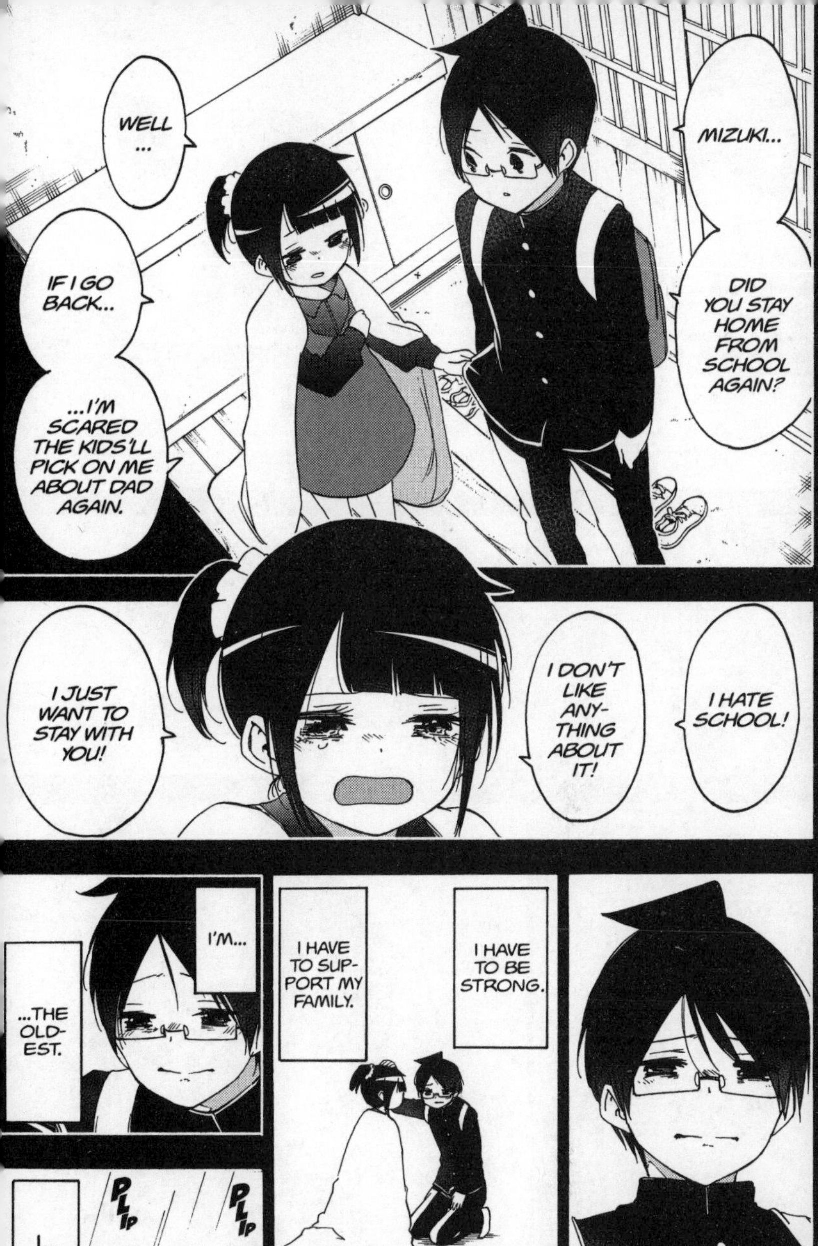
MIZUKI...
DID YOU STAY HOME FROM SCHOOL AGAIN?
WELL ...
IF I GO BACK...
...I'M SCARED THE KIDS'LL PICK ON ME ABOUT DAD AGAIN.
I HATE SCHOOL!
I DON'T LIKE ANYTHING ABOUT IT!
I JUST WANT TO STAY WITH YOU!
I HAVE TO BE STRONG.
I HAVE TO SUPPORT MY FAMILY.
I'M...
...THE OLDEST.
PLIP
PLIP
I...

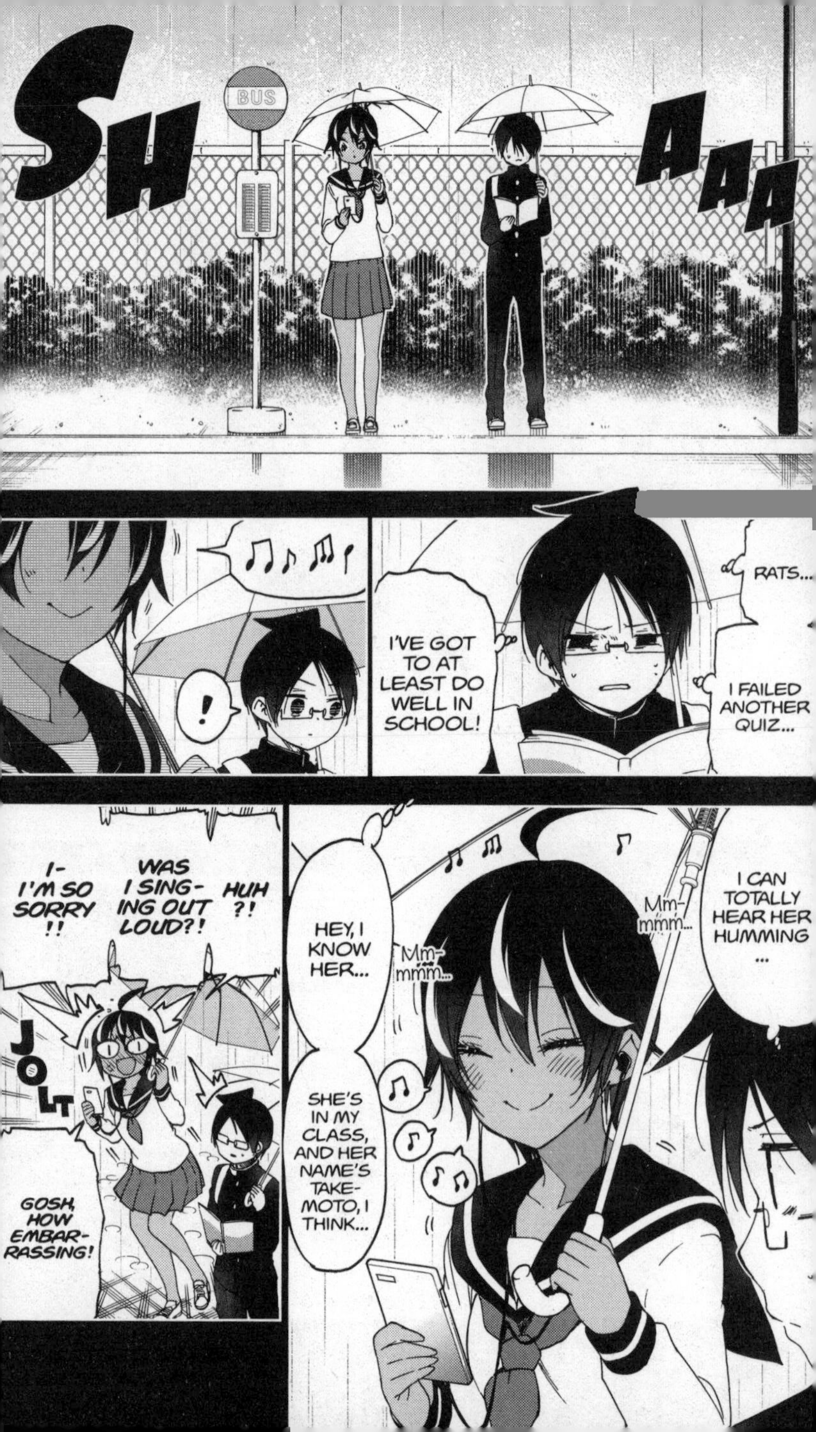
SHAAAA
BUS
RATS...
I FAILED ANOTHER QUIZ...
I'VE GOT TO AT LEAST DO WELL IN SCHOOL!
!
I CAN TOTALLY HEAR HER HUMMING...
Mm-mmm...
HEY, I KNOW HER...
Mm-mmm...
SHE'S IN MY CLASS, AND HER NAME'S TAKEMOTO, I THINK...
HUH?!
WAS I SINGING OUT LOUD?!
I- I'M SO SORRY!!
JOLT
GOSH, HOW EMBARRASSING!

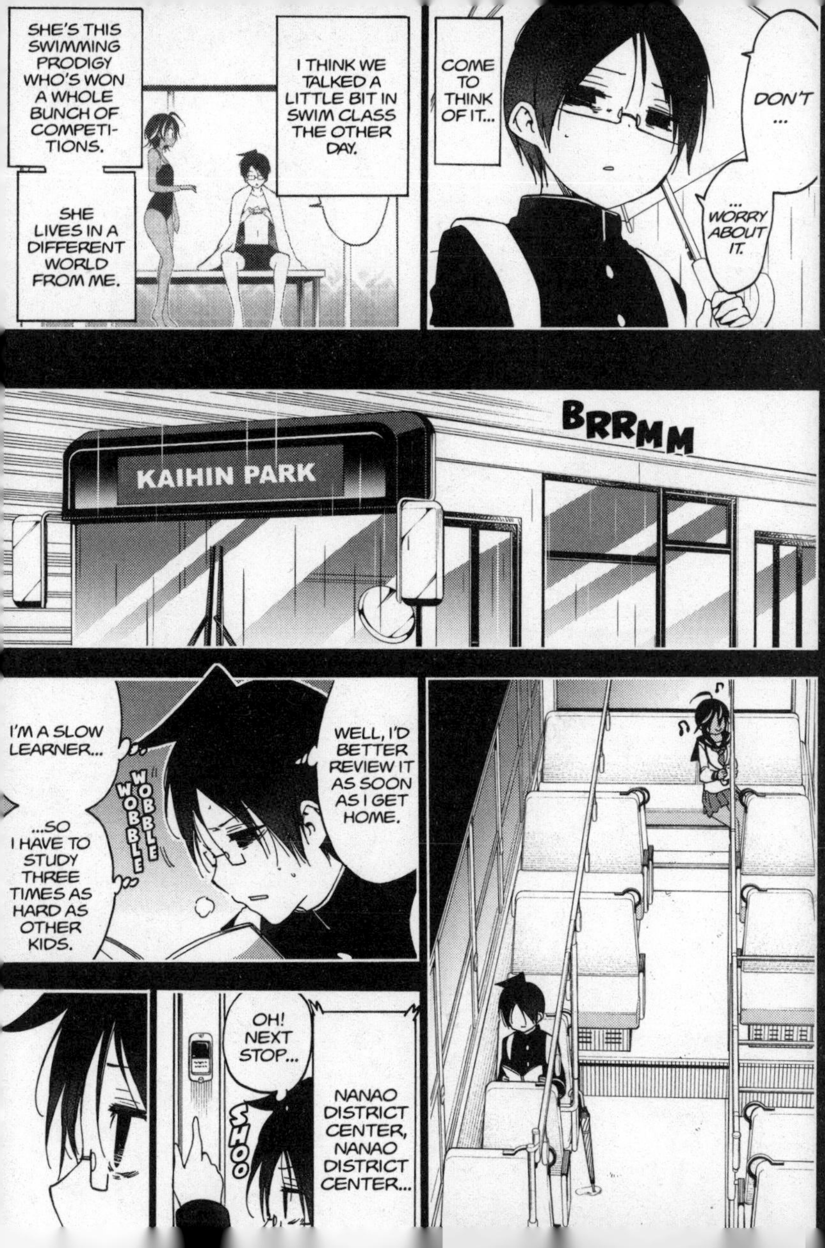
DON'T ...
... WORRY ABOUT IT.
COME TO THINK OF IT...
I THINK WE TALKED A LITTLE BIT IN SWIM CLASS THE OTHER DAY.
SHE'S THIS SWIMMING PRODIGY WHO'S WON A WHOLE BUNCH OF COMPETITIONS.
SHE LIVES IN A DIFFERENT WORLD FROM ME.
BRRMM
KAIHIN PARK
WELL, I'D BETTER REVIEW IT AS SOON AS I GET HOME.
I'M A SLOW LEARNER...
WOBBLE WOBBLE
...SO I HAVE TO STUDY THREE TIMES AS HARD AS OTHER KIDS.
NANAO DISTRICT CENTER, NANAO DISTRICT CENTER...
OH! NEXT STOP...
SHOO

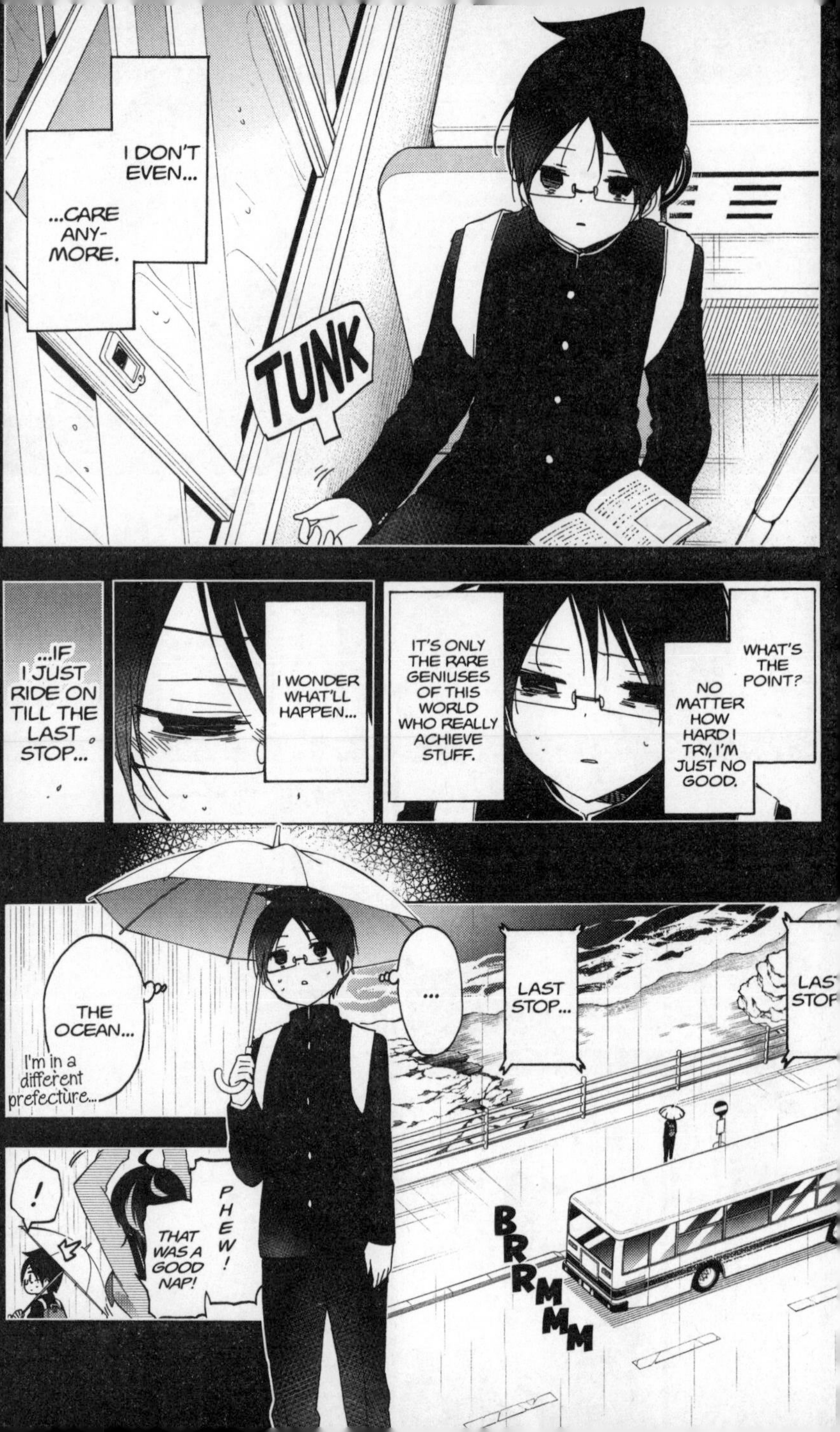
I DON'T EVEN...
...CARE ANY-MORE.
TUNK
WHAT'S THE POINT?
NO MATTER HOW HARD I TRY, I'M JUST NO GOOD.
IT'S ONLY THE RARE GENIUSES OF THIS WORLD WHO REALLY ACHIEVE STUFF.
I WONDER WHAT'LL HAPPEN...
...IF I JUST RIDE ON TILL THE LAST STOP...
LAST STO
LAST STOP...
BRRMMM
...
THE OCEAN...
I'm in a different prefecture...
!
PHEW!
THAT WAS A GOOD NAP!

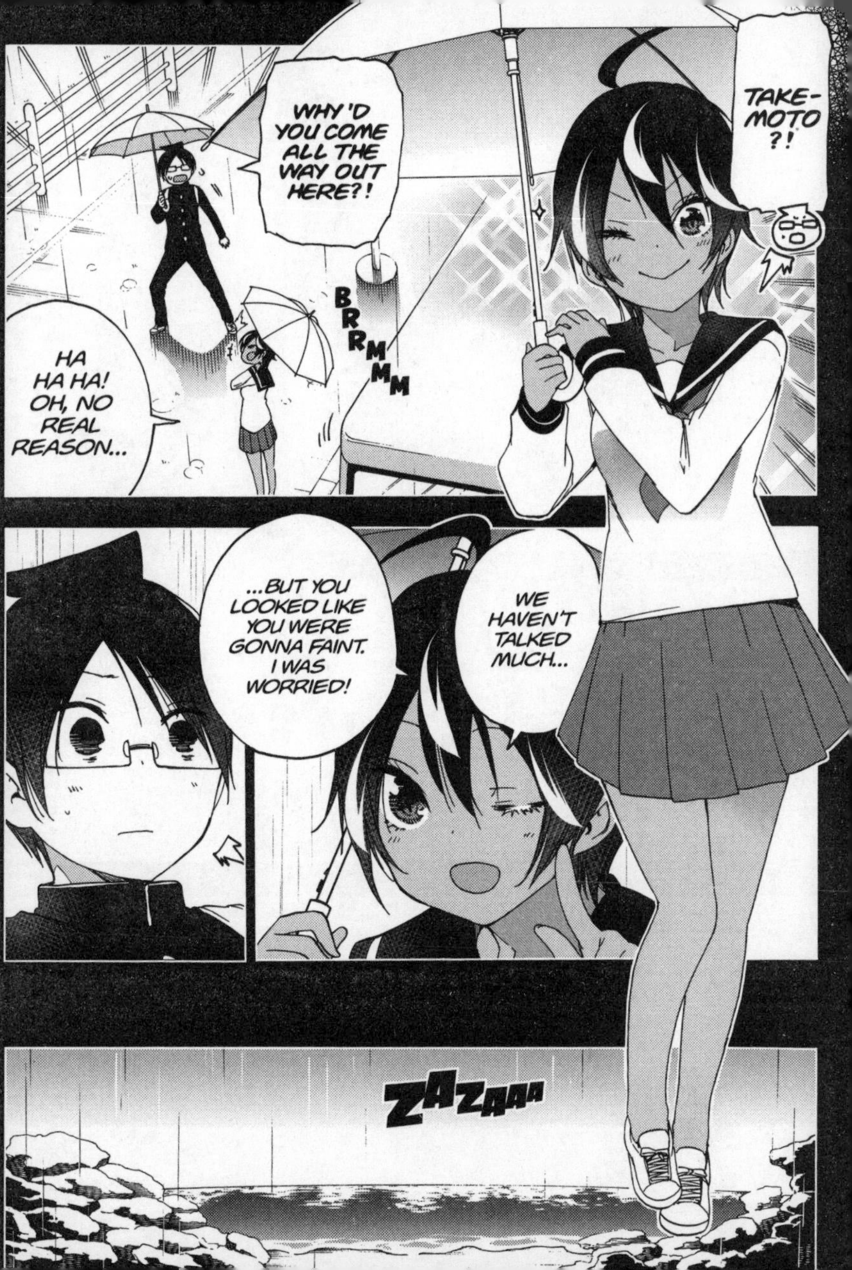
TAKE-MOTO?!
WHY 'D YOU COME ALL THE WAY OUT HERE?!
BRRMMM
HA HA HA! OH, NO REAL REASON...
WE HAVEN'T TALKED MUCH...
...BUT YOU LOOKED LIKE YOU WERE GONNA FAINT. I WAS WORRIED!
ZAZAAA

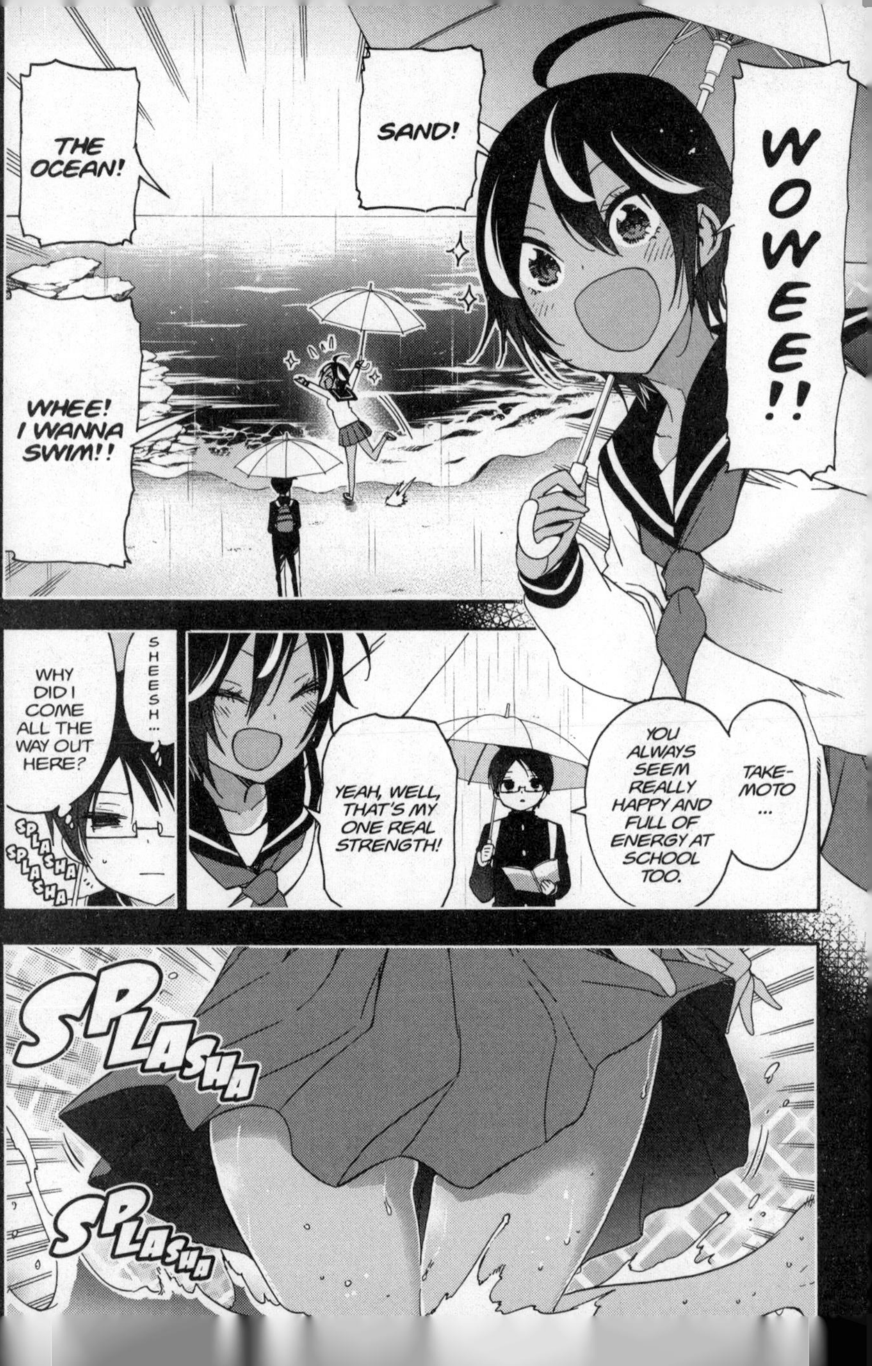
WOWEE!!
SAND!
THE OCEAN!
WHEE! I WANNA SWIM!!
TAKE-MOTO ...
YOU ALWAYS SEEM REALLY HAPPY AND FULL OF ENERGY AT SCHOOL TOO.
YEAH, WELL, THAT'S MY ONE REAL STRENGTH!
SHEESH...
WHY DID I COME ALL THE WAY OUT HERE?
SPLASHA
SPLASHA
SPLASHA
SPLASHA

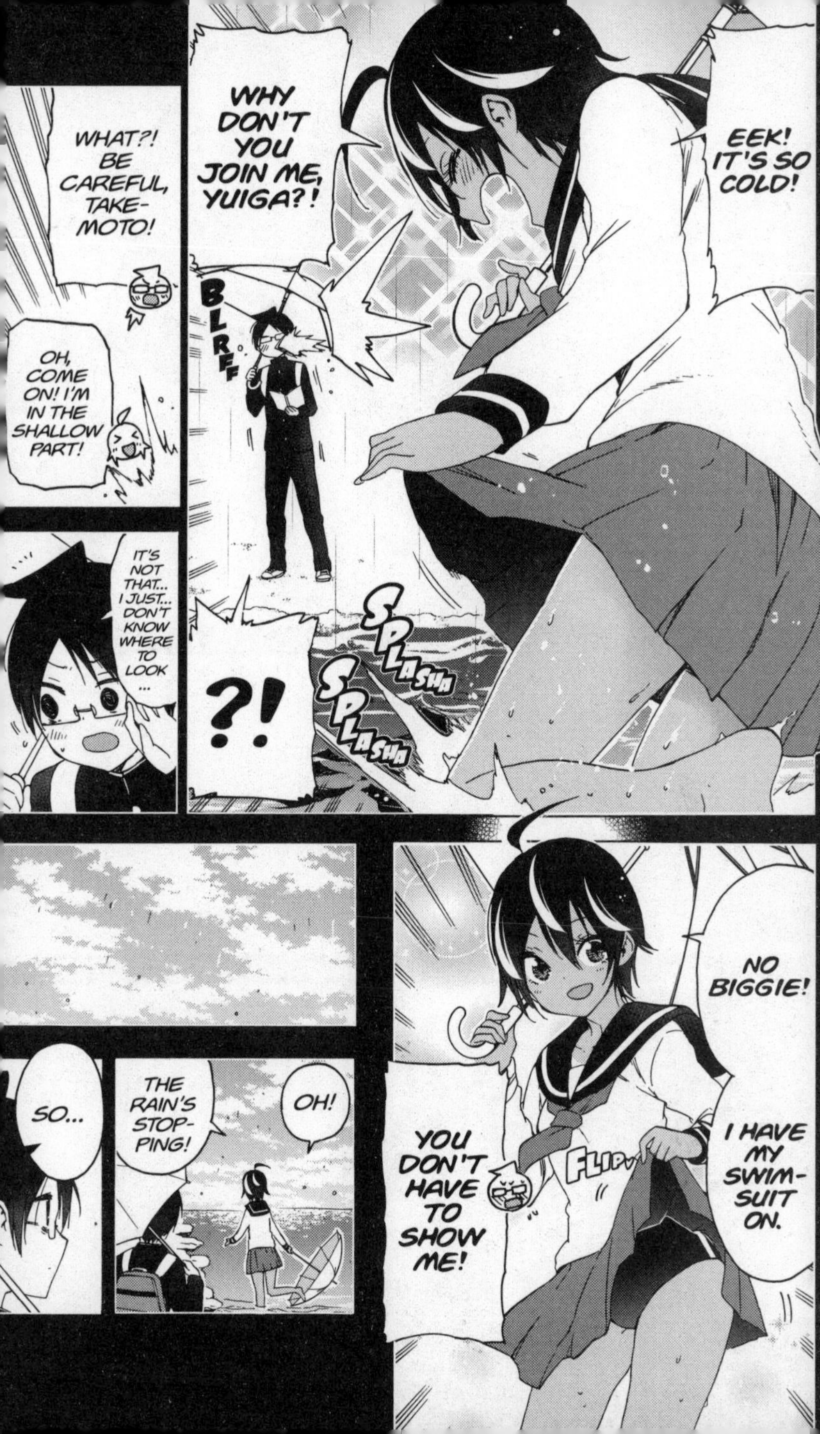
EEK! IT'S SO COLD!
WHY DON'T YOU JOIN ME, YUIGA?!
BLRFF
SPLASHA
SPLASHA
?!
WHAT?! BE CAREFUL, TAKE-MOTO!
OH, COME ON! I'M IN THE SHALLOW PART!
IT'S NOT THAT... I JUST... DON'T KNOW WHERE TO LOOK...
NO BIGGIE!
I HAVE MY SWIM-SUIT ON.
FLIP
YOU DON'T HAVE TO SHOW ME!
OH!
THE RAIN'S STOP-PING!
SO...

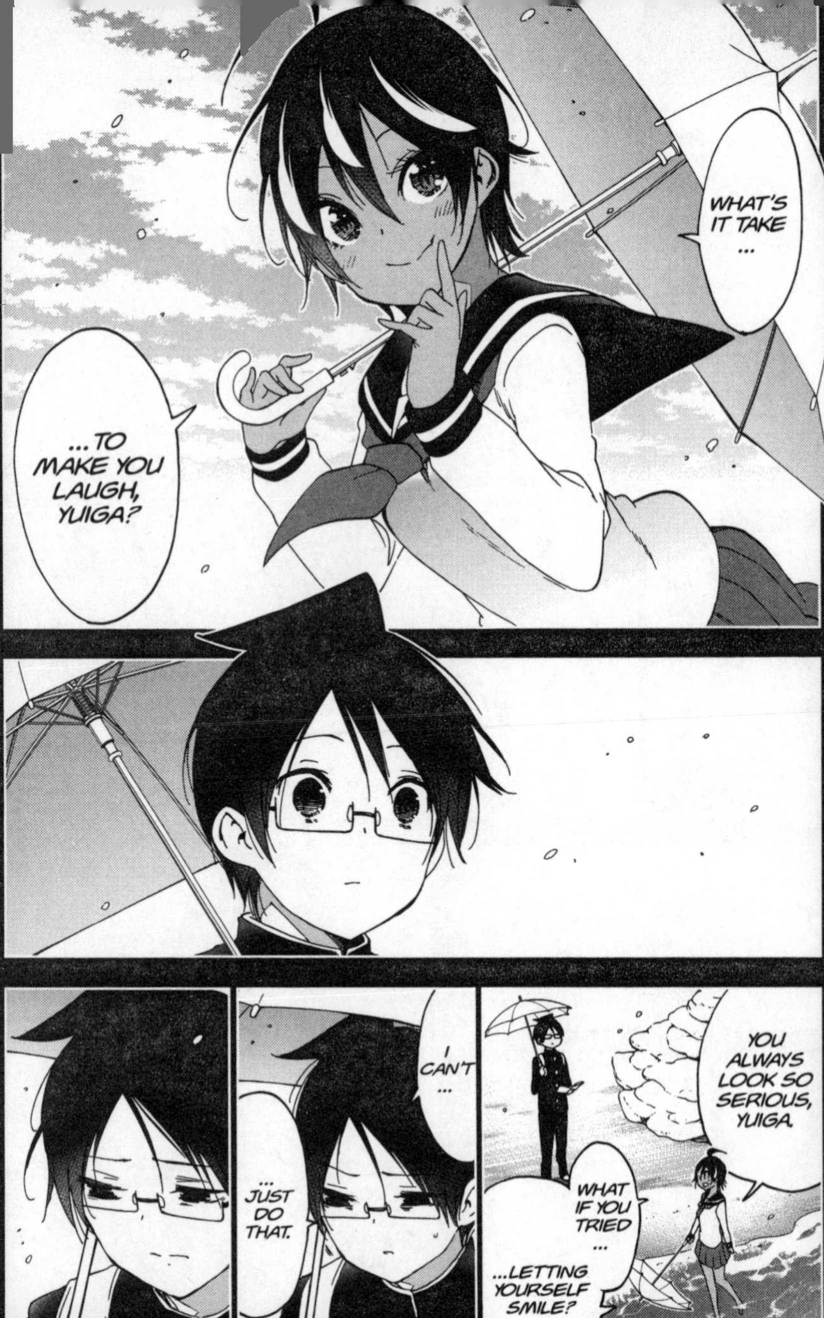
WHAT'S IT TAKE ...
...TO MAKE YOU LAUGH, YUIGA?
YOU ALWAYS LOOK SO SERIOUS, YUIGA.
WHAT IF YOU TRIED ...
...LETTING YOURSELF SMILE?
I CAN'T ...
... JUST DO THAT.

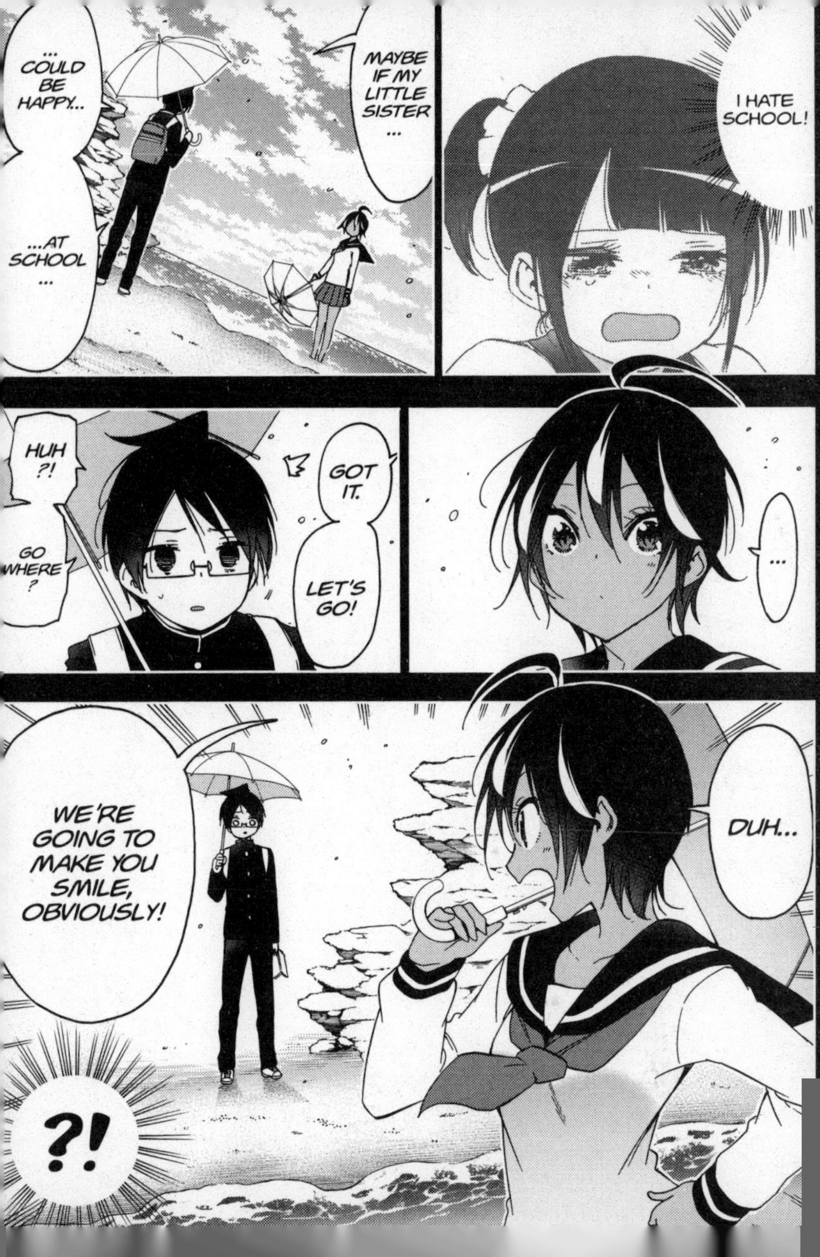
I HATE SCHOOL!
MAYBE IF MY LITTLE SISTER ...
... COULD BE HAPPY...
...AT SCHOOL ...
...
GOT IT.
LET'S GO!
HUH ?!
GO WHERE ?
DUH...
WE'RE GOING TO MAKE YOU SMILE, OBVIOUSLY!
?!

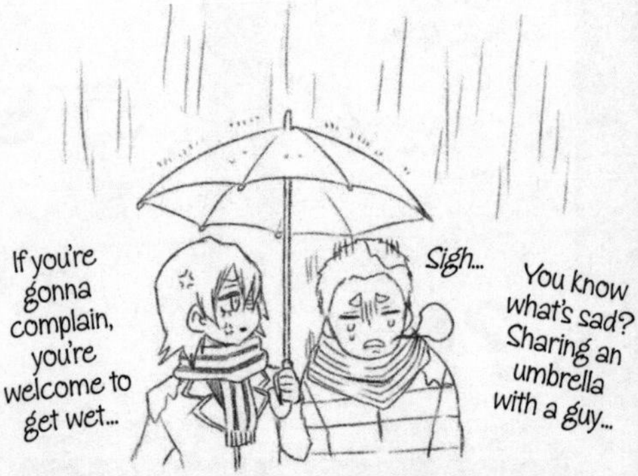
You know what's sad? Sharing an umbrella with a guy...
Sigh...
If you're gonna complain, you're welcome to get wet...

Question 146: The Ephemeral Mermaid Sprinkles into the Promised [X], Part 5

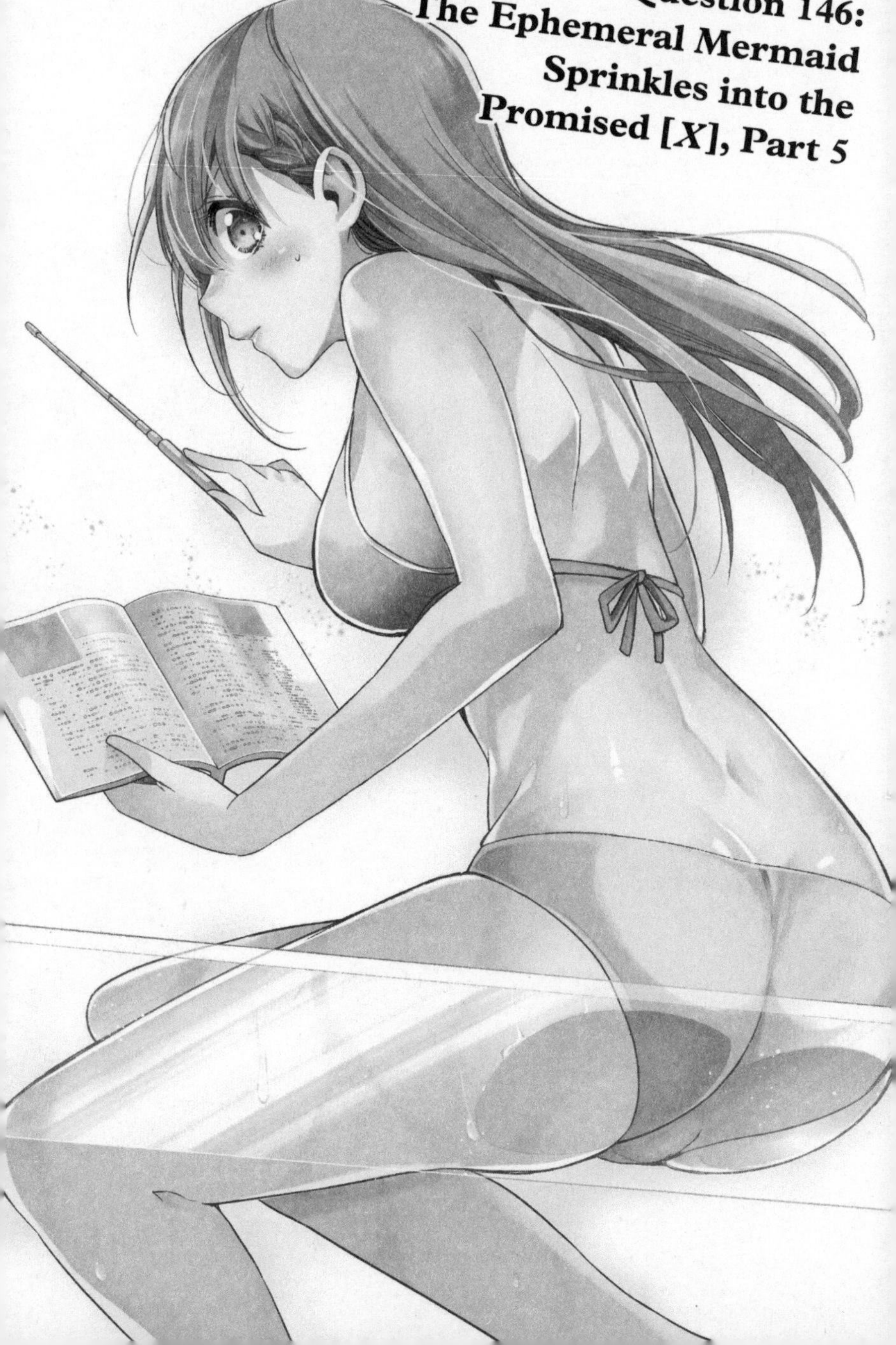

[x] We
Never
Learn

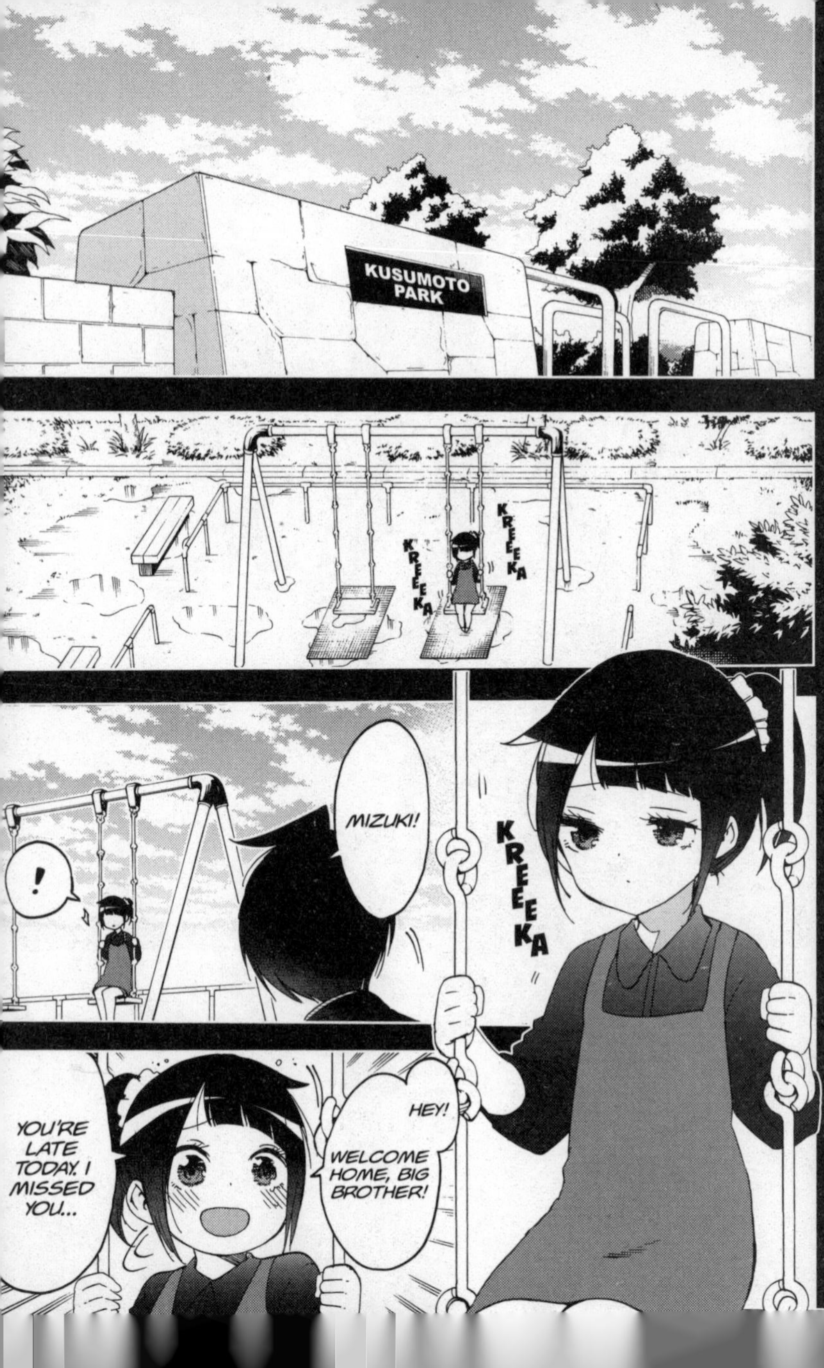
KUSUMOTO PARK
KREEKA
KREEKA
MIZUKI!
!
KREEKA
HEY!
WELCOME HOME, BIG BROTHER!
YOU'RE LATE TODAY. I MISSED YOU...

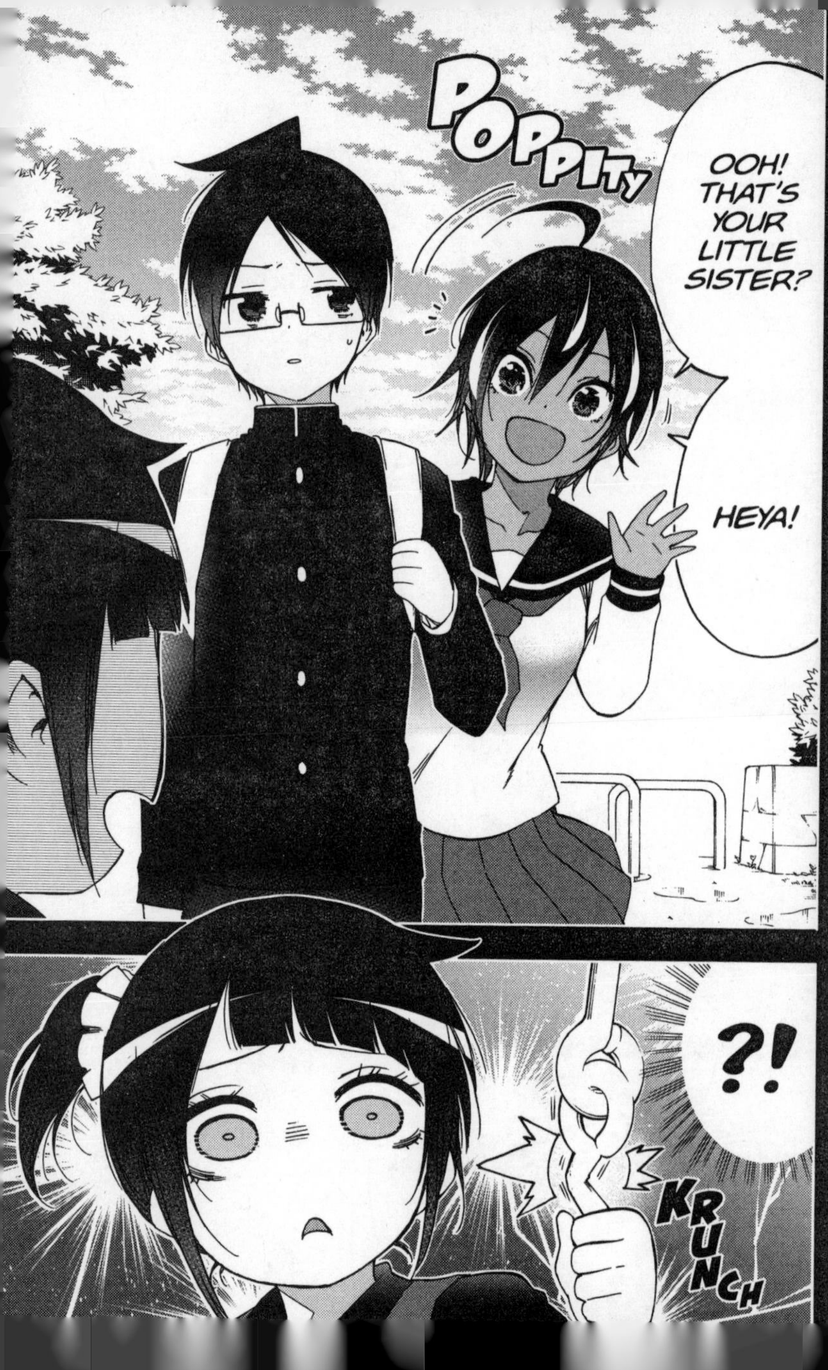
POPPITY
OOH! THAT'S YOUR LITTLE SISTER?
HEYA!
?!
KRUNCH

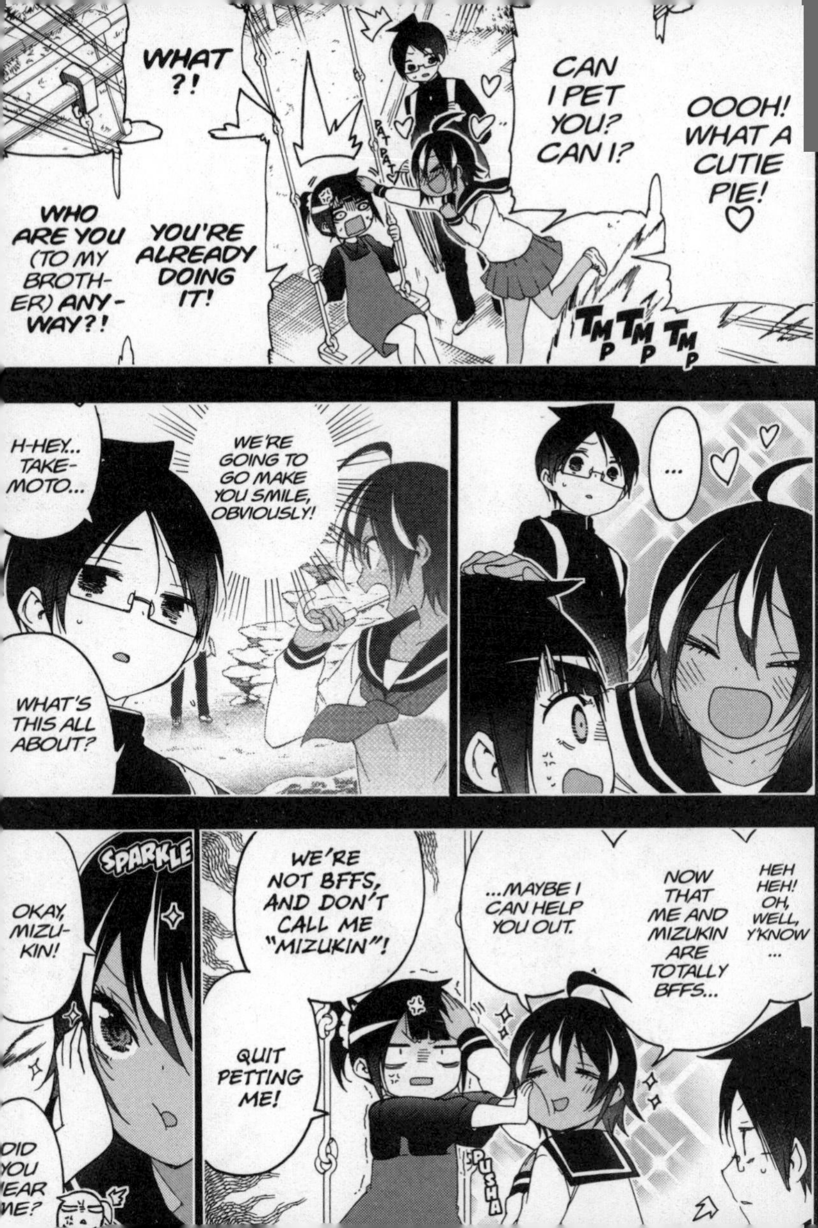
OOOH! WHAT A CUTIE PIE! ♡
CAN I PET YOU? CAN I?
PAT PAT
WHAT?!
YOU'RE ALREADY DOING IT!
WHO ARE YOU (TO MY BROTHER) ANYWAY?!
TMP TMP TMP
...
WE'RE GOING TO GO MAKE YOU SMILE, OBVIOUSLY!
H-HEY... TAKEMOTO...
WHAT'S THIS ALL ABOUT?
HEH HEH! OH, WELL, Y'KNOW...
NOW THAT ME AND MIZUKIN ARE TOTALLY BFFS...
...MAYBE I CAN HELP YOU OUT.
WE'RE NOT BFFS, AND DON'T CALL ME "MIZUKIN"!
QUIT PETTING ME!
PUSHA
SPARKLE
OKAY, MIZUKIN!
DID YOU HEAR ME?

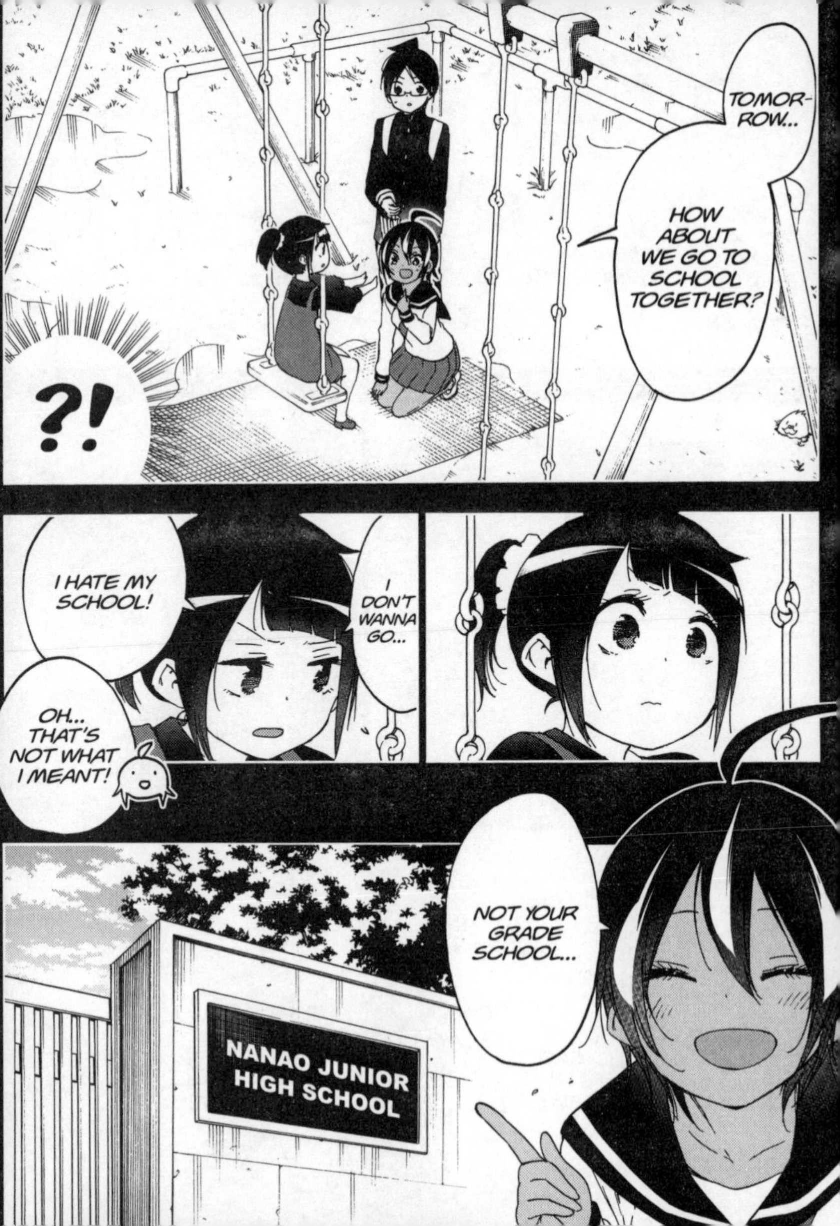
TOMOR-ROW...
HOW ABOUT WE GO TO SCHOOL TOGETHER?
?!
I DON'T WANNA GO...
I HATE MY SCHOOL!
OH... THAT'S NOT WHAT I MEANT!
NOT YOUR GRADE SCHOOL...
NANAO JUNIOR HIGH SCHOOL

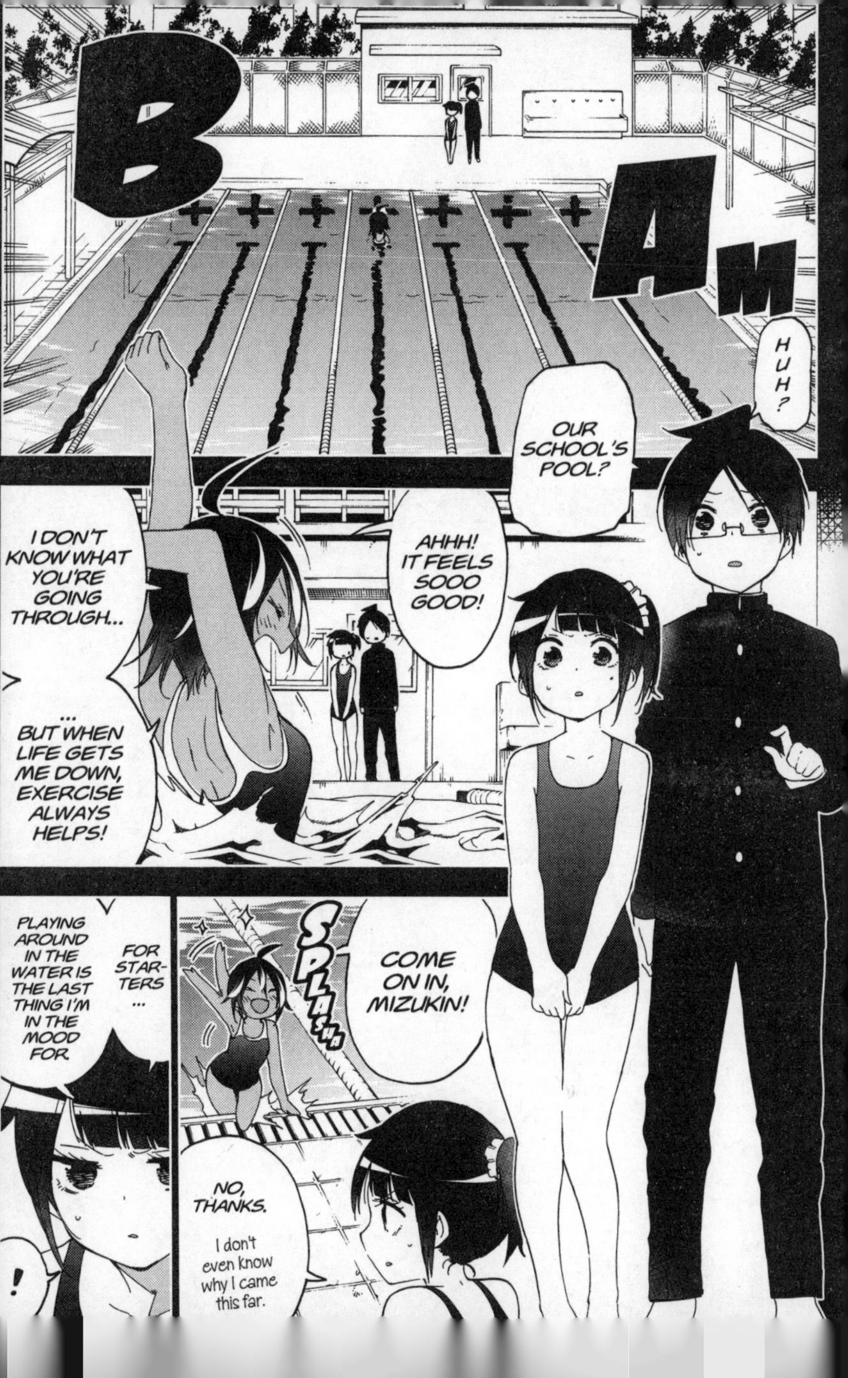
BAM
HUH?
OUR SCHOOL'S POOL?
AHHH! IT FEELS SOOO GOOD!
I DON'T KNOW WHAT YOU'RE GOING THROUGH...
...BUT WHEN LIFE GETS ME DOWN, EXERCISE ALWAYS HELPS!
COME ON IN, MIZUKIN!
SPLASHA
NO, THANKS.
I don't even know why I came this far.
FOR STARTERS...
PLAYING AROUND IN THE WATER IS THE LAST THING I'M IN THE MOOD FOR.

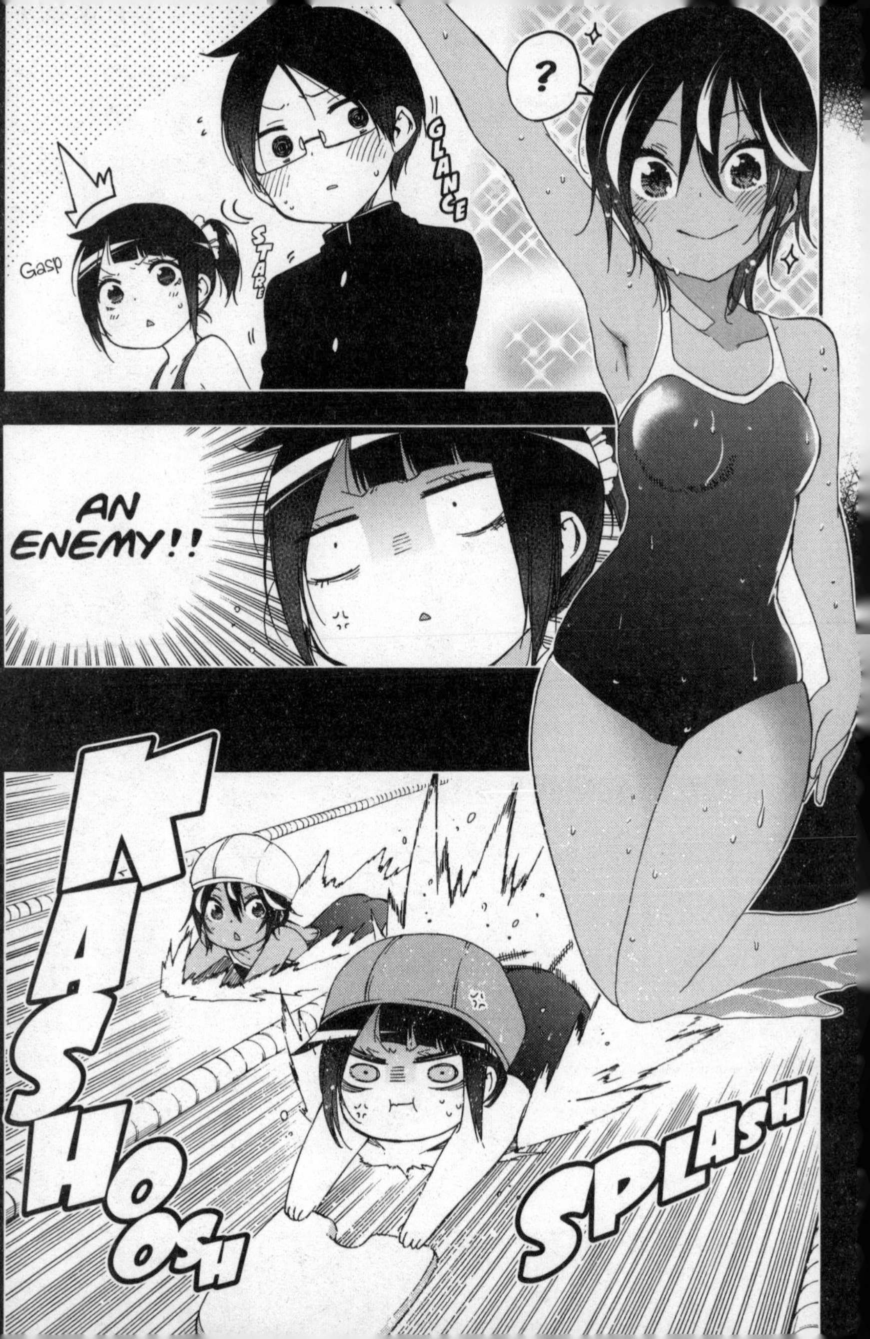
?
GLANCE
STARE
Gasp
AN ENEMY!!
KASHOOSH
SPLASH

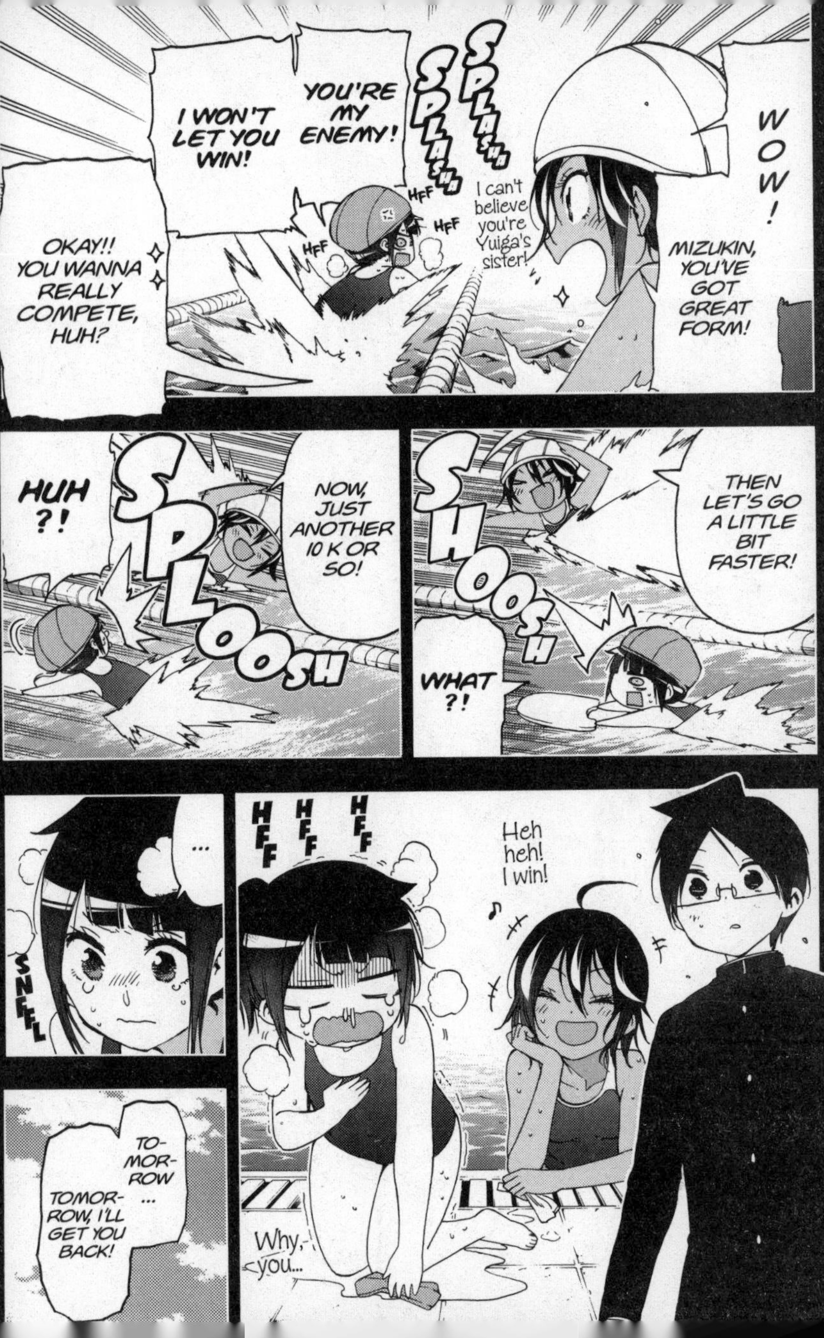
WOW!
MIZUKIN, YOU'VE GOT GREAT FORM!
I can't believe you're Yuiga's sister!
SPLASH
SPLASH
HFF HFF HFF
YOU'RE MY ENEMY!
I WON'T LET YOU WIN!
OKAY!! YOU WANNA REALLY COMPETE, HUH?
THEN LET'S GO A LITTLE BIT FASTER!
SHOOOSH
WHAT?!
NOW, JUST ANOTHER 10 K OR SO!
SPLOOSH
HUH?!
Heh heh! I win!
HFF HFF HFF
Why, you...
...
SNFFL
TO-MOR-ROW...
TOMORROW, I'LL GET YOU BACK!

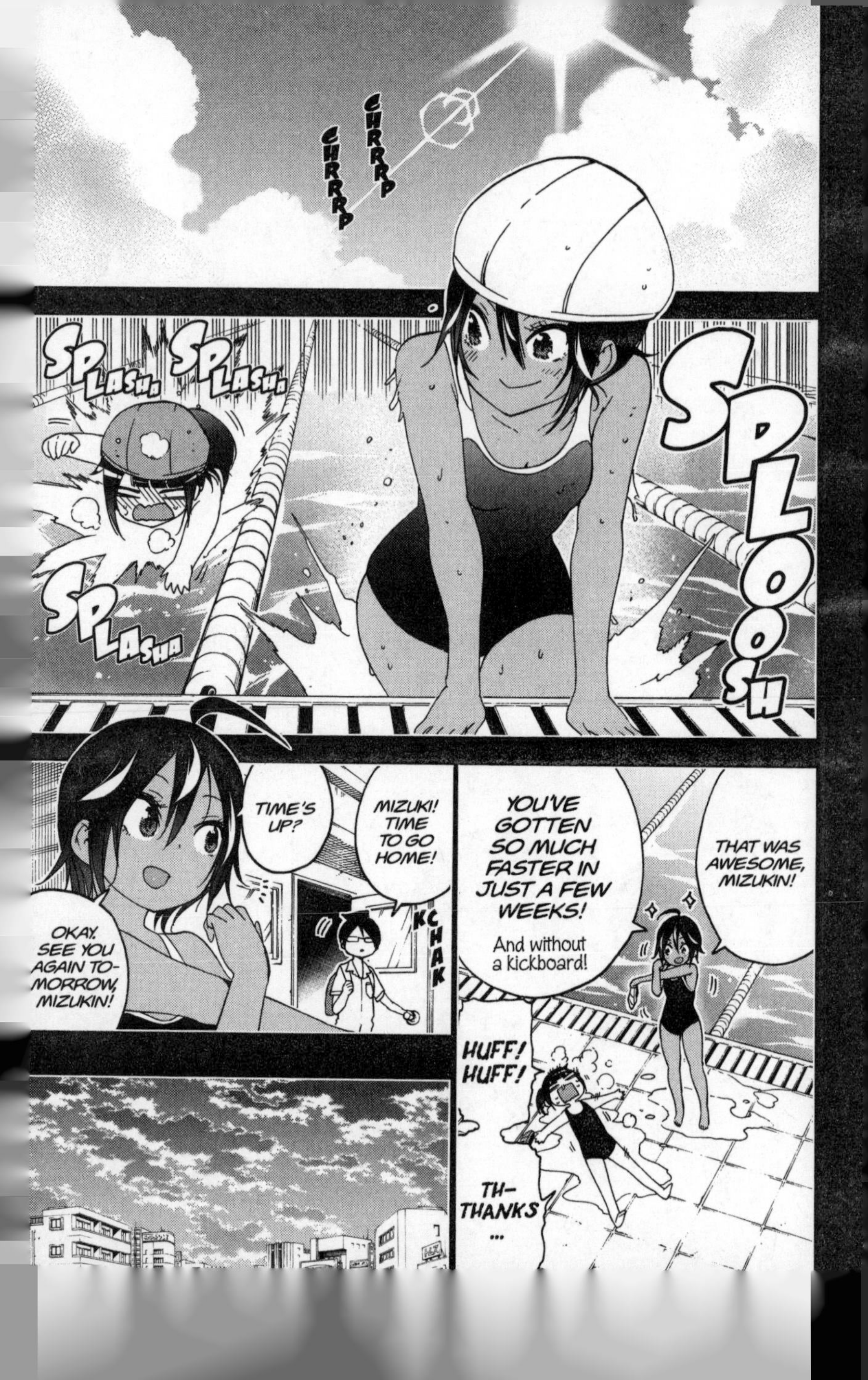
CHRRRP
CHRRRP
SPLOOSH
SPLASHA
SPLASHA
SPLASHA
THAT WAS AWESOME, MIZUKIN!
YOU'VE GOTTEN SO MUCH FASTER IN JUST A FEW WEEKS!
And without a kickboard!
HUFF! HUFF!
TH- THANKS ...
MIZUKI! TIME TO GO HOME!
KCHAK
TIME'S UP?
OKAY. SEE YOU AGAIN TO-MORROW, MIZUKIN!

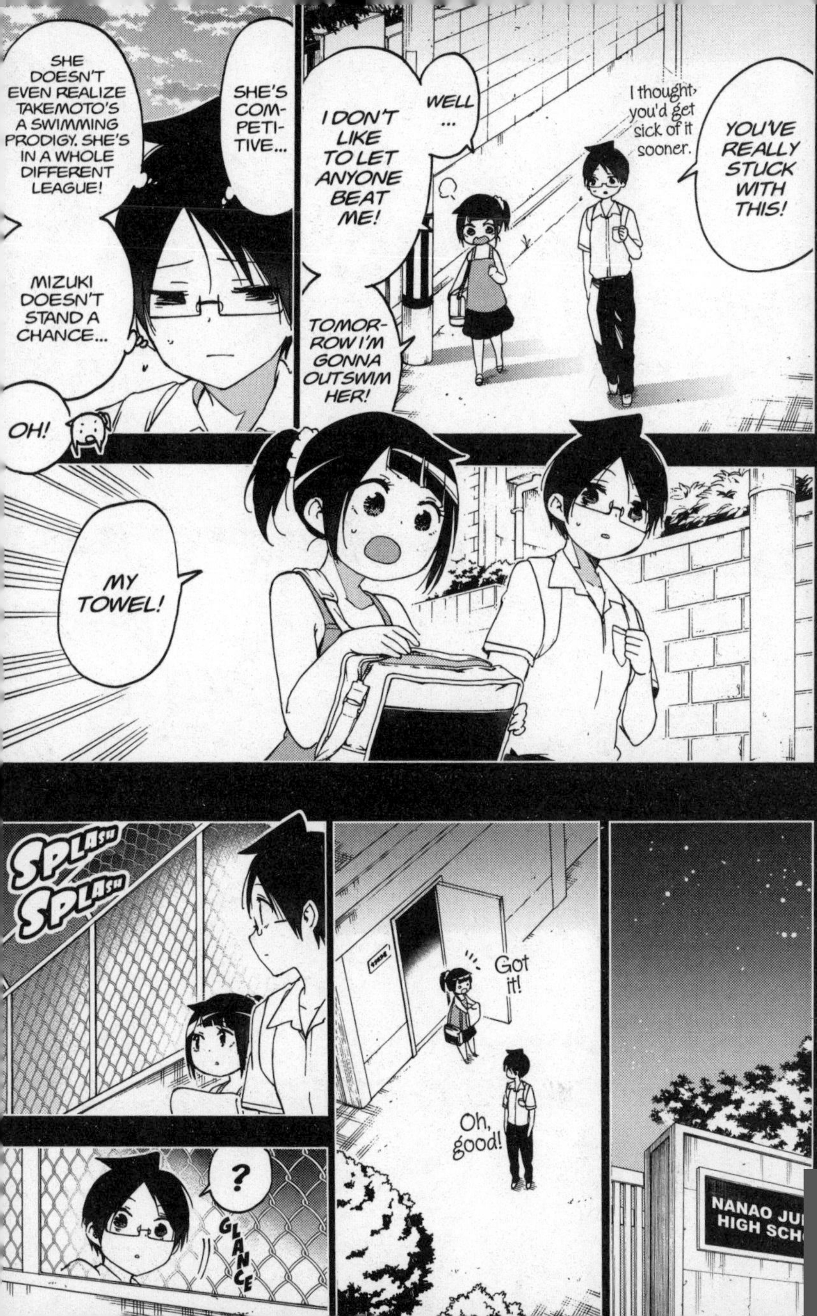
YOU'VE REALLY STUCK WITH THIS!
I thought you'd get sick of it sooner.
WELL...
I DON'T LIKE TO LET ANYONE BEAT ME!
TOMORROW I'M GONNA OUTSWIM HER!
SHE'S COMPETITIVE...
SHE DOESN'T EVEN REALIZE TAKEMOTO'S A SWIMMING PRODIGY. SHE'S IN A WHOLE DIFFERENT LEAGUE!
MIZUKI DOESN'T STAND A CHANCE...
OH!
MY TOWEL!
NANAO JU
HIGH SCH
Got it!
Oh, good!
SPLASH
SPLASH
?
GLANCE

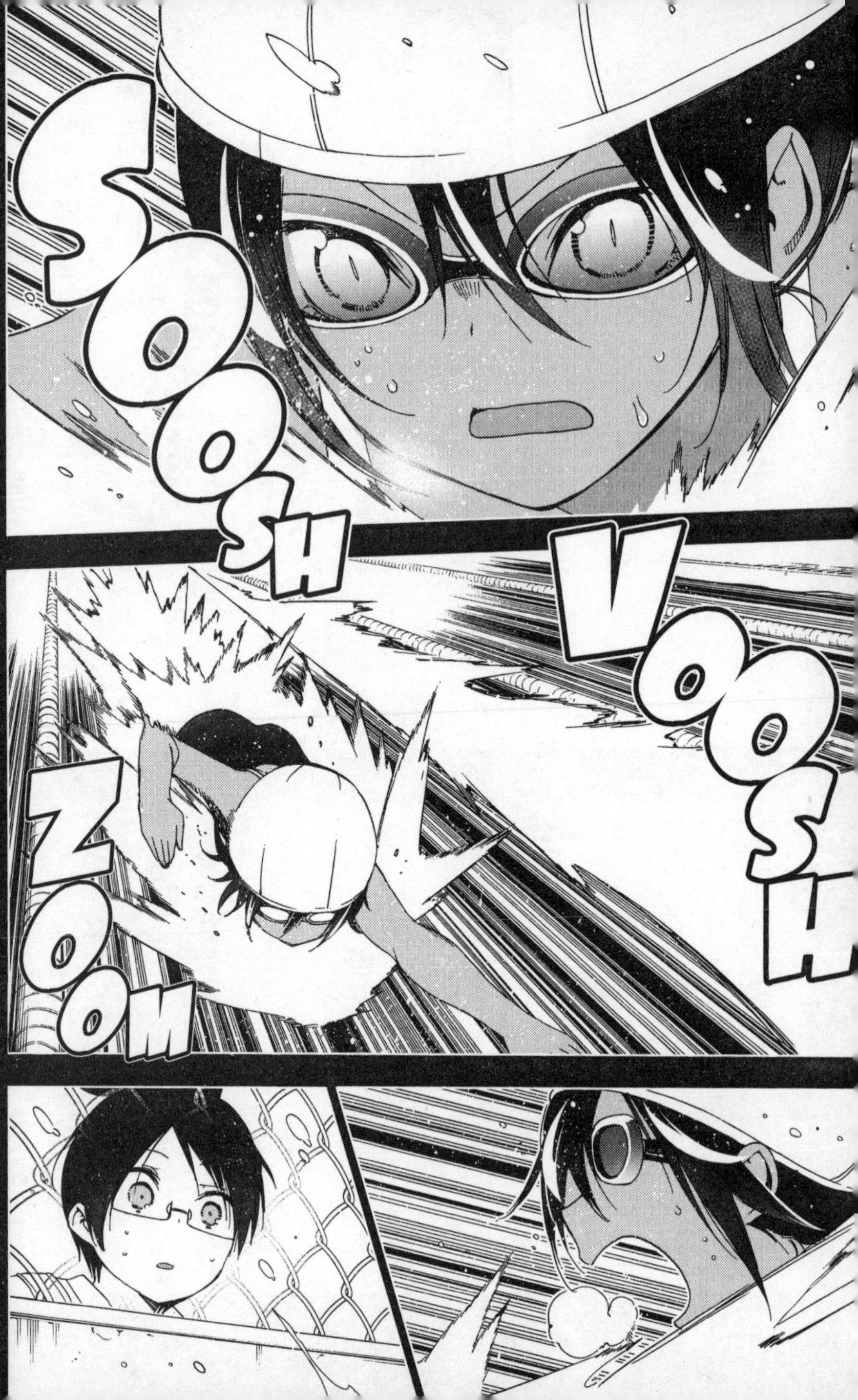
SWOOOSH
VOOOSH
ZOOOM

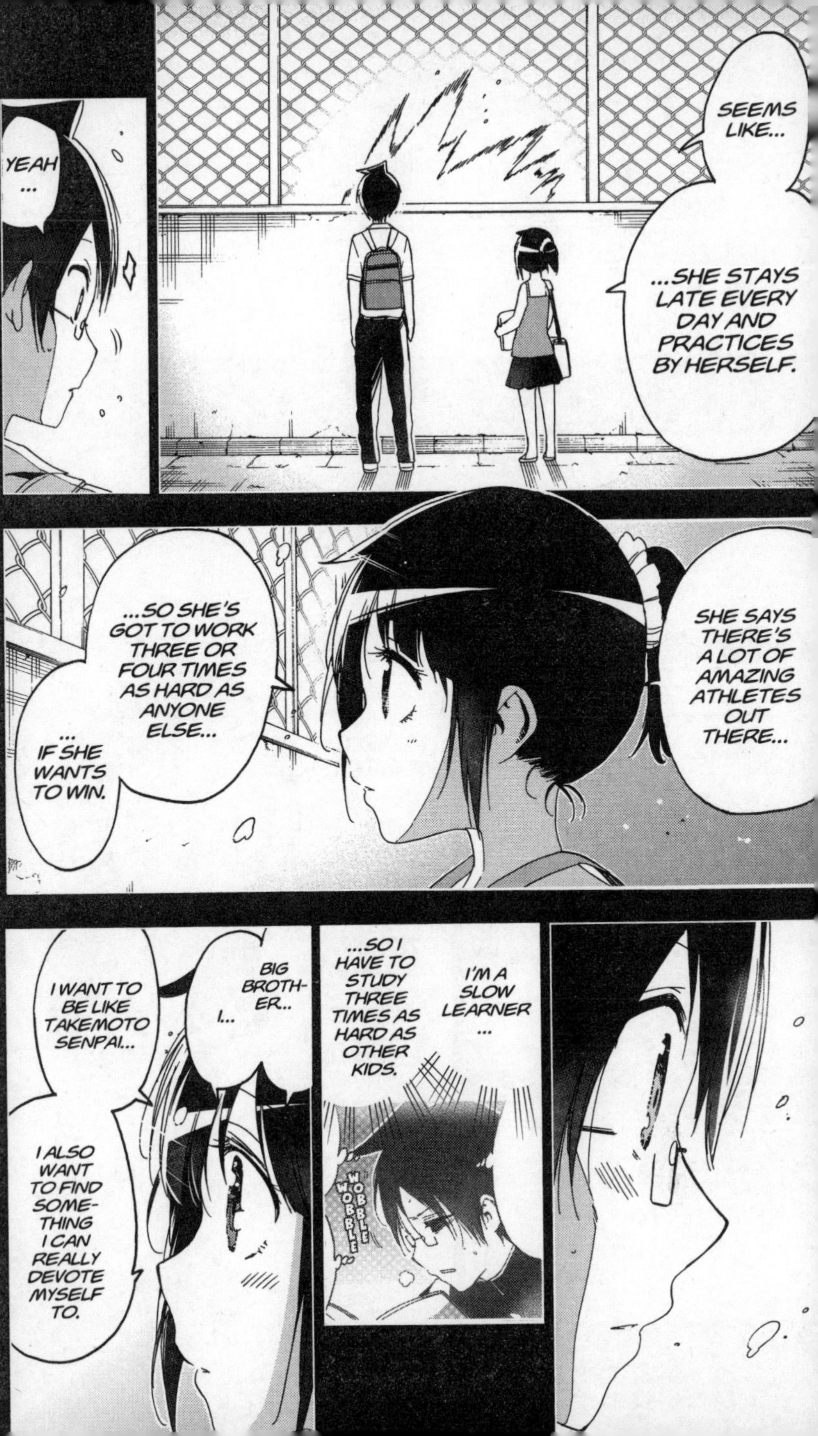
SEEMS LIKE...
...SHE STAYS LATE EVERY DAY AND PRACTICES BY HERSELF.
YEAH ...
SHE SAYS THERE'S A LOT OF AMAZING ATHLETES OUT THERE...
...SO SHE'S GOT TO WORK THREE OR FOUR TIMES AS HARD AS ANYONE ELSE...
... IF SHE WANTS TO WIN.
I'M A SLOW LEARNER ...
...SO I HAVE TO STUDY THREE TIMES AS HARD AS OTHER KIDS.
WOBBLE WOBBLE
BIG BROTH-ER...
I...
I WANT TO BE LIKE TAKEMOTO SENPAI...
I ALSO WANT TO FIND SOME-THING I CAN REALLY DEVOTE MYSELF TO.

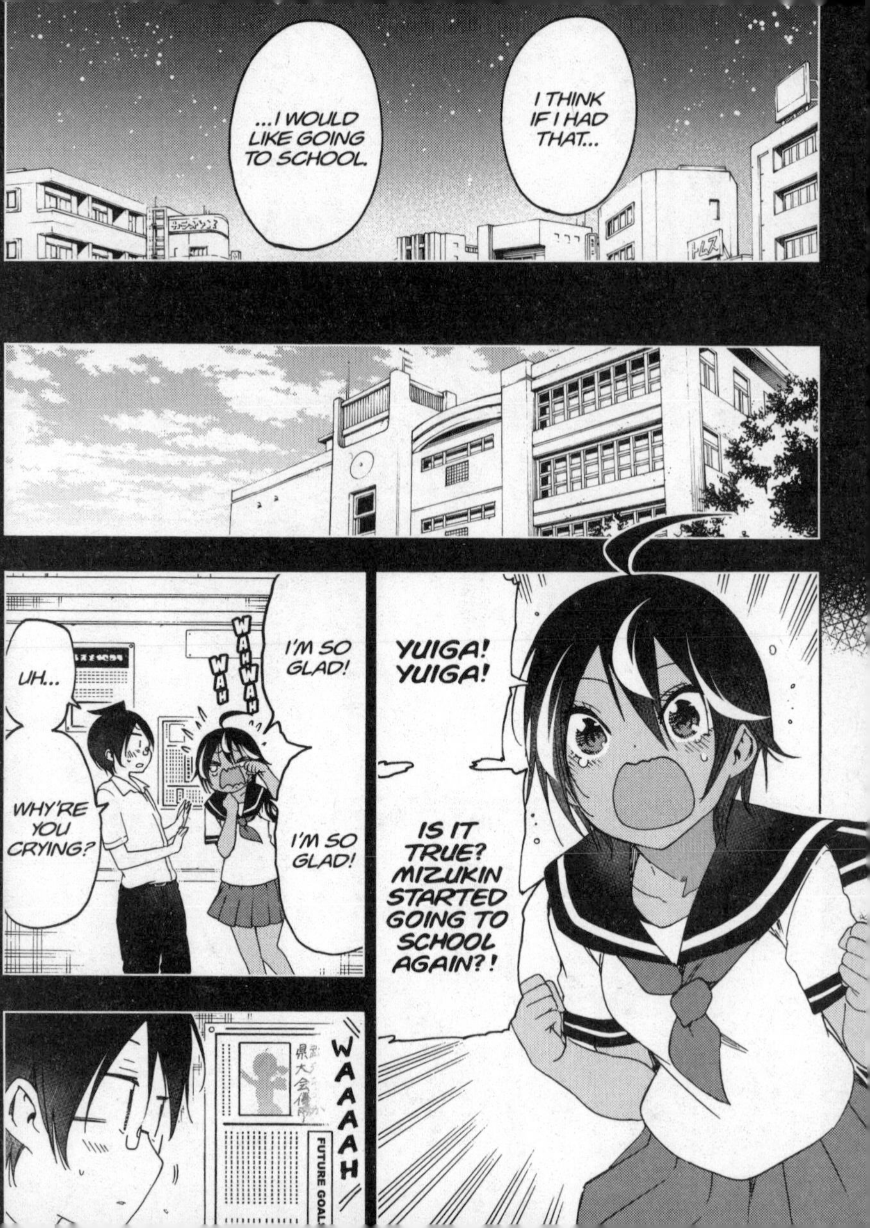
I THINK IF I HAD THAT...
...I WOULD LIKE GOING TO SCHOOL.
YUIGA! YUIGA!
IS IT TRUE? MIZUKIN STARTED GOING TO SCHOOL AGAIN?!
I'M SO GLAD!
WAHWAH
WAH
I'M SO GLAD!
UH...
WHY'RE YOU CRYING?
WAAAAAH
FUTURE GOAL

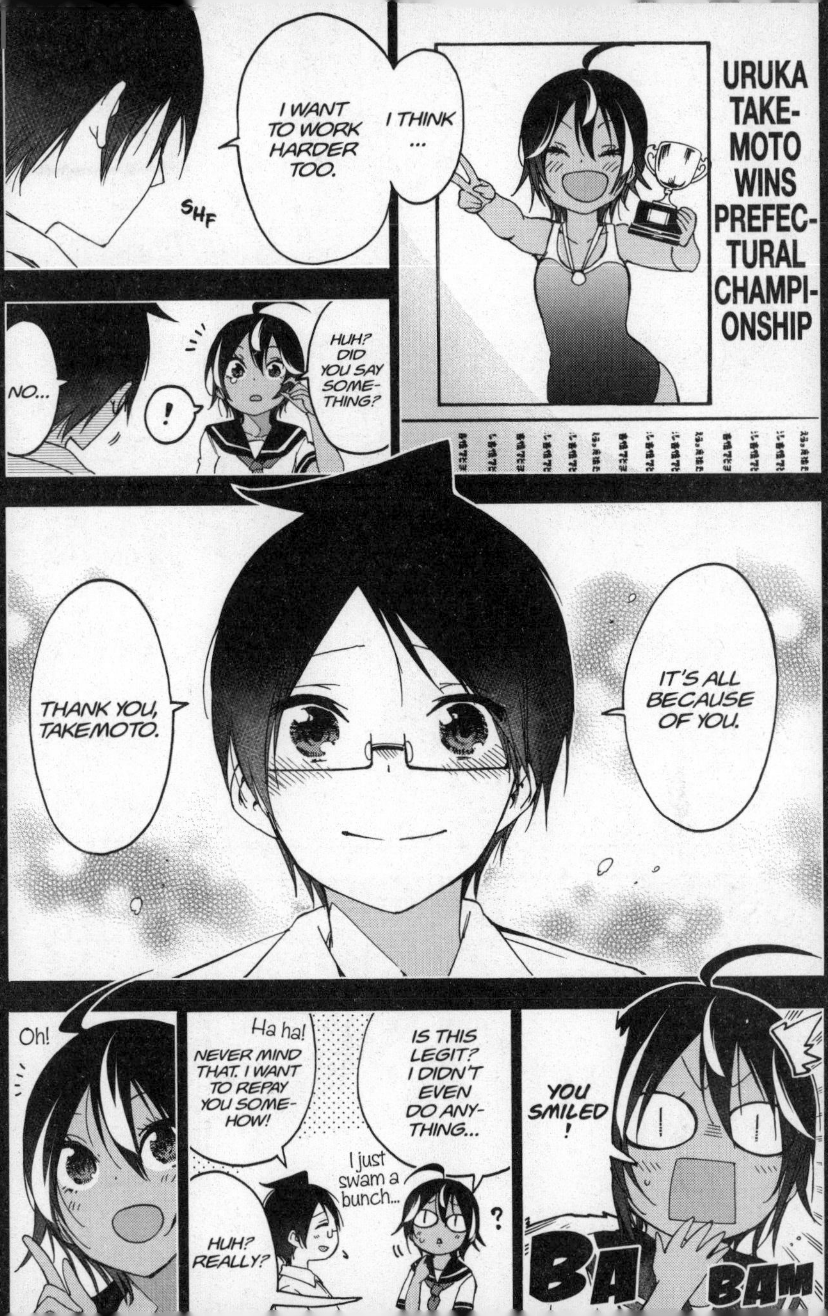
URUKA TAKEMOTO WINS PREFECTURAL CHAMPIONSHIP
I THINK ...
I WANT TO WORK HARDER TOO.
SHF
HUH? DID YOU SAY SOMETHING?
!
NO...
IT'S ALL BECAUSE OF YOU.
THANK YOU, TAKEMOTO.
YOU SMILED!
BA
BAM
IS THIS LEGIT? I DIDN'T EVEN DO ANYTHING...
Ha ha!
NEVER MIND THAT. I WANT TO REPAY YOU SOMEHOW!
I just swam a bunch...
?
HUH? REALLY?
Oh!

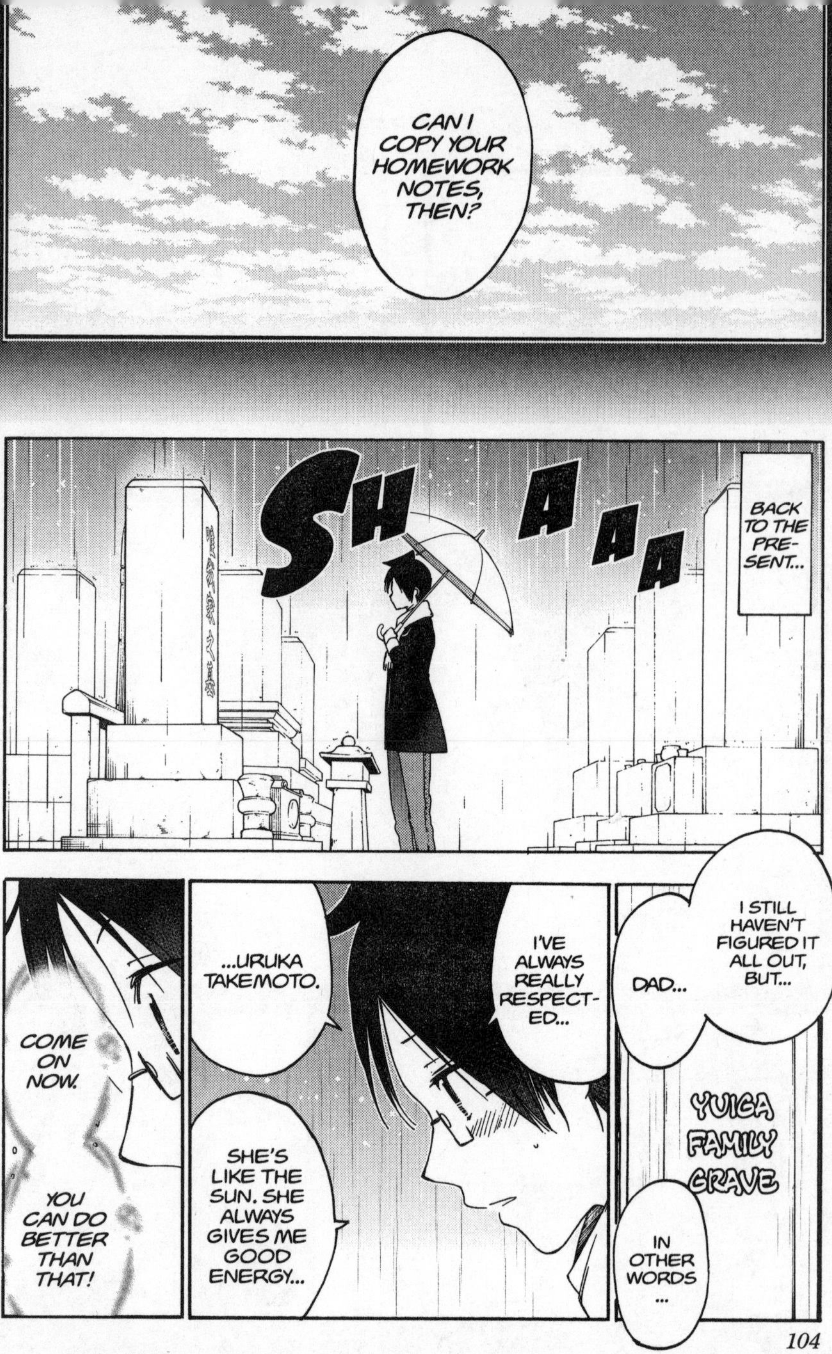
CAN I COPY YOUR HOMEWORK NOTES, THEN?
BACK TO THE PRE-SENT...
SHAAA
I STILL HAVEN'T FIGURED IT ALL OUT, BUT...
DAD...
YUIGA FAMILY GRAVE
IN OTHER WORDS ...
I'VE ALWAYS REALLY RESPECT-ED...
...URUKA TAKEMOTO.
SHE'S LIKE THE SUN. SHE ALWAYS GIVES ME GOOD ENERGY...
COME ON NOW.
YOU CAN DO BETTER THAN THAT!

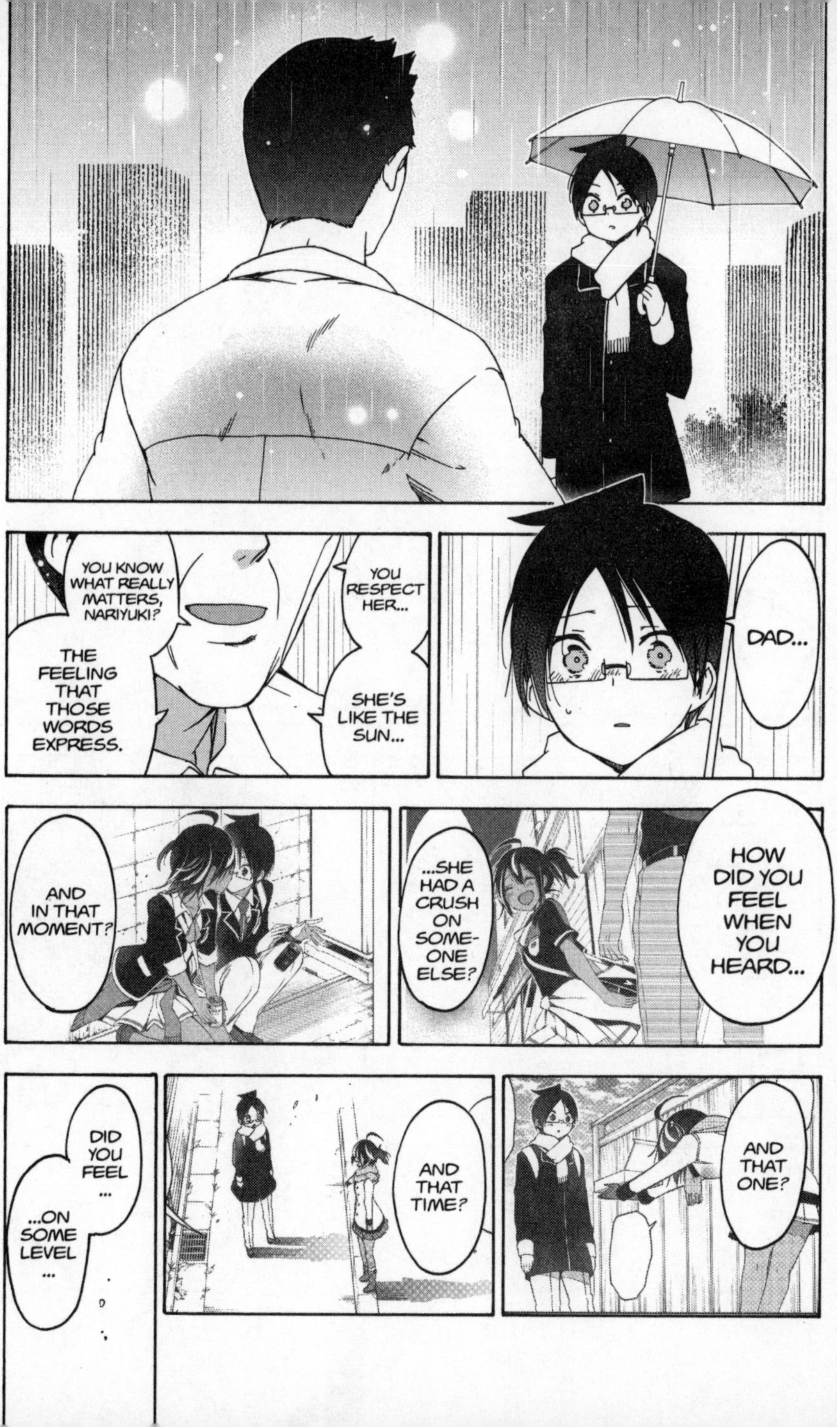
DAD...
YOU RESPECT HER...
SHE'S LIKE THE SUN...
YOU KNOW WHAT REALLY MATTERS, NARIYUKI?
THE FEELING THAT THOSE WORDS EXPRESS.
HOW DID YOU FEEL WHEN YOU HEARD...
...SHE HAD A CRUSH ON SOME-ONE ELSE?
AND IN THAT MOMENT?
AND THAT ONE?
AND THAT TIME?
DID YOU FEEL ...
...ON SOME LEVEL ...

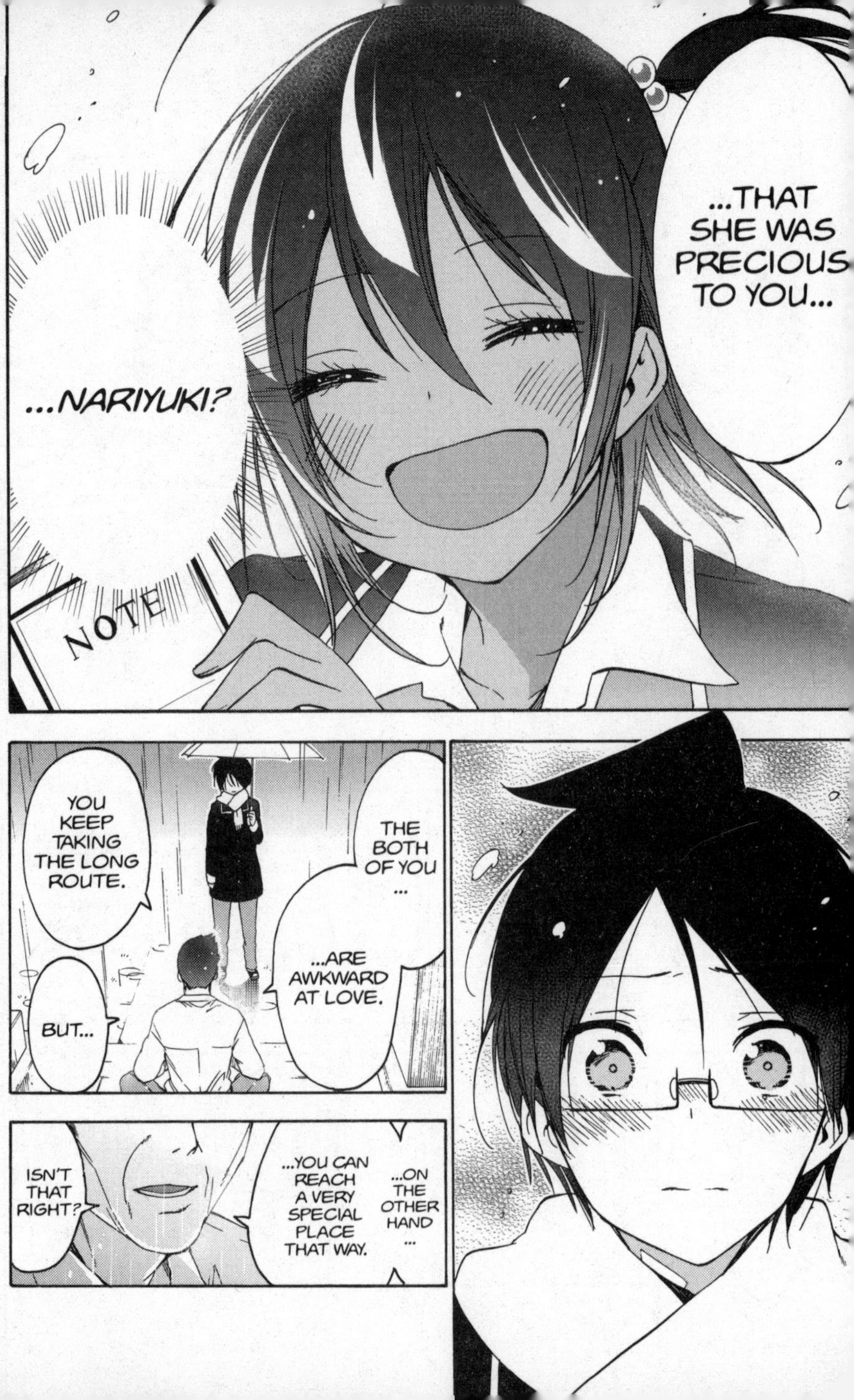
...THAT SHE WAS PRECIOUS TO YOU...
...NARIYUKI?
NOTE
THE BOTH OF YOU ...
...ARE AWKWARD AT LOVE.
YOU KEEP TAKING THE LONG ROUTE.
BUT...
...ON THE OTHER HAND ...
...YOU CAN REACH A VERY SPECIAL PLACE THAT WAY.
ISN'T THAT RIGHT?

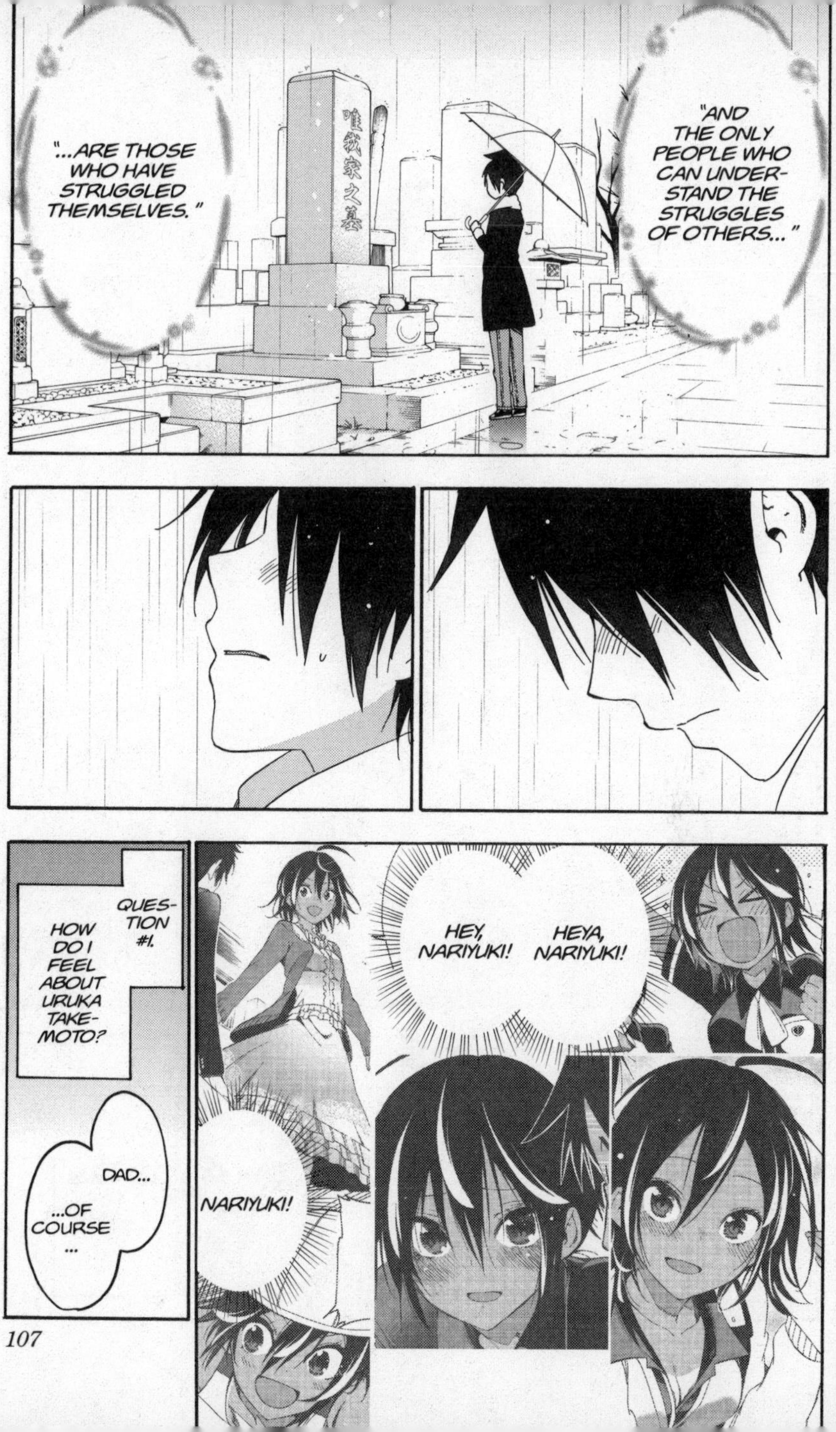
"AND THE ONLY PEOPLE WHO CAN UNDERSTAND THE STRUGGLES OF OTHERS..."
唯我家之墓
"...ARE THOSE WHO HAVE STRUGGLED THEMSELVES."
HEYA, NARIYUKI!
HEY, NARIYUKI!
NARIYUKI!
QUESTION #1.
HOW DO I FEEL ABOUT URUKA TAKEMOTO?
DAD...
...OF COURSE ...

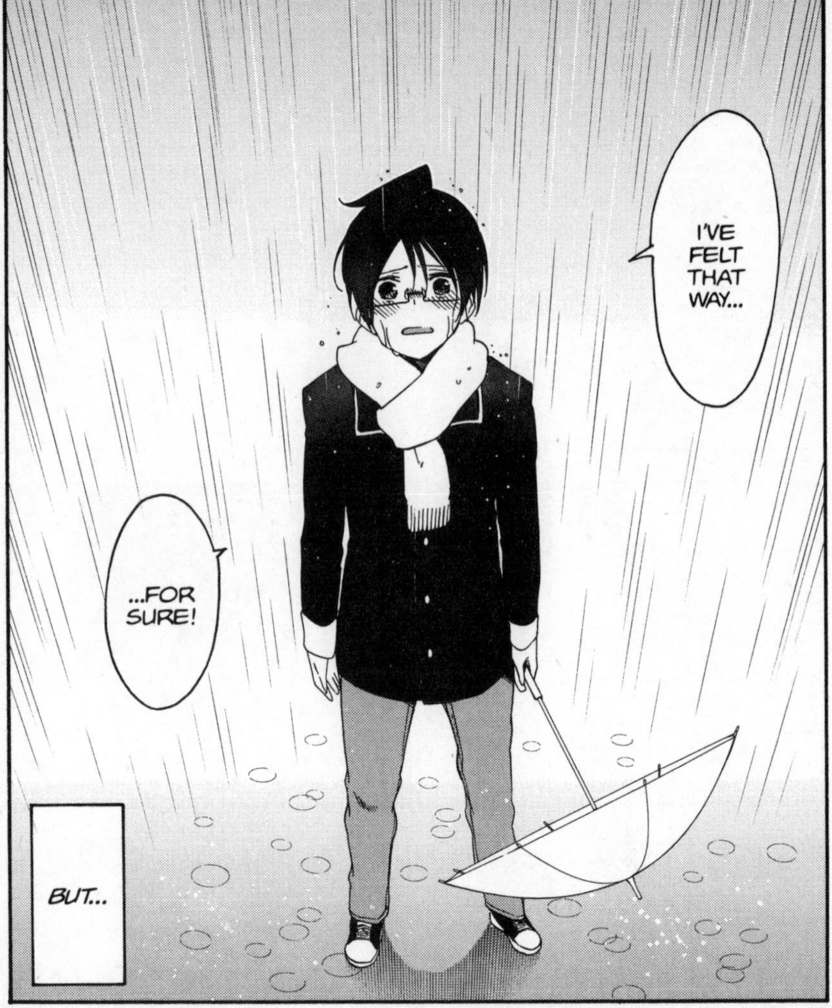
I'VE FELT THAT WAY...
...FOR SURE!
BUT...

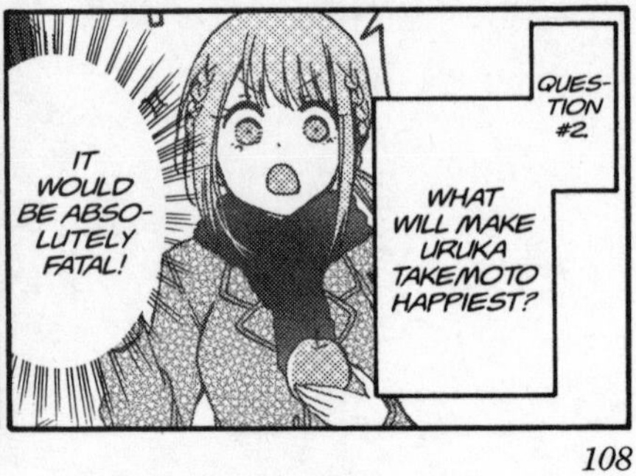
QUES-TION #2.
WHAT WILL MAKE URUKA TAKEMOTO HAPPIEST?
IT WOULD BE ABSO-LUTELY FATAL!

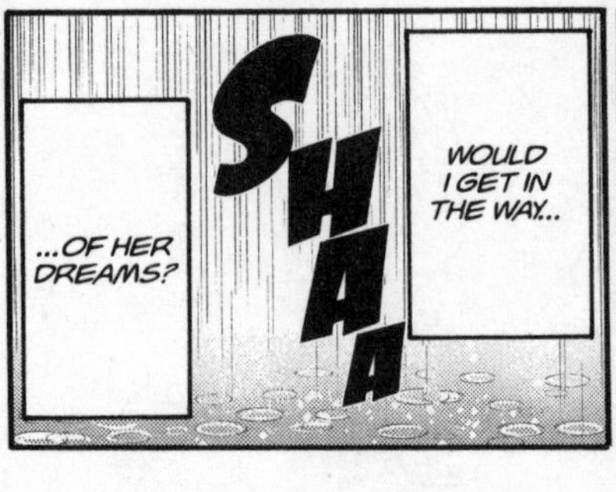
WOULD I GET IN THE WAY...
SHAA
...OF HER DREAMS?

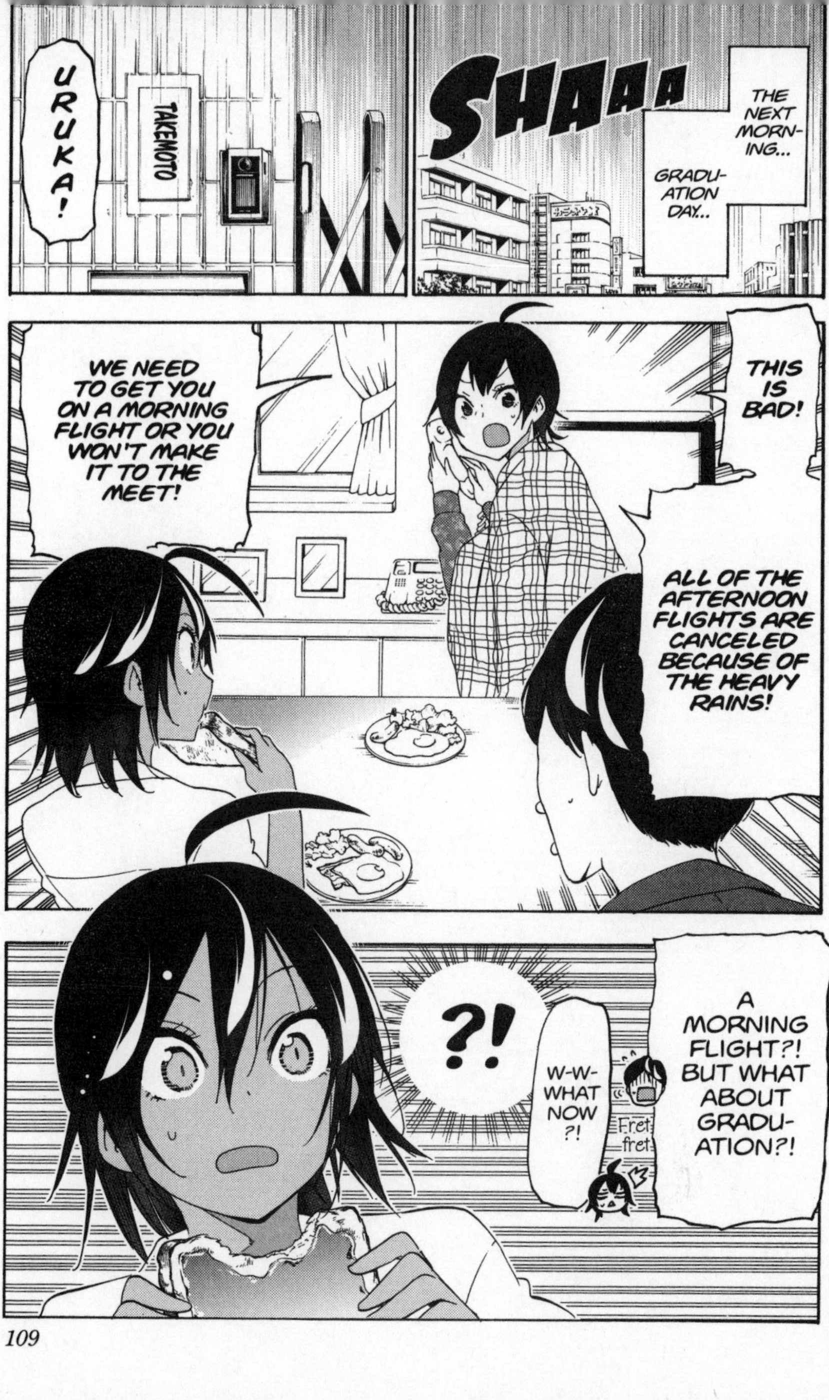
SHAAA
THE NEXT MORNING...
GRADUATION DAY...
URUKA!
TAKEMOTO
THIS IS BAD!
ALL OF THE AFTERNOON FLIGHTS ARE CANCELED BECAUSE OF THE HEAVY RAINS!
WE NEED TO GET YOU ON A MORNING FLIGHT OR YOU WON'T MAKE IT TO THE MEET!
A MORNING FLIGHT?! BUT WHAT ABOUT GRADUATION?!
W-W-WHAT NOW?!
Fret fret
?!

Club Registration

Swim team

Grade 5, Class 1
Mizuki Yuiga

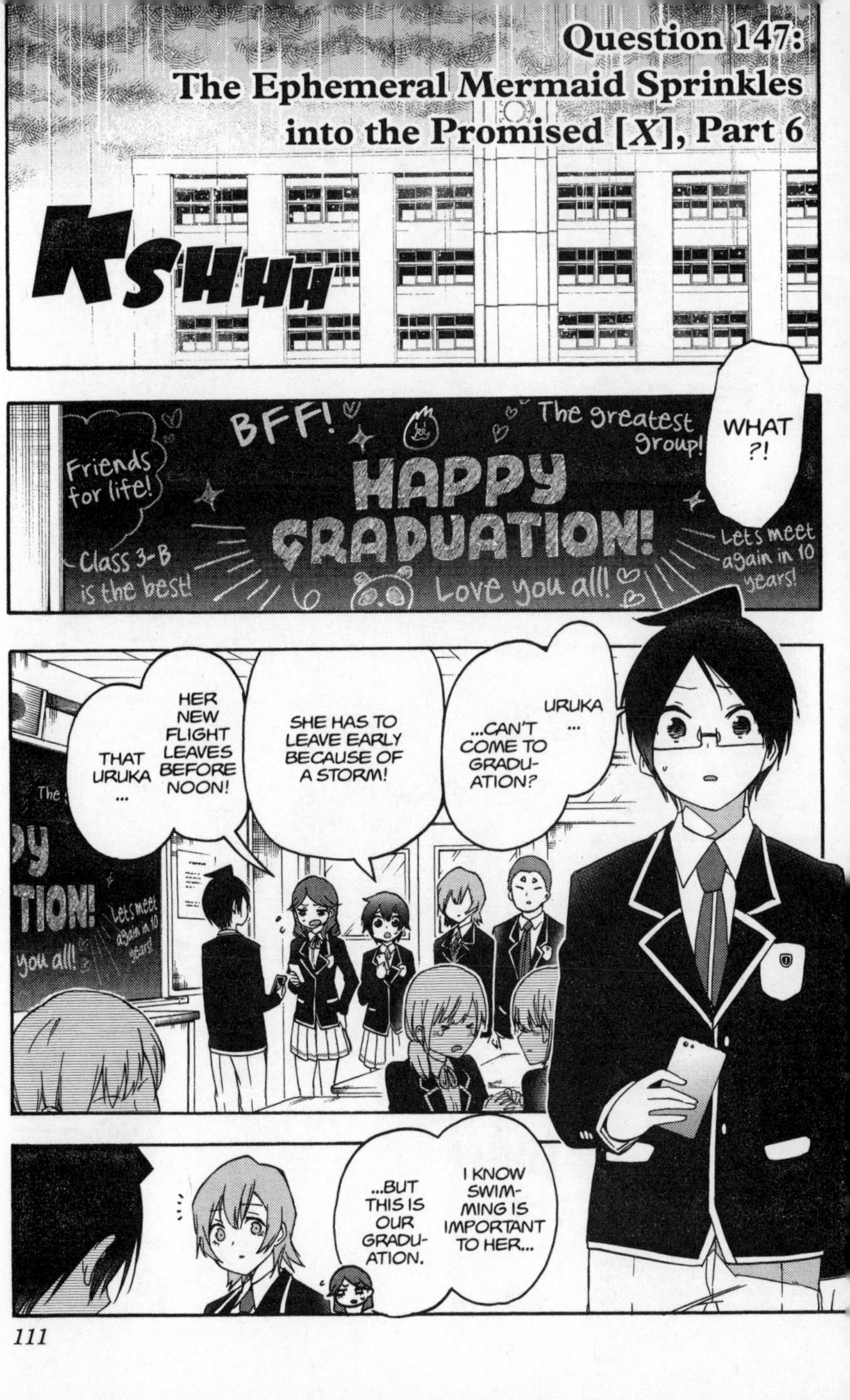
Question 147:
The Ephemeral Mermaid Sprinkles into the Promised [X], Part 6
KSHHH
WHAT ?!
The greatest group!
BFF!
Friends for life!
HAPPY GRADUATION!
Lets meet again in 10 years!
Love you all!
Class 3-B is the best!
URUKA ...
...CAN'T COME TO GRADU-ATION?
SHE HAS TO LEAVE EARLY BECAUSE OF A STORM!
HER NEW FLIGHT LEAVES BEFORE NOON!
THAT URUKA ...
I KNOW SWIM-MING IS IMPORTANT TO HER...
...BUT THIS IS OUR GRADU-ATION.

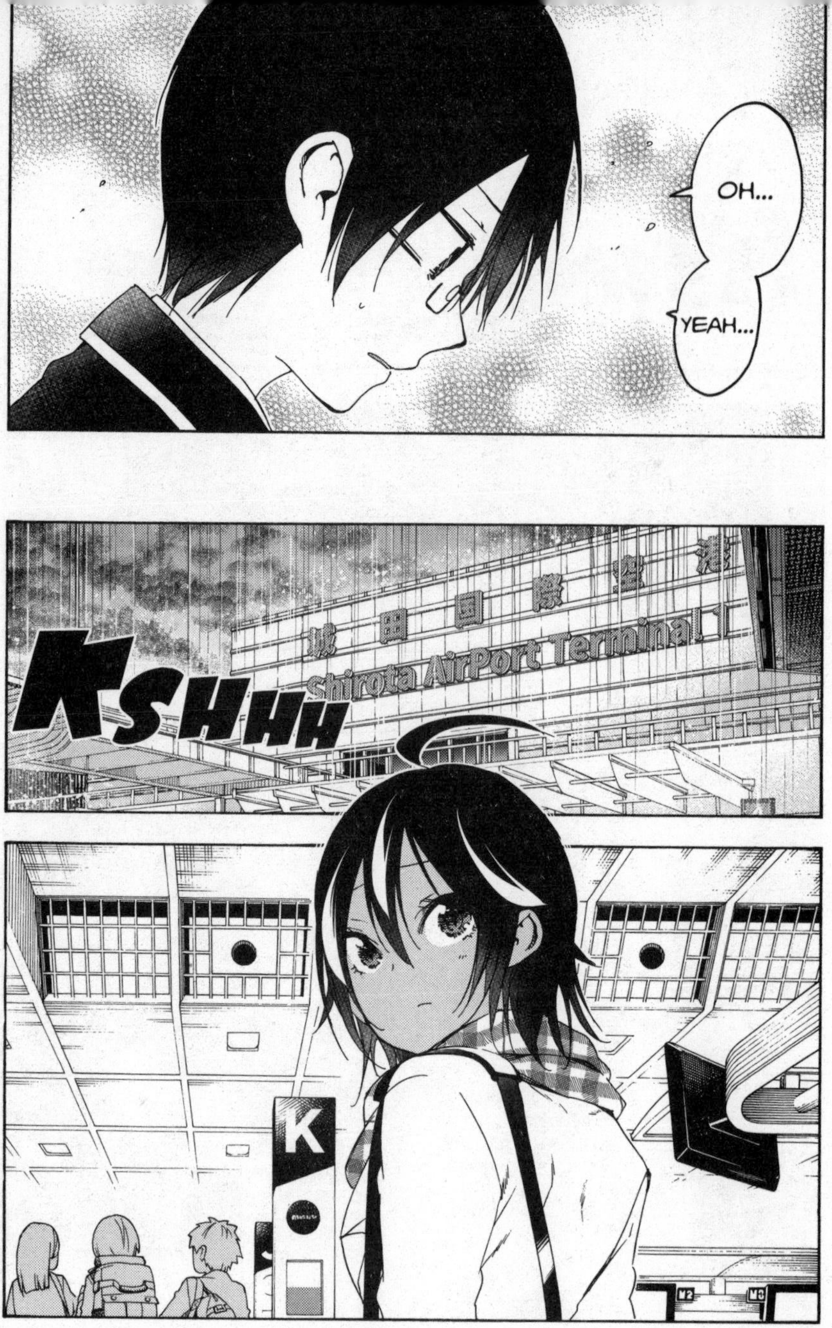
OH...
YEAH...
城田国際空港
Shirota AirPort Terminal 1
KSHHH
K

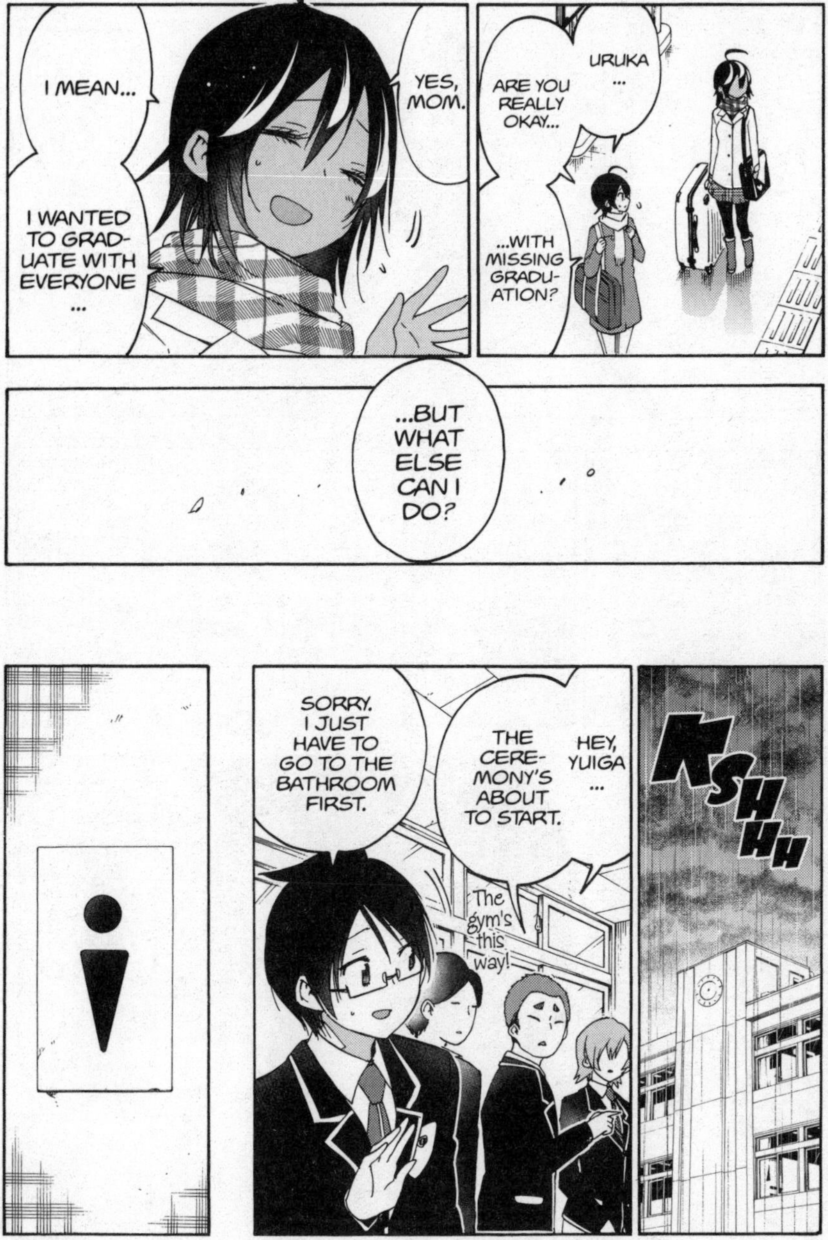
URUKA ...
ARE YOU REALLY OKAY...
...WITH MISSING GRADUATION?
YES, MOM.
I MEAN...
I WANTED TO GRADUATE WITH EVERYONE ...
...BUT WHAT ELSE CAN I DO?
KSHHH
HEY, YUIGA ...
THE CEREMONY'S ABOUT TO START.
The gym's this way!
SORRY. I JUST HAVE TO GO TO THE BATHROOM FIRST.

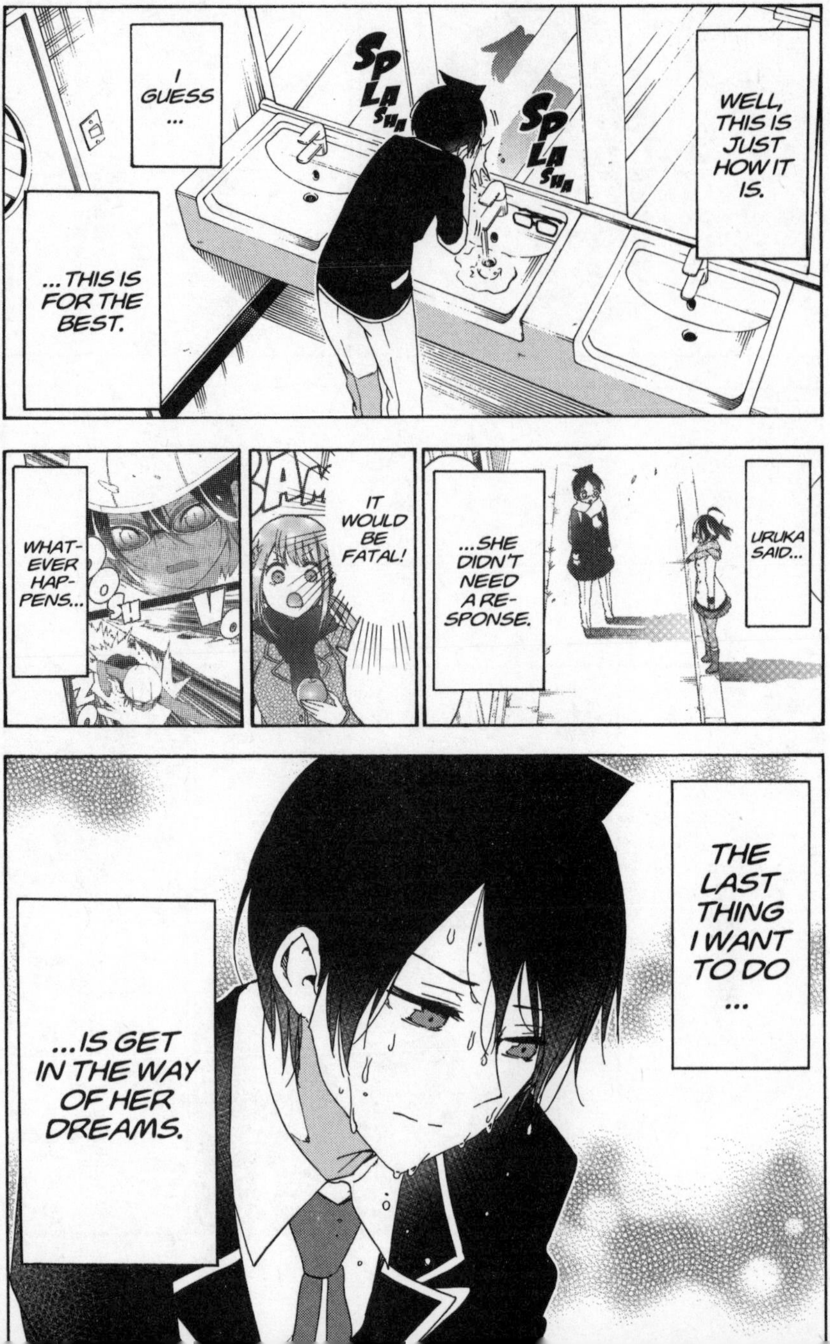
WELL, THIS IS JUST HOW IT IS.
SPLASHA
SPLASHA
I GUESS ...
...THIS IS FOR THE BEST.
URUKA SAID...
...SHE DIDN'T NEED A RE-SPONSE.
IT WOULD BE FATAL!
WHAT-EVER HAP-PENS...
THE LAST THING I WANT TO DO ...
...IS GET IN THE WAY OF HER DREAMS.

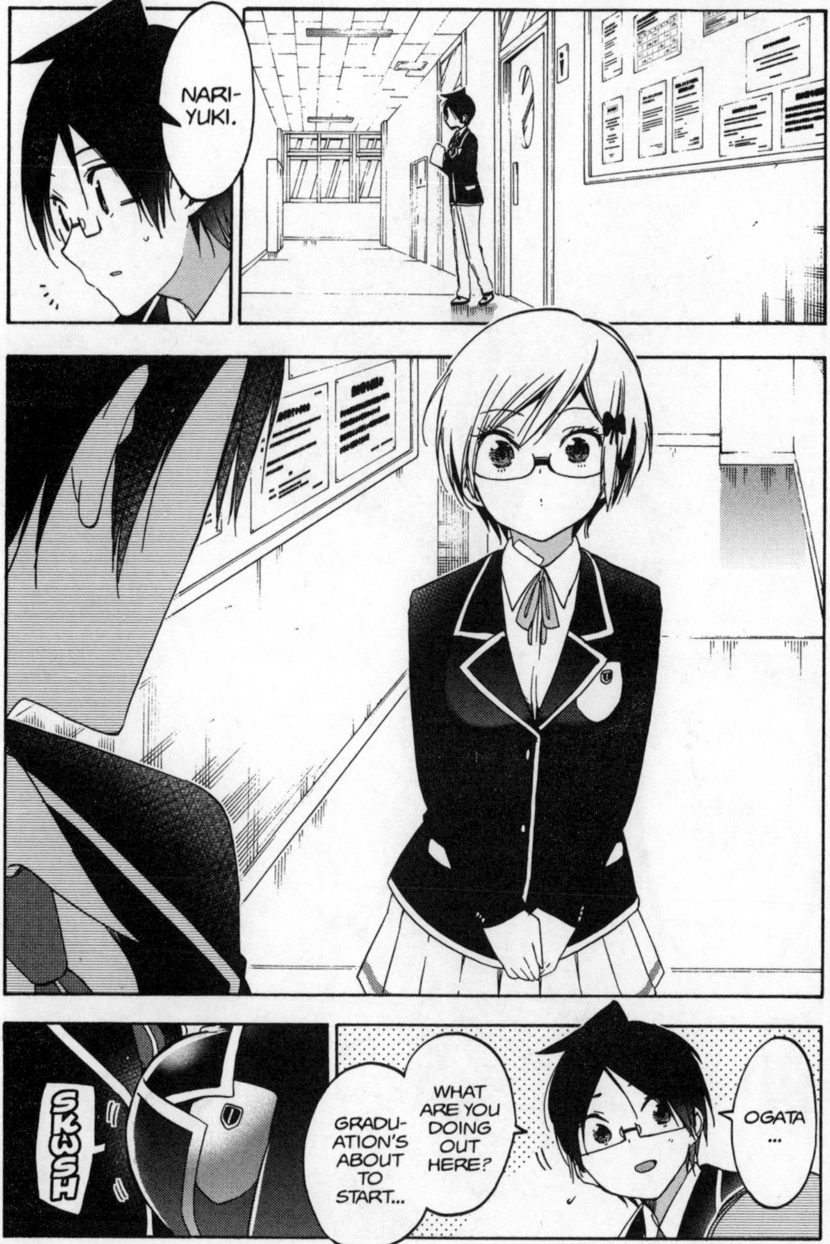
NARI-YUKI.
OGATA ...
WHAT ARE YOU DOING OUT HERE?
GRADUATION'S ABOUT TO START...
SKWSH

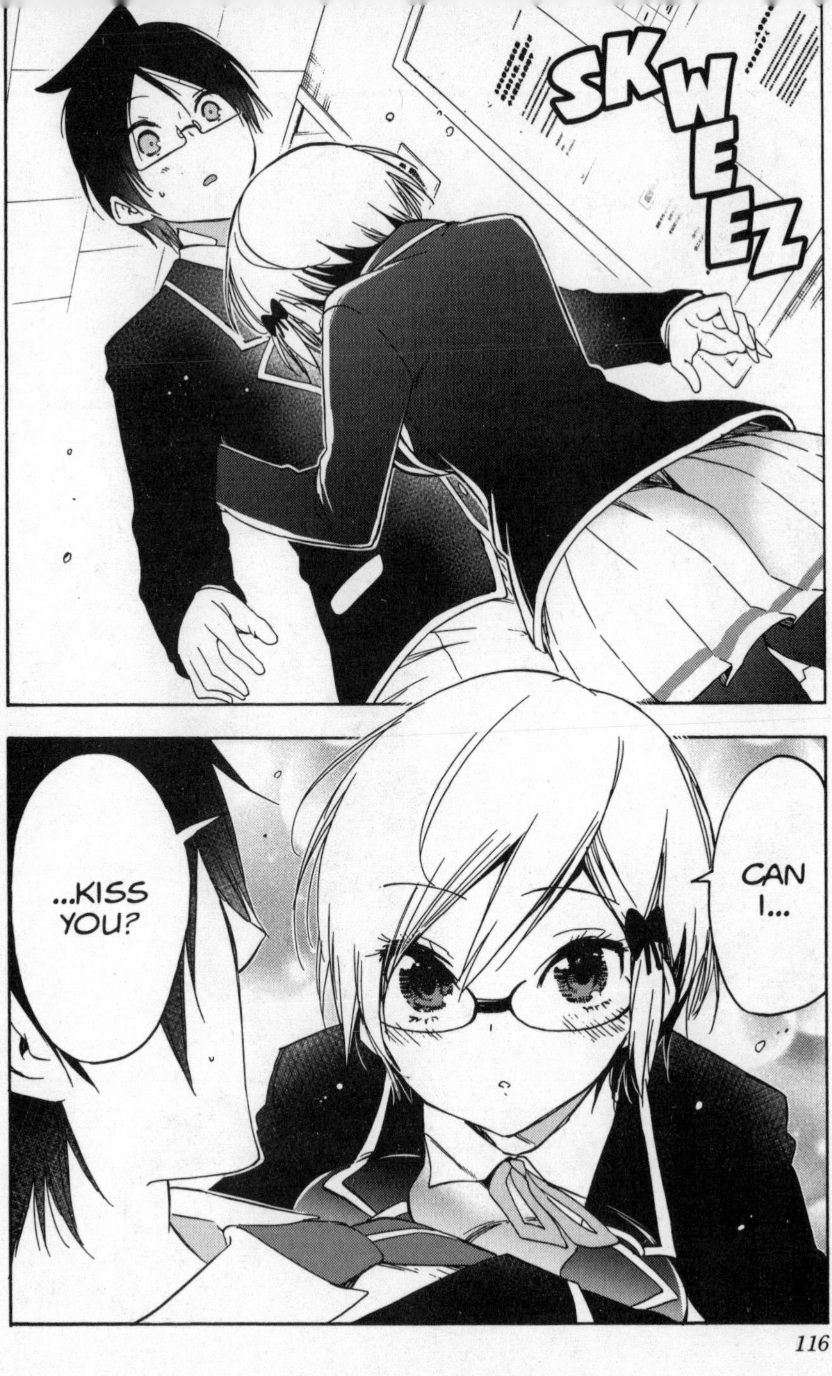
SKWEEZ
CAN I...
...KISS YOU?

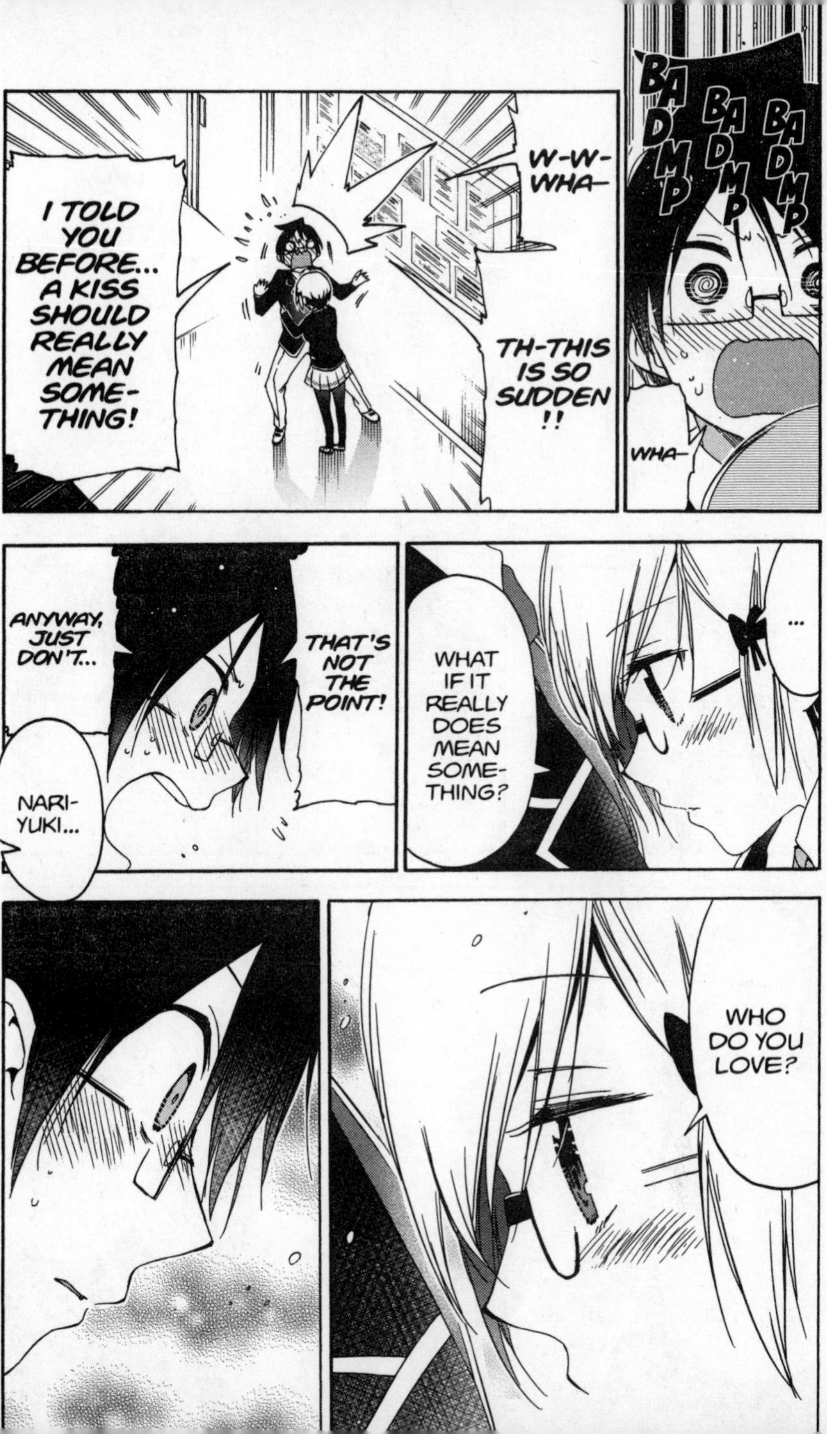
BADMP
BADMP
BADMP
WHA-
W-W-WHA-
TH-THIS IS SO SUDDEN!!
I TOLD YOU BEFORE... A KISS SHOULD REALLY MEAN SOME-THING!
...
WHAT IF IT REALLY DOES MEAN SOME-THING?
THAT'S NOT THE POINT!
ANYWAY, JUST DON'T...
NARI-YUKI...
WHO DO YOU LOVE?

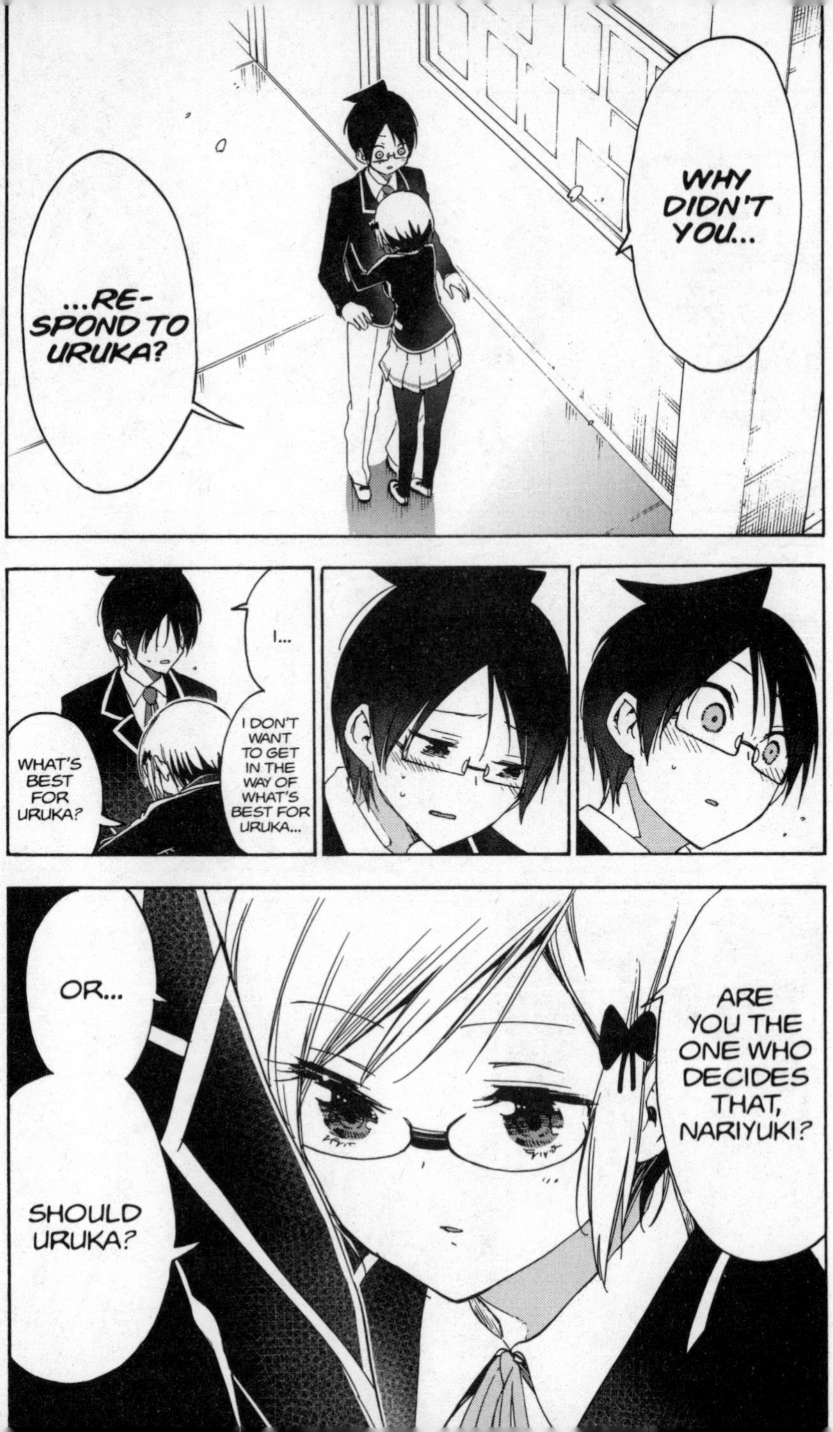
WHY DIDN'T YOU...
...RE-SPOND TO URUKA?
I...
I DON'T WANT TO GET IN THE WAY OF WHAT'S BEST FOR URUKA...
WHAT'S BEST FOR URUKA?
ARE YOU THE ONE WHO DECIDES THAT, NARIYUKI?
OR...
SHOULD URUKA?

TO HELL WITH KNOWING WHAT'S BEST FOR SOMEONE ELSE!

RIGHT?

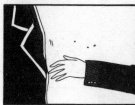

WAS THAT...

DO YOU...

I'M KID-DING.

O-OGATA...?!

YOU...

TMP

...JUST A JOKE.

IT'S ALL...

I...

119

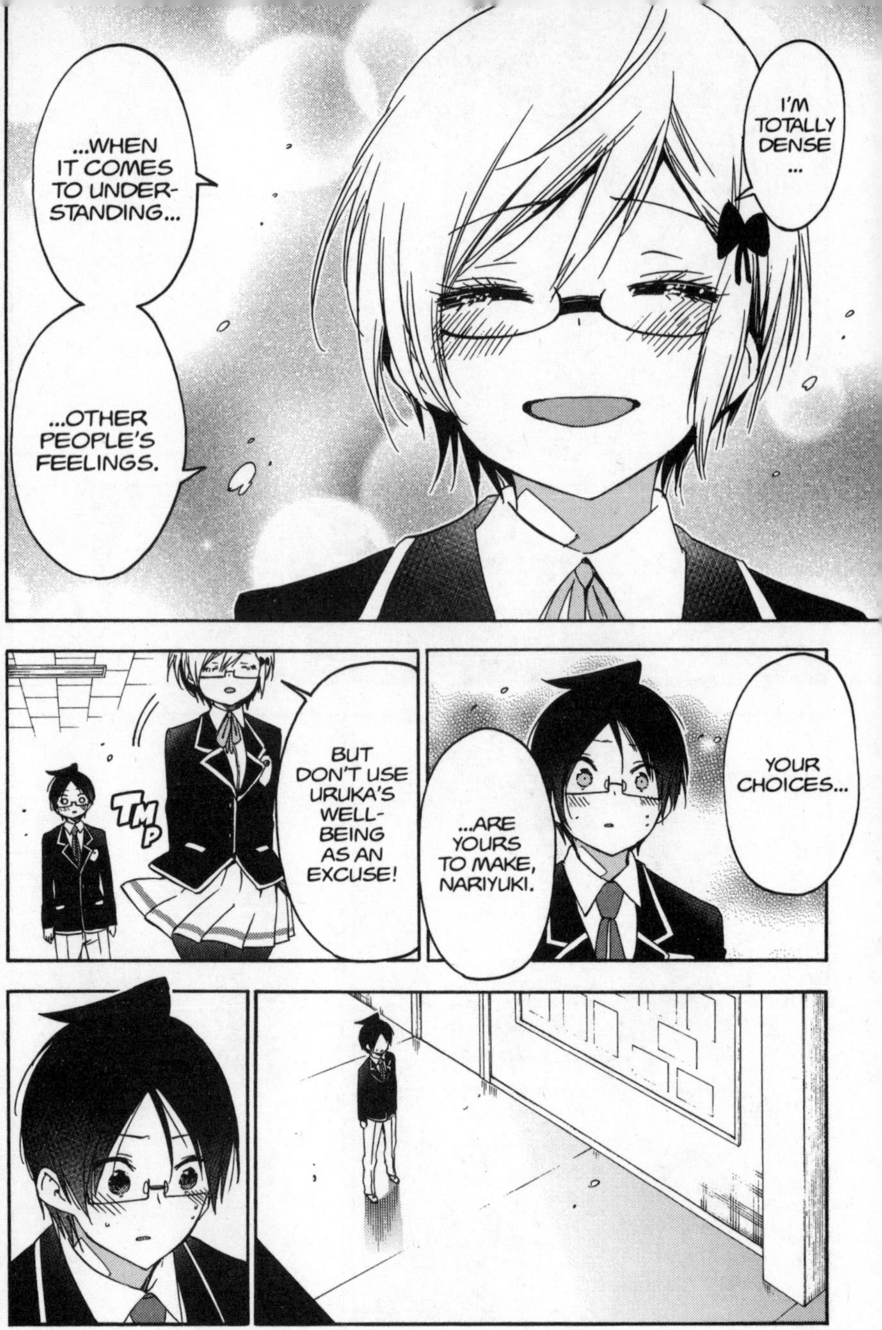
I'M TOTALLY DENSE...
...WHEN IT COMES TO UNDER-STANDING...
...OTHER PEOPLE'S FEELINGS.
YOUR CHOICES...
...ARE YOURS TO MAKE, NARIYUKI.
BUT DON'T USE URUKA'S WELL-BEING AS AN EXCUSE!
TMP

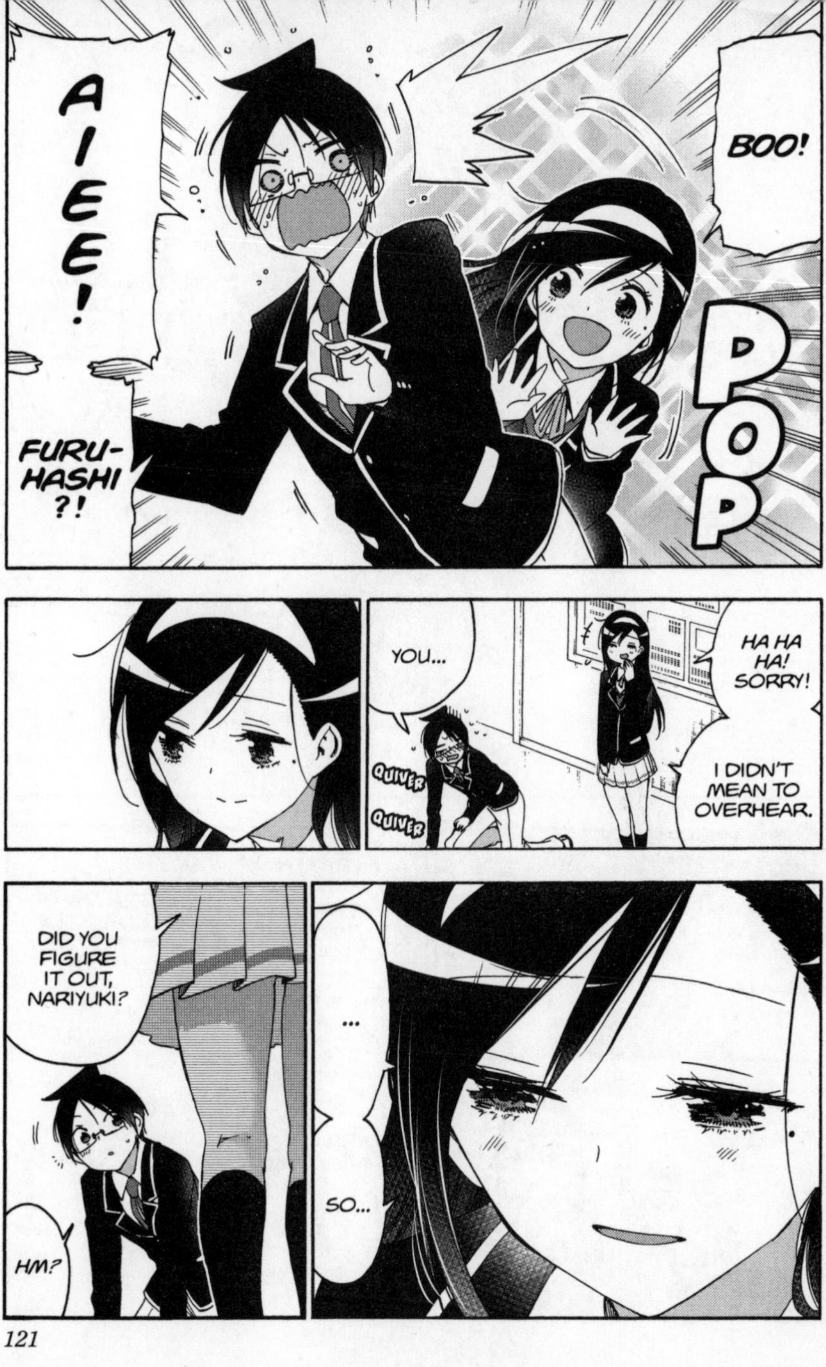
BOO!
POP
AIEE!
FURU-HASHI?!
HA HA HA! SORRY!
I DIDN'T MEAN TO OVERHEAR.
YOU...
QUIVER
QUIVER
...
SO...
DID YOU FIGURE IT OUT, NARIYUKI?
HM?

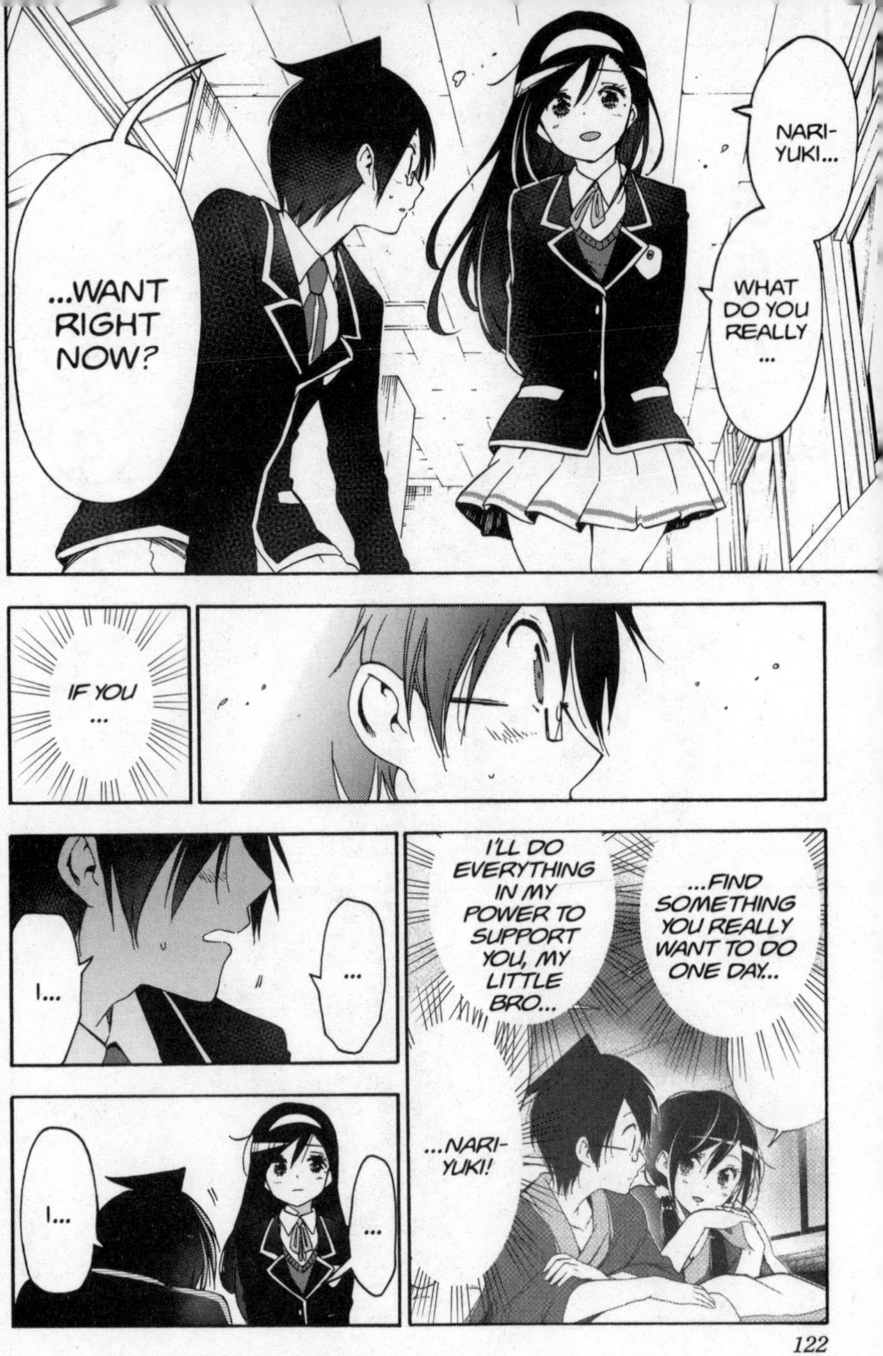
NARI-YUKI...
WHAT DO YOU REALLY ...
...WANT RIGHT NOW?
IF YOU ...
...FIND SOMETHING YOU REALLY WANT TO DO ONE DAY...
I'LL DO EVERYTHING IN MY POWER TO SUPPORT YOU, MY LITTLE BRO...
...NARI-YUKI!
...
I...
...
I...

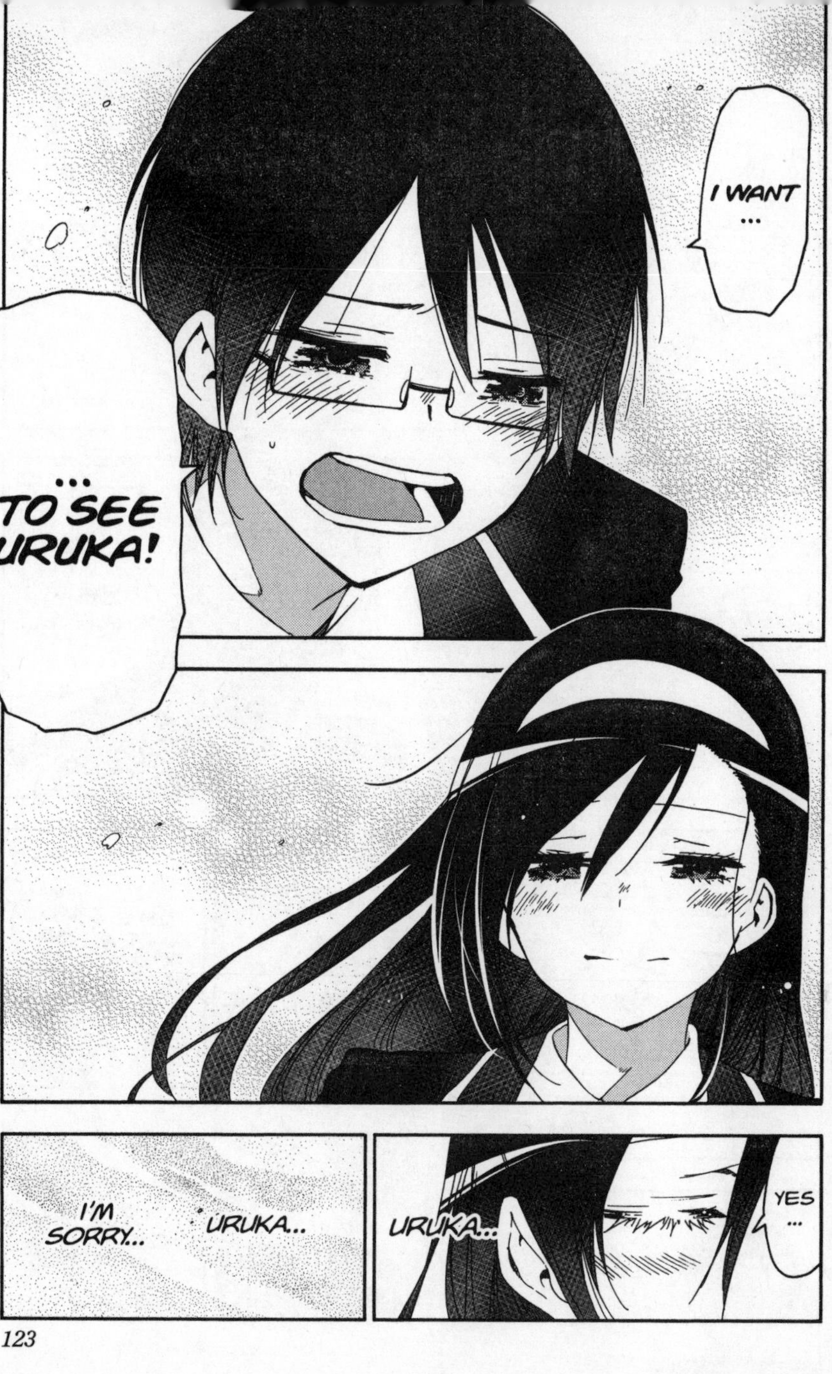
I WANT ...
... TO SEE URUKA!
YES ...
URUKA...
URUKA...
I'M SORRY...

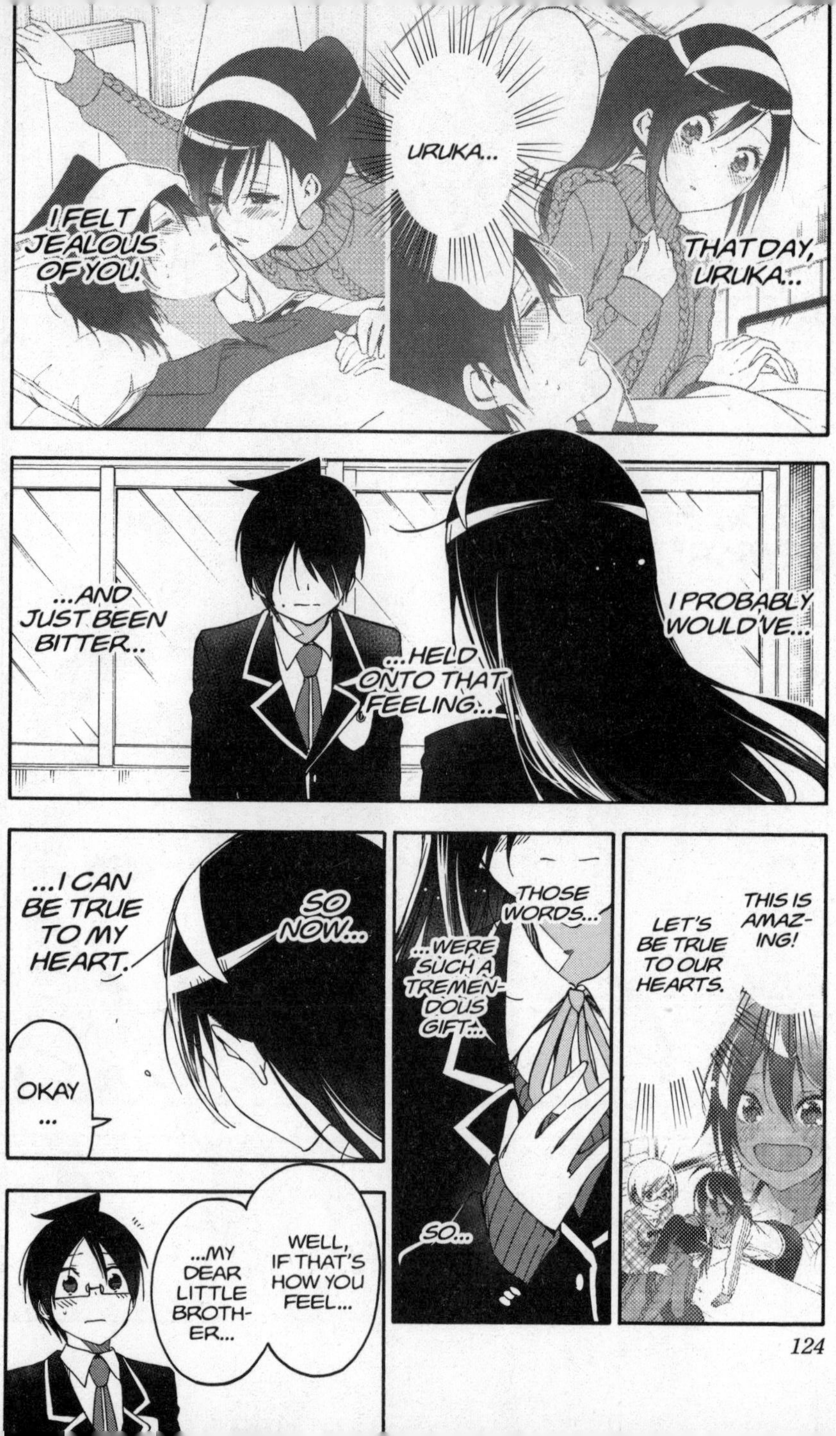
URUKA...
THAT DAY, URUKA...
I FELT JEALOUS OF YOU.
I PROBABLY WOULD'VE...
...HELD ONTO THAT FEELING...
...AND JUST BEEN BITTER...
THIS IS AMAZING!
LET'S BE TRUE TO OUR HEARTS.
THOSE WORDS...
...WERE SUCH A TREMENDOUS GIFT...
SO...
SO NOW...
...I CAN BE TRUE TO MY HEART.
OKAY ...
WELL, IF THAT'S HOW YOU FEEL...
...MY DEAR LITTLE BROTHER...

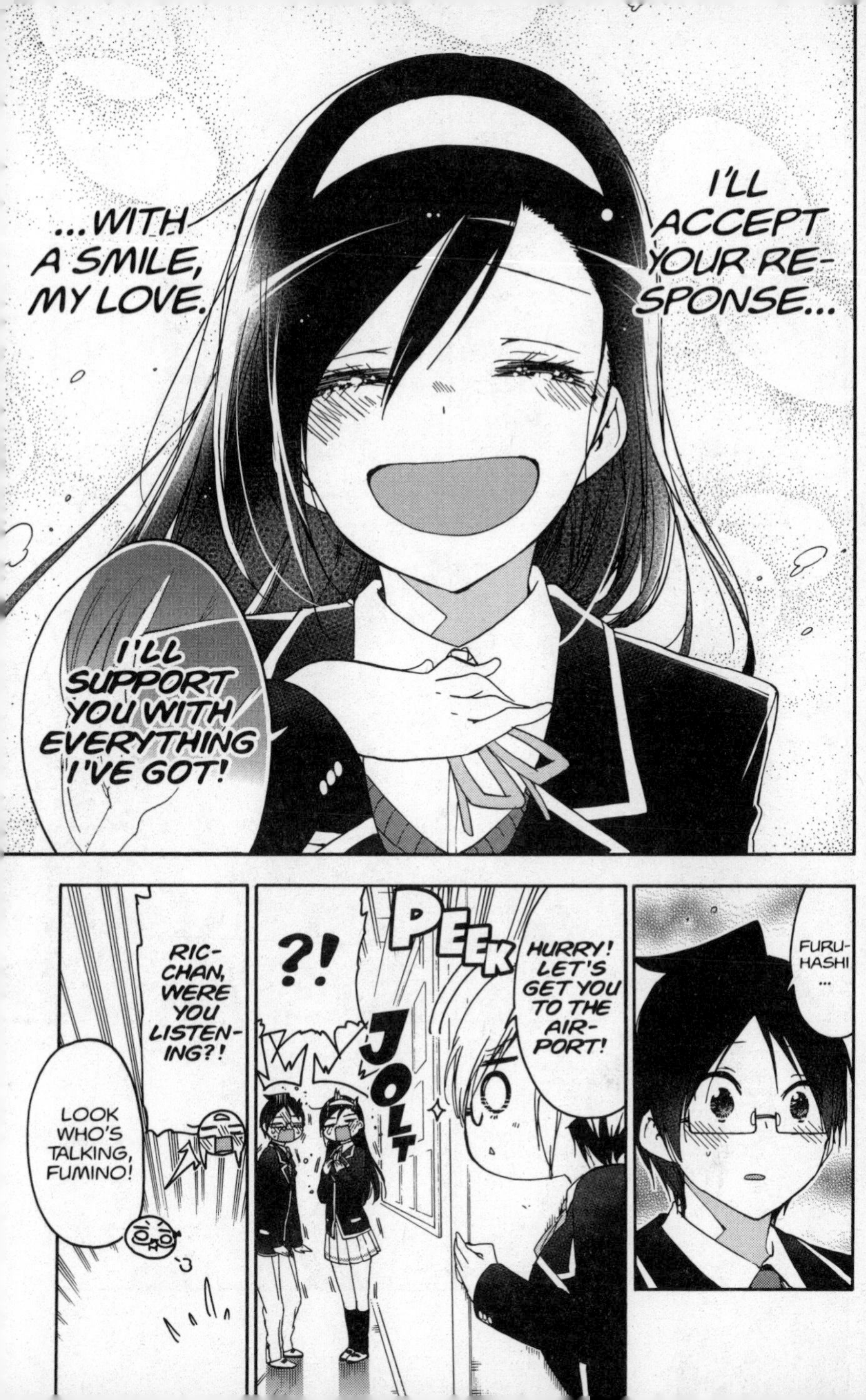
I'LL ACCEPT YOUR RE-SPONSE...
...WITH A SMILE, MY LOVE.
I'LL SUPPORT YOU WITH EVERYTHING I'VE GOT!
FURU-HASHI ...
PEEK
HURRY! LET'S GET YOU TO THE AIR-PORT!
?!
JOLT
RIC-CHAN, WERE YOU LISTEN-ING?!
LOOK WHO'S TALKING, FUMINO!

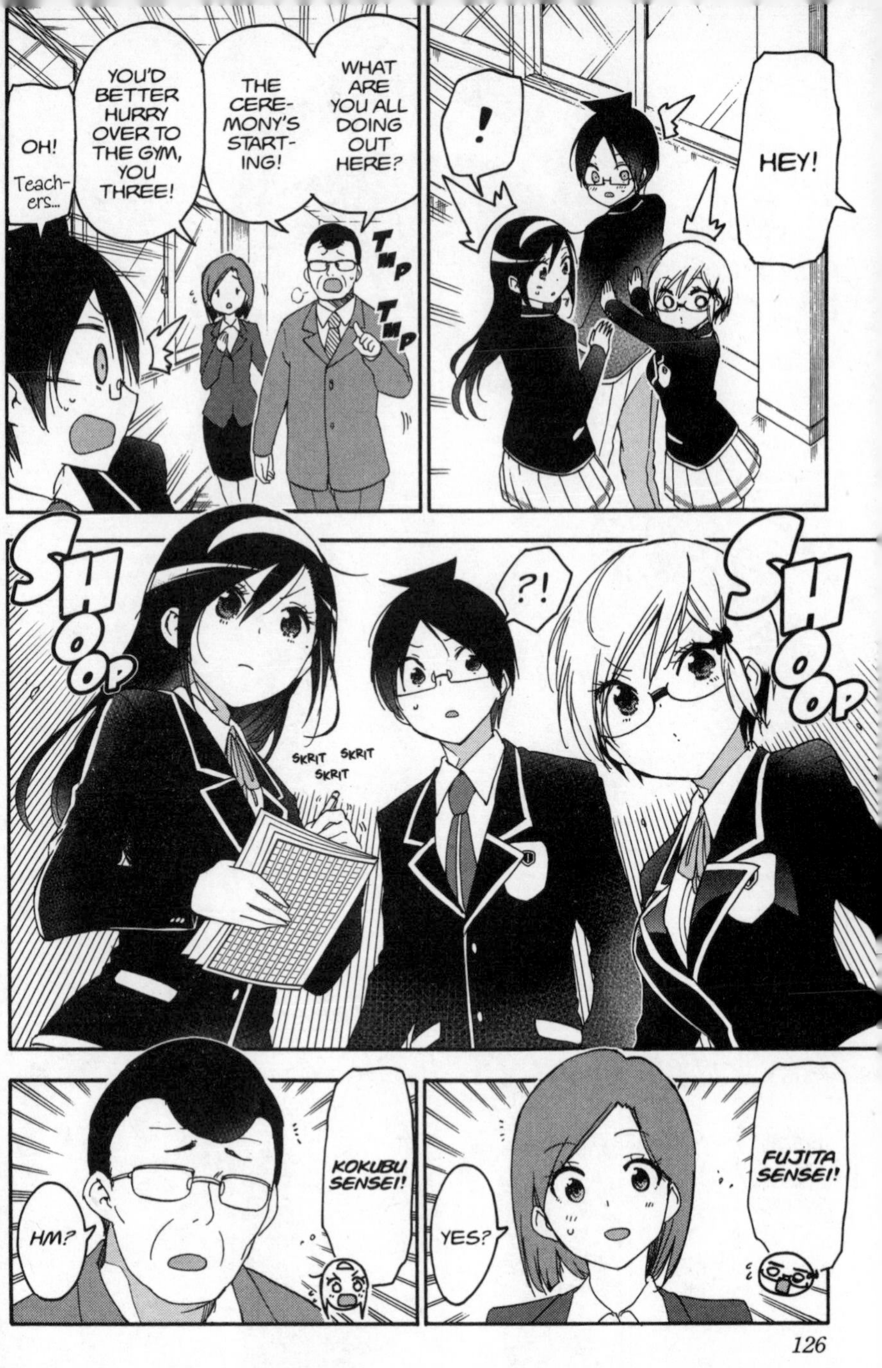
HEY!
!
WHAT ARE YOU ALL DOING OUT HERE?
THE CEREMONY'S STARTING!
YOU'D BETTER HURRY OVER TO THE GYM, YOU THREE!
TMP TMP
OH! Teachers...
SHOOP
?!
SKRIT SKRIT SKRIT
SHOOP
FUJITA SENSEI!
YES?
KOKUBU SENSEI!
HM?

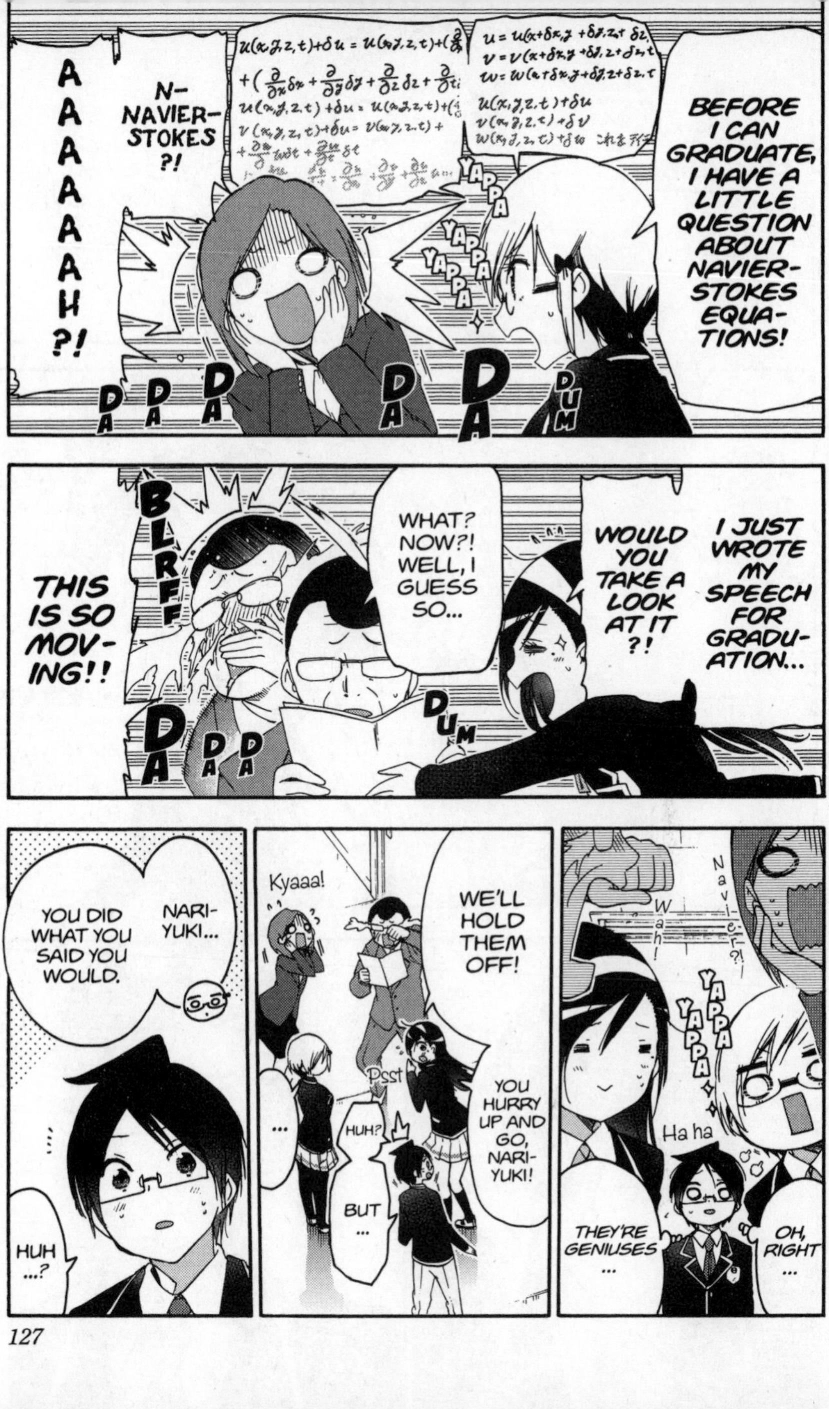
BEFORE I CAN GRADUATE, I HAVE A LITTLE QUESTION ABOUT NAVIER-STOKES EQUATIONS!
DUM
YAPPA YAPPA YAPPA
N-NAVIER-STOKES?!
AAAAAAAH?!
DA DA DA DA DA
I JUST WROTE MY SPEECH FOR GRADUATION...
WOULD YOU TAKE A LOOK AT IT?!
WHAT? NOW?! WELL, I GUESS SO...
DUM
BLRFF
THIS IS SO MOVING!!
DA DA DA
Navier?!
YAPPA YAPPA
Wah!
OH, RIGHT...
THEY'RE GENIUSES...
Ha ha
WE'LL HOLD THEM OFF!
Kyaaa!
YOU HURRY UP AND GO, NARI-YUKI!
Psst
HUH?
...
BUT...
NARI-YUKI...
YOU DID WHAT YOU SAID YOU WOULD.
...
HUH...?

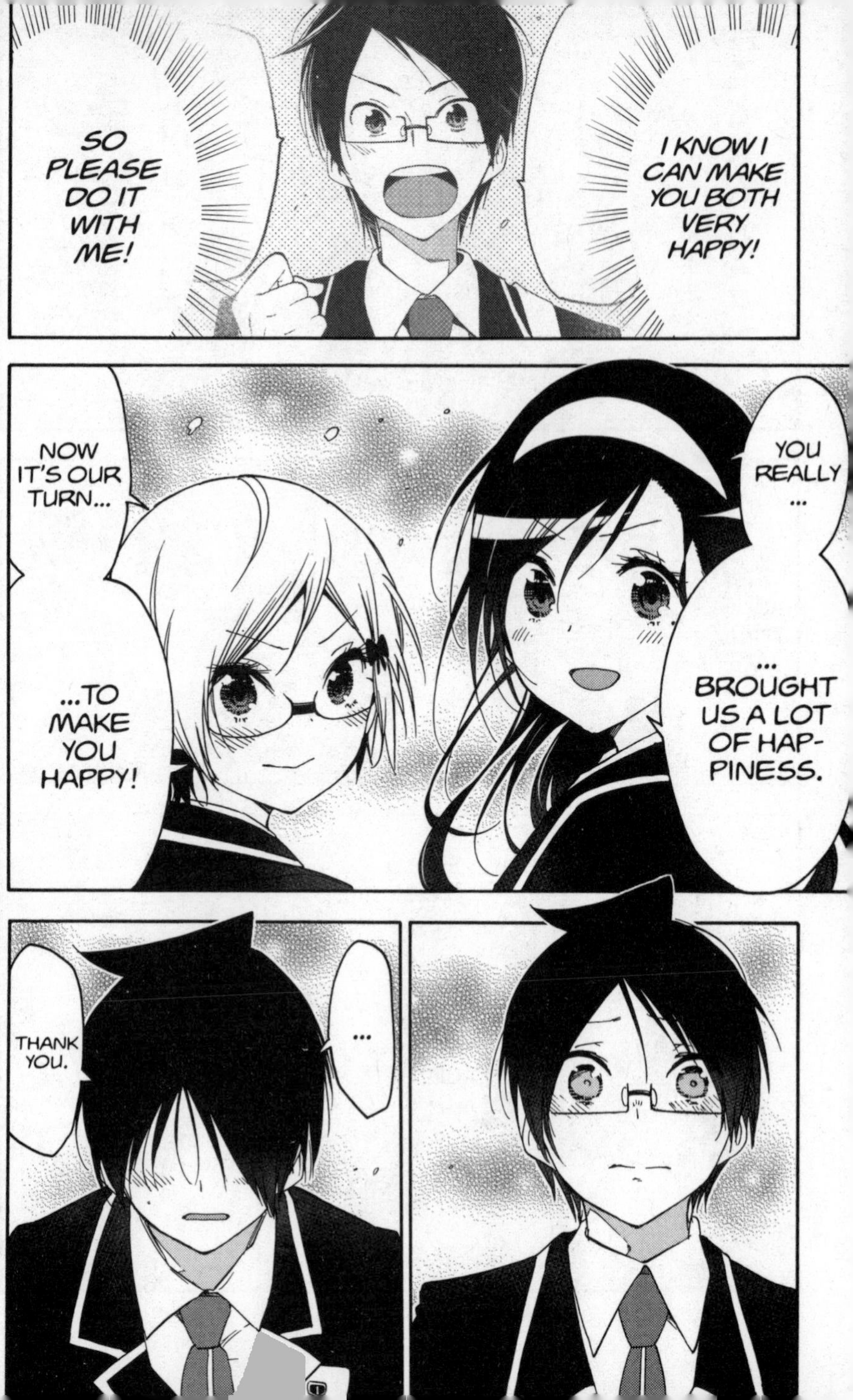
I KNOW I CAN MAKE YOU BOTH VERY HAPPY!
SO PLEASE DO IT WITH ME!
YOU REALLY ...
... BROUGHT US A LOT OF HAP-PINESS.
NOW IT'S OUR TURN...
...TO MAKE YOU HAPPY!
...
THANK YOU.

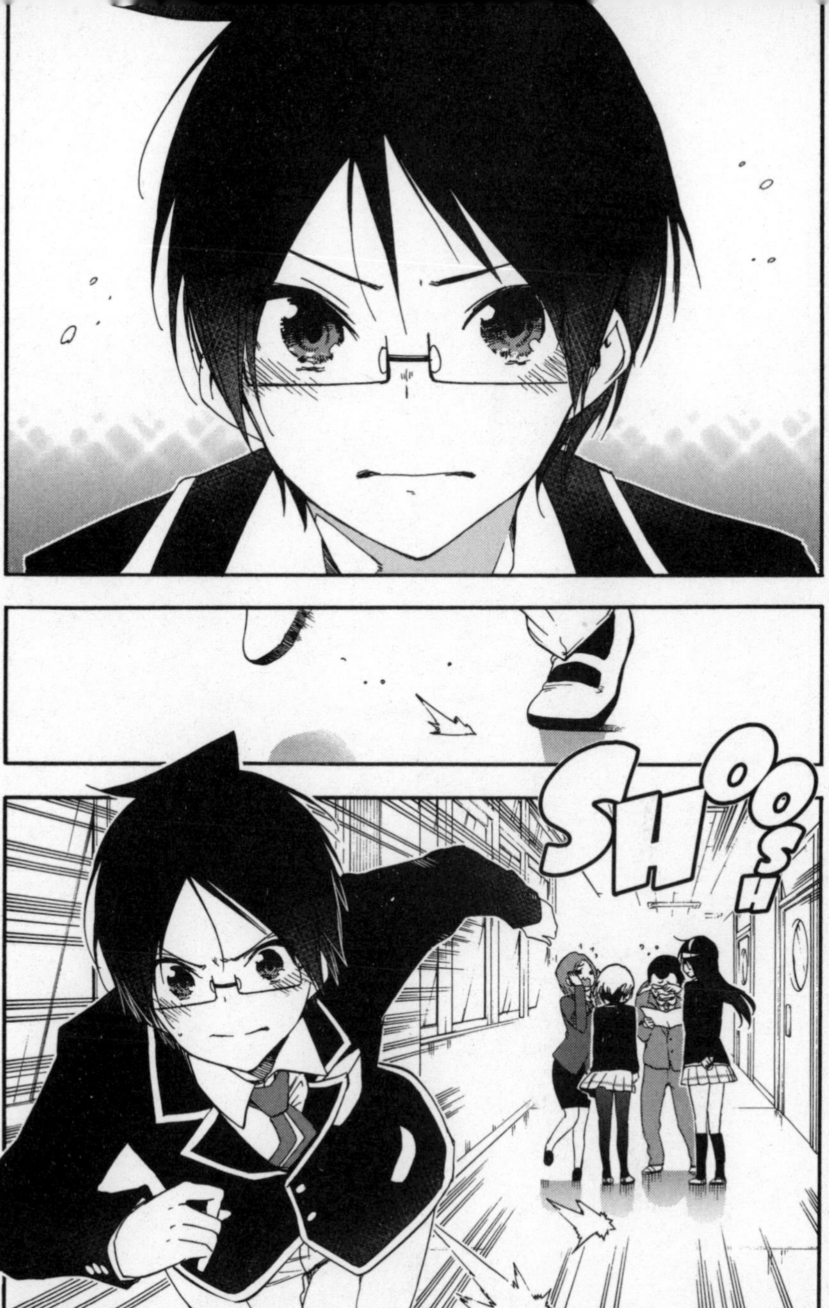
SHOOOSH

Question 148: The Ephemeral Mermaid Sprinkles into the Promised [X], Part 7

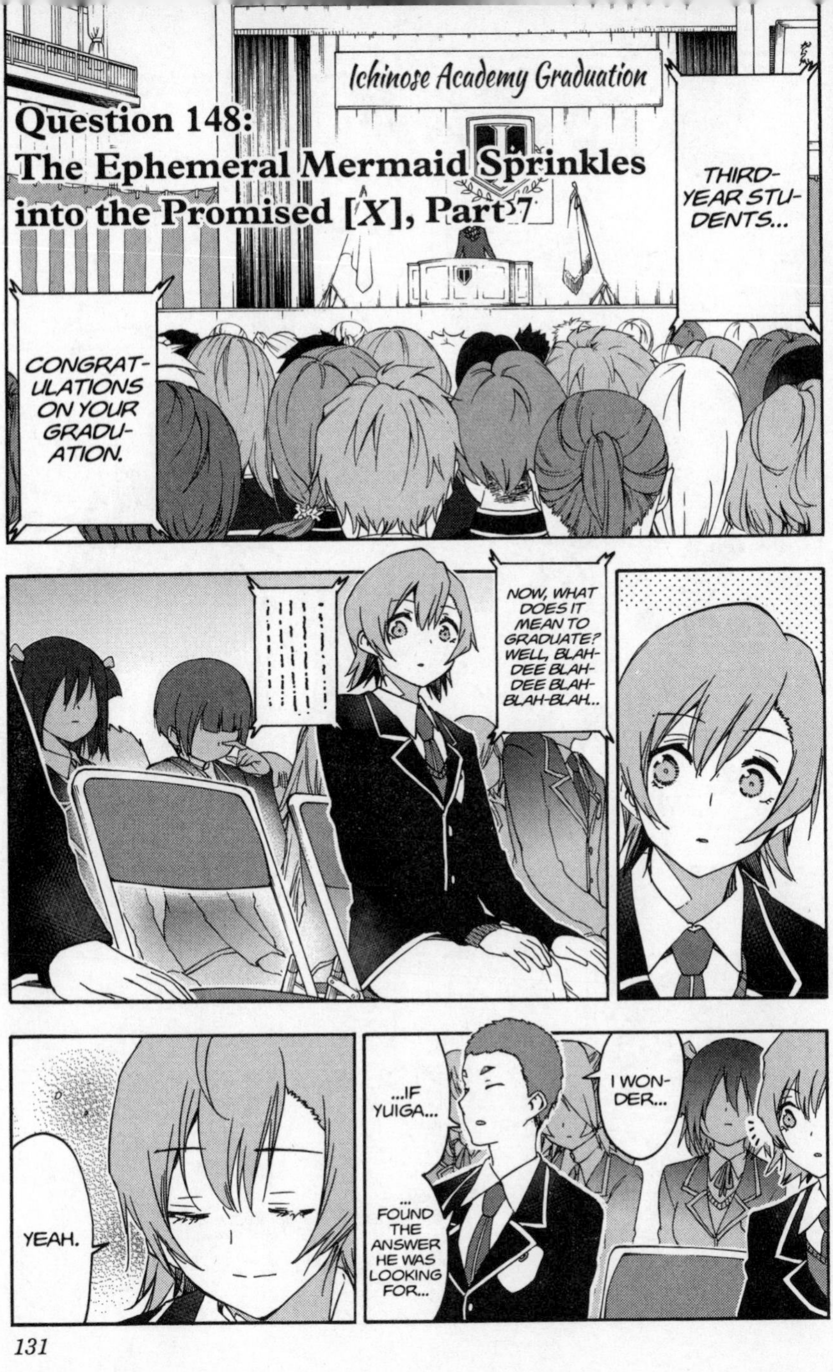

Ichinose Academy Graduation
THIRD-YEAR STUDENTS...
CONGRATULATIONS ON YOUR GRADUATION.
NOW, WHAT DOES IT MEAN TO GRADUATE? WELL, BLAH-DEE BLAH-DEE BLAH-BLAH-BLAH...
I WONDER...
...IF YUIGA...
...FOUND THE ANSWER HE WAS LOOKING FOR...
YEAH.

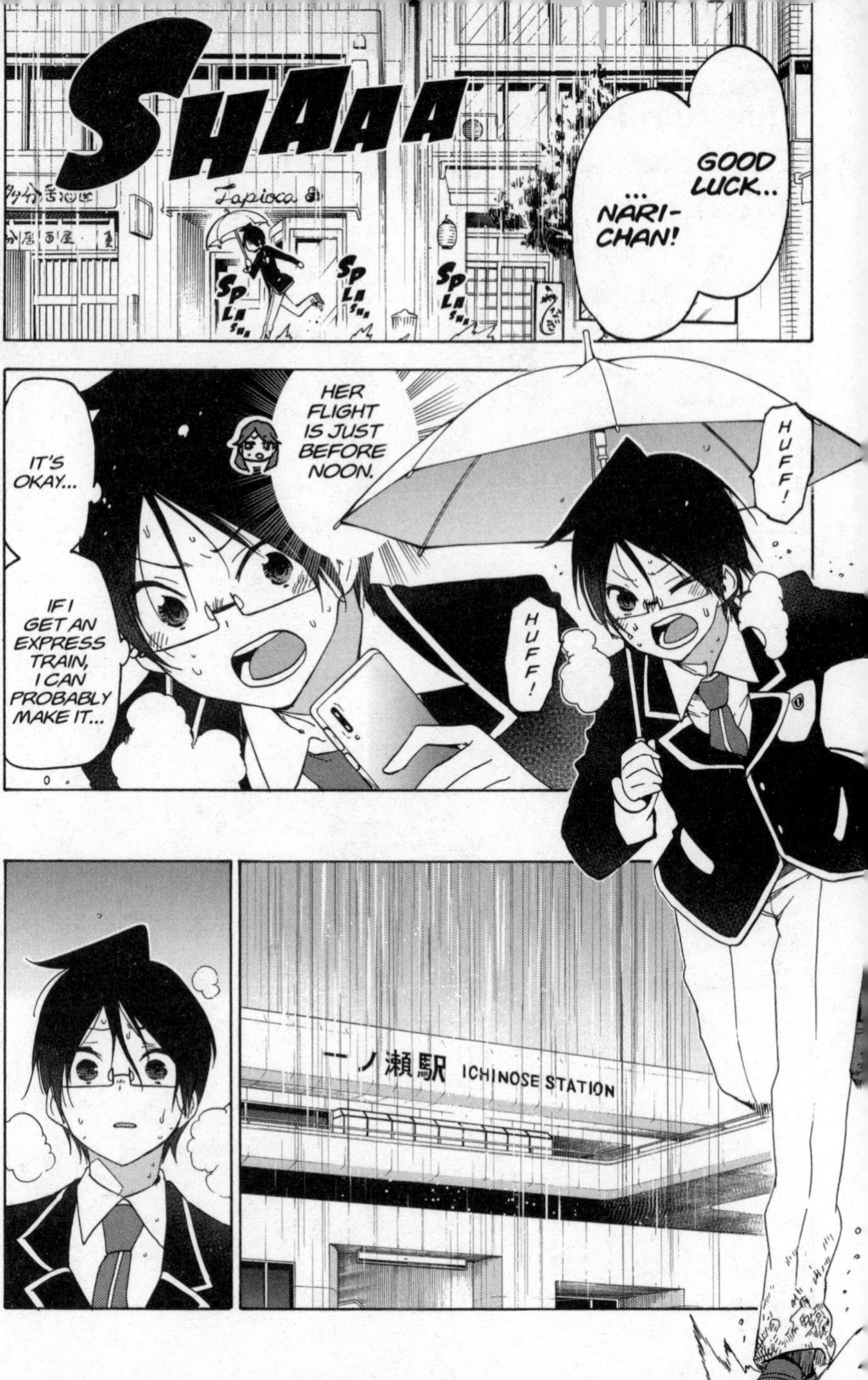
GOOD LUCK...
... NARI-CHAN!
SHAAA
Tapioca
SPLASH
SPLASH
SPLASH
HUFF!
HUFF!
HER FLIGHT IS JUST BEFORE NOON.
IT'S OKAY...
IF I GET AN EXPRESS TRAIN, I CAN PROBABLY MAKE IT...
一ノ瀬駅 ICHINOSE STATION

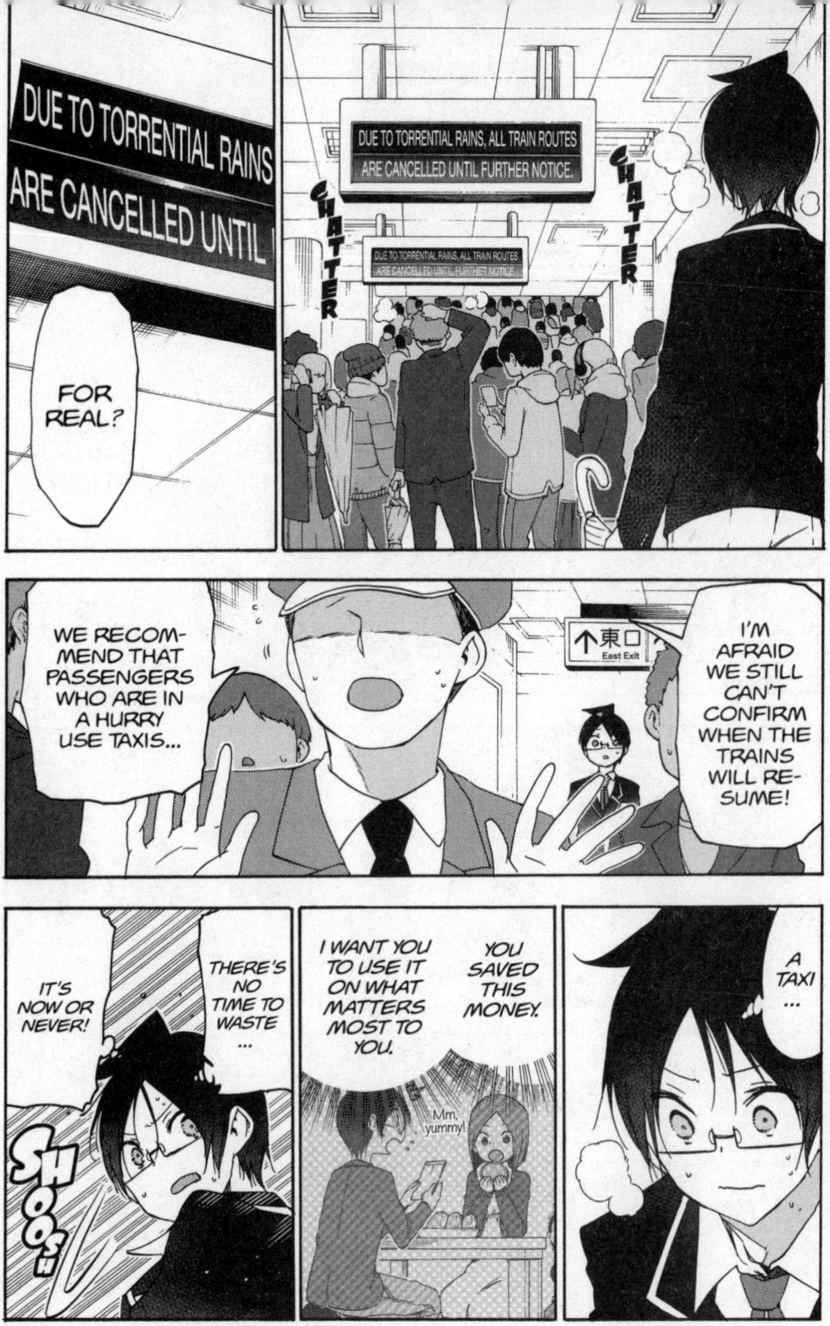
DUE TO TORRENTIAL RAINS, ALL TRAIN ROUTES
ARE CANCELLED UNTIL FURTHER NOTICE.
CHATTER
CHATTER
DUE TO TORRENTIAL RAINS, ALL TRAIN ROUTES
ARE CANCELLED UNTIL FURTHER NOTICE.
DUE TO TORRENTIAL RAINS
ARE CANCELLED UNTIL
FOR REAL?
I'M AFRAID WE STILL CAN'T CONFIRM WHEN THE TRAINS WILL RE-SUME!
↑東口 East Exit
WE RECOM-MEND THAT PASSENGERS WHO ARE IN A HURRY USE TAXIS...
A TAXI ...
YOU SAVED THIS MONEY.
I WANT YOU TO USE IT ON WHAT MATTERS MOST TO YOU.
Mm, yummy!
THERE'S NO TIME TO WASTE ...
IT'S NOW OR NEVER!
SHOOSH

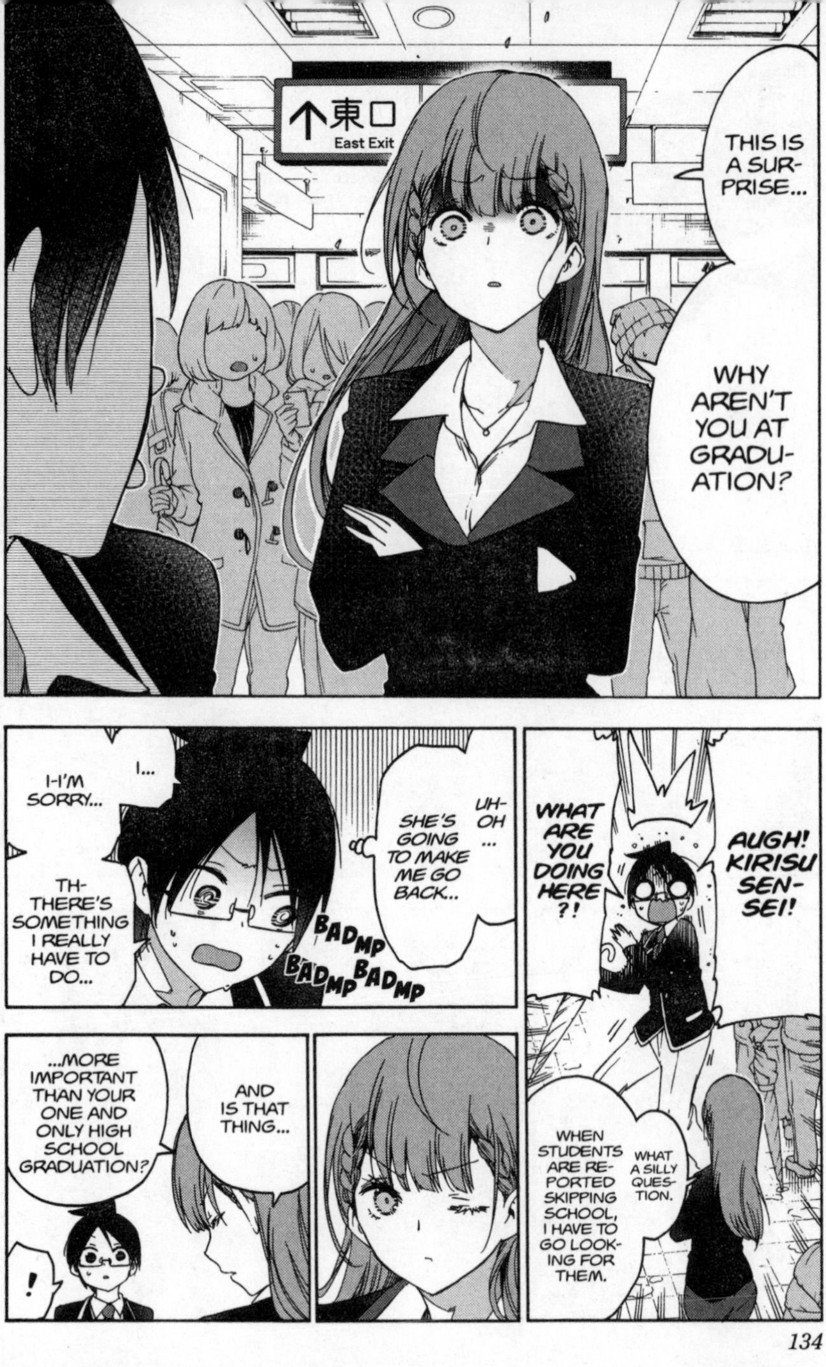
東口
East Exit
THIS IS A SURPRISE...
WHY AREN'T YOU AT GRADUATION?
AUGH! KIRISU SENSEI!
WHAT ARE YOU DOING HERE?!
WHAT A SILLY QUESTION.
WHEN STUDENTS ARE REPORTED SKIPPING SCHOOL, I HAVE TO GO LOOKING FOR THEM.
UH-OH...
SHE'S GOING TO MAKE ME GO BACK...
BADMP BADMP BADMP
I...
I-I'M SORRY...
TH-THERE'S SOMETHING I REALLY HAVE TO DO...
AND IS THAT THING...
...MORE IMPORTANT THAN YOUR ONE AND ONLY HIGH SCHOOL GRADUATION?
!

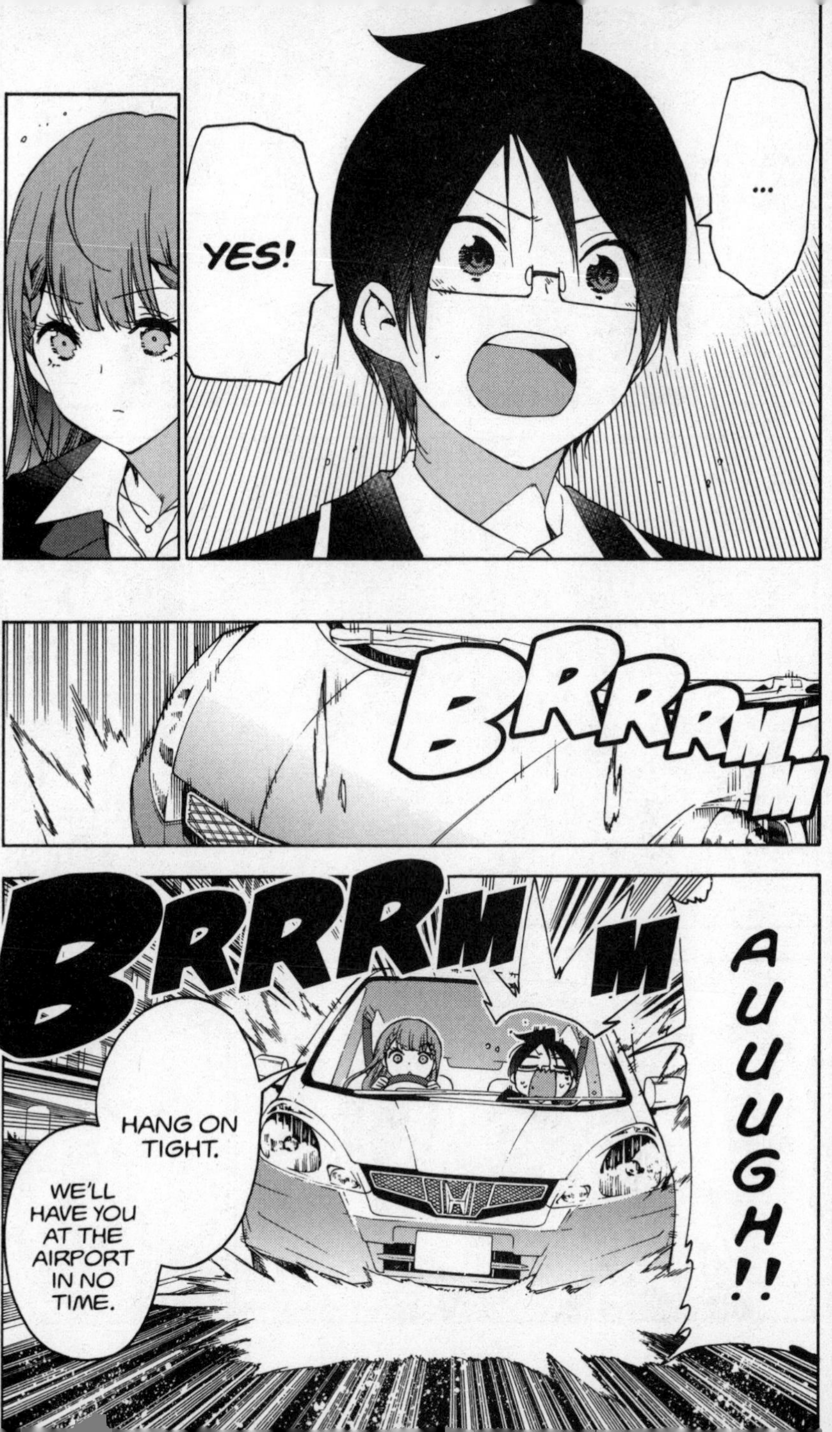
...
YES!
BRRRMM
BRRRMM
AUUUGH!!
HANG ON TIGHT.
WE'LL HAVE YOU AT THE AIRPORT IN NO TIME.

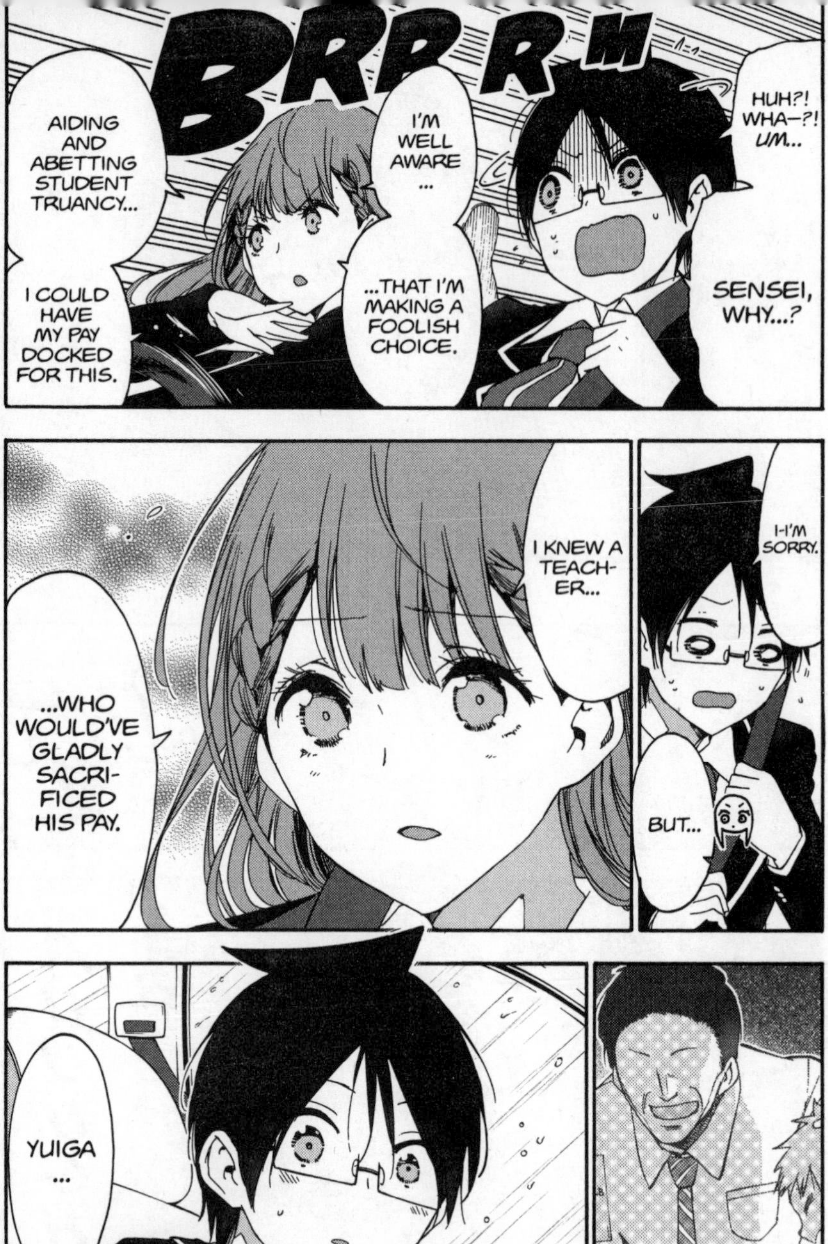
BRRRM
HUH?! WHA–?! UM...
SENSEI, WHY...?
I'M WELL AWARE...
...THAT I'M MAKING A FOOLISH CHOICE.
AIDING AND ABETTING STUDENT TRUANCY...
I COULD HAVE MY PAY DOCKED FOR THIS.
I-I'M SORRY.
BUT...
I KNEW A TEACHER...
...WHO WOULD'VE GLADLY SACRIFICED HIS PAY.
YUIGA...

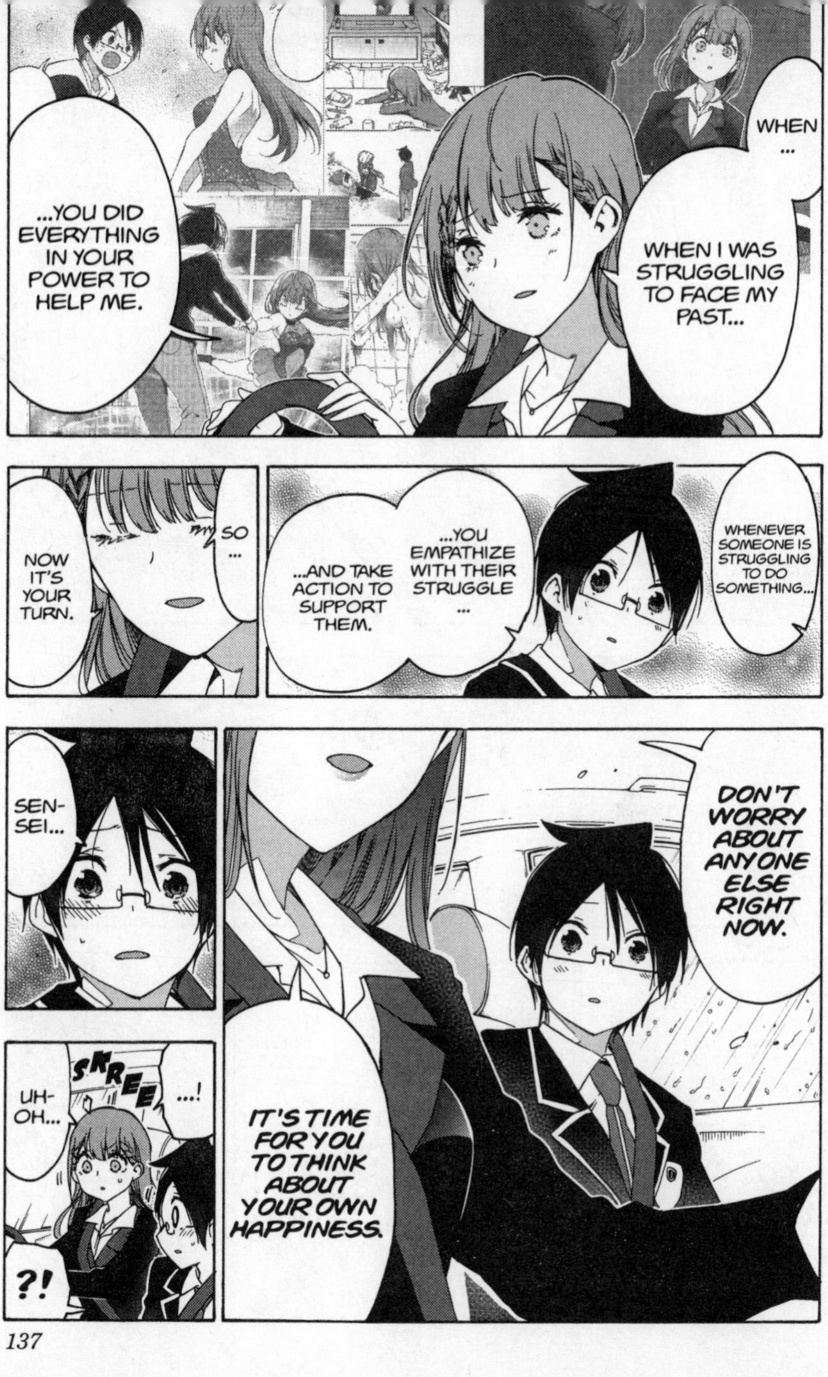
WHEN ...
WHEN I WAS STRUGGLING TO FACE MY PAST...
...YOU DID EVERYTHING IN YOUR POWER TO HELP ME.
WHENEVER SOMEONE IS STRUGGLING TO DO SOMETHING...
...YOU EMPATHIZE WITH THEIR STRUGGLE ...
...AND TAKE ACTION TO SUPPORT THEM.
SO ...
NOW IT'S YOUR TURN.
DON'T WORRY ABOUT ANYONE ELSE RIGHT NOW.
IT'S TIME FOR YOU TO THINK ABOUT YOUR OWN HAPPINESS.
SEN-SEI...
...!
SKREE
UH-OH...
?!

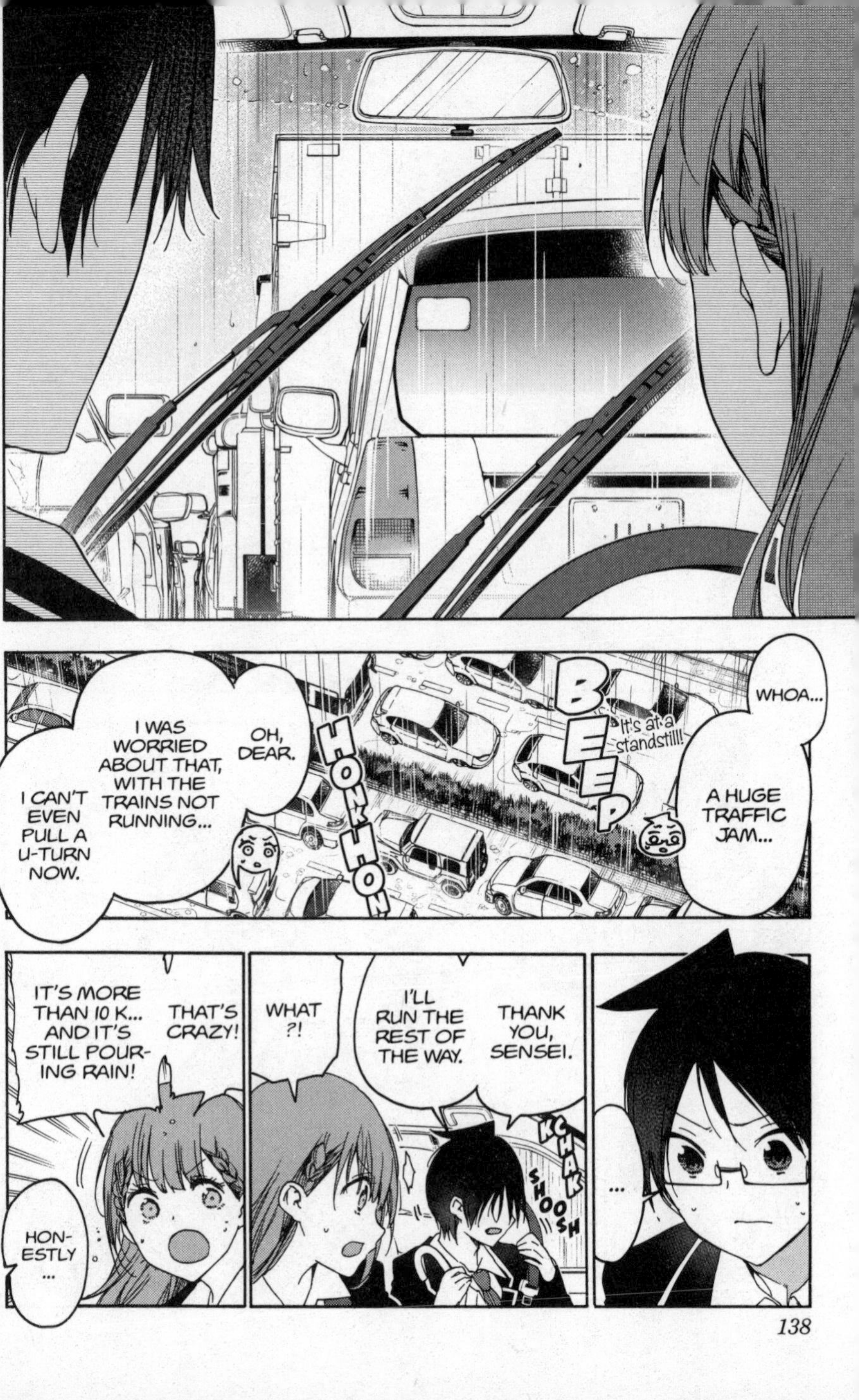
WHOA...
A HUGE TRAFFIC JAM...
It's at a standstill!!
BEEP
HONK HONK
OH, DEAR.
I WAS WORRIED ABOUT THAT, WITH THE TRAINS NOT RUNNING...
I CAN'T EVEN PULL A U-TURN NOW.
...
THANK YOU, SENSEI.
I'LL RUN THE REST OF THE WAY.
KCHAK
SHOOSH
WHAT?!
THAT'S CRAZY!
IT'S MORE THAN 10 K... AND IT'S STILL POURING RAIN!
HONESTLY...

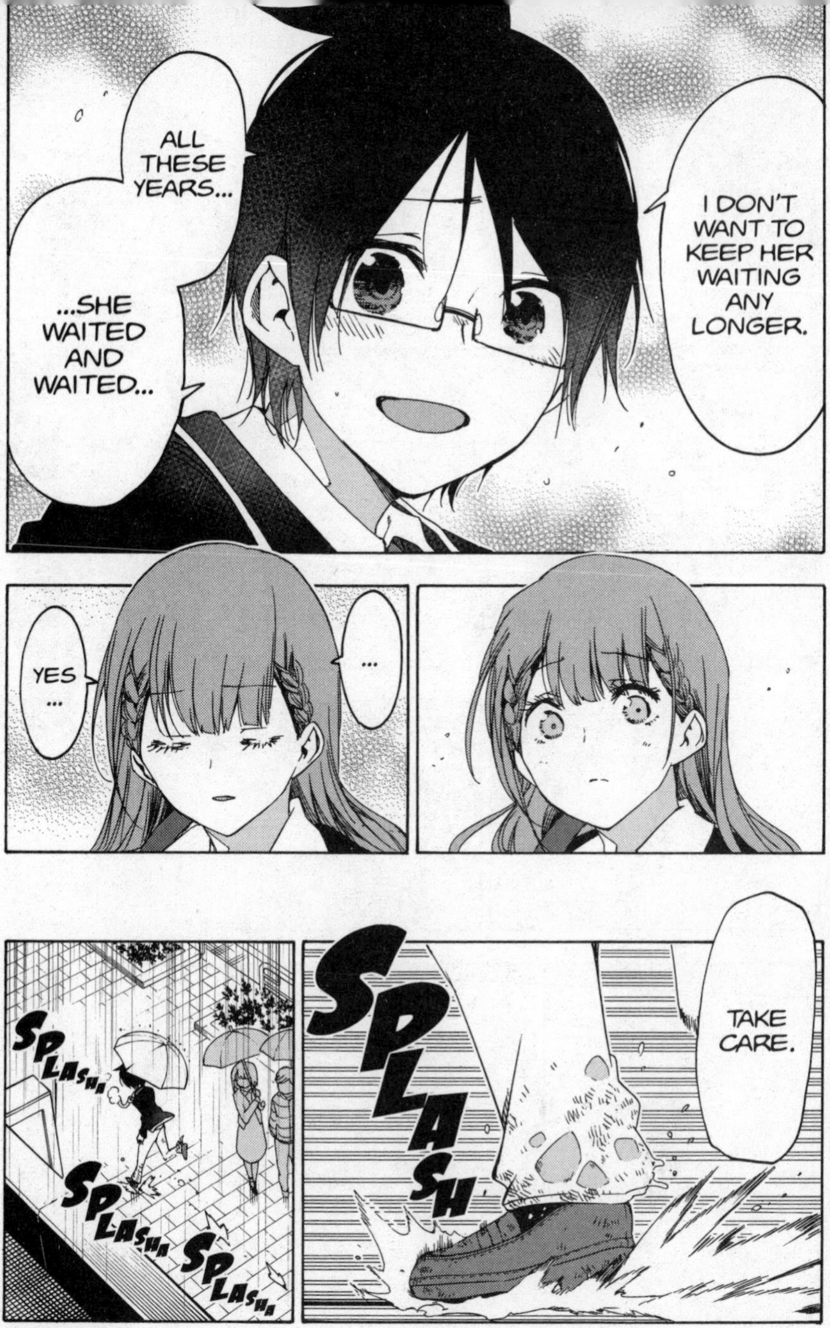
I DON'T WANT TO KEEP HER WAITING ANY LONGER.
ALL THESE YEARS...
...SHE WAITED AND WAITED...
...
YES ...
TAKE CARE.
SPLASH
SPLASH
SPLASH
SPLASH
SPLASH

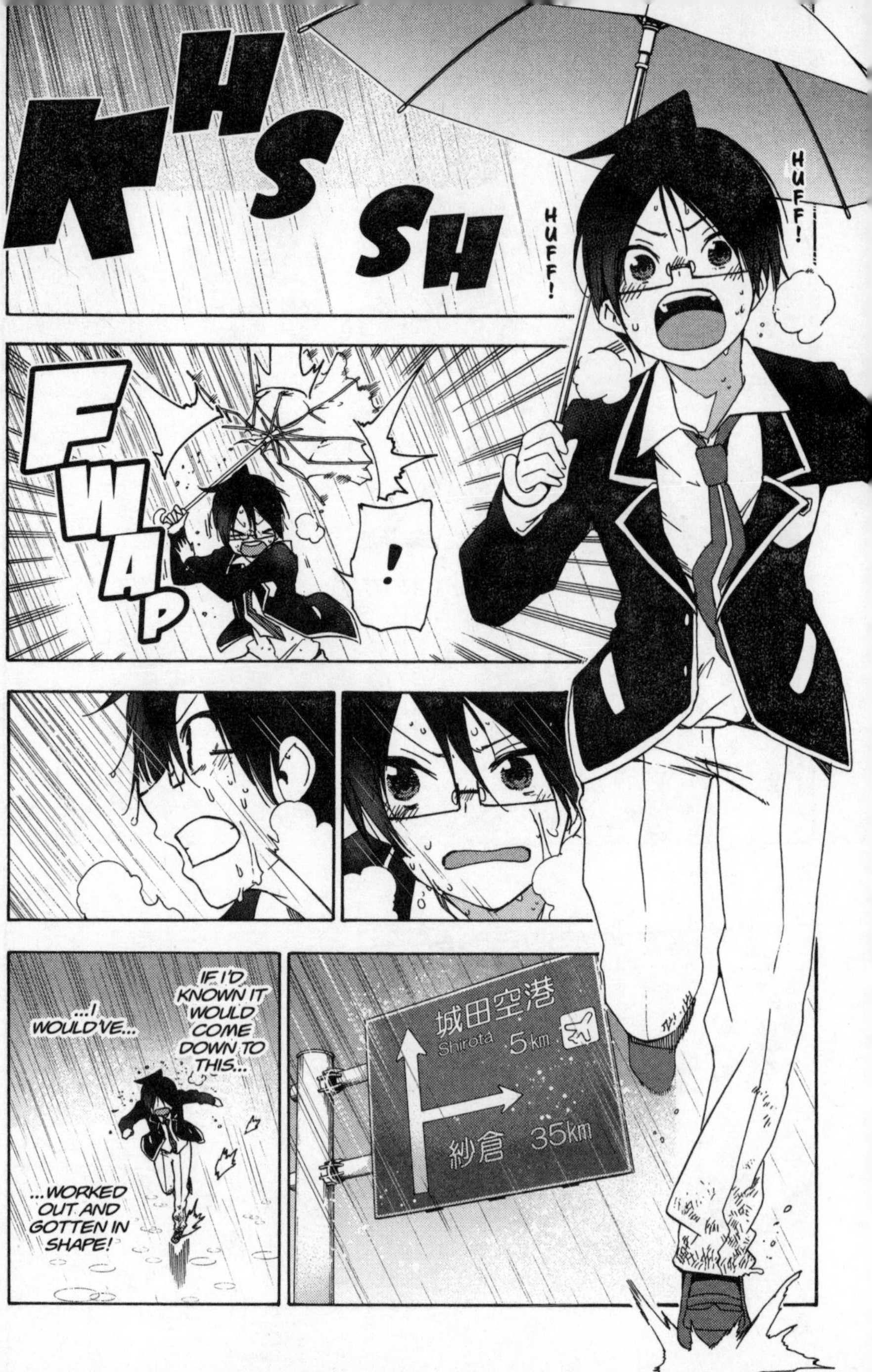
HUFF!
HUFF!
KHSSH
FWAP
!
城田空港
Shirota 5km
紗倉 35km
IF I'D KNOWN IT WOULD COME DOWN TO THIS...
...I WOULD'VE...
...WORKED OUT AND GOTTEN IN SHAPE!

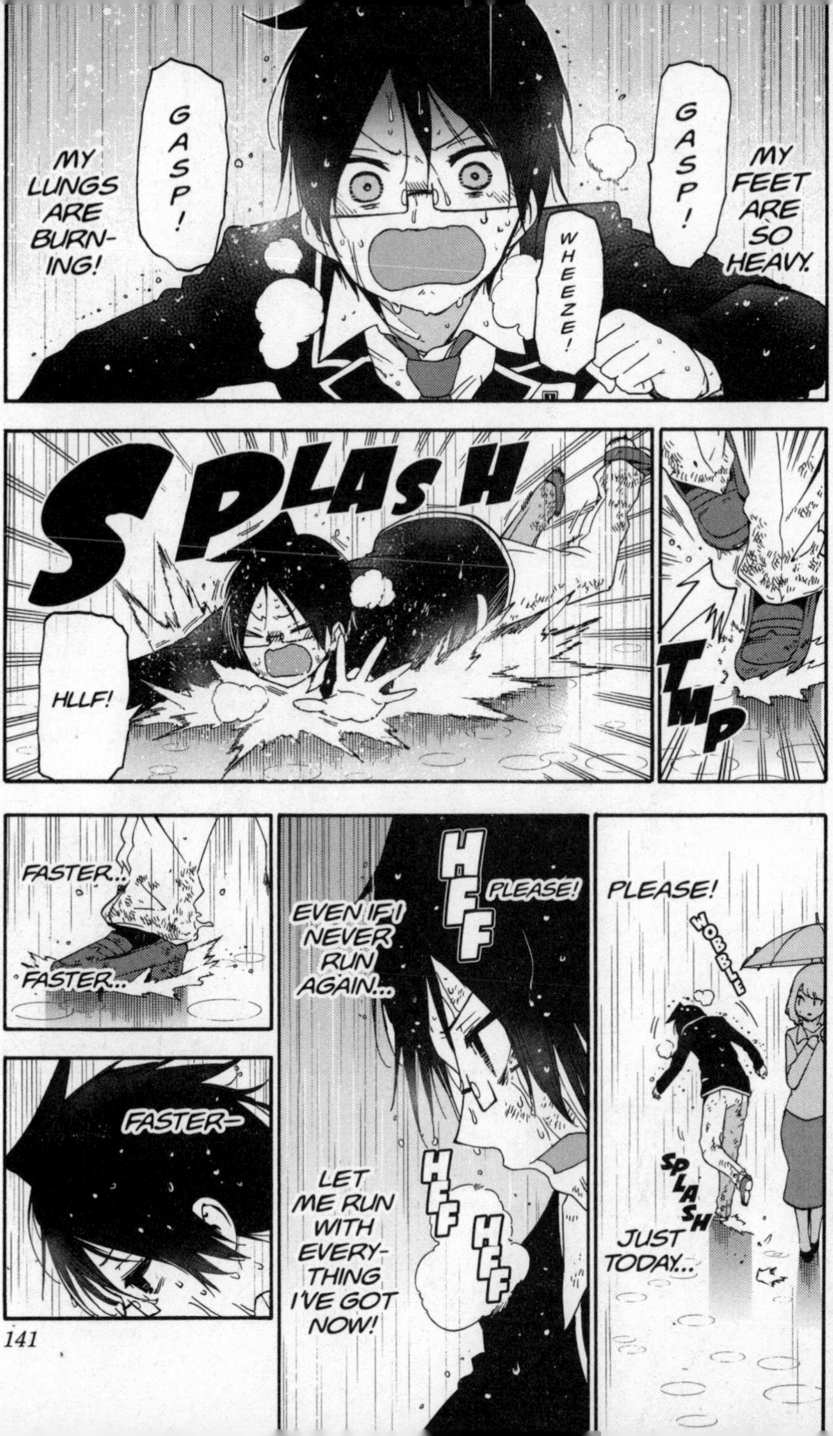
MY FEET ARE SO HEAVY.
GASP!
WHEEZE!
GASP!
MY LUNGS ARE BURNING!
TMP
SPLASH
HLLF!
PLEASE!
WOBBLE
SPLASH
JUST TODAY...
HFF
PLEASE!
EVEN IF I NEVER RUN AGAIN...
HFF
HFF
HFF
LET ME RUN WITH EVERY-THING I'VE GOT NOW!
FASTER...
FASTER...
FASTER-

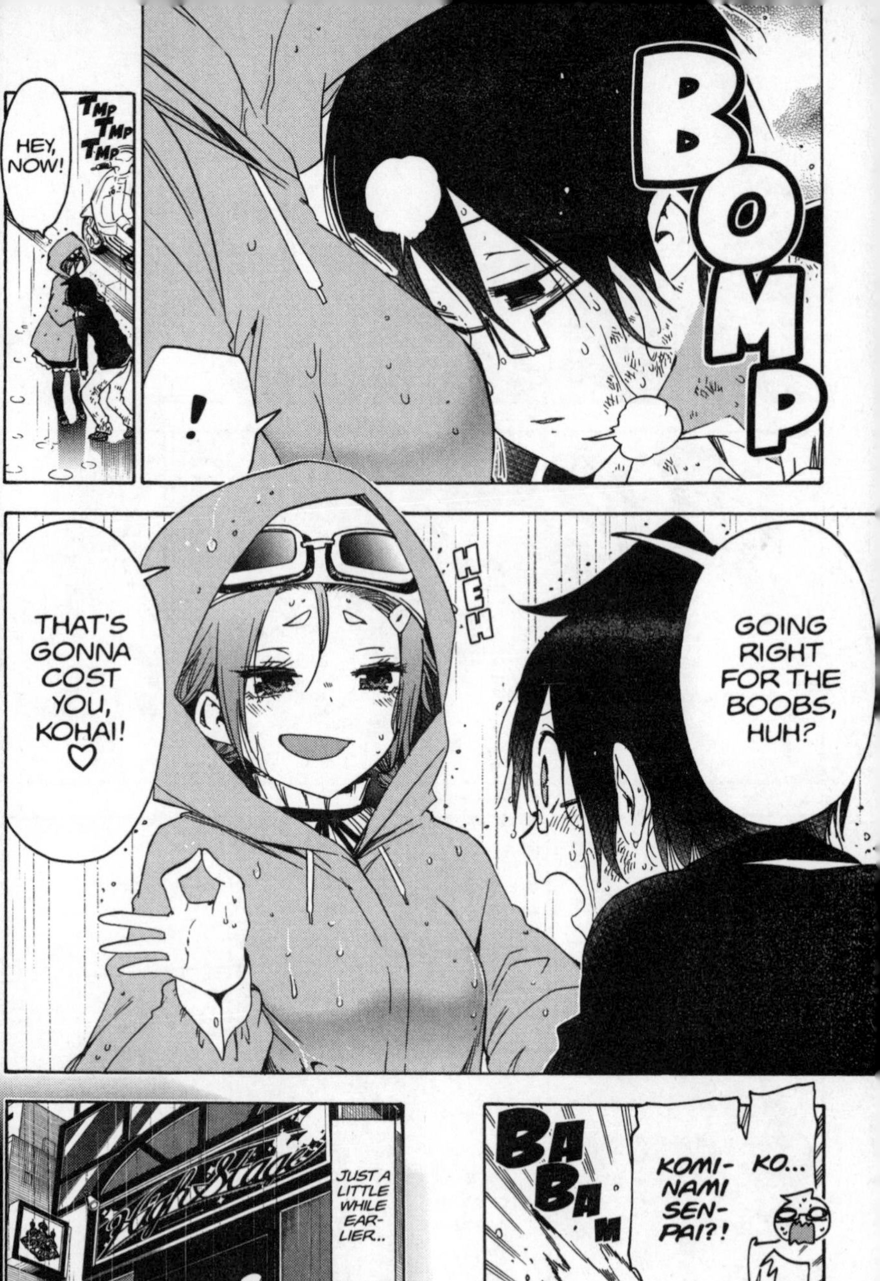
BOMP
!
TMP TMP TMP
HEY, NOW!
GOING RIGHT FOR THE BOOBS, HUH?
HEH
THAT'S GONNA COST YOU, KOHAI! ♡
BABAM
KO...
KOMI-NAMI SEN-PAI?!
High Stage
JUST A LITTLE WHILE EAR-LIER...

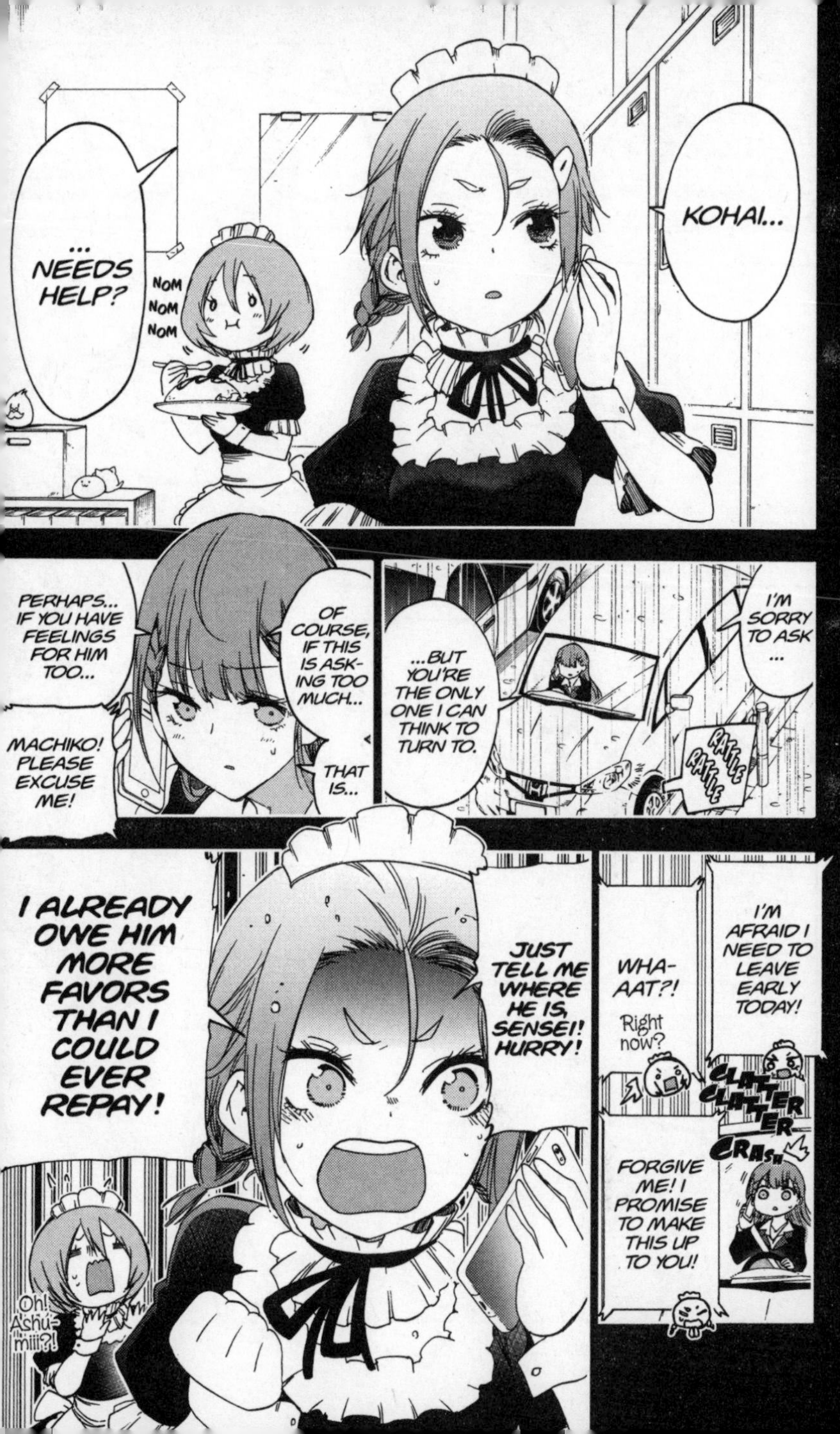
KOHAI...
...NEEDS HELP?
NOM NOM NOM
I'M SORRY TO ASK ...
RATTLE RATTLE
...BUT YOU'RE THE ONLY ONE I CAN THINK TO TURN TO.
OF COURSE, IF THIS IS ASK-ING TOO MUCH...
THAT IS...
PERHAPS... IF YOU HAVE FEELINGS FOR HIM TOO...
MACHIKO! PLEASE EXCUSE ME!
I'M AFRAID I NEED TO LEAVE EARLY TODAY!
WHA-AAT?!
Right now?
CLATTER CLATTER CRASH
FORGIVE ME! I PROMISE TO MAKE THIS UP TO YOU!
JUST TELL ME WHERE HE IS, SENSEI! HURRY!
I ALREADY OWE HIM MORE FAVORS THAN I COULD EVER REPAY!
Oh! Ashu-miii?!

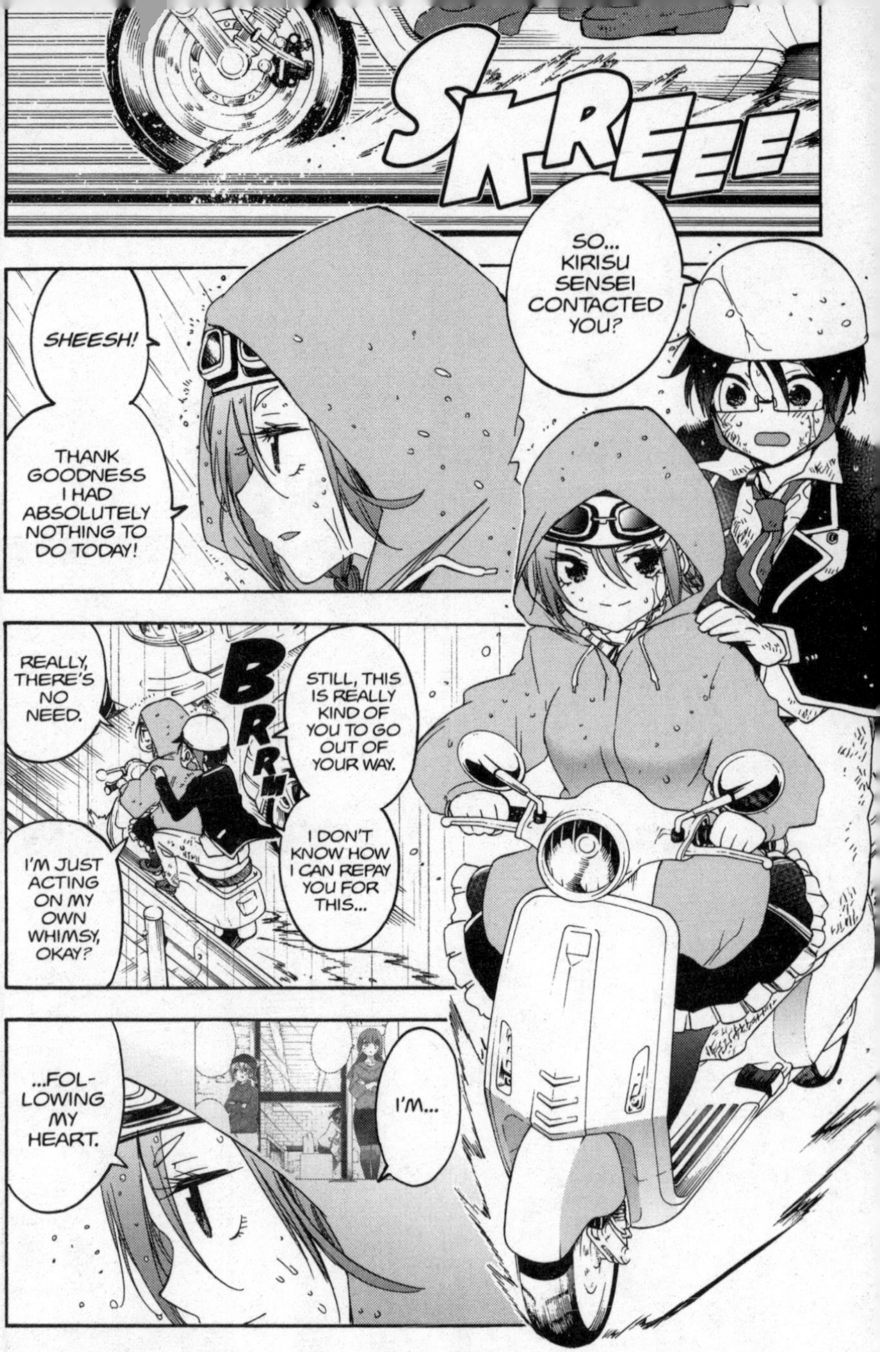
SKREEE
SO... KIRISU SENSEI CONTACTED YOU?
SHEESH!
THANK GOODNESS I HAD ABSOLUTELY NOTHING TO DO TODAY!
STILL, THIS IS REALLY KIND OF YOU TO GO OUT OF YOUR WAY.
I DON'T KNOW HOW I CAN REPAY YOU FOR THIS...
BRRM
REALLY, THERE'S NO NEED.
I'M JUST ACTING ON MY OWN WHIMSY, OKAY?
I'M...
...FOL-LOWING MY HEART.

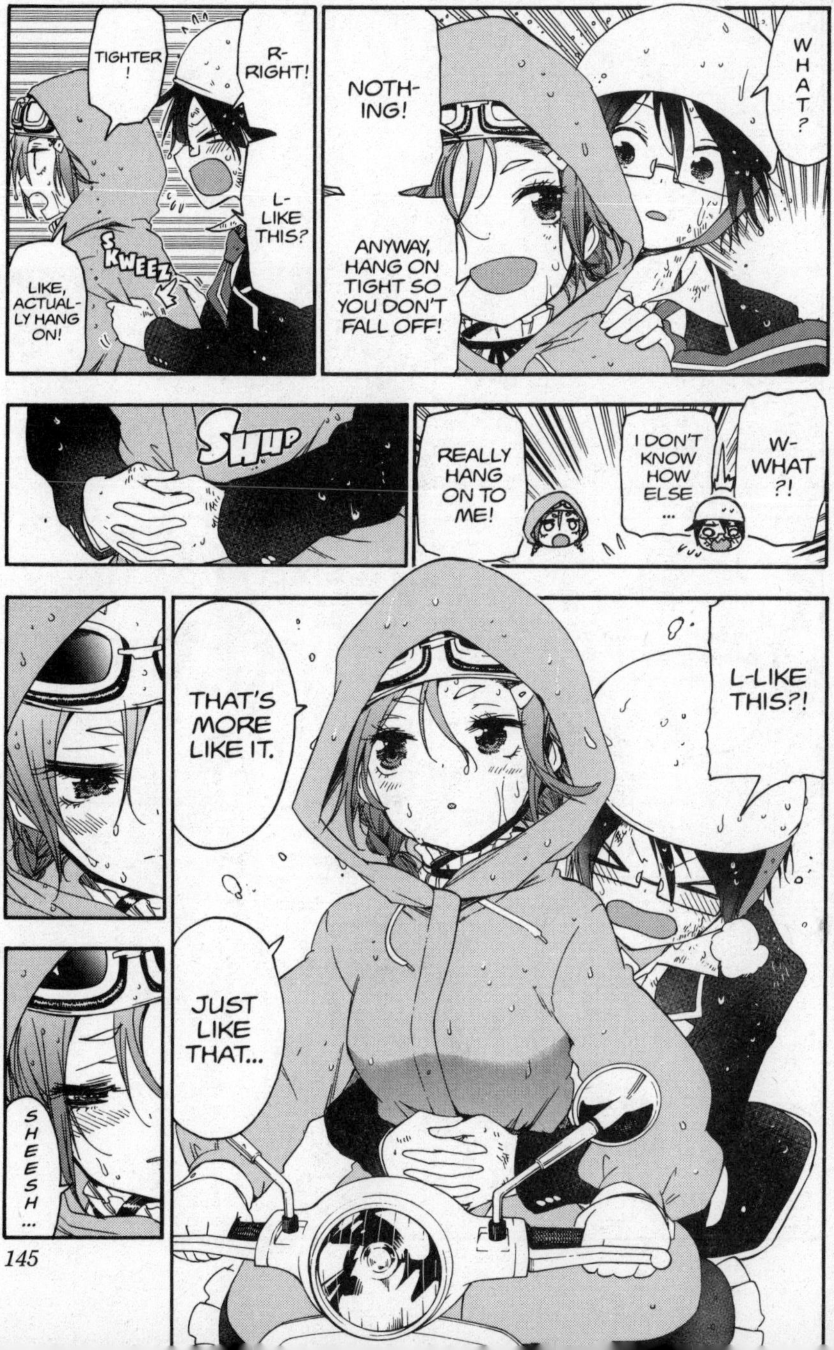
WHAT?
NOTH-ING!
ANYWAY, HANG ON TIGHT SO YOU DON'T FALL OFF!
R-RIGHT!
TIGHTER!
L-LIKE THIS?
SKWEEZ
LIKE, ACTUAL-LY HANG ON!
W-WHAT?!
I DON'T KNOW HOW ELSE...
REALLY HANG ON TO ME!
SHUP
L-LIKE THIS?!
THAT'S MORE LIKE IT.
JUST LIKE THAT...
SHEESH...

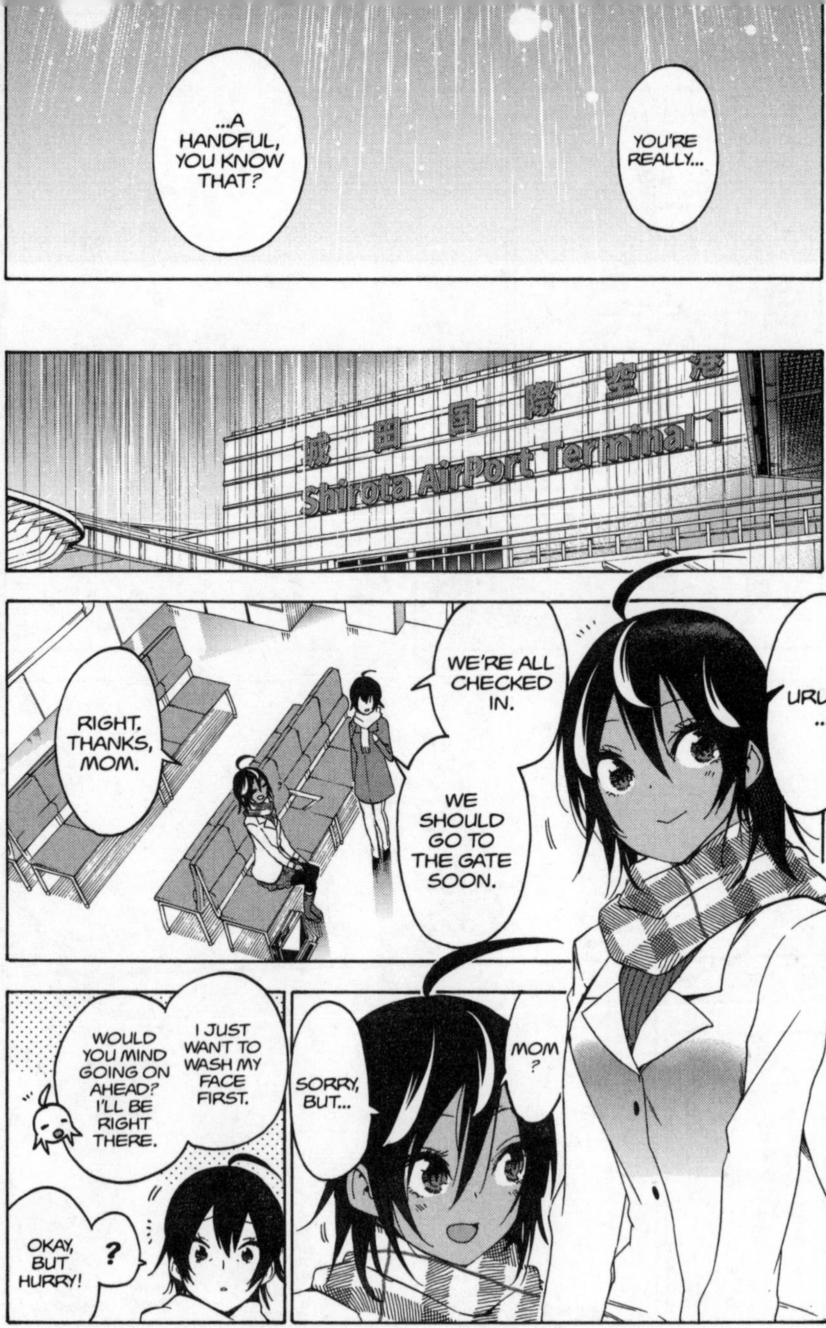
YOU'RE REALLY...
...A HANDFUL, YOU KNOW THAT?
城田国際空港
Shirota AirPort Terminal 1
WE'RE ALL CHECKED IN.
WE SHOULD GO TO THE GATE SOON.
RIGHT. THANKS, MOM.
URUKA ...
MOM ?
SORRY, BUT...
I JUST WANT TO WASH MY FACE FIRST.
WOULD YOU MIND GOING ON AHEAD? I'LL BE RIGHT THERE.
OKAY, BUT HURRY!
?

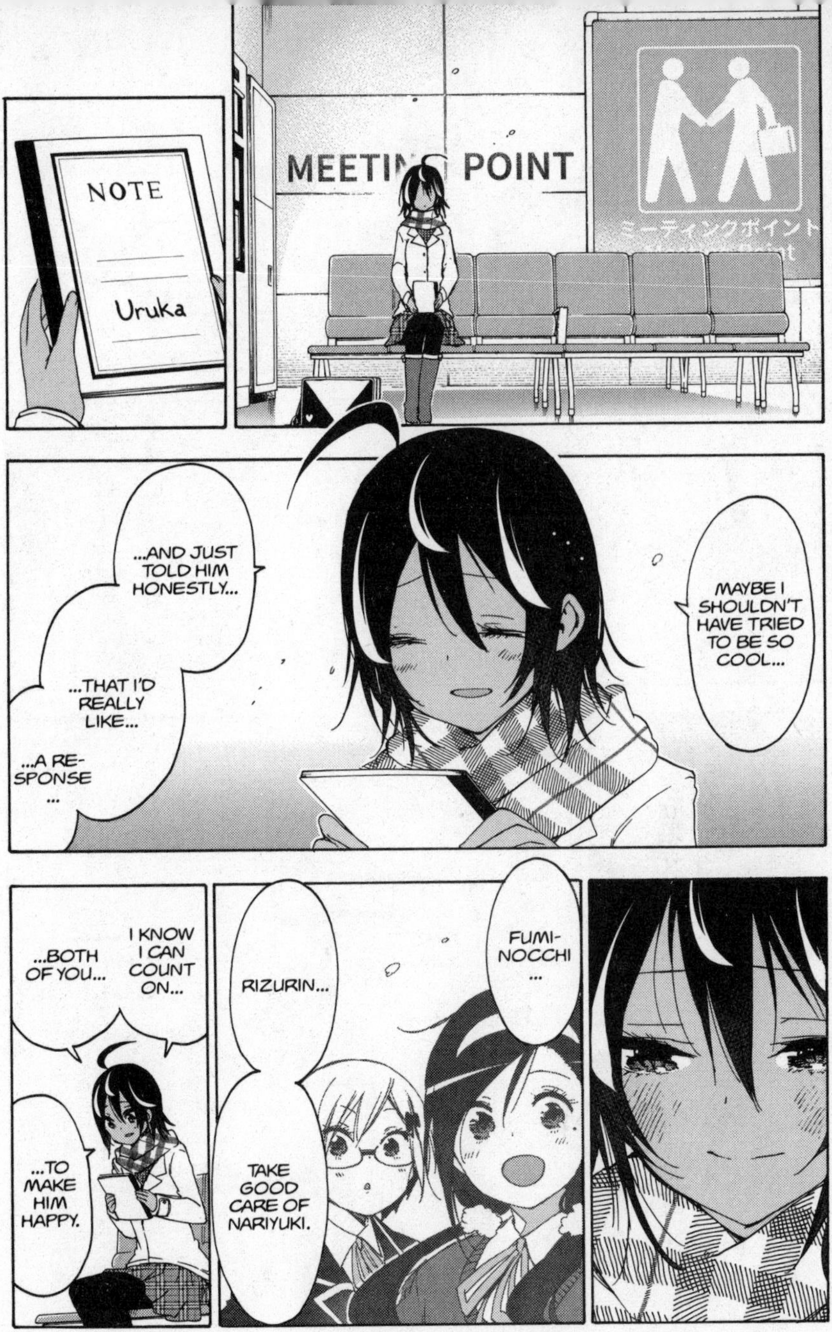
MEETING POINT
ミーティングポイント
NOTE
Uruka
MAYBE I SHOULDN'T HAVE TRIED TO BE SO COOL...
...AND JUST TOLD HIM HONESTLY...
...THAT I'D REALLY LIKE...
...A RE-SPONSE ...
FUMI-NOCCHI ...
RIZURIN...
TAKE GOOD CARE OF NARIYUKI.
I KNOW I CAN COUNT ON...
...BOTH OF YOU...
...TO MAKE HIM HAPPY.

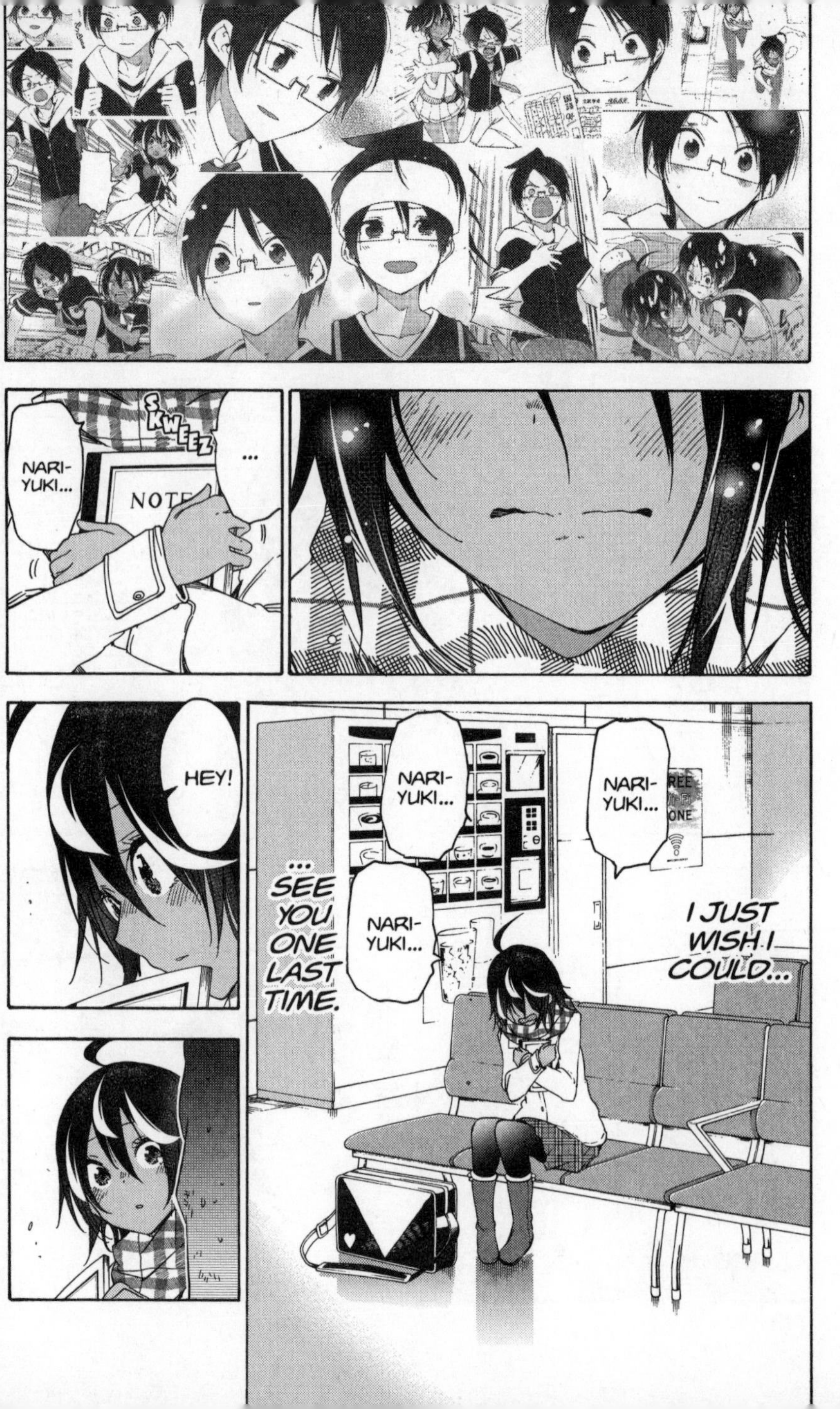
SKWEEZ
...
NARI-YUKI...
NARI-YUKI...
NARI-YUKI...
I JUST WISH I COULD...
...SEE YOU ONE LAST TIME.
NARI-YUKI...
HEY!

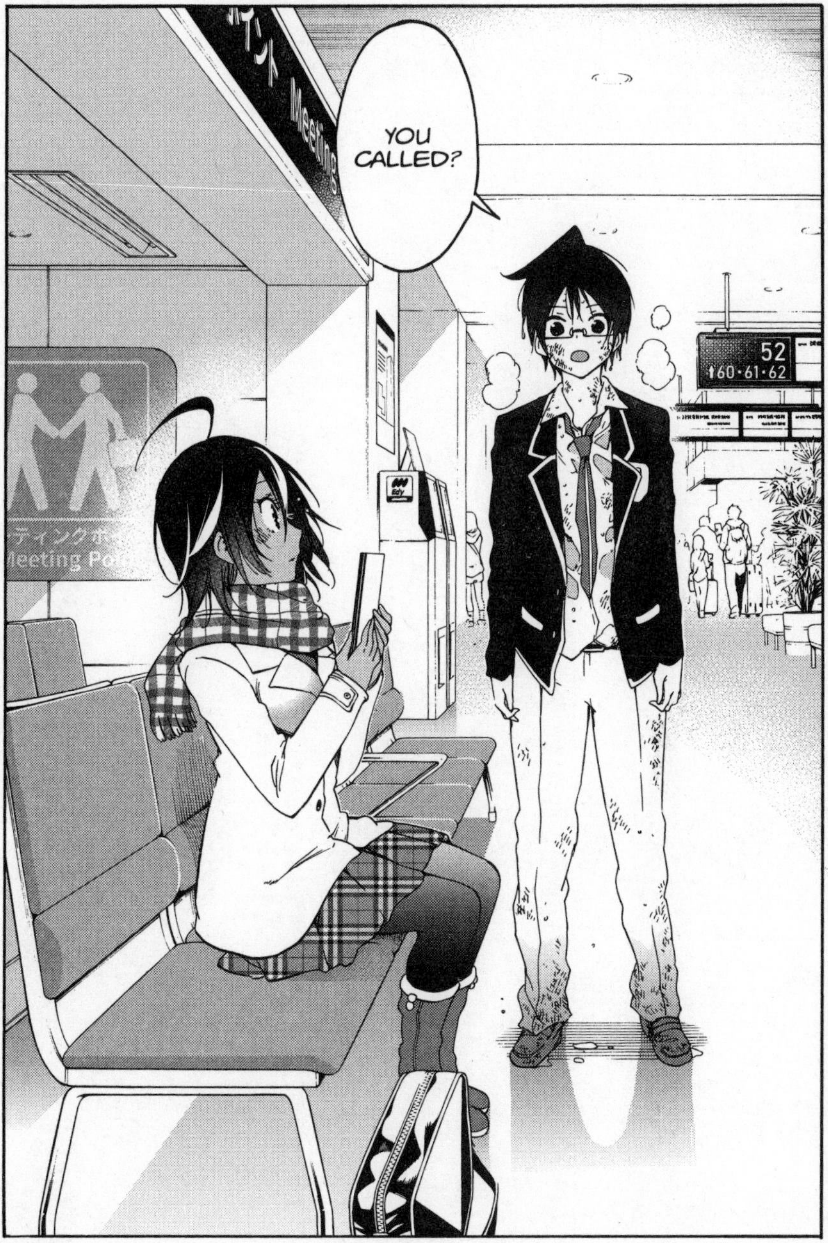
YOU CALLED?
52
↑60・61・62

Terminal 1

Question 149: The Ephemeral Mermaid Sprinkles into the Promised [X], Part 8

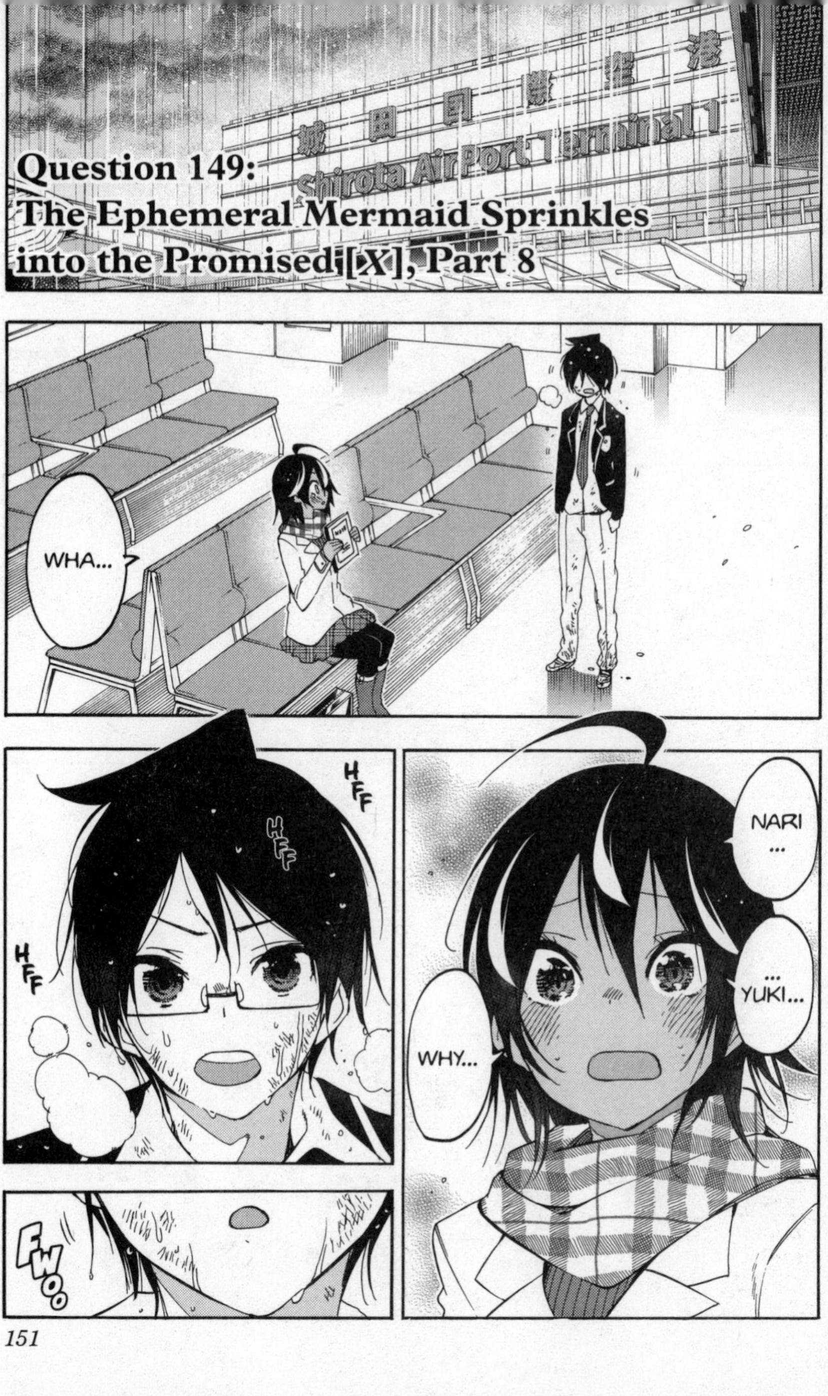

Shirota Air Port Terminal1
WHA...
NARI ...
... YUKI...
WHY...
HFF
HFF
HFF
FWOO

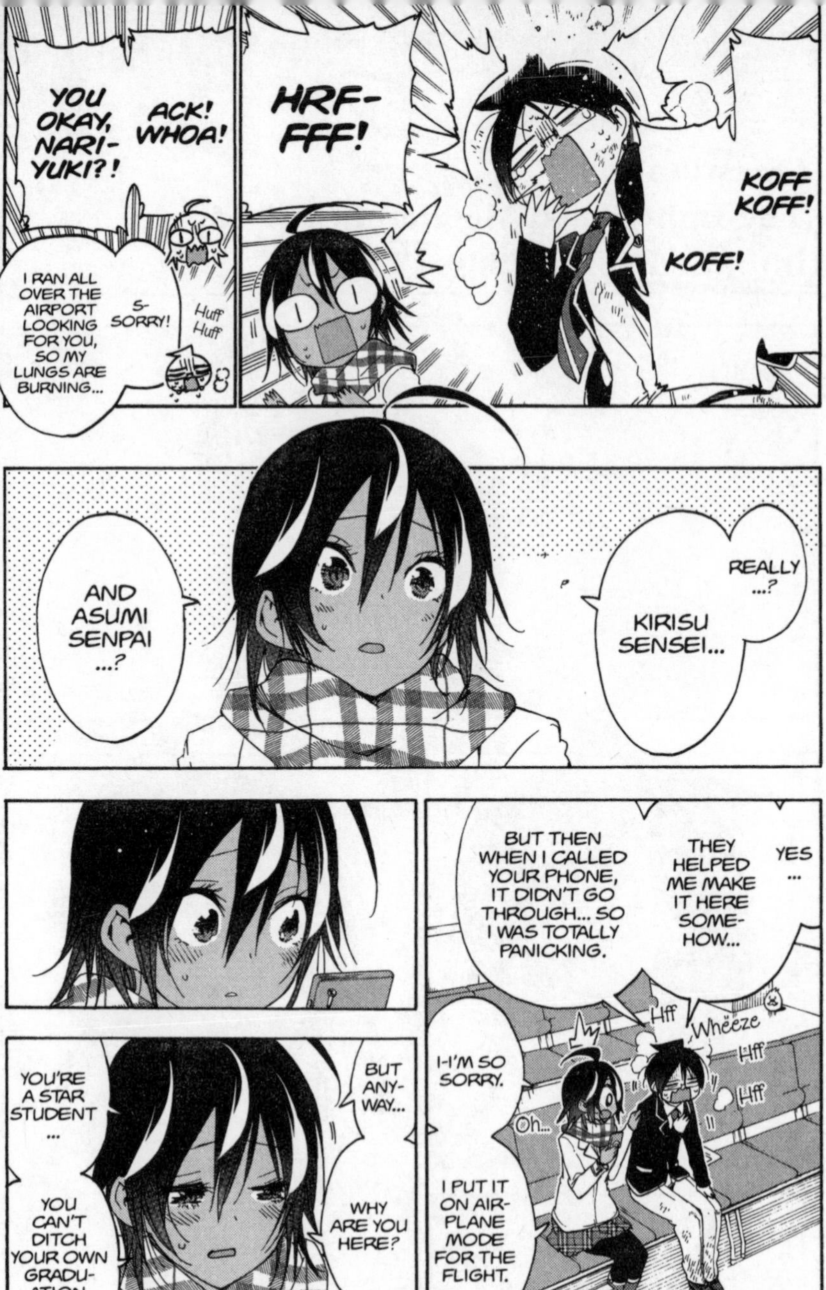
KOFF KOFF!
KOFF!
HRF-FFF!
ACK! WHOA!
YOU OKAY, NARI-YUKI?!
S-SORRY!
Huff Huff
I RAN ALL OVER THE AIRPORT LOOKING FOR YOU, SO MY LUNGS ARE BURNING...
REALLY ...?
KIRISU SENSEI...
AND ASUMI SENPAI ...?
YES ...
THEY HELPED ME MAKE IT HERE SOME-HOW...
BUT THEN WHEN I CALLED YOUR PHONE, IT DIDN'T GO THROUGH... SO I WAS TOTALLY PANICKING.
Hff
Wheeze
Hff
Hff
I-I'M SO SORRY.
Oh...
I PUT IT ON AIR-PLANE MODE FOR THE FLIGHT.
BUT ANY-WAY...
WHY ARE YOU HERE?
YOU'RE A STAR STUDENT ...
YOU CAN'T DITCH YOUR OWN GRADU-ATION.

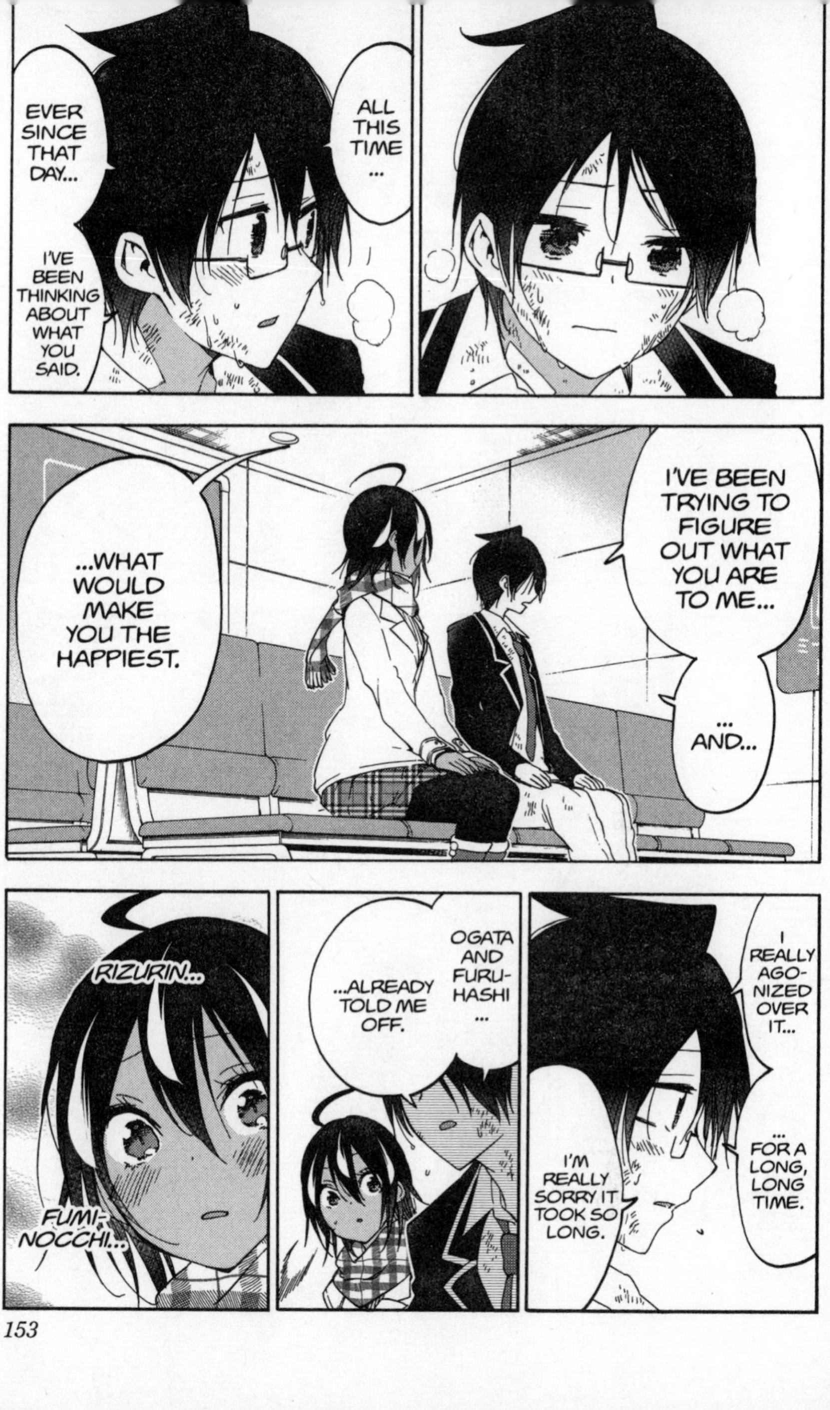
ALL THIS TIME ...
EVER SINCE THAT DAY...
I'VE BEEN THINKING ABOUT WHAT YOU SAID.
I'VE BEEN TRYING TO FIGURE OUT WHAT YOU ARE TO ME...
... AND...
...WHAT WOULD MAKE YOU THE HAPPIEST.
I REALLY AGO-NIZED OVER IT...
... FOR A LONG, LONG TIME.
I'M REALLY SORRY IT TOOK SO LONG.
OGATA AND FURU-HASHI ...
...ALREADY TOLD ME OFF.
RIZURIN...
FUMI-NOCCHI...

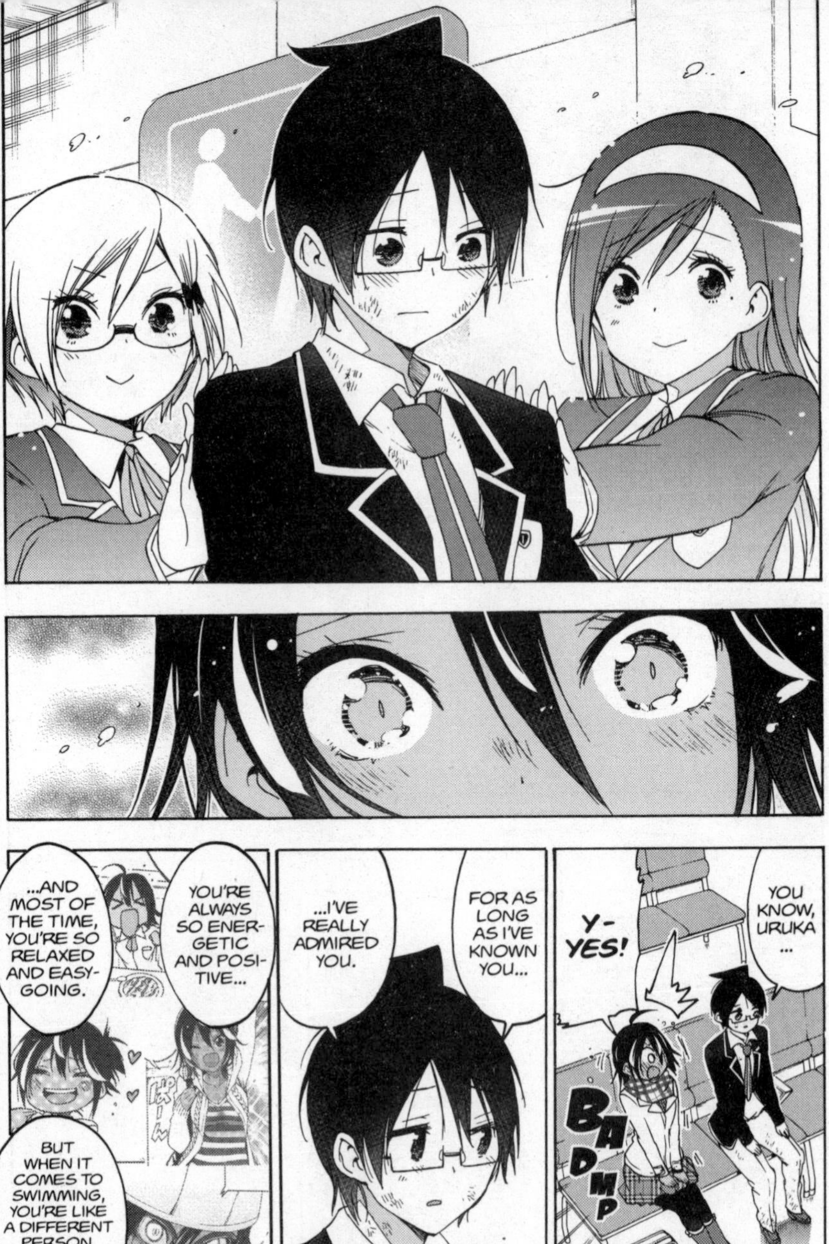
YOU KNOW, URUKA ...
Y-YES!
BADMP
FOR AS LONG AS I'VE KNOWN YOU...
...I'VE REALLY ADMIRED YOU.
YOU'RE ALWAYS SO ENERGETIC AND POSITIVE...
...AND MOST OF THE TIME, YOU'RE SO RELAXED AND EASY-GOING.
BUT WHEN IT COMES TO SWIMMING, YOU'RE LIKE A DIFFERENT PERSON. YOU'RE INCREDIBLE ...

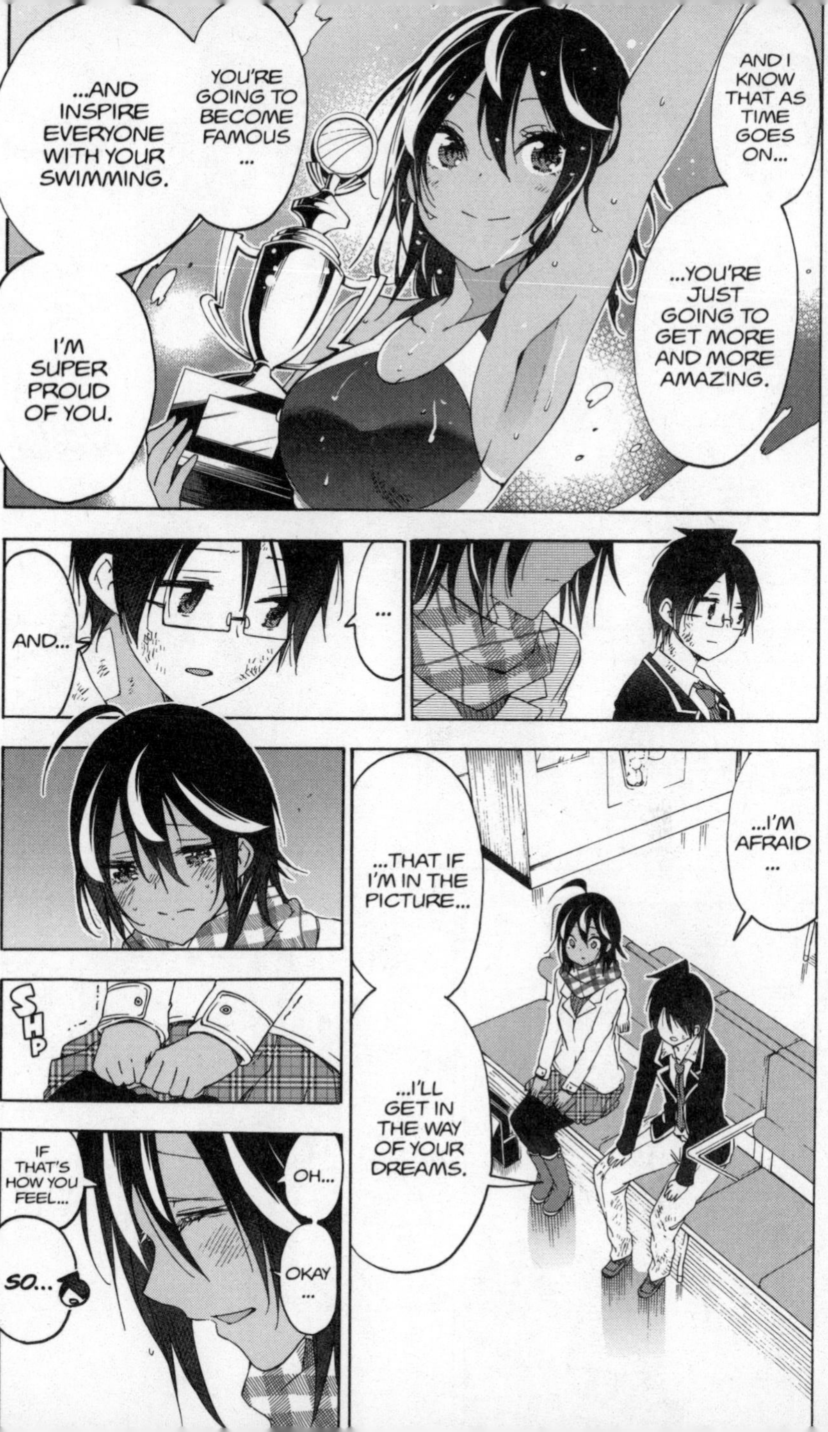
AND I KNOW THAT AS TIME GOES ON...
...YOU'RE JUST GOING TO GET MORE AND MORE AMAZING.
YOU'RE GOING TO BECOME FAMOUS ...
...AND INSPIRE EVERYONE WITH YOUR SWIMMING.
I'M SUPER PROUD OF YOU.
...
AND...
...I'M AFRAID ...
...THAT IF I'M IN THE PICTURE...
...I'LL GET IN THE WAY OF YOUR DREAMS.
SHP
OH...
OKAY ...
IF THAT'S HOW YOU FEEL...
SO...

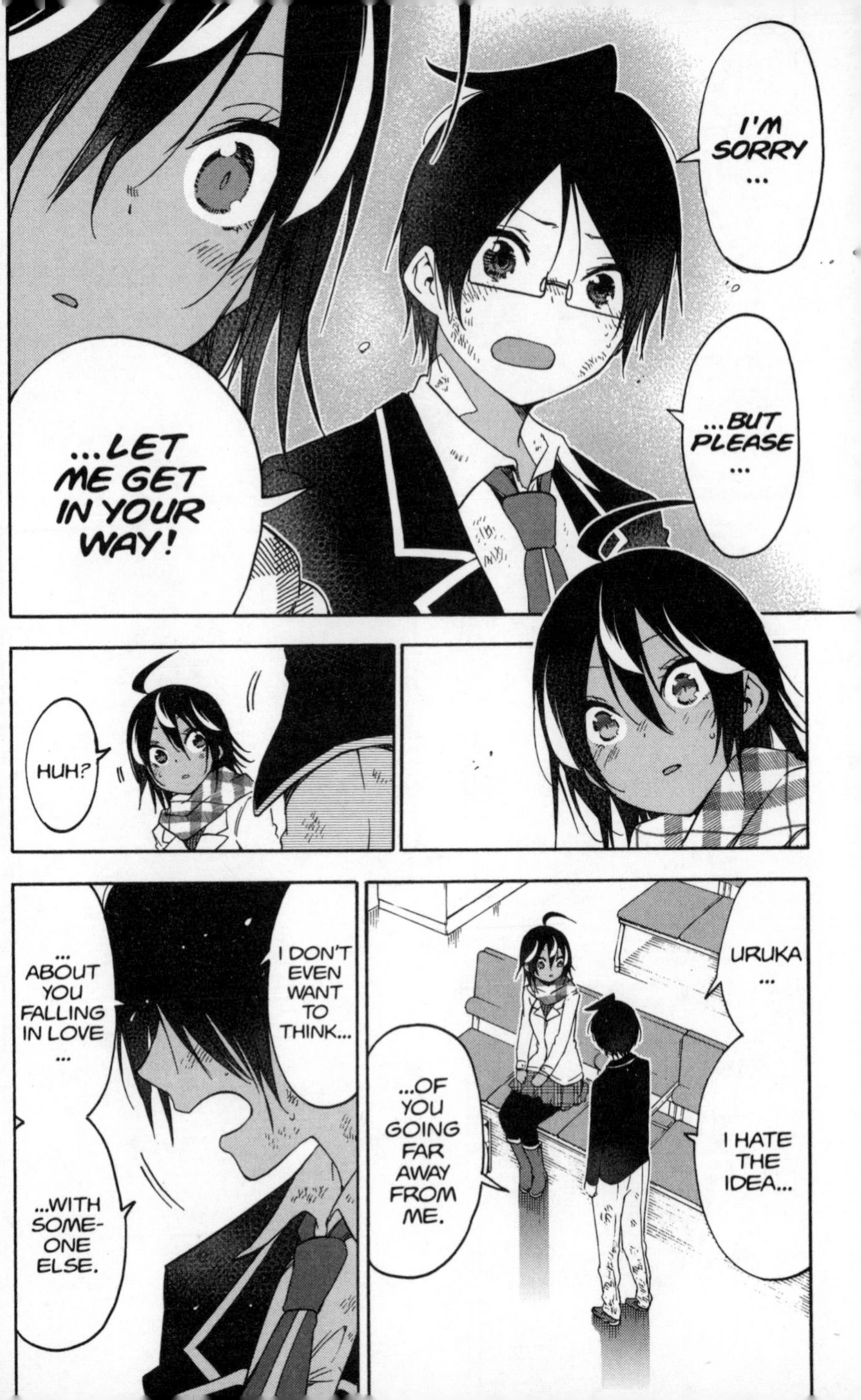
I'M SORRY ...
...BUT PLEASE ...
...LET ME GET IN YOUR WAY!
HUH?
URUKA ...
I HATE THE IDEA...
...OF YOU GOING FAR AWAY FROM ME.
I DON'T EVEN WANT TO THINK...
... ABOUT YOU FALLING IN LOVE ...
...WITH SOME-ONE ELSE.

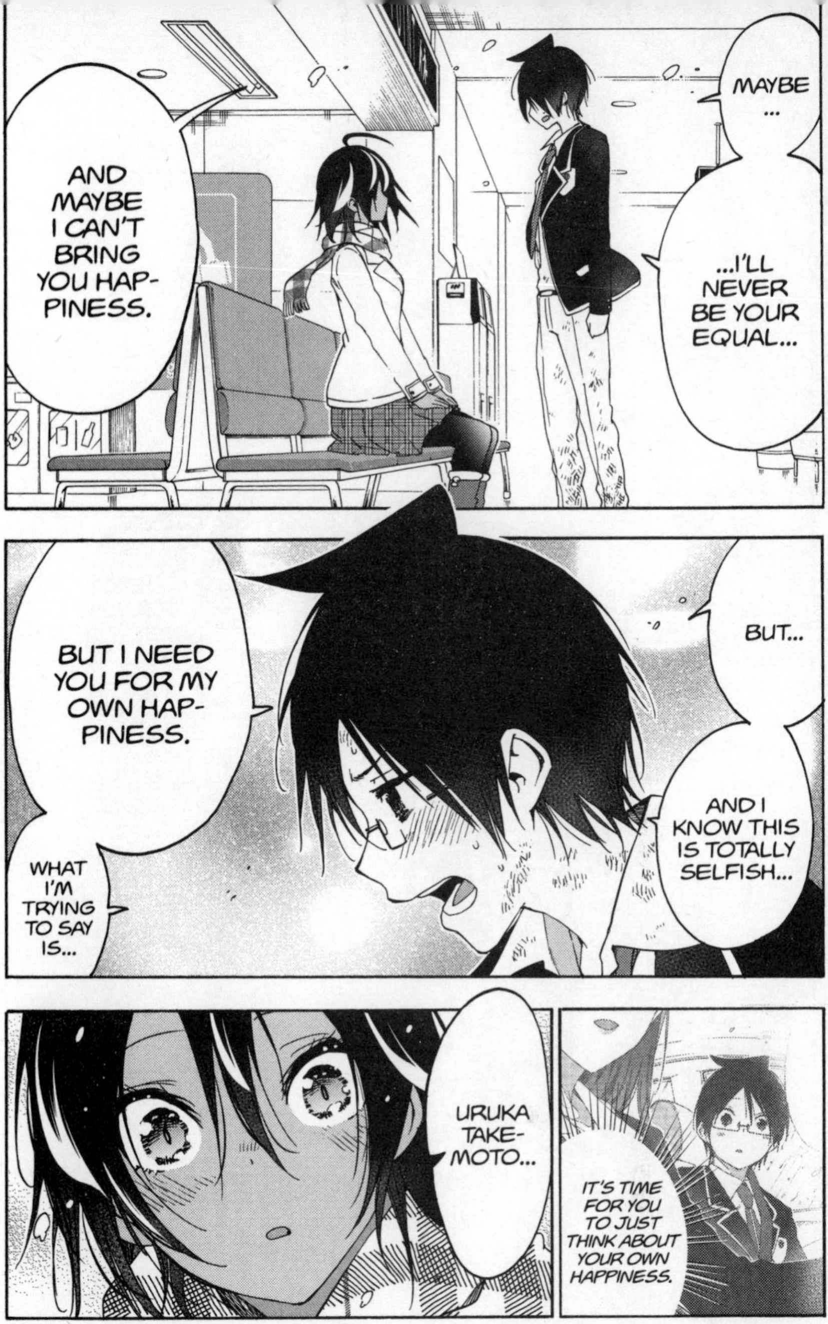
MAYBE...
...I'LL NEVER BE YOUR EQUAL...
AND MAYBE I CAN'T BRING YOU HAP-PINESS.
BUT...
AND I KNOW THIS IS TOTALLY SELFISH...
BUT I NEED YOU FOR MY OWN HAP-PINESS.
WHAT I'M TRYING TO SAY IS...
IT'S TIME FOR YOU TO JUST THINK ABOUT YOUR OWN HAPPINESS.
URUKA TAKE-MOTO...

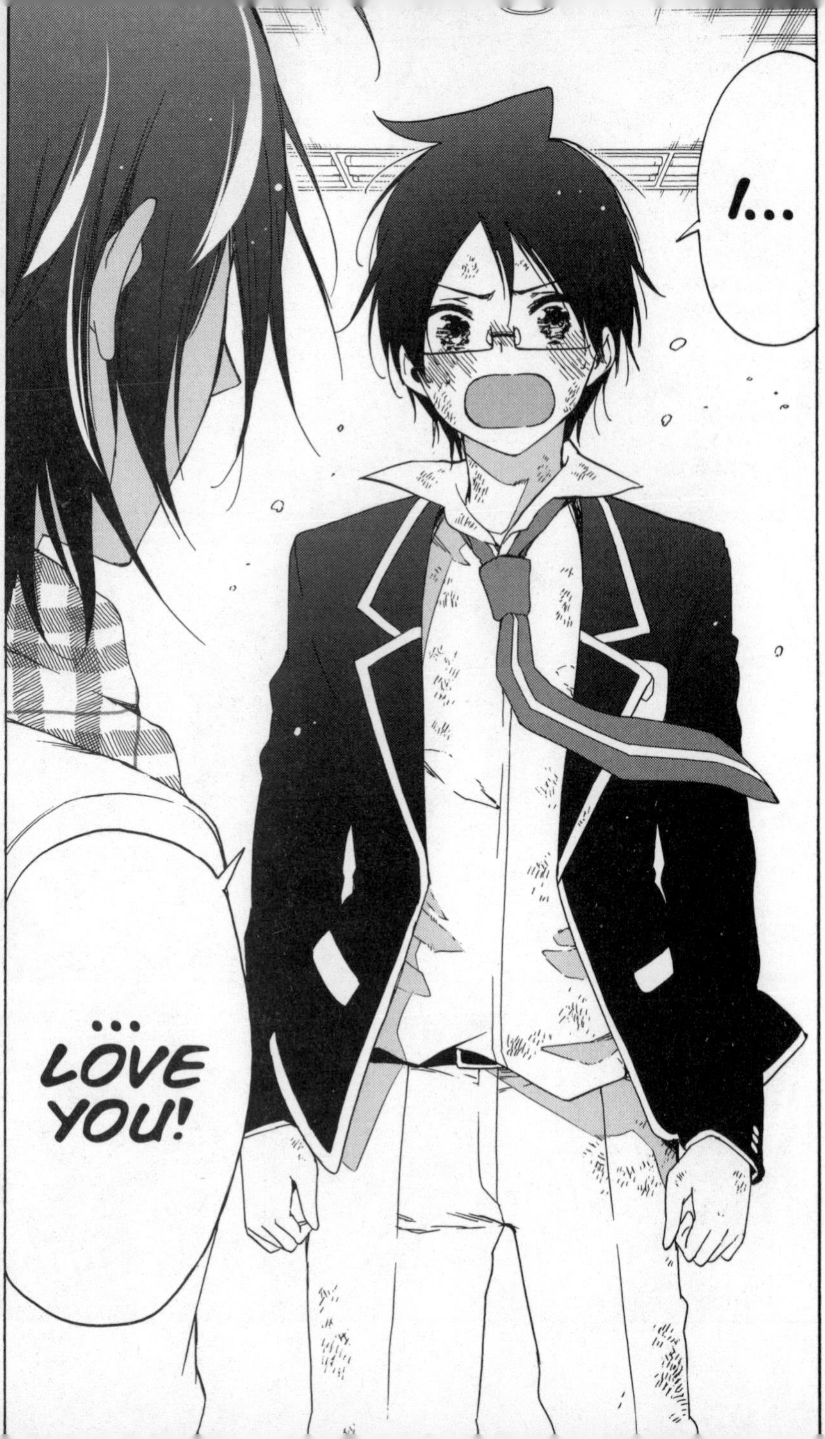
I...
...LOVE YOU!

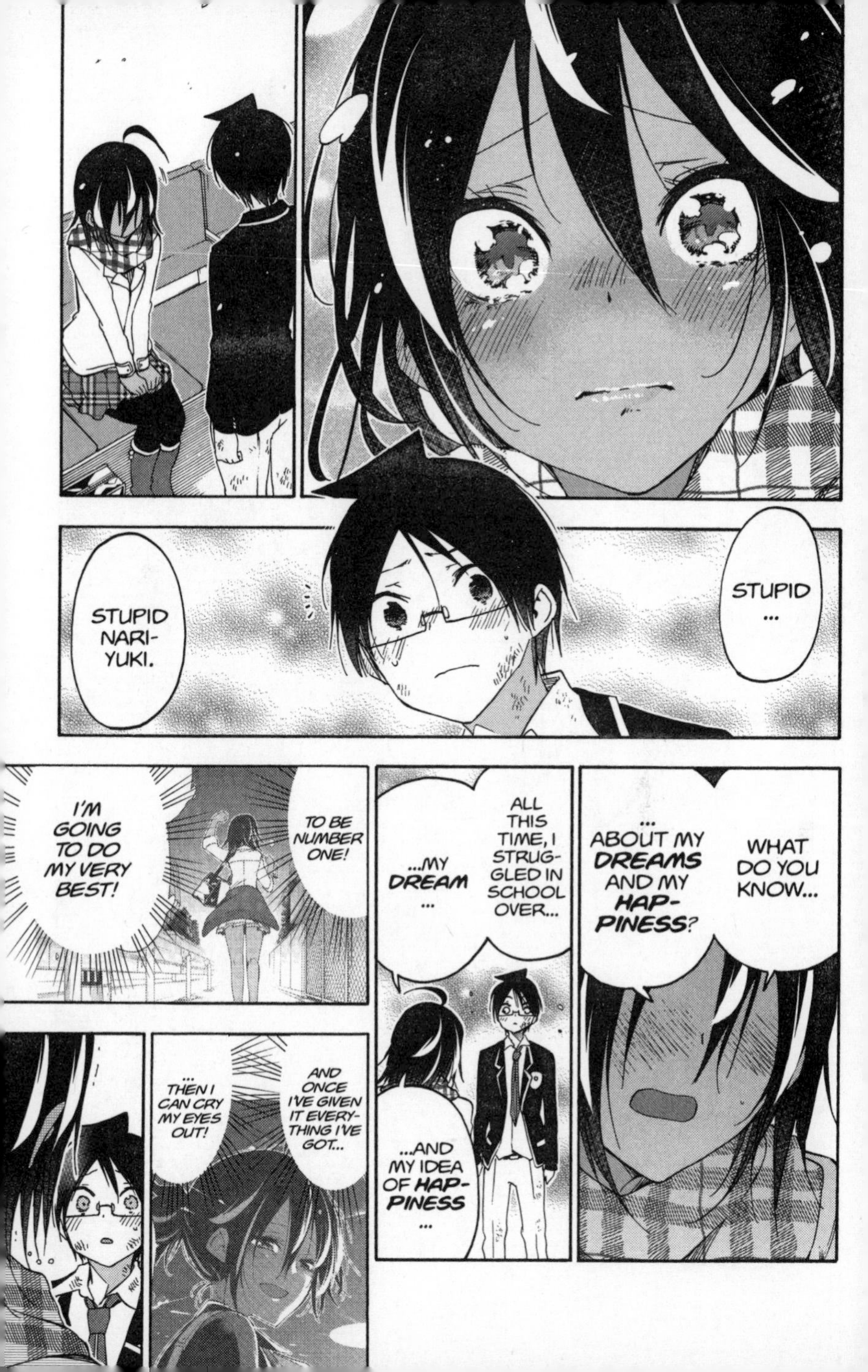
STUPID ...
STUPID NARI-YUKI.
WHAT DO YOU KNOW...
... ABOUT MY DREAMS AND MY HAP-PINESS?
ALL THIS TIME, I STRUG-GLED IN SCHOOL OVER...
...MY DREAM ...
...AND MY IDEA OF HAP-PINESS ...
TO BE NUMBER ONE!
I'M GOING TO DO MY VERY BEST!
AND ONCE I'VE GIVEN IT EVERY-THING I'VE GOT...
... THEN I CAN CRY MY EYES OUT!

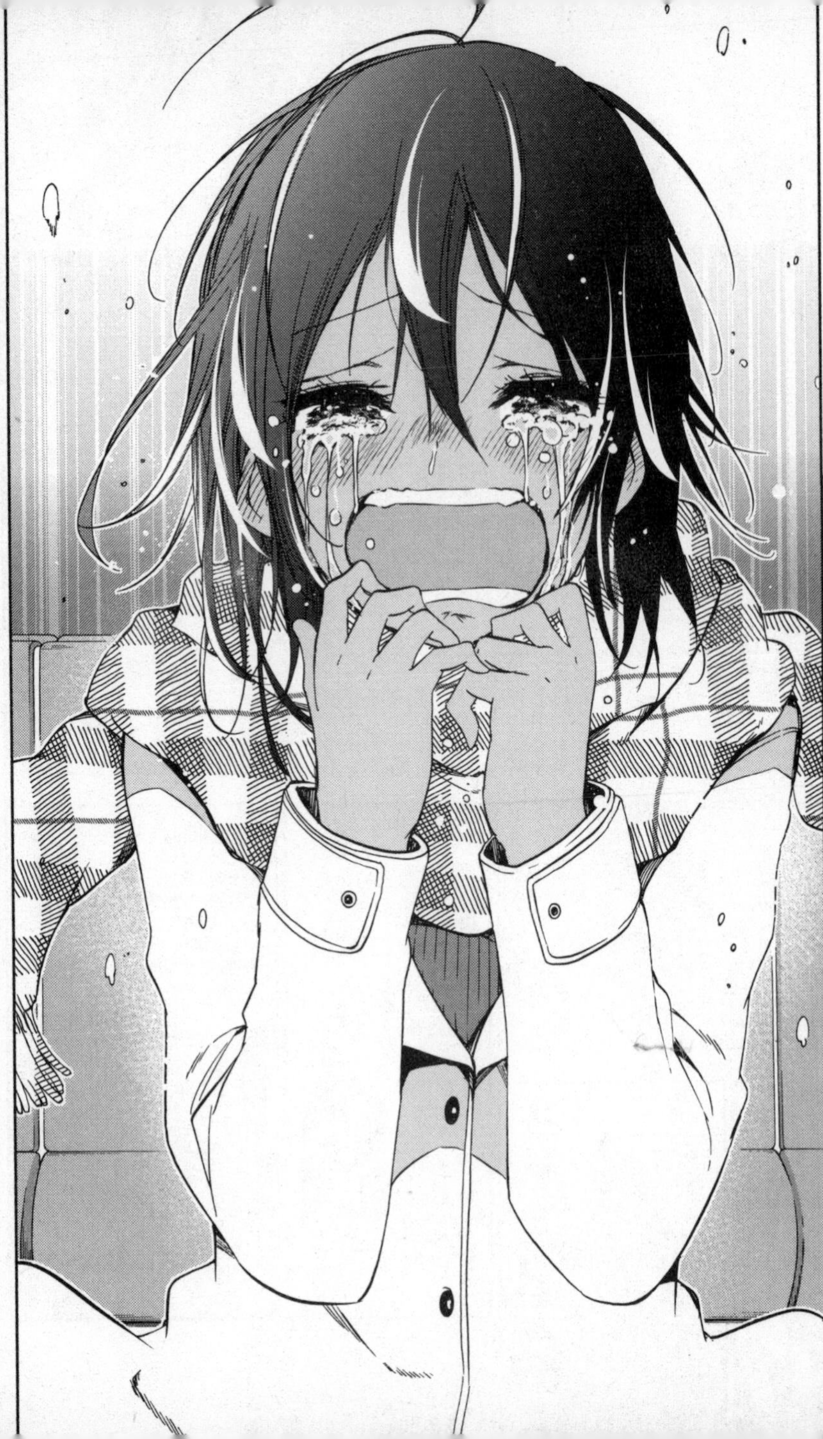

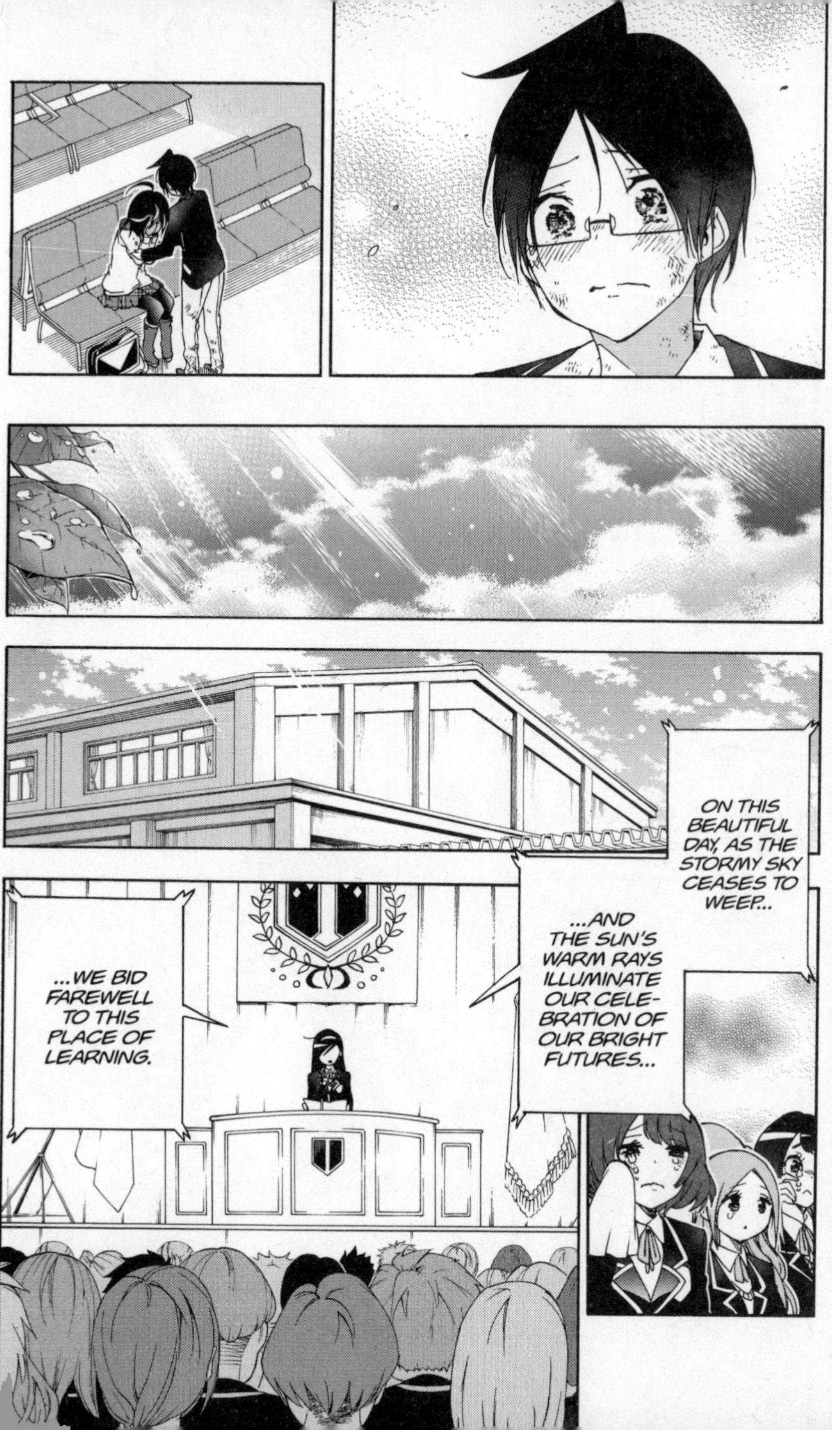
ON THIS BEAUTIFUL DAY, AS THE STORMY SKY CEASES TO WEEP...
...AND THE SUN'S WARM RAYS ILLUMINATE OUR CELE- BRATION OF OUR BRIGHT FUTURES...
...WE BID FAREWELL TO THIS PLACE OF LEARNING.

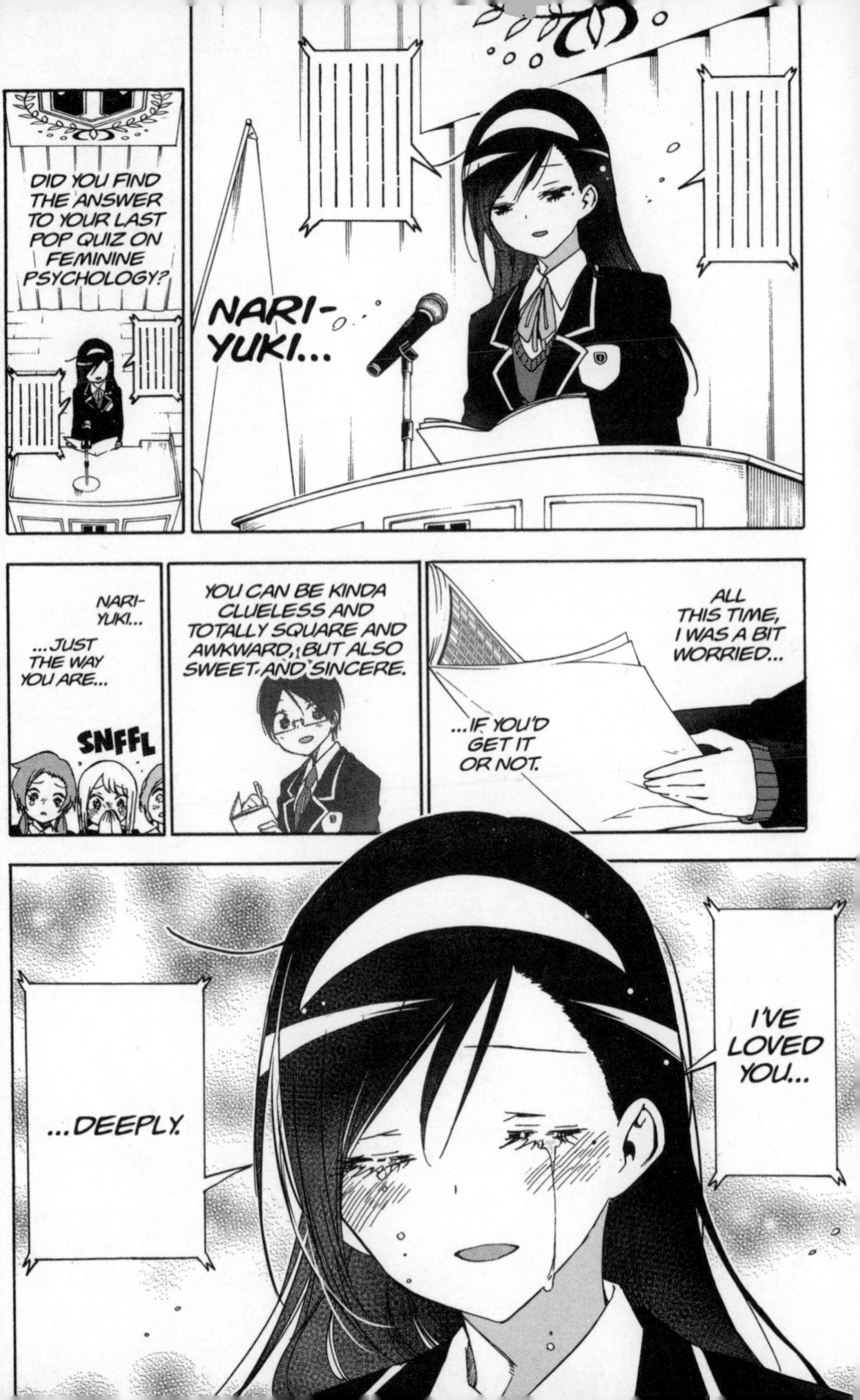
NARI-YUKI...
DID YOU FIND THE ANSWER TO YOUR LAST POP QUIZ ON FEMININE PSYCHOLOGY?
ALL THIS TIME, I WAS A BIT WORRIED...
...IF YOU'D GET IT OR NOT.
YOU CAN BE KINDA CLUELESS AND TOTALLY SQUARE AND AWKWARD, BUT ALSO SWEET AND SINCERE.
NARI-YUKI...
...JUST THE WAY YOU ARE...
SNFFL
I'VE LOVED YOU...
...DEEPLY.

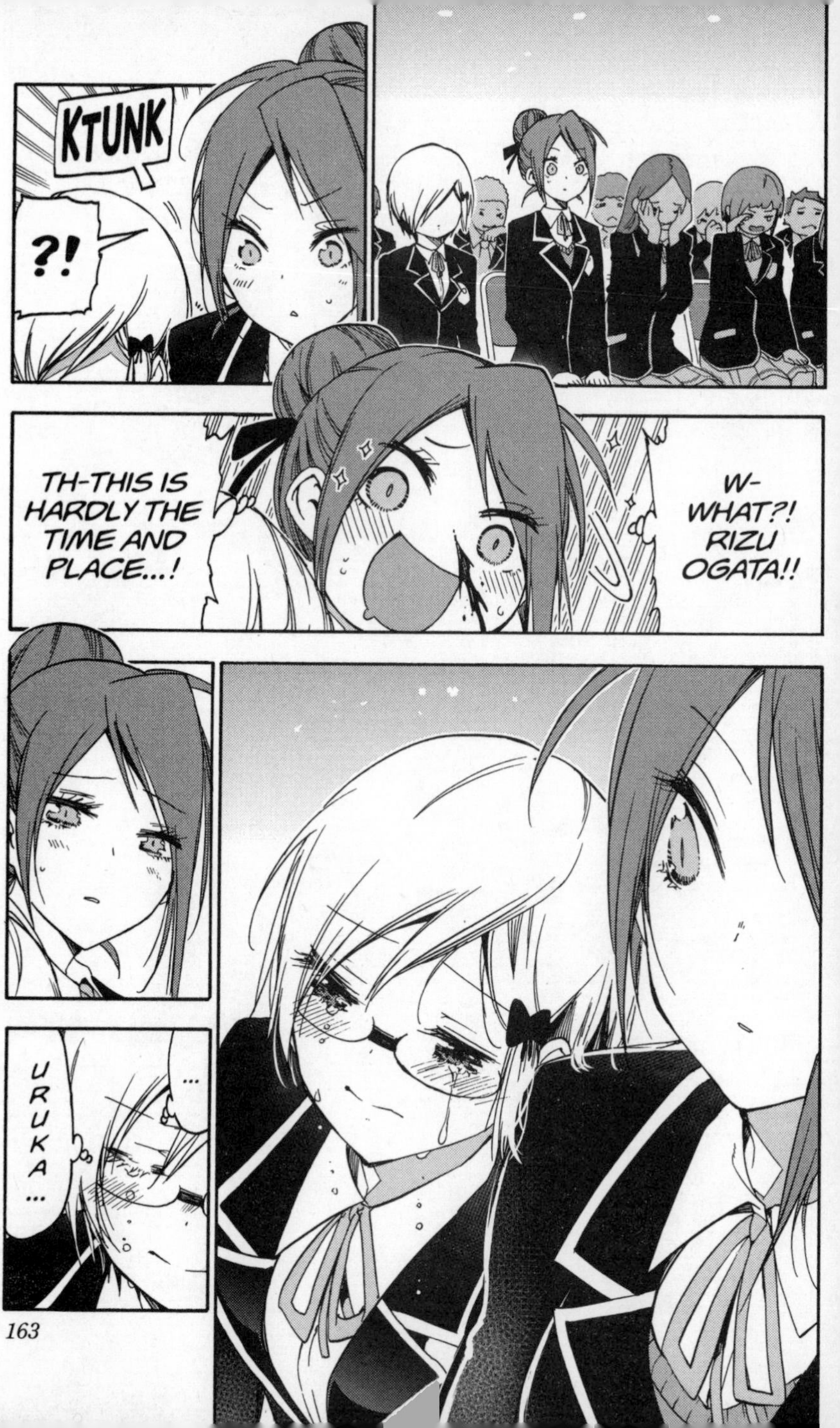
KTUNK
?!
W-WHAT?! RIZU OGATA!!
TH-THIS IS HARDLY THE TIME AND PLACE...!
...
URUKA...

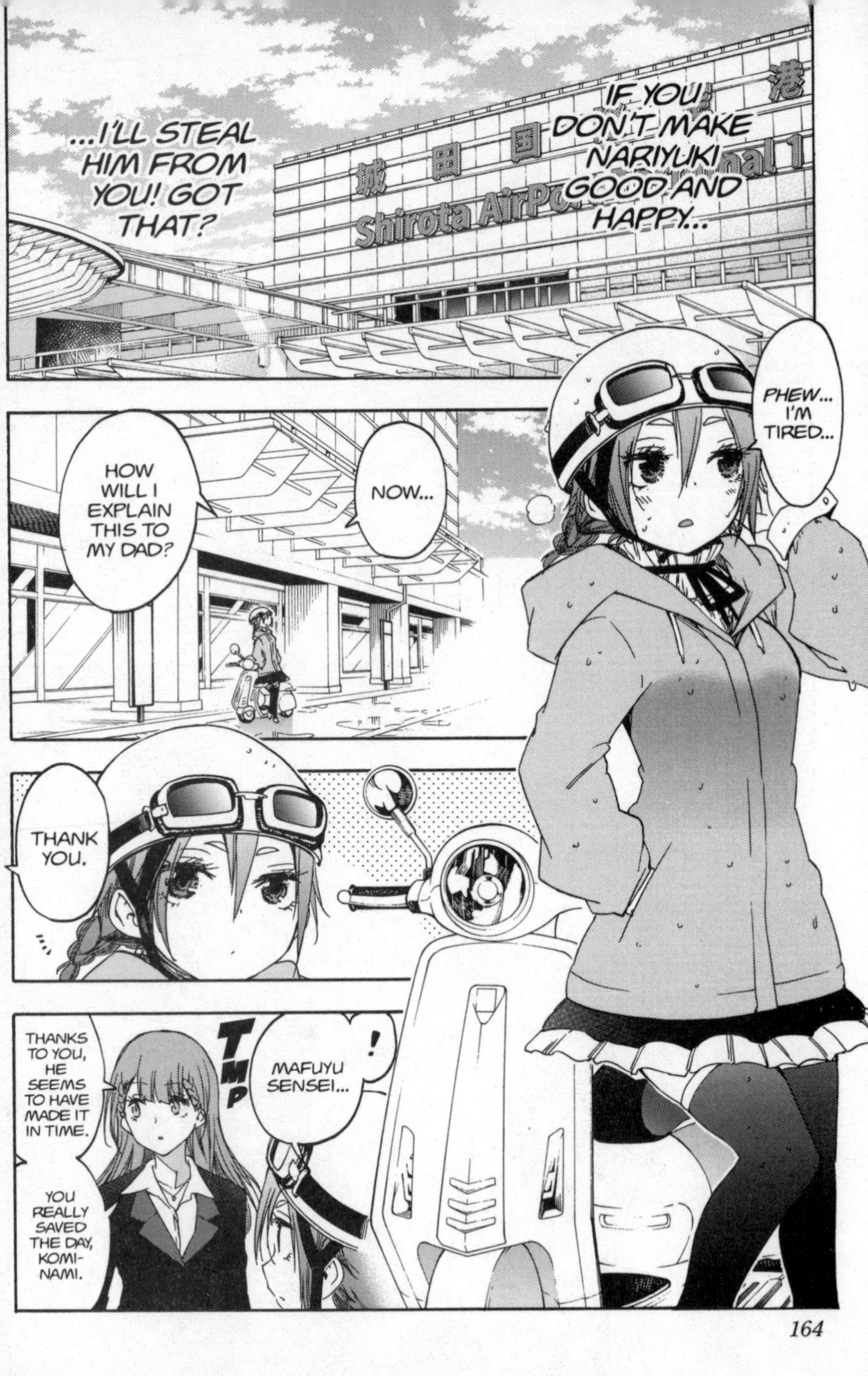
IF YOU DON'T MAKE NARIYUKI GOOD AND HAPPY...
...I'LL STEAL HIM FROM YOU! GOT THAT?
PHEW... I'M TIRED...
NOW...
HOW WILL I EXPLAIN THIS TO MY DAD?
THANK YOU.
...
!
MAFUYU SENSEI...
TMP
THANKS TO YOU, HE SEEMS TO HAVE MADE IT IN TIME.
YOU REALLY SAVED THE DAY, KOMINAMI.

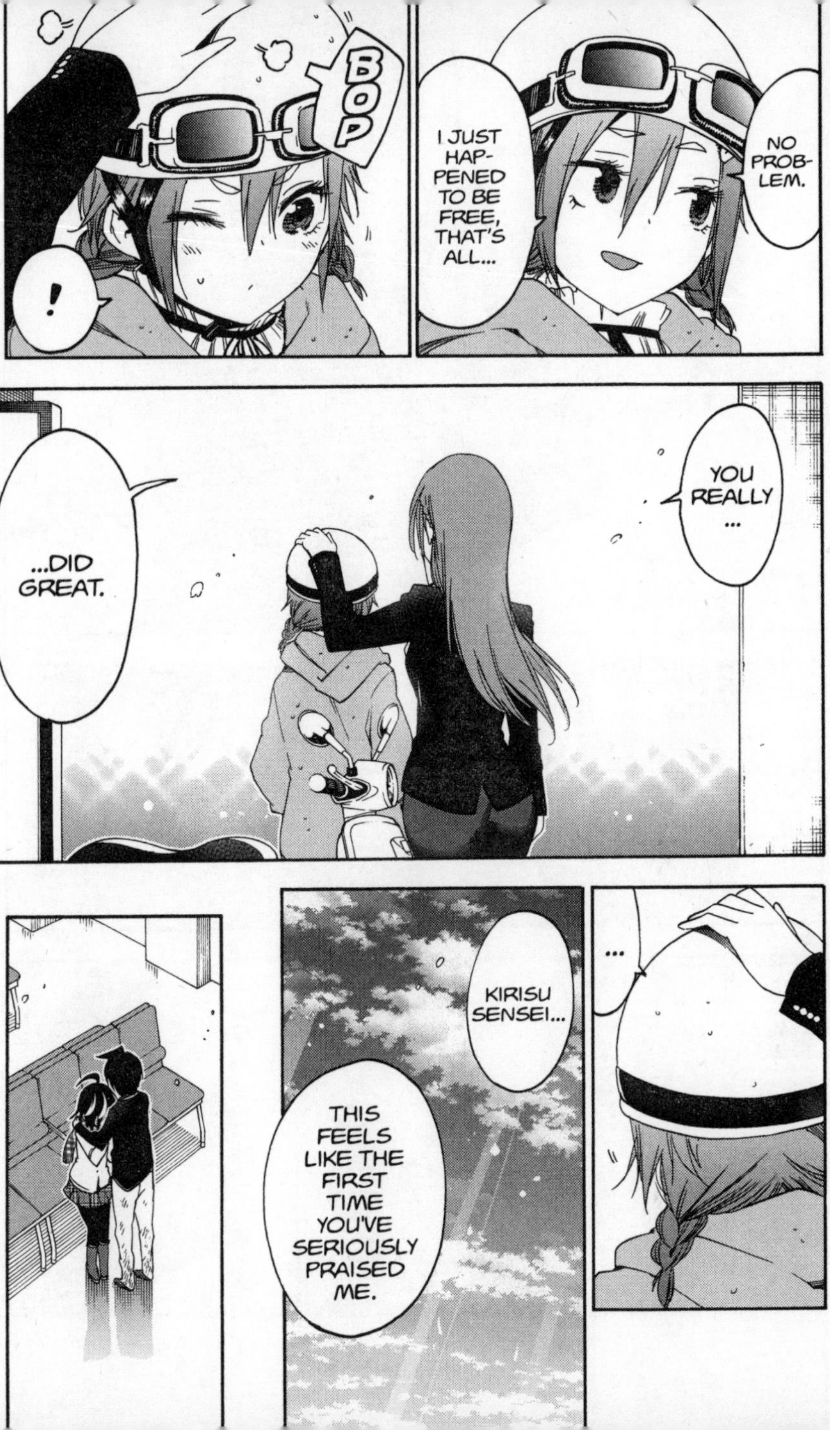
NO PROB-LEM.
I JUST HAP-PENED TO BE FREE, THAT'S ALL...
BOP
!
YOU REALLY...
...DID GREAT.
...
KIRISU SENSEI...
THIS FEELS LIKE THE FIRST TIME YOU'VE SERIOUSLY PRAISED ME.

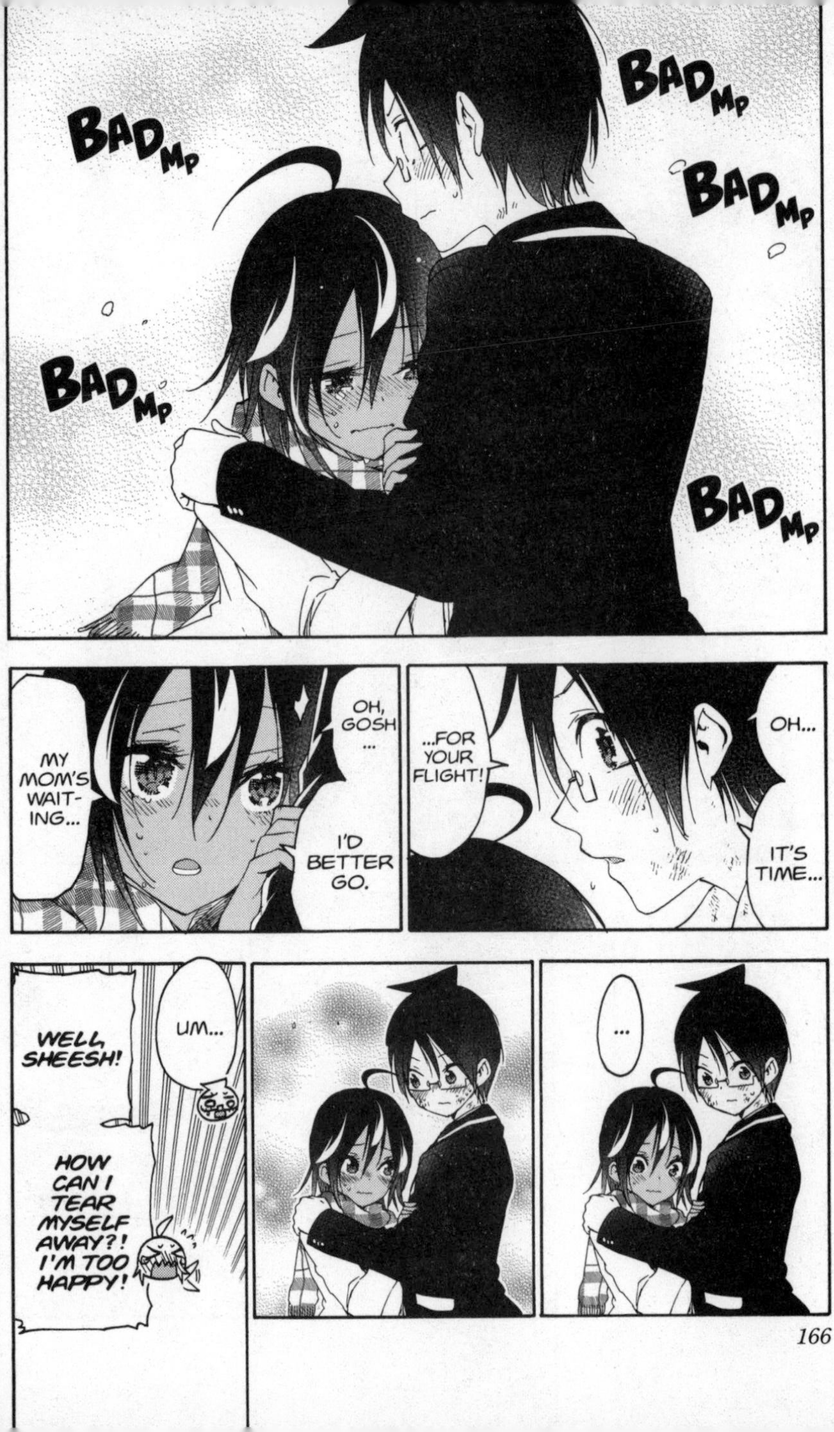
BADMP
BADMP
BADMP
BADMP
BADMP
OH...
IT'S TIME...
...FOR YOUR FLIGHT!
OH, GOSH...
I'D BETTER GO.
MY MOM'S WAITING...
...
UM...
WELL, SHEESH!
HOW CAN I TEAR MYSELF AWAY?! I'M TOO HAPPY!

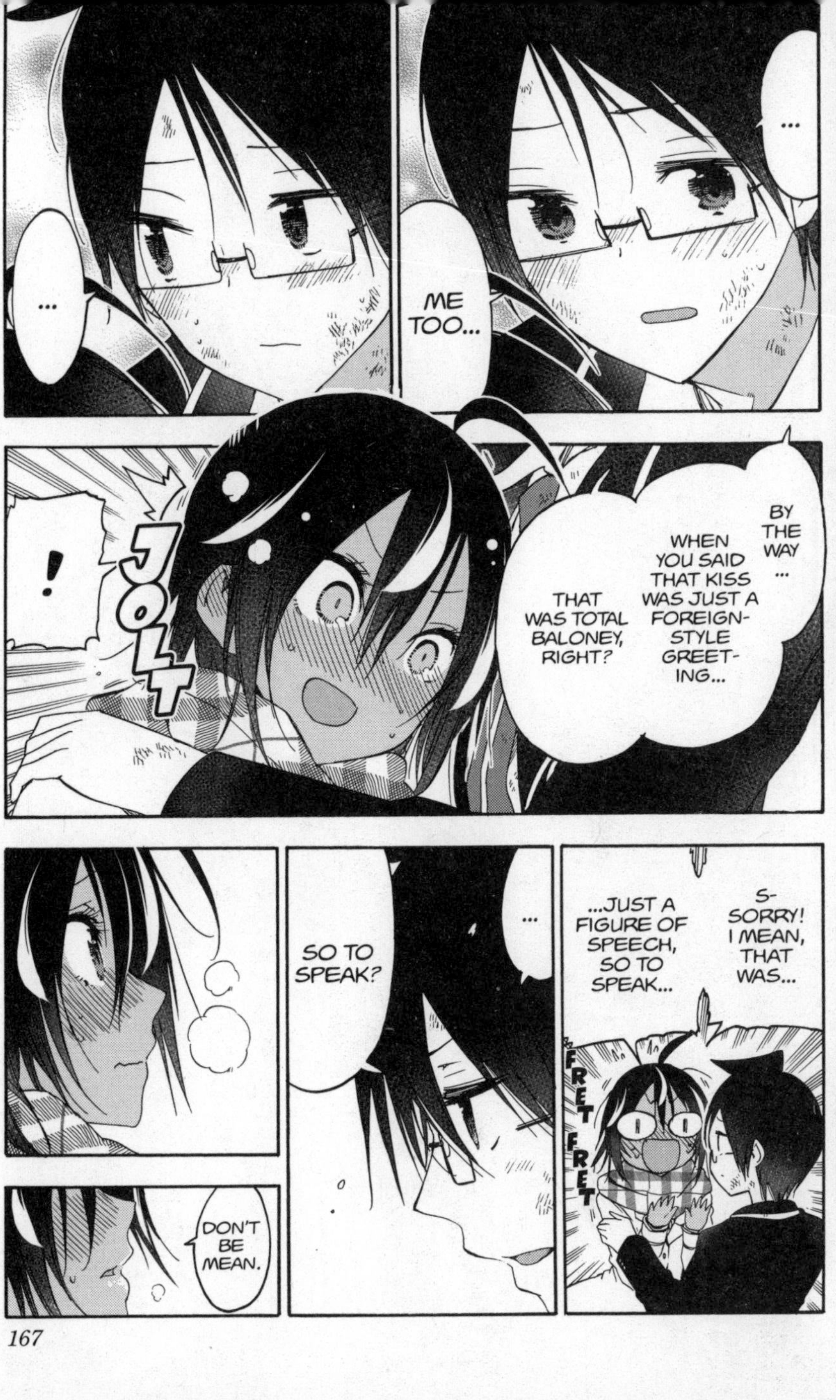
...
ME TOO...
...
BY THE WAY ... WHEN YOU SAID THAT KISS WAS JUST A FOREIGN-STYLE GREETING...
THAT WAS TOTAL BALONEY, RIGHT?
JOLT
!
S-SORRY! I MEAN, THAT WAS...
...JUST A FIGURE OF SPEECH, SO TO SPEAK...
FRET FRET
...
SO TO SPEAK?
DON'T BE MEAN.

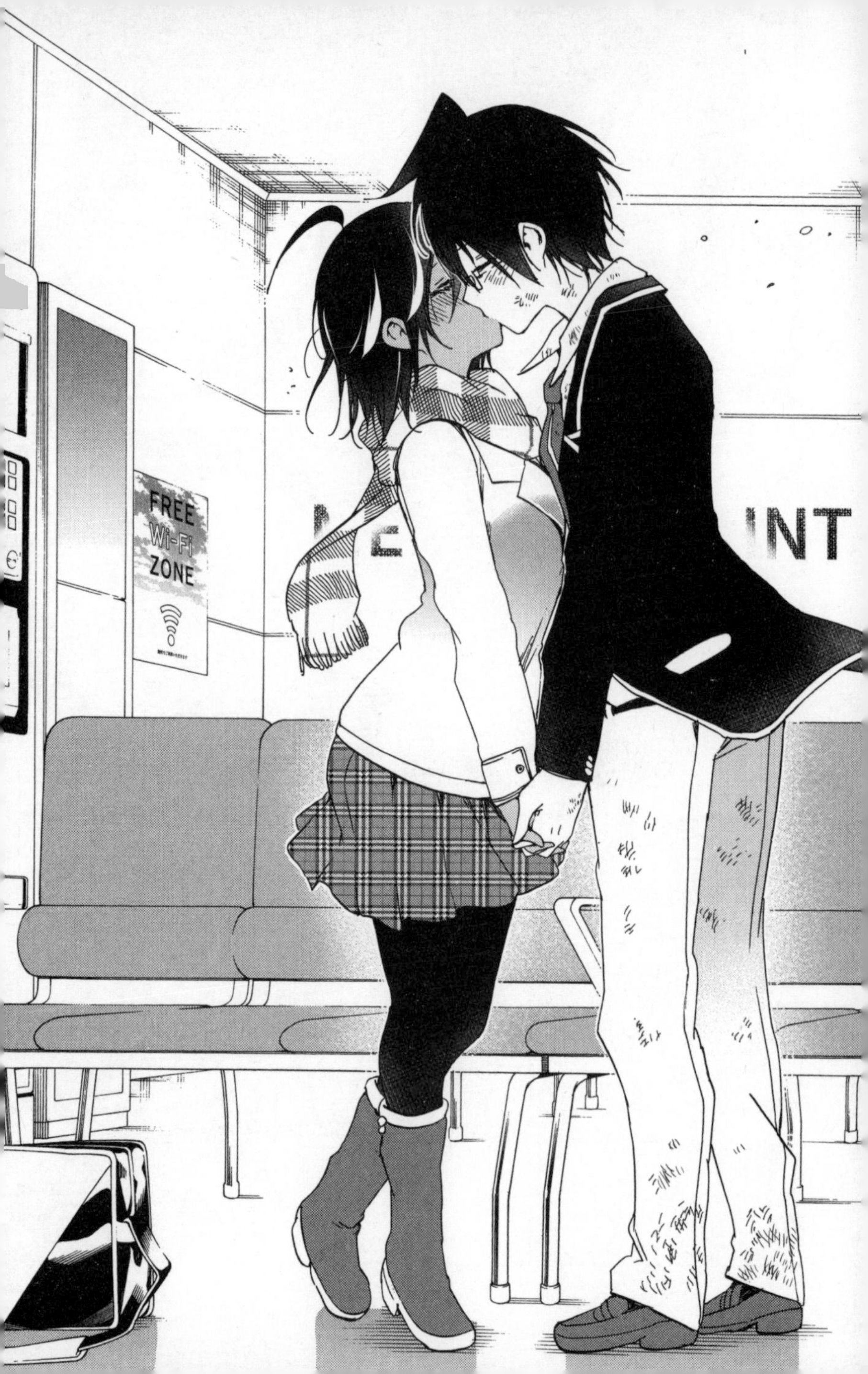
FREE
Wi-Fi
ZONE

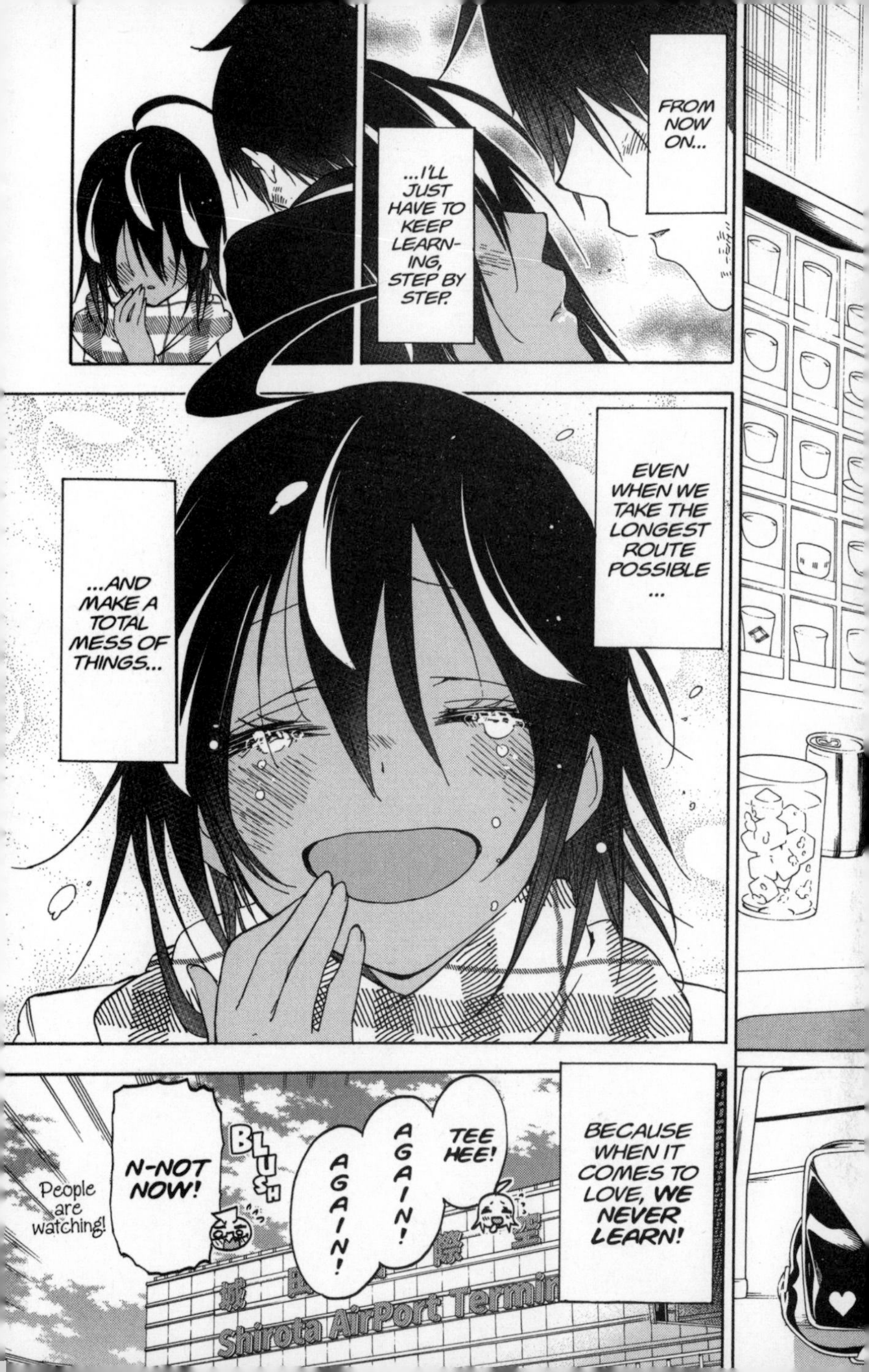
FROM NOW ON...
...I'LL JUST HAVE TO KEEP LEARNING, STEP BY STEP.
EVEN WHEN WE TAKE THE LONGEST ROUTE POSSIBLE...
...AND MAKE A TOTAL MESS OF THINGS...
BECAUSE WHEN IT COMES TO LOVE, WE NEVER LEARN!
TEE HEE!
AGAIN! AGAIN!
BLUSH
N-NOT NOW!
People are watching!
Shirota AirPort Termin

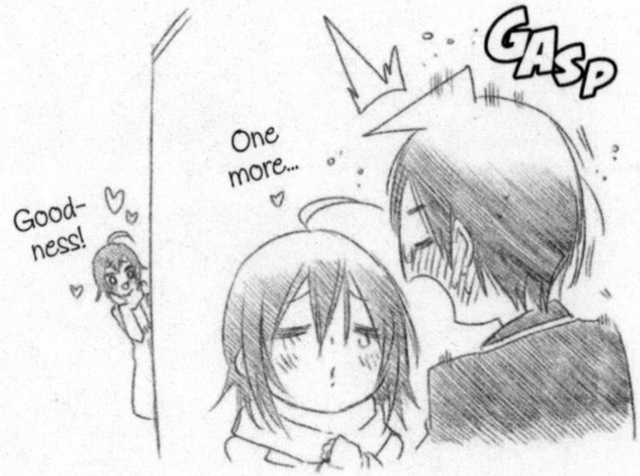
GASP
One more...
Good-
ness!

Question 150: [*X*] = ...

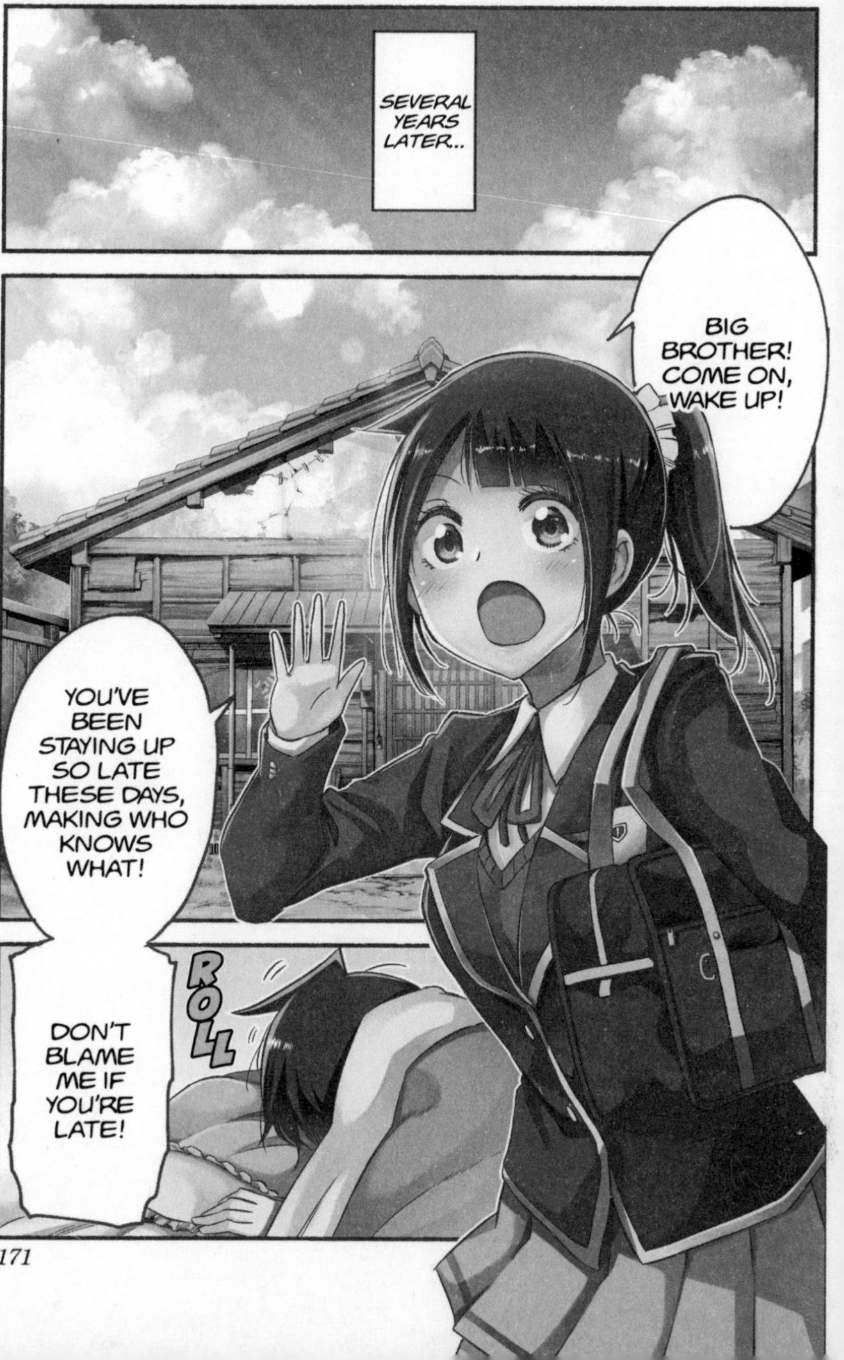
SEVERAL YEARS LATER...
BIG BROTHER! COME ON, WAKE UP!
YOU'VE BEEN STAYING UP SO LATE THESE DAYS, MAKING WHO KNOWS WHAT!
ROLL
DON'T BLAME ME IF YOU'RE LATE!

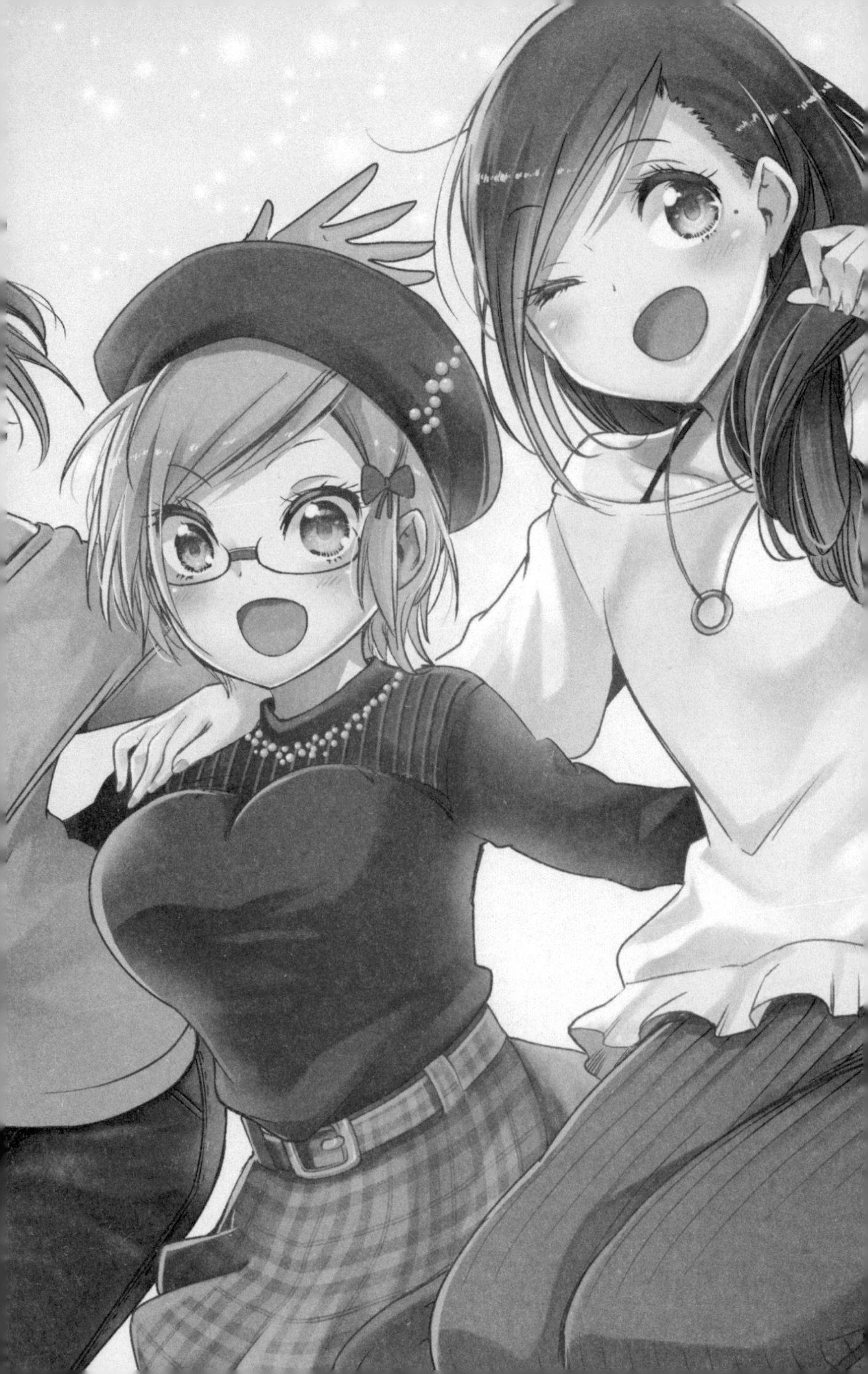

Question 150: [X] = …

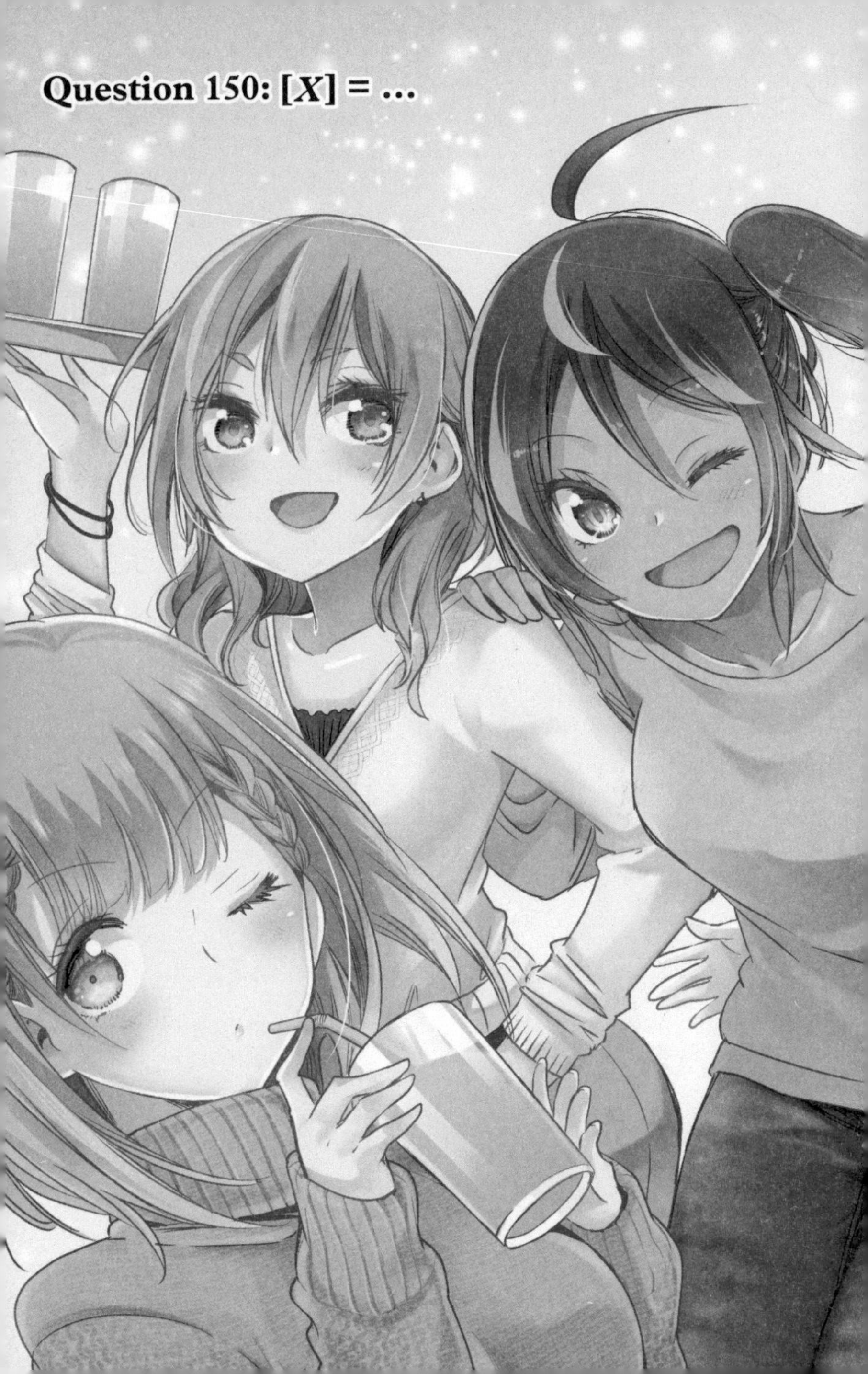

[x] We + Never ÷ × Learn

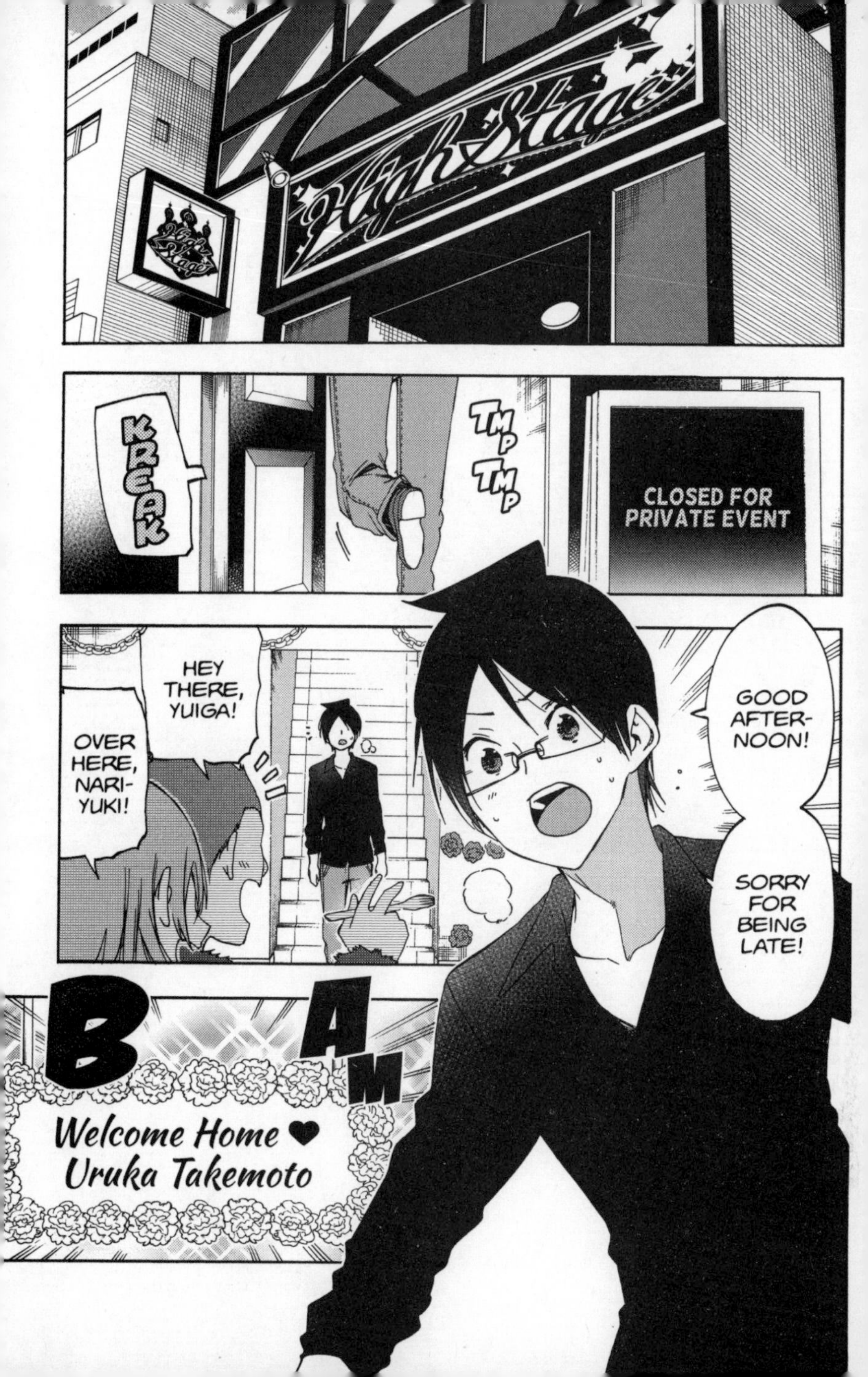
High Stage
CLOSED FOR PRIVATE EVENT
TMP TMP
KREAK
GOOD AFTER-NOON!
SORRY FOR BEING LATE!
HEY THERE, YUIGA!
OVER HERE, NARI-YUKI!
BAM
Welcome Home ❤ Uruka Takemoto

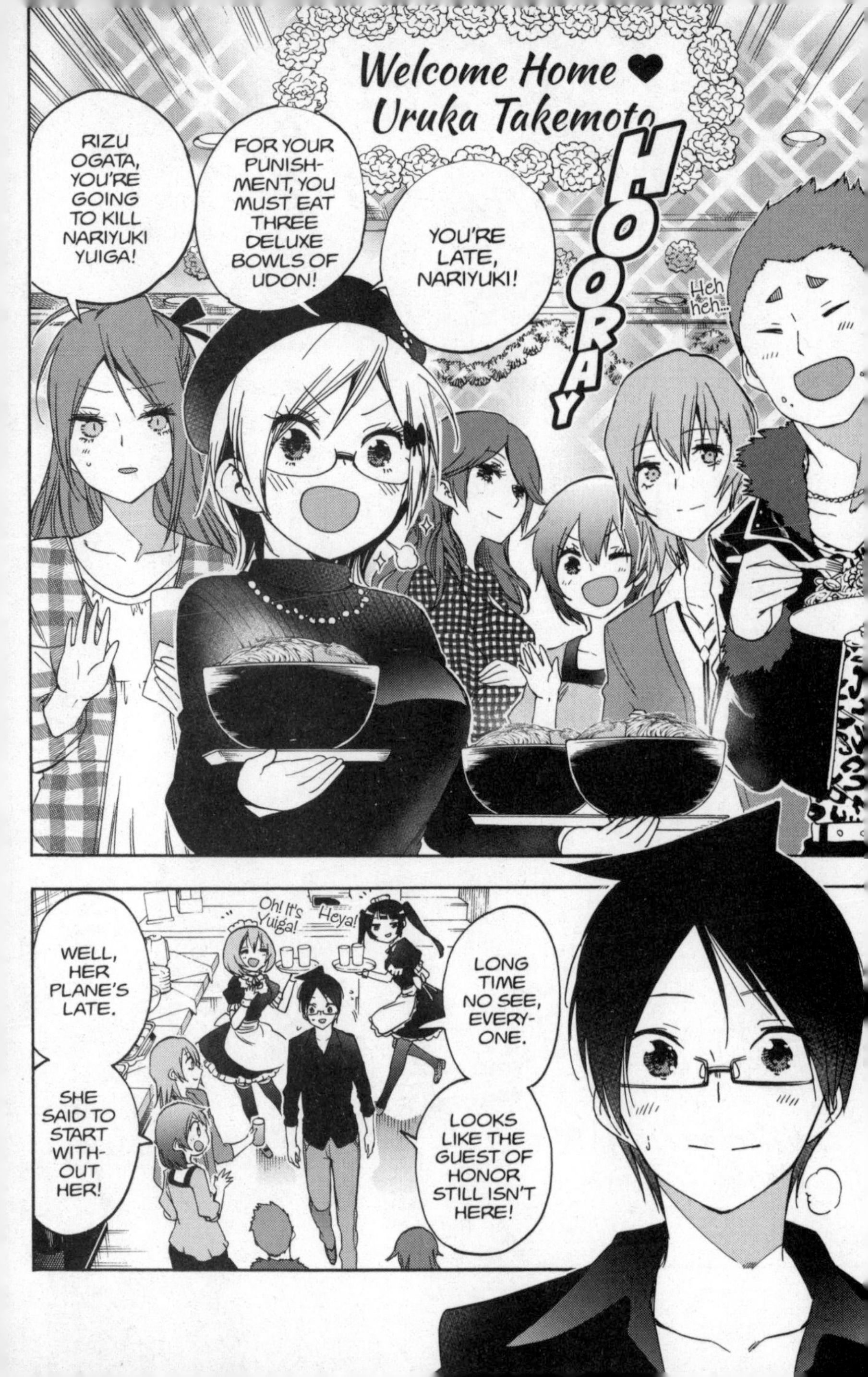
Welcome Home ♥ Uruka Takemoto
HOORAY
Heh heh...
YOU'RE LATE, NARIYUKI!
FOR YOUR PUNISHMENT, YOU MUST EAT THREE DELUXE BOWLS OF UDON!
RIZU OGATA, YOU'RE GOING TO KILL NARIYUKI YUIGA!
LONG TIME NO SEE, EVERYONE.
Heya!
Oh! It's Yuiga!
WELL, HER PLANE'S LATE.
LOOKS LIKE THE GUEST OF HONOR STILL ISN'T HERE!
SHE SAID TO START WITHOUT HER!

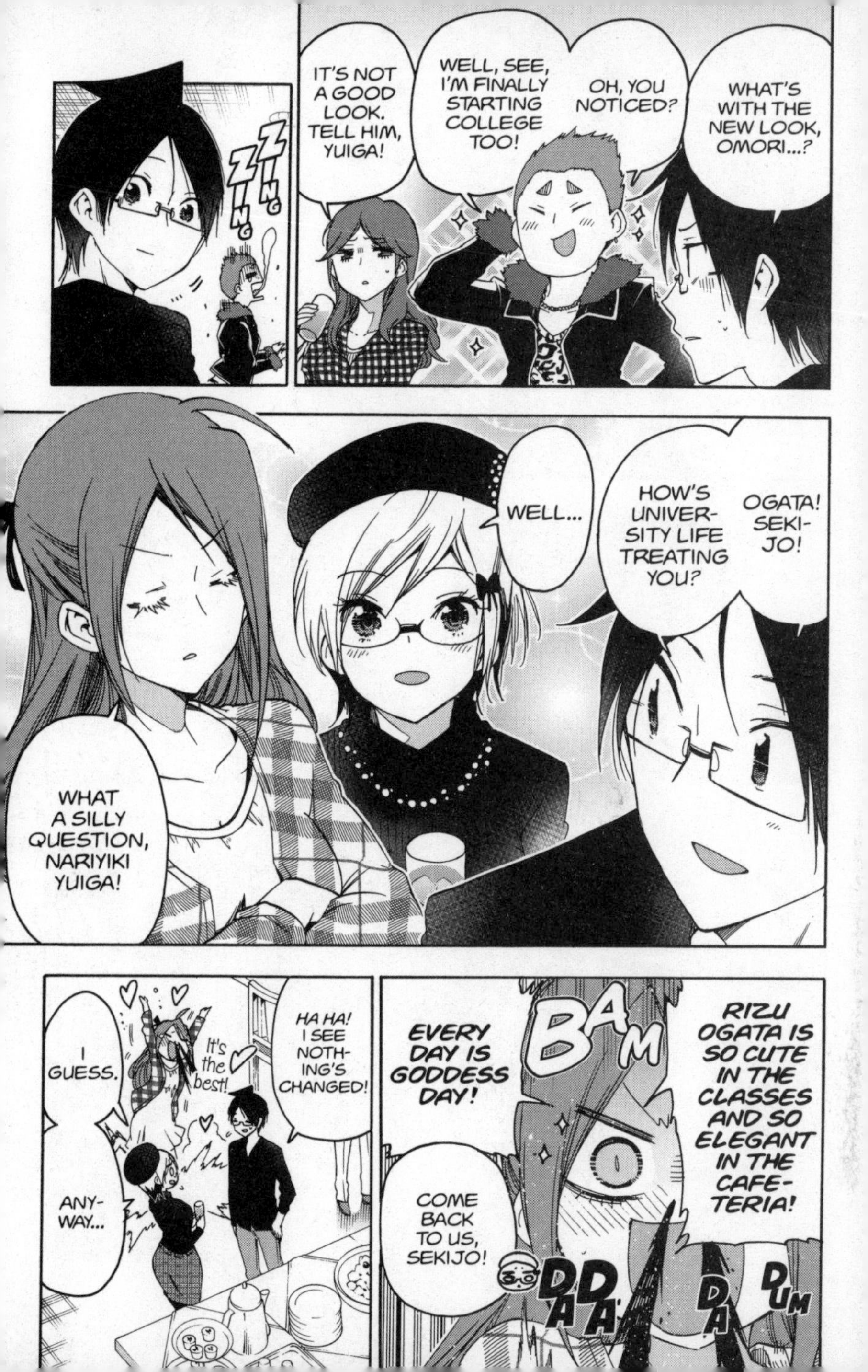
WHAT'S WITH THE NEW LOOK, OMORI...?
OH, YOU NOTICED?
WELL, SEE, I'M FINALLY STARTING COLLEGE TOO!
IT'S NOT A GOOD LOOK. TELL HIM, YUIGA!
ZING
ZING
OGATA! SEKIJO!
HOW'S UNIVERSITY LIFE TREATING YOU?
WELL...
WHAT A SILLY QUESTION, NARIYIKI YUIGA!
RIZU OGATA IS SO CUTE IN THE CLASSES AND SO ELEGANT IN THE CAFETERIA!
BAM
EVERY DAY IS GODDESS DAY!
COME BACK TO US, SEKIJO!
DA DA DA DA DUM
HA HA! I SEE NOTHING'S CHANGED!
It's the best!
I GUESS.
ANYWAY...

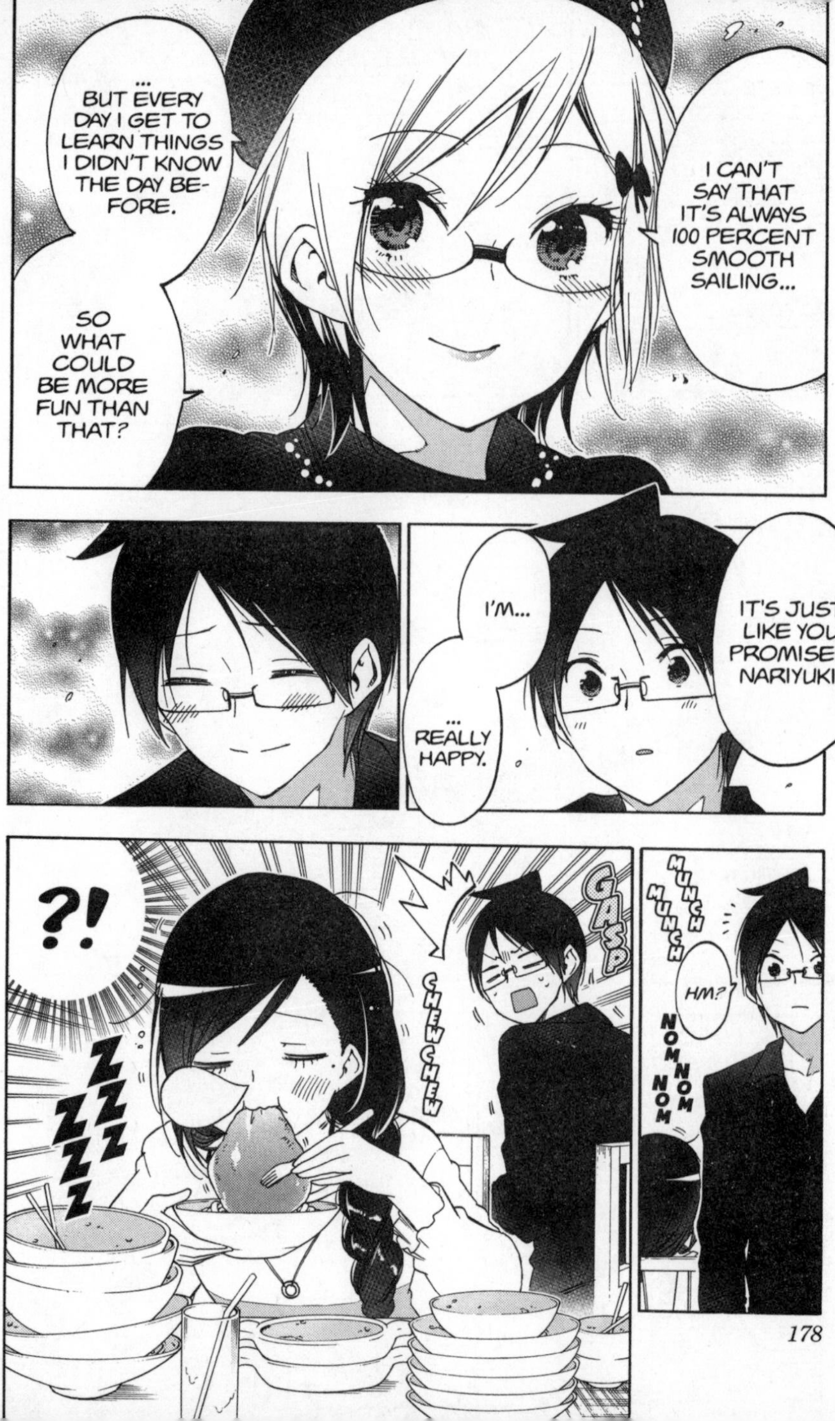
I CAN'T SAY THAT IT'S ALWAYS 100 PERCENT SMOOTH SAILING...
...BUT EVERY DAY I GET TO LEARN THINGS I DIDN'T KNOW THE DAY BE-FORE.
SO WHAT COULD BE MORE FUN THAN THAT?
IT'S JUST LIKE YOU PROMISED, NARIYUKI!
I'M...
...REALLY HAPPY.
MUNCH MUNCH
HM?
NOM NOM NOM NOM
GASP
CHEW CHEW
?!

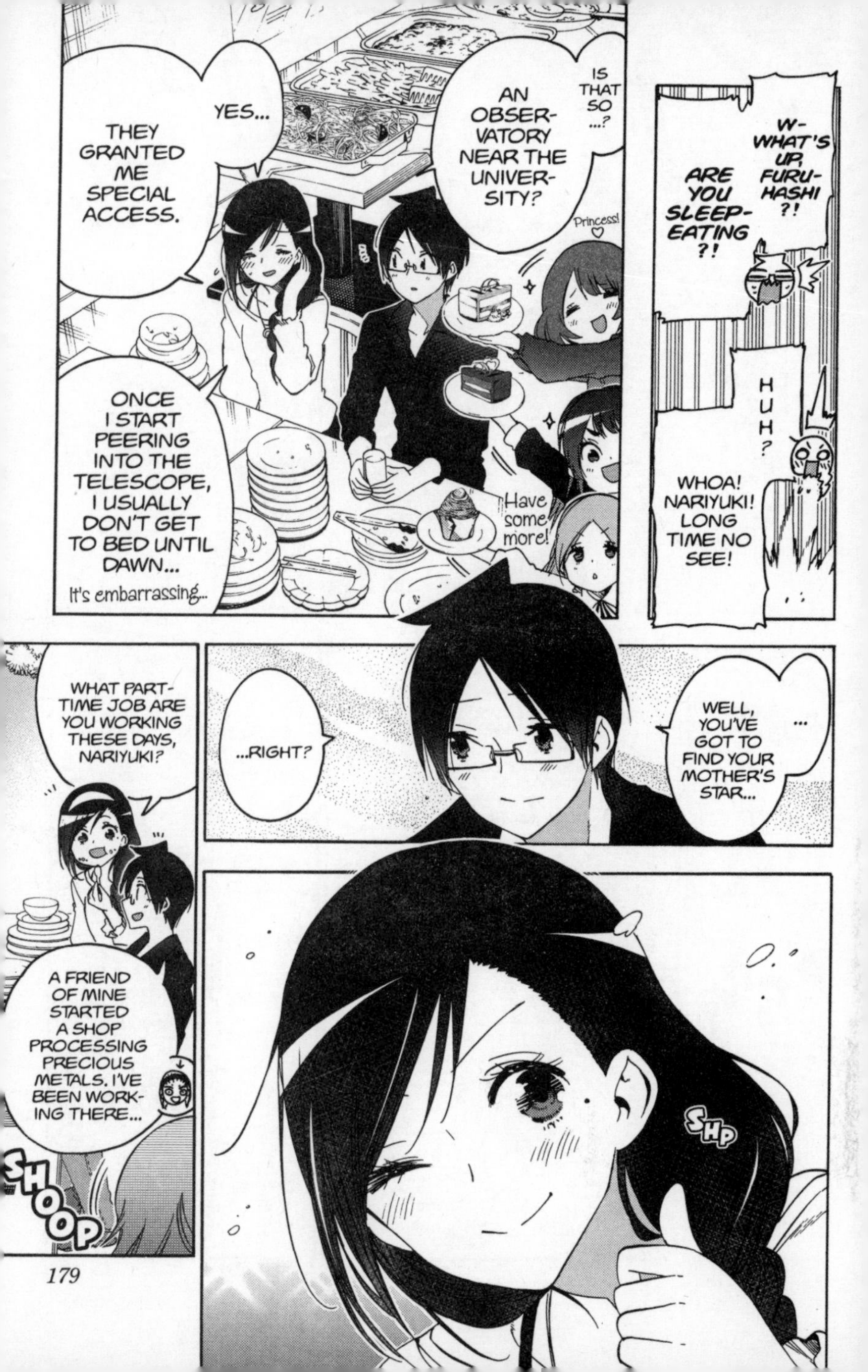

W-WHAT'S UP, FURU-HASHI?!
ARE YOU SLEEP-EATING?!
HUH?
WHOA! NARIYUKI! LONG TIME NO SEE!
AN OBSER-VATORY NEAR THE UNIVER-SITY?
IS THAT SO...?
YES...
THEY GRANTED ME SPECIAL ACCESS.
Princess!
Have some more!
ONCE I START PEERING INTO THE TELESCOPE, I USUALLY DON'T GET TO BED UNTIL DAWN...
It's embarrassing...
WELL, YOU'VE GOT TO FIND YOUR MOTHER'S STAR...
...
...RIGHT?
SHP
WHAT PART-TIME JOB ARE YOU WORKING THESE DAYS, NARIYUKI?
A FRIEND OF MINE STARTED A SHOP PROCESSING PRECIOUS METALS. I'VE BEEN WORK-ING THERE...
SHOOP

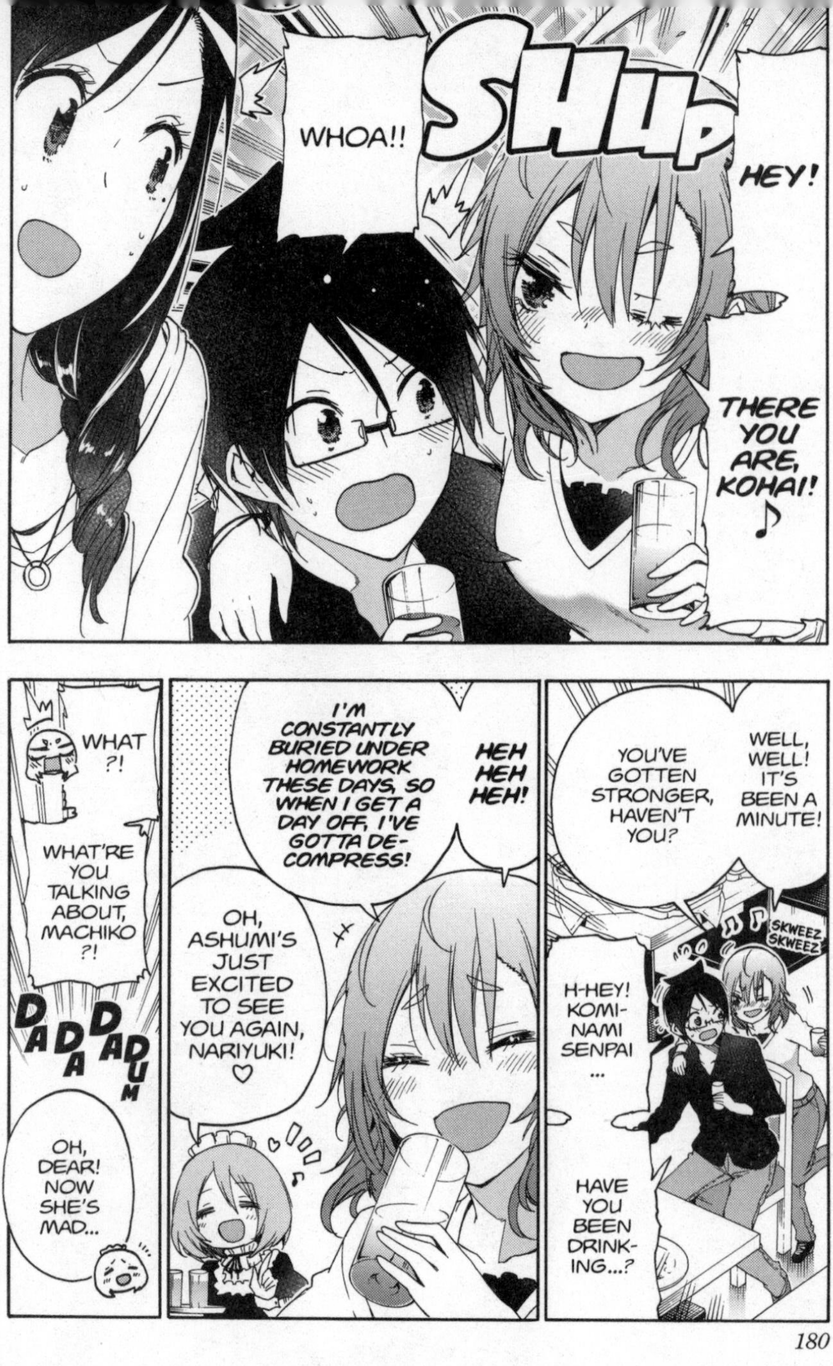
SHUP
HEY!
THERE YOU ARE, KOHAI! ♪
WHOA!!
WELL, WELL! IT'S BEEN A MINUTE!
YOU'VE GOTTEN STRONGER, HAVEN'T YOU?
SKWEEZ SKWEEZ
H-HEY! KOMINAMI SENPAI...
HAVE YOU BEEN DRINKING...?
HEH HEH HEH!
I'M CONSTANTLY BURIED UNDER HOMEWORK THESE DAYS, SO WHEN I GET A DAY OFF, I'VE GOTTA DE-COMPRESS!
OH, ASHUMI'S JUST EXCITED TO SEE YOU AGAIN, NARIYUKI! ♡
WHAT?!
WHAT'RE YOU TALKING ABOUT, MACHIKO?!
DA DA DA DA DUM
OH, DEAR! NOW SHE'S MAD...

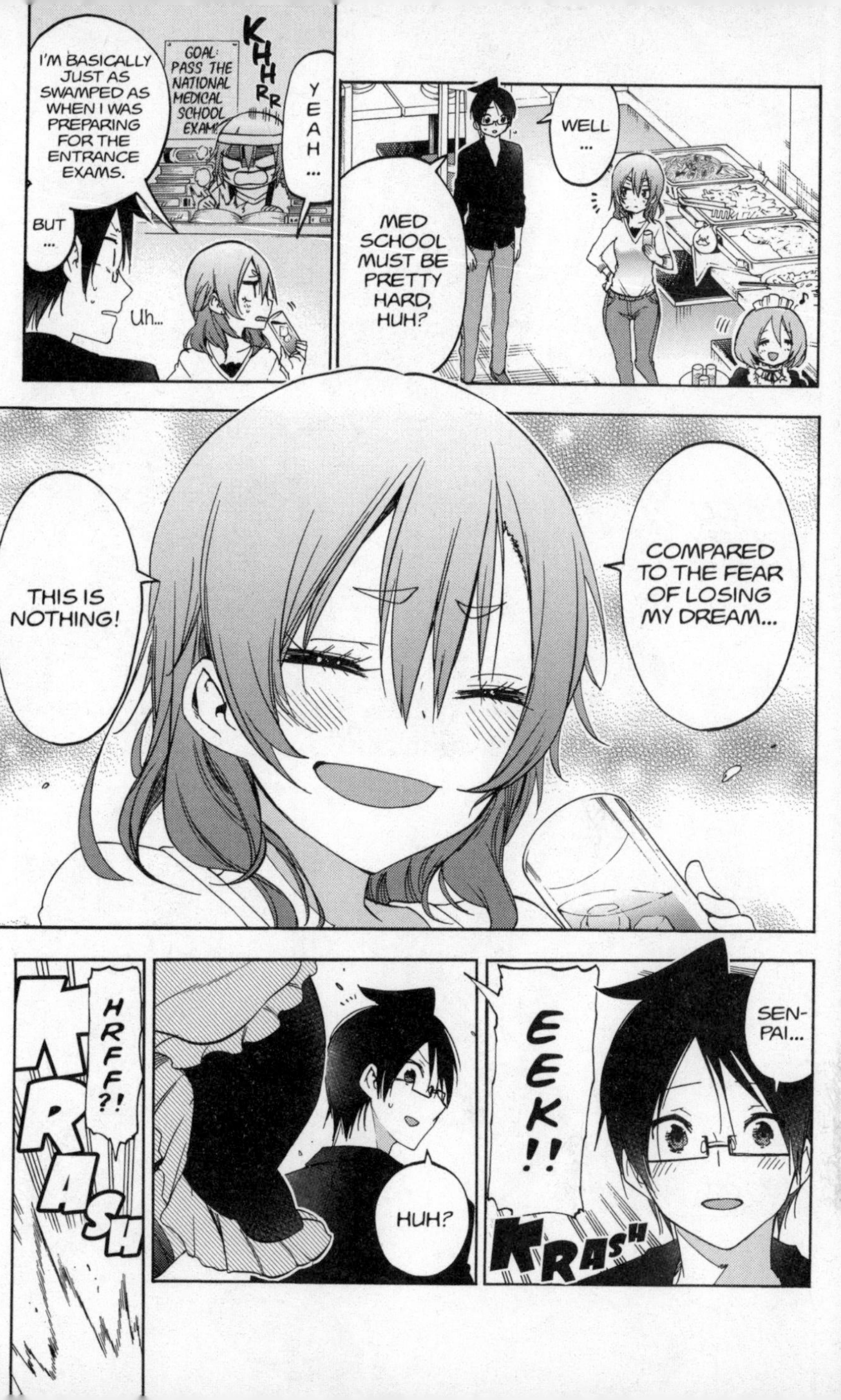
WELL ...
MED SCHOOL MUST BE PRETTY HARD, HUH?
YEAH ...
KHHRR
GOAL: PASS THE NATIONAL MEDICAL SCHOOL EXAM!
I'M BASICALLY JUST AS SWAMPED AS WHEN I WAS PREPARING FOR THE ENTRANCE EXAMS.
BUT ...
Uh...
COMPARED TO THE FEAR OF LOSING MY DREAM...
THIS IS NOTHING!
SEN-PAI...
EEK!!
KRASH
HUH?
HRFF?!
KRASH

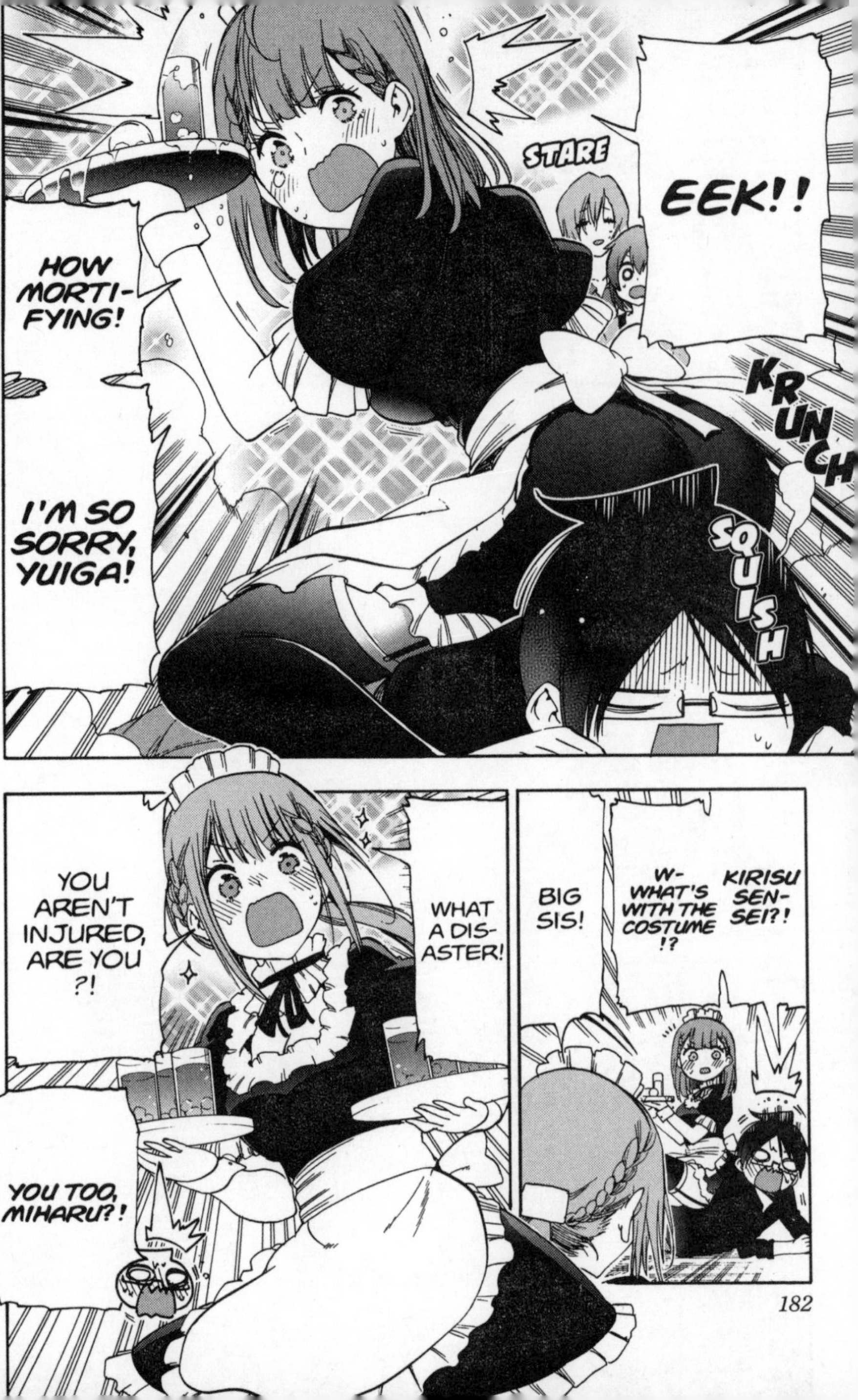
EEK!!
KRUNCH
STARE
SQUISH
HOW MORTI-FYING!
I'M SO SORRY, YUIGA!
KIRISU SEN-SEI?!
W-WHAT'S WITH THE COSTUME!?
BIG SIS!
WHAT A DIS-ASTER!
YOU AREN'T INJURED, ARE YOU?!
YOU TOO, MIHARU?!

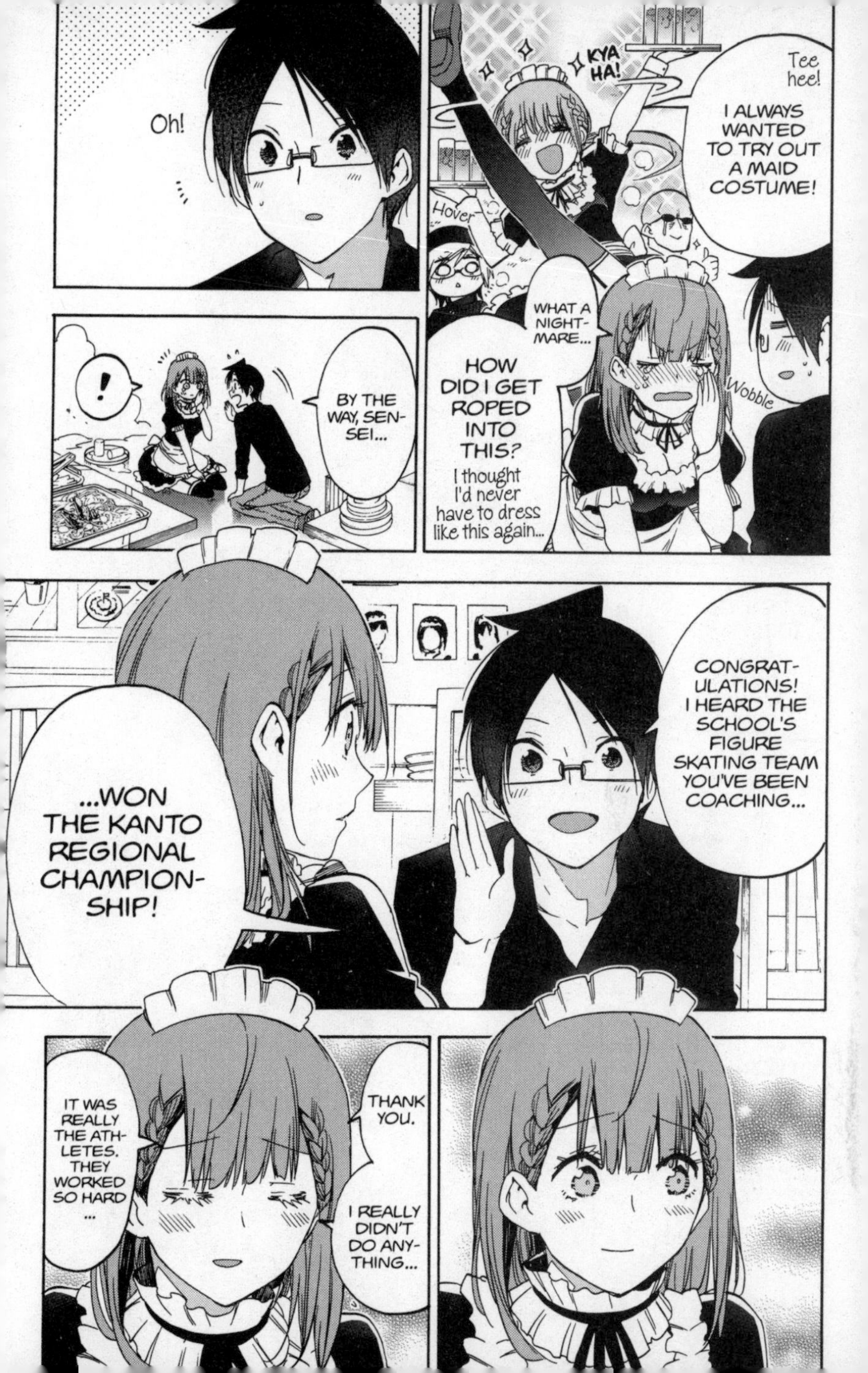
KYA HA!
Tee hee!
I ALWAYS WANTED TO TRY OUT A MAID COSTUME!
Hover
WHAT A NIGHT-MARE...
HOW DID I GET ROPED INTO THIS?
I thought I'd never have to dress like this again...
Wobble
Oh!
...
!
BY THE WAY, SEN-SEI...
CONGRAT-ULATIONS! I HEARD THE SCHOOL'S FIGURE SKATING TEAM YOU'VE BEEN COACHING...
...WON THE KANTO REGIONAL CHAMPION-SHIP!
THANK YOU.
IT WAS REALLY THE ATH-LETES. THEY WORKED SO HARD ...
I REALLY DIDN'T DO ANY-THING...

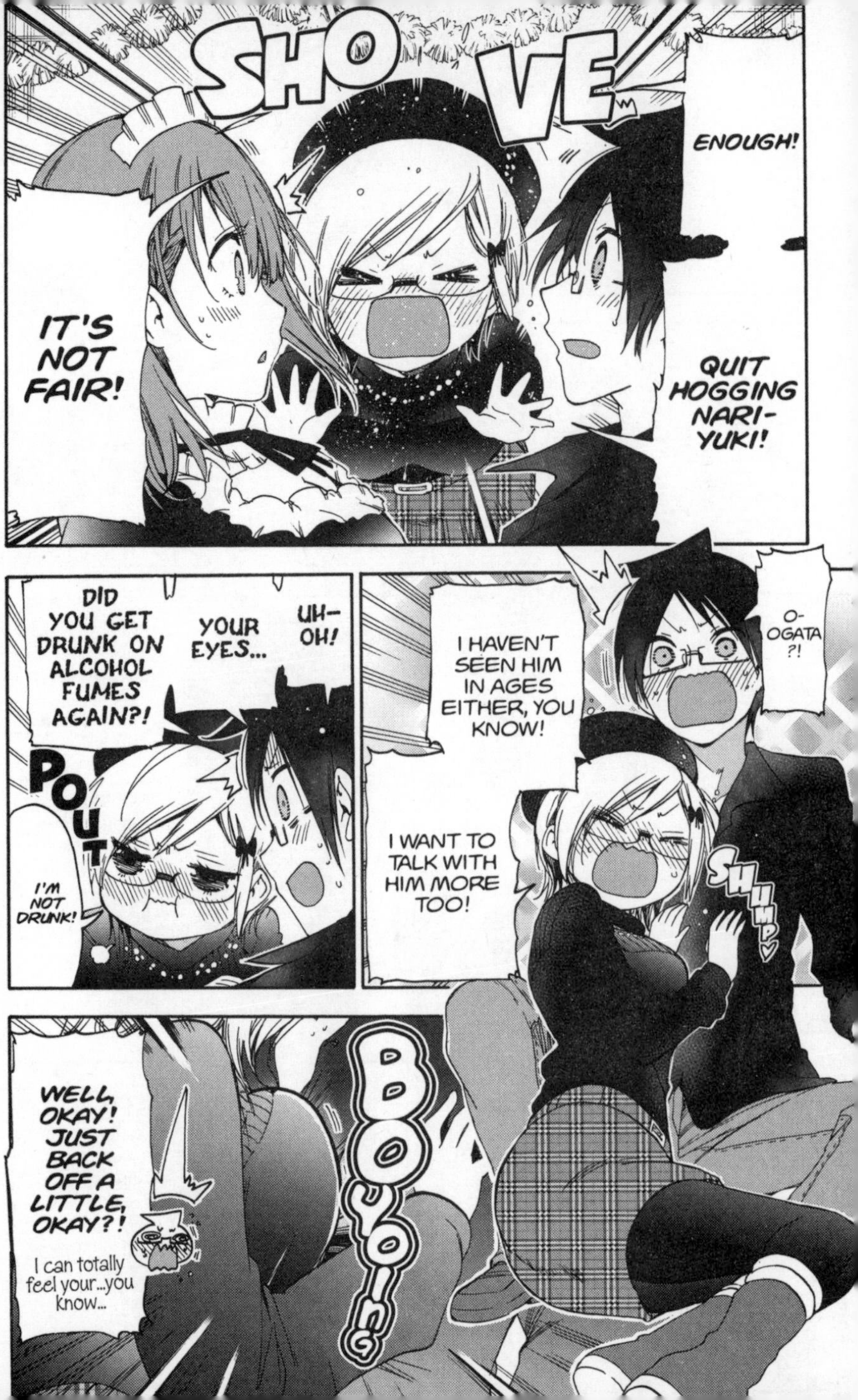
SHOVE
ENOUGH!
QUIT HOGGING NARI-YUKI!
IT'S NOT FAIR!
O-OGATA?!
I HAVEN'T SEEN HIM IN AGES EITHER, YOU KNOW!
I WANT TO TALK WITH HIM MORE TOO!
SHUMP
UH-OH!
YOUR EYES...
DID YOU GET DRUNK ON ALCOHOL FUMES AGAIN?!
POUT
I'M NOT DRUNK!
BOYOING
WELL, OKAY! JUST BACK OFF A LITTLE, OKAY?!
I can totally feel your...you know...

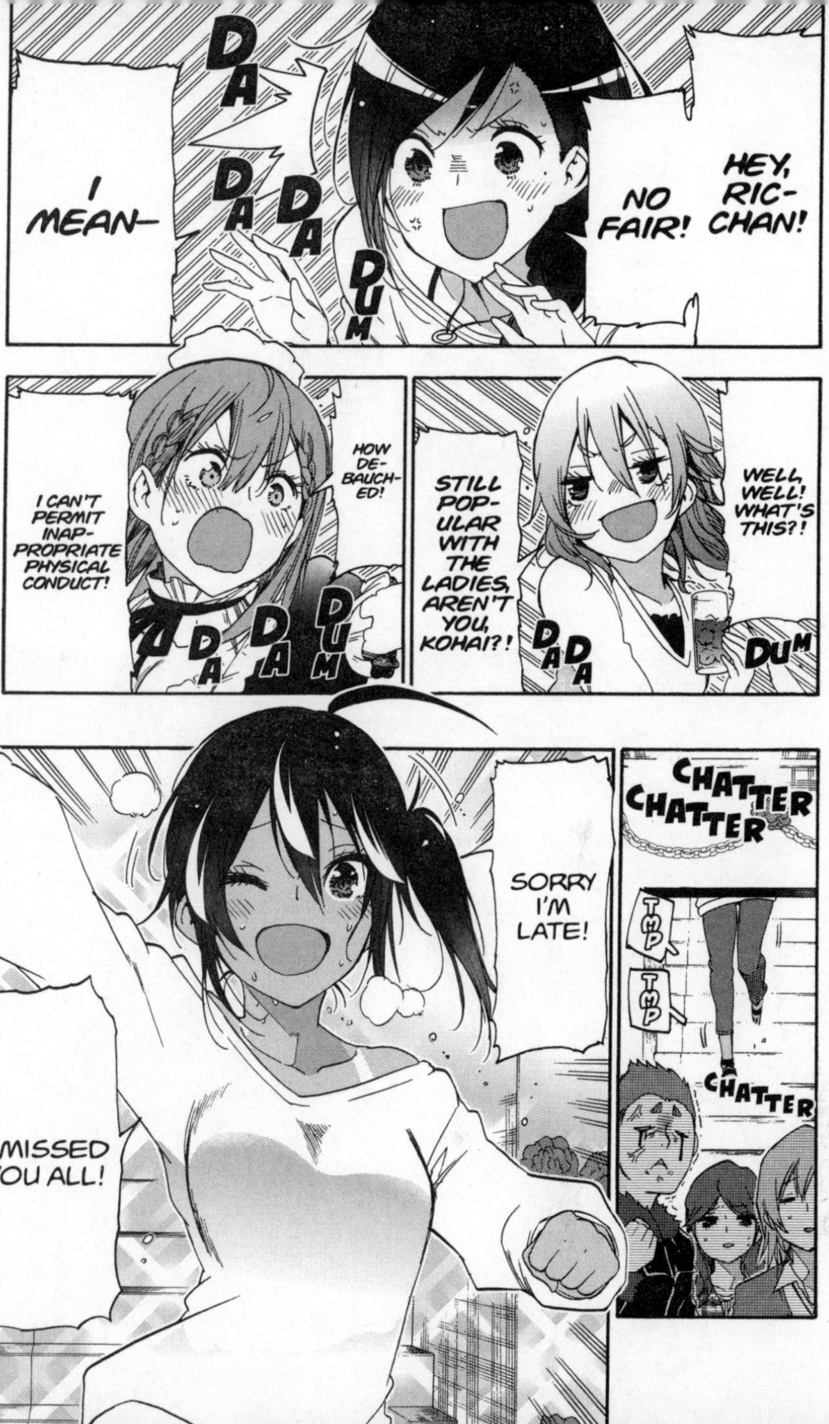
HEY, RIC-CHAN!
NO FAIR!
DA DA DA DA DUM
I MEAN—
WELL, WELL! WHAT'S THIS?!
STILL POPULAR WITH THE LADIES, AREN'T YOU, KOHAI?!
DA DA DUM
HOW DEBAUCHED!
I CAN'T PERMIT INAPPROPRIATE PHYSICAL CONDUCT!
DA DA DA DUM
CHATTER CHATTER
TMP TMP
CHATTER
SORRY I'M LATE!
I MISSED YOU ALL!

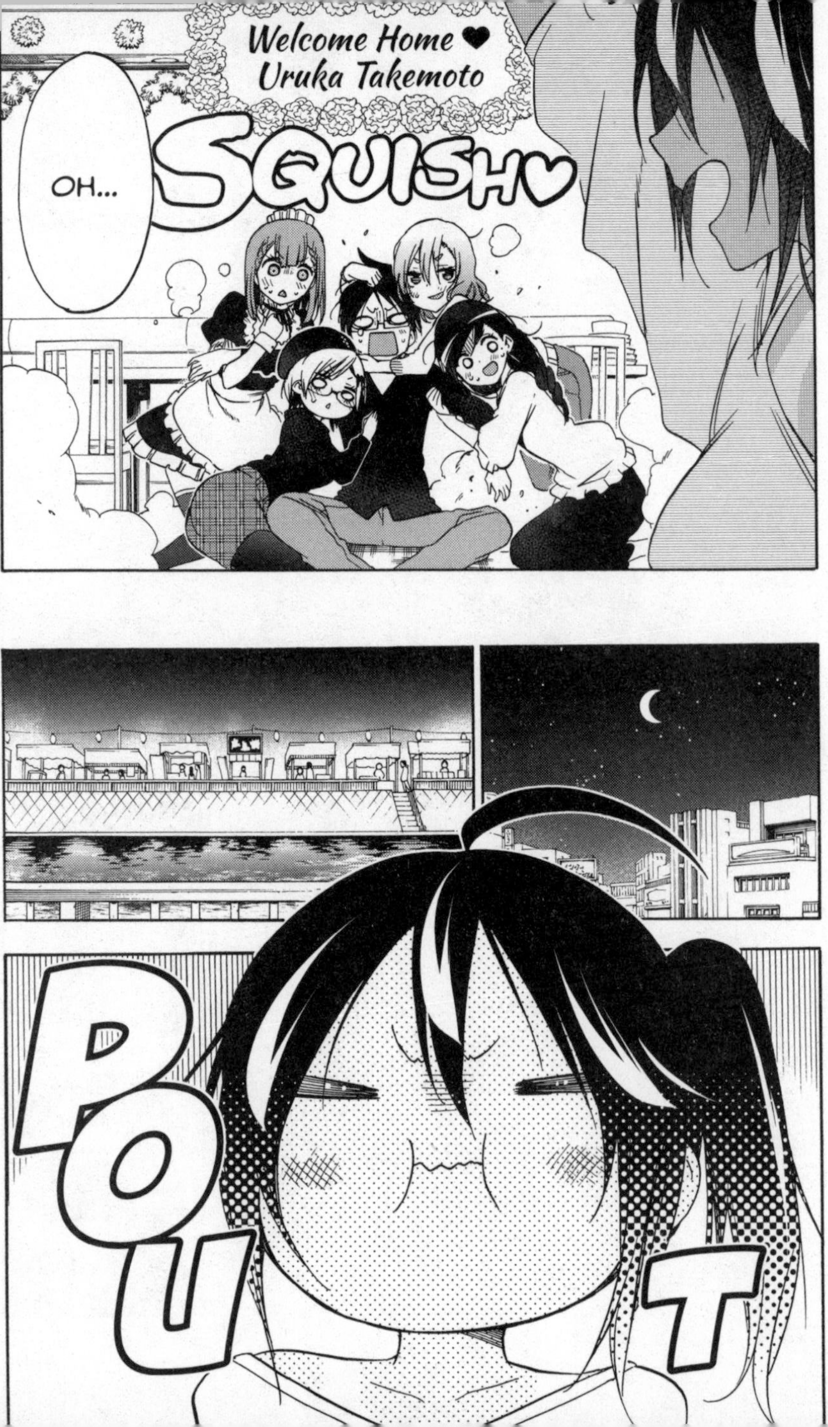
Welcome Home ♥
Uruka Takemoto
SQUISH♥
OH...
POUT

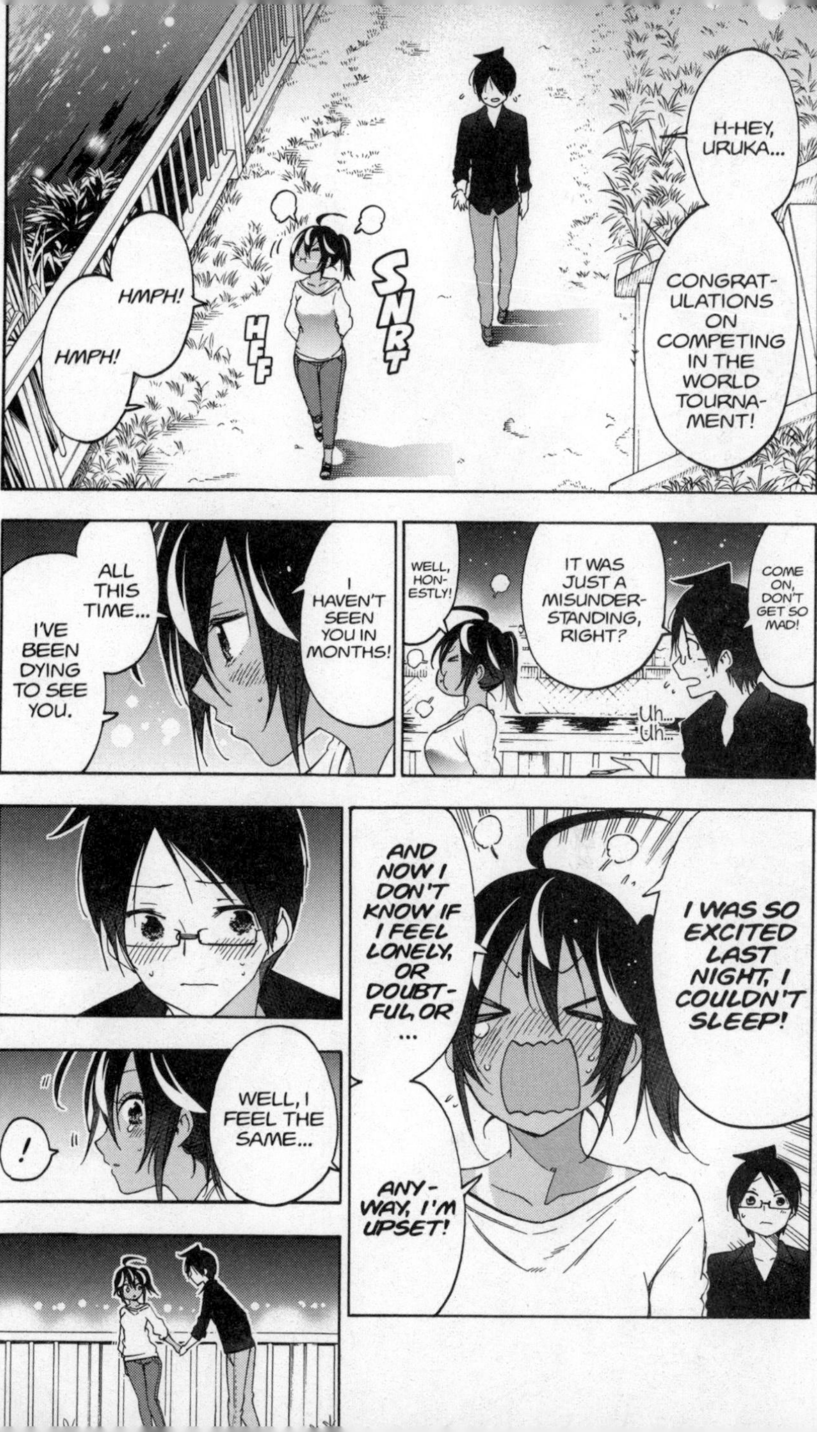
H-HEY, URUKA...
CONGRATULATIONS ON COMPETING IN THE WORLD TOURNAMENT!
SNRT
HFF
HMPH!
HMPH!
COME ON, DON'T GET SO MAD!
IT WAS JUST A MISUNDERSTANDING, RIGHT?
Uh... Uh...
WELL, HONESTLY!
I HAVEN'T SEEN YOU IN MONTHS!
ALL THIS TIME...
I'VE BEEN DYING TO SEE YOU.
I WAS SO EXCITED LAST NIGHT, I COULDN'T SLEEP!
AND NOW I DON'T KNOW IF I FEEL LONELY, OR DOUBTFUL, OR ...
ANYWAY, I'M UPSET!
WELL, I FEEL THE SAME...
!

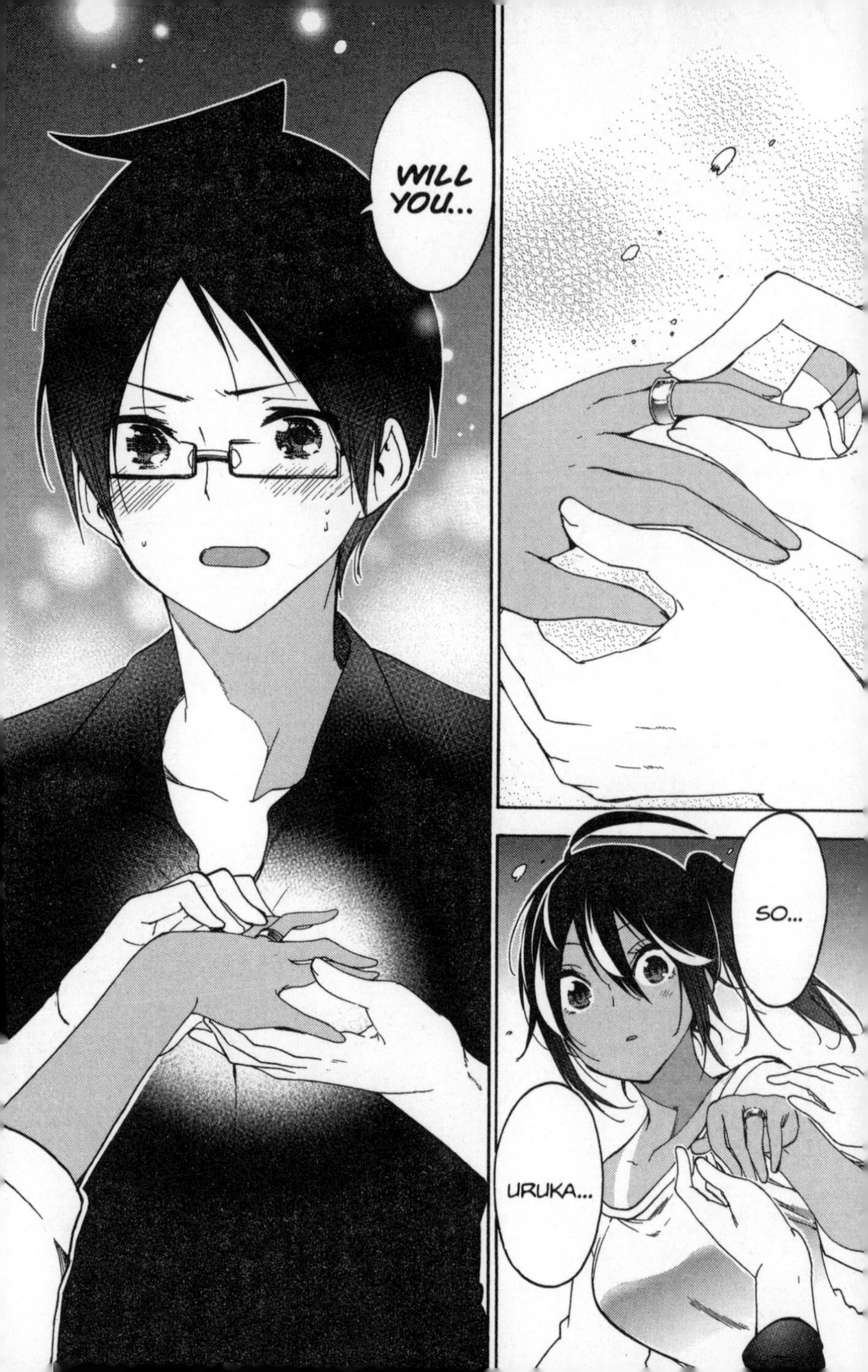
SO...
URUKA...
WILL YOU...

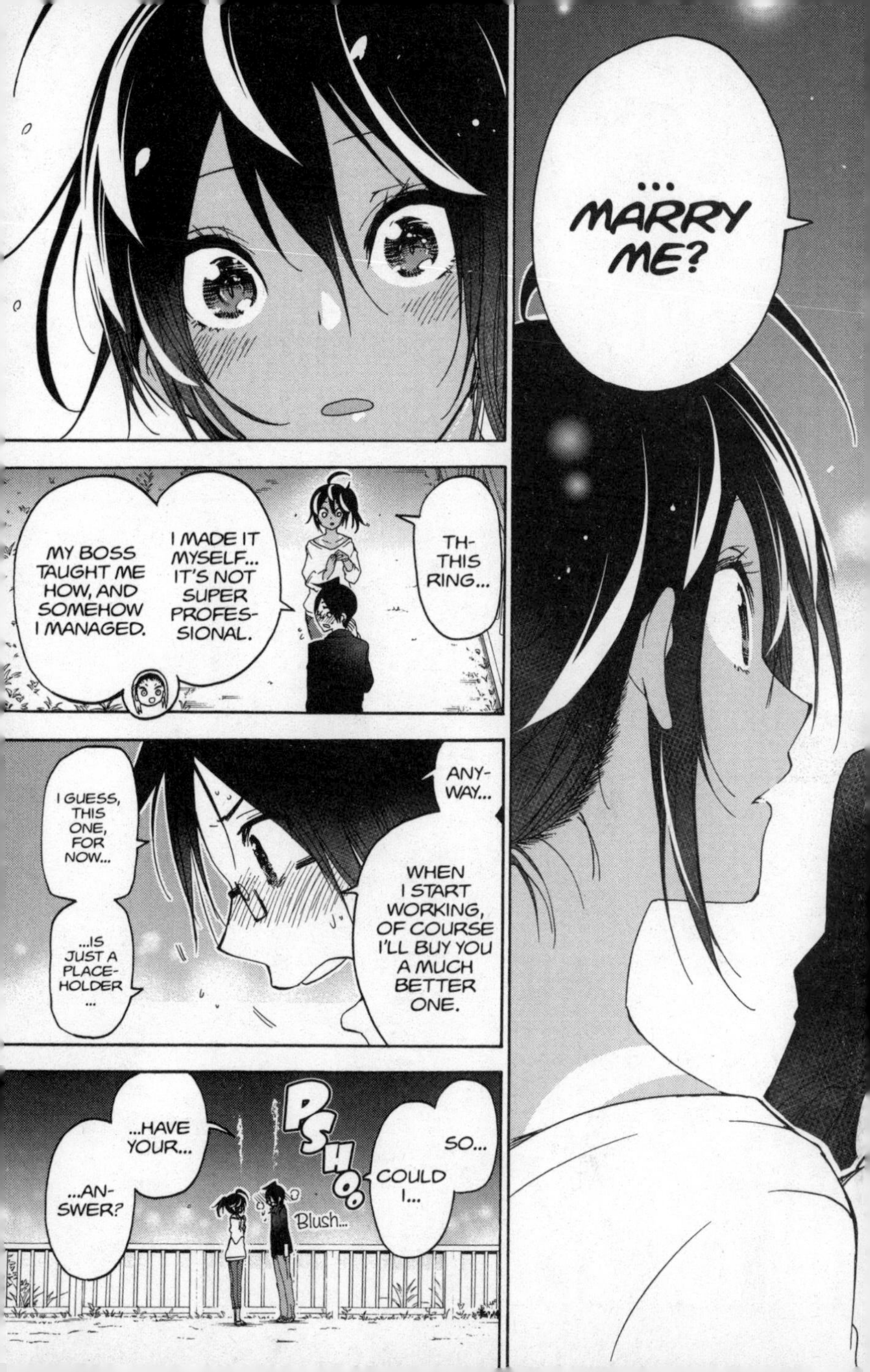
...MARRY ME?
TH-THIS RING...
I MADE IT MYSELF... IT'S NOT SUPER PROFESSIONAL.
MY BOSS TAUGHT ME HOW, AND SOMEHOW I MANAGED.
ANYWAY...
WHEN I START WORKING, OF COURSE I'LL BUY YOU A MUCH BETTER ONE.
I GUESS, THIS ONE, FOR NOW...
...IS JUST A PLACEHOLDER...
SO...
COULD I...
PSHOO
Blush...
...HAVE YOUR...
...ANSWER?

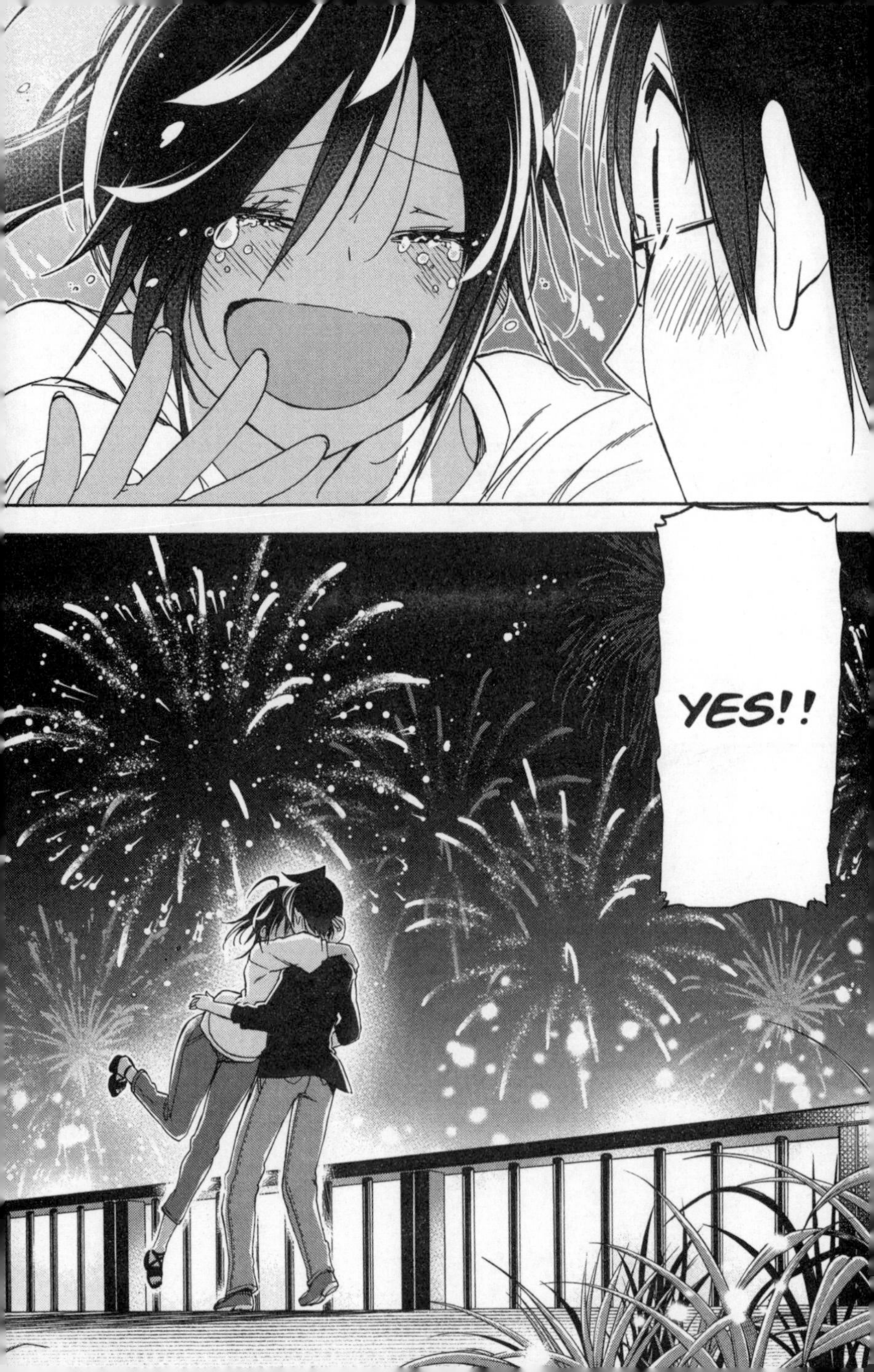
YES!!

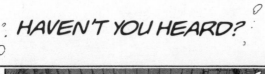

HAVEN'T YOU HEARD?
WHEN THEY SHOOT OFF THE FIRST FIREWORK ON THE FINAL NIGHT OF THE FESTIVAL...
...IF A BOY AND GIRL ARE TOUCHING WHEN IT EXPLODES...
...THEY'LL BE BOUND BY FATE.

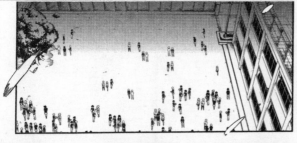

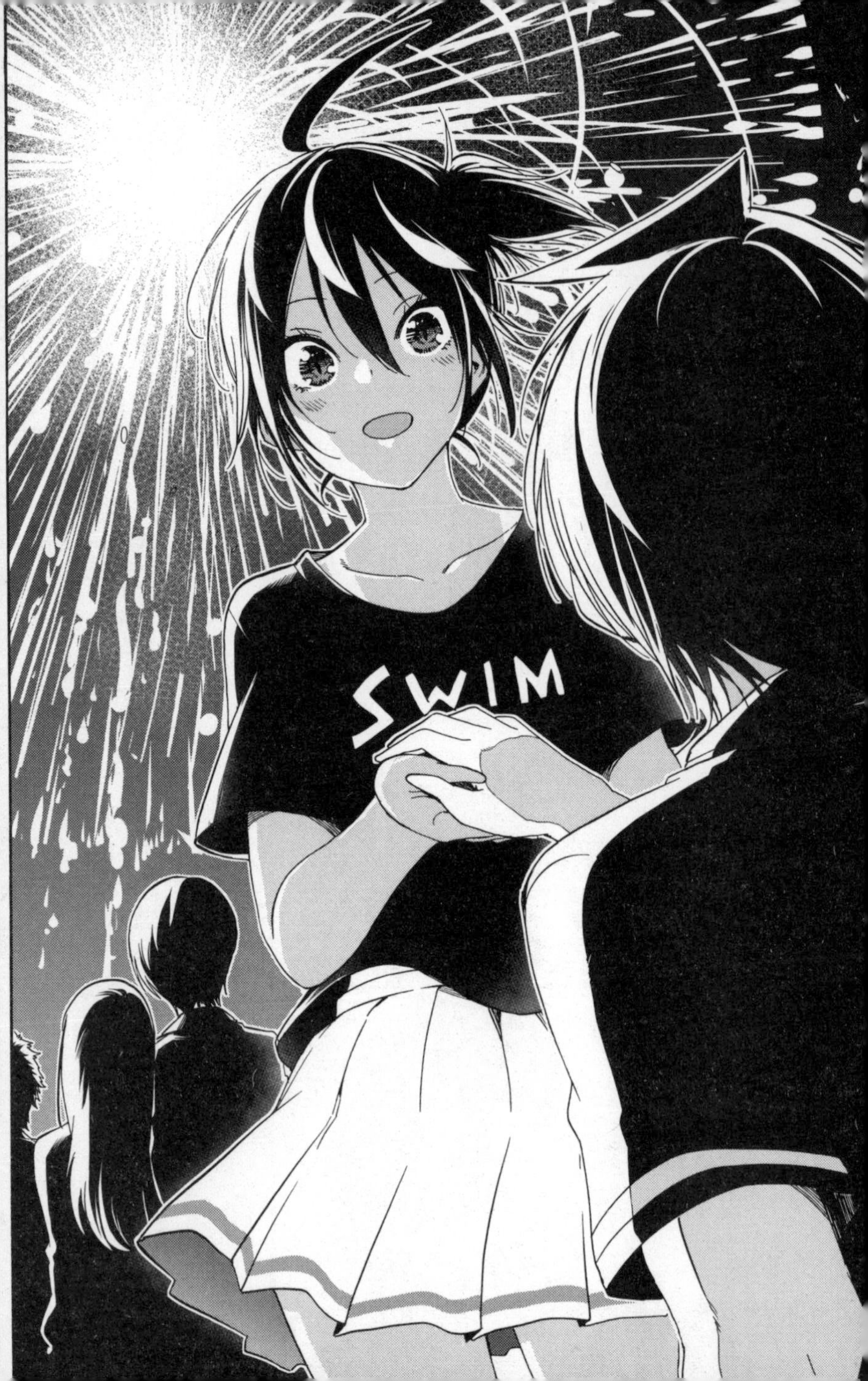
SWIM

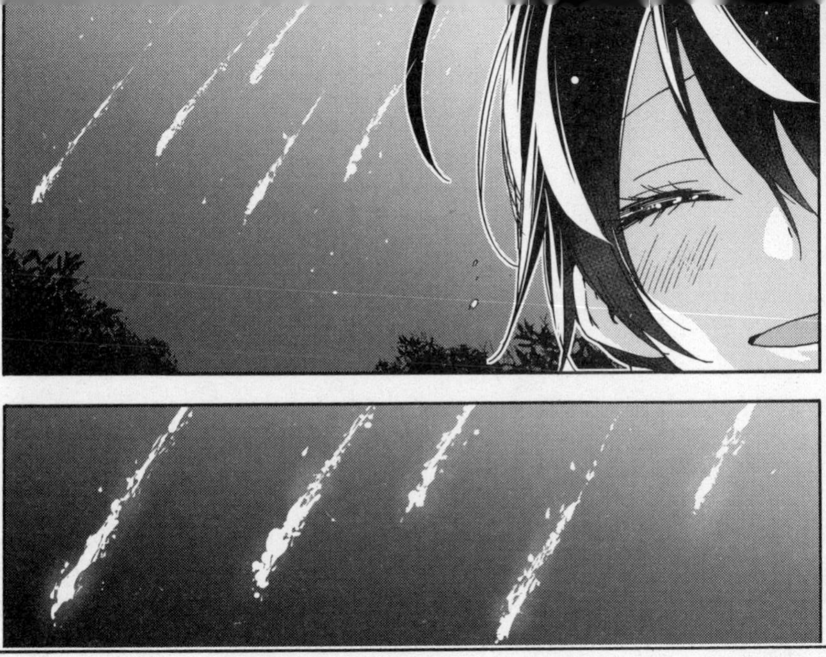

ROUTE: 1/5

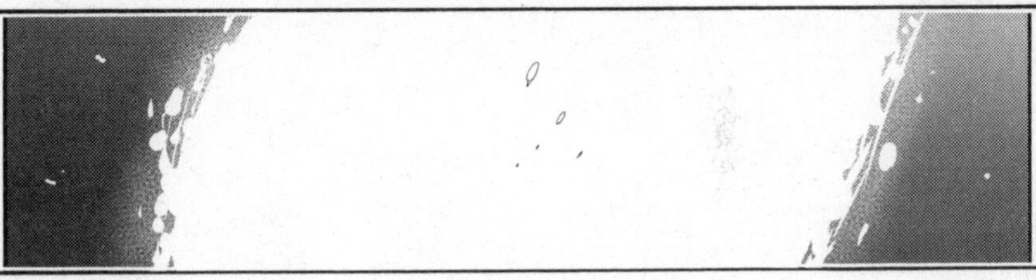

[X] = The Shimmering Ebony Mermaid Princess Arc

- END -

[x] We Never Learn

We Never Learn 17

STAFF LIST

STAFF

Taishi Tsutsui

Yu Kato

Naoki Ochiai

Sachiko

Yukki

Satoshi Okazaki

HELP

Paripoi

Akaya-siki

Chikomichi

SPY × FAMILY

STORY AND ART BY TATSUYA ENDO

An action-packed comedy about a fake family made up of a spy, an assassin and a telepath!

Master spy Twilight is unparalleled when it comes to going undercover on dangerous missions for the betterment of the world. But when he receives the ultimate assignment— to get married and have a kid—he may finally be in over his head!

RATED
T+
OLDER TEEN

VIZ

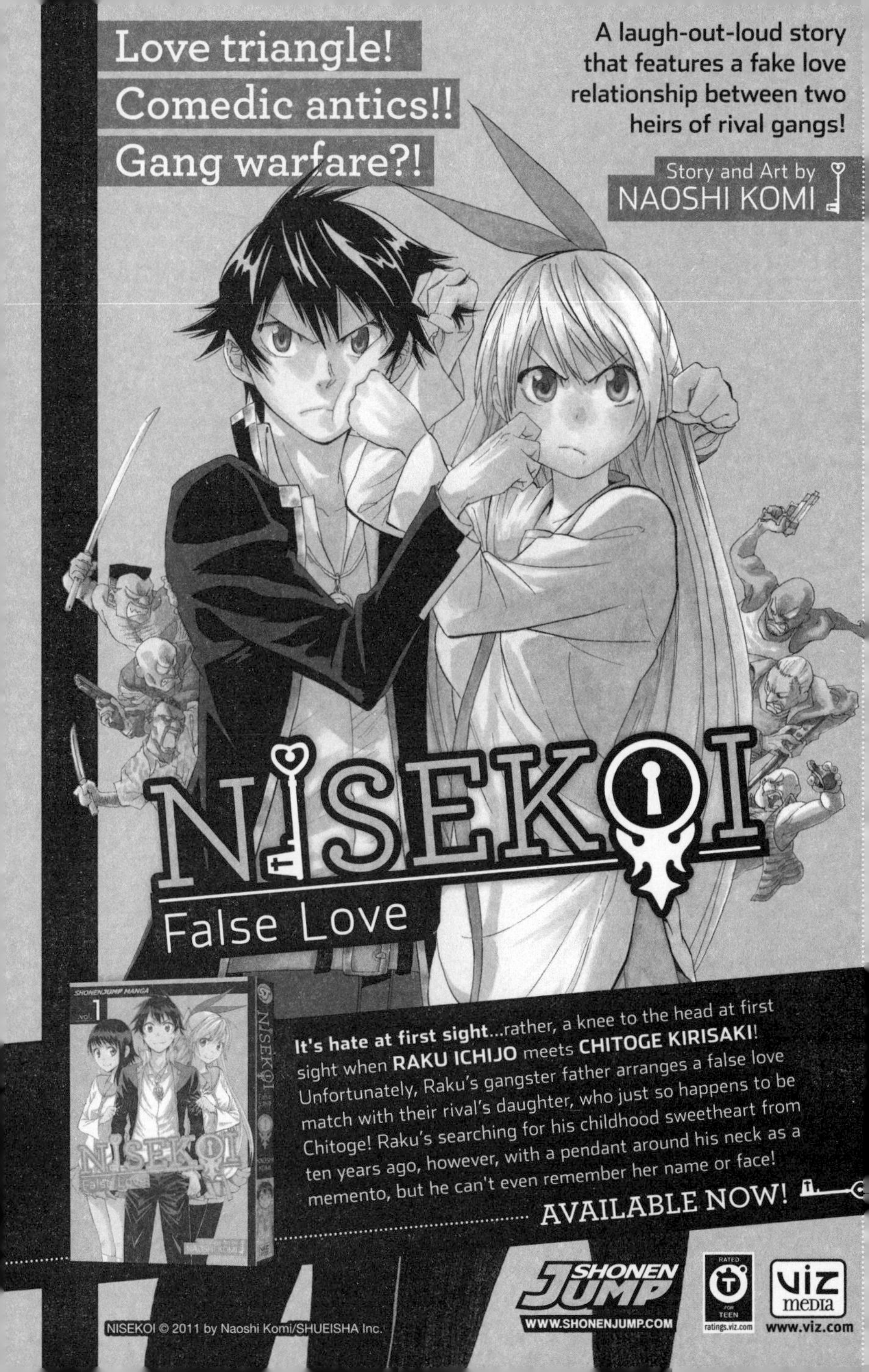

Love triangle!
Comedic antics!!
Gang warfare?!
A laugh-out-loud story that features a fake love relationship between two heirs of rival gangs!
Story and Art by
NAOSHI KOMI
NISEKOI
False Love
SHONENJUMP MANGA
vol. 1
NISEKOI
False Love
It's hate at first sight...rather, a knee to the head at first sight when RAKU ICHIJO meets CHITOGE KIRISAKI! Unfortunately, Raku's gangster father arranges a false love match with their rival's daughter, who just so happens to be Chitoge! Raku's searching for his childhood sweetheart from ten years ago, however, with a pendant around his neck as a memento, but he can't even remember her name or face!
AVAILABLE NOW!
SHONEN JUMP
WWW.SHONENJUMP.COM
RATED T FOR TEEN
ratings.viz.com
VIZ media
www.viz.com
NISEKOI © 2011 by Naoshi Komi/SHUEISHA Inc.

ASSASSINATION CLASSROOM

COMPLETE BOX SET

STORY AND ART BY YUSEI MATSUI

The complete bestselling *Assassination Classroom* series is now available in a boldly designed, value-priced box set!

· Includes all 21 volumes of this unique tale of a mysterious, smiley-faced, tentacled, superpowered teacher who guides a group of misfit students to find themselves—while doing their best to assassinate him.

· Also includes an exclusive, full-color, mini "yearbook" filled with images of favorite characters in different art styles and contexts (previously unreleased in the English editions).